Hungary
a country study

Foreign Area Studies
The American University
Coauthors
Eugene K. Keefe, Lyle E. Brenneman,
William Giloane, Anne K. Long,
James M. Moore, Jr., Neda A. Walpole
Research completed February 1973

On the cover: Parliament House, Budapest

Illustration prepared by Marty Ittner.

First Edition, 1973; Fifth Printing, 1987.

Library of Congress Catalog Card Number: 73–600190

Headquarters, Department of the Army
DA Pam 550–165

For sale by the Superintendent of Documents, U.S. Government Printing Office
Washington, D.C. 20402

Foreword

This volume is one in a continuing series of books now being prepared by the Federal Research Division of the Library of Congress under the Country Studies—Area Handbook Program. This book, however, is a reprint of a book written by members of the research staff of Foreign Area Studies, The American University. The last page of this book lists the other published studies.

Most books in the series deal with a particular foreign country, describing and analyzing its political, economic, social, and national security systems and institutions, and the interrelationships of those systems and the ways they are shaped by cultural factors. Each study is written by a multidisciplinary team of social scientists. The authors seek to provide a basic understanding of the observed society, striving for a dynamic rather than a static portrayal. Particular attention is devoted to the people who make up the society, their origins, dominant beliefs and values, their common interests and the issues on which they are divided, the nature and extent of their involvement with national institutions, and their attitudes toward each other and toward their social system and political order.

The books represent the analysis of the authors and should not be construed as an expression of an official United States government position, policy, or decision. The authors have sought to adhere to accepted standards of scholarly objectivity. Corrections, additions, and suggestions for changes from readers will be welcomed for use in future editions.

Chief
Federal Research Division
Library of Congress
Washington, D.C. 20540

PREFACE

The Hungarian People's Republic was created in 1949 after the Communists had taken over operation of the country. The first communist regime, cast in a Stalinist mold, was repressive to a degree that ultimately brought about a popular uprising in 1956. The revolt was put down by Soviet military might, and a new regime selected by the Soviet Union was installed. That regime was still in power in 1973. After a period of hard-line reconstruction following the revolt, the leadership moderated its policies in order to placate the people and stabilize the government.

By 1973 the stability of the government seemed to be unquestioned. To all outward appearances, Hungary was among the most loyal of the allies of the Soviet Union and continued to be heavily influenced by it.

The *Area Handbook for Hungary* is an effort to explain the workings of the Hungarian communist system, that is, the post-1949 system; however, historical factors are introduced where considered helpful to an understanding of the period. Chapter 2, Historical Setting, is, of necessity, a very brief sketch of Hungary's long history intended to aid in the comprehension of the present. The authors have conscientiously attempted to set aside preconceptions in order to present an objective overview of Hungarian life.

English usage follows *Webster's Seventh New Collegiate Dictionary*. The spelling of place names conforms to the rulings of the United States Board on Geographic Names, but diacritical marks have been omitted. Measurements are given in standard American or British terms. Tonnages are in metric tons unless otherwise specified.

COUNTRY SUMMARY

1. COUNTRY: Communist state closely associated with the Soviet Union. Long established monarchy, under a regent after 1919, formally terminated in 1946. Became Hungarian People's Republic in 1949 with Soviet-style constitution.

2. SIZE AND LOCATION: Area about 35,920 square miles; located in Eastern Europe in middle basin of Danube River. Landlocked with 1,400 miles of border touching on Romania, Yugoslavia, Austria, Czechoslovakia, and the Soviet Union.

3. TOPOGRAPHY: Mean elevation is low. Major topographic regions include Great Plain east of Danube River, Transdanubian rolling hills west of the river. Elevations in mountains along northern border rarely exceed 3,000 feet.

4. CLIMATE: Generally East European continental, characterized by hot summers and cold winters. Moderated by Mediterranean and Atlantic maritime systems, particularly during summer months.

5. POPULATION: About 10.4 million in 1972, with density of 290 persons per square mile. Annual growth rate is a low 0.3 percent.

6. ETHNIC GROUPS AND LANGUAGES: 96 percent of population is Magyar, or Hungarian. Persons of German, Slovak, Serb, Croat, and Romanian origin are guaranteed the right to use their languages and to preserve their cultural heritage, but Hungarian, the official language, is spoken by the entire population.

7. RELIGION: Two-thirds of population is Roman Catholic, one-third is Protestant. Of the latter, two-thirds are Calvinist and one-third Lutheran. There are some 60,000 Jews and some 60,000 Eastern Orthodox. Influence of religion on people is declining as the society becomes increasingly secular.

8. GOVERNMENT: Two-branch government headed by the National Assembly, a unicameral legislature, and the Council of Ministers, which is the executive branch. Real power held by the Communist Party, headed by its first secretary, the Political Bureau (Politburo), the Secretariat, and the Central Committee.

9. ADMINISTRATIVE DIVISIONS: Nineteen counties and five towns of county rank are subdivided into 183 districts and towns of district rank. Districts are subdivided into 3,135 villages. Governmental administration is by local councils at each level.

10. INTERNATIONAL ORGANIZATIONS: Member of the Warsaw

Treaty Organization (Warsaw Pact), the Council for Mutual Economic Assistance (COMECON), and the United Nations (UN), including several UN specialized agencies.

11. JUSTICE: Three-level court system includes Supreme Court and courts at county and district levels. Military and labor courts fall in special category responsible only to Supreme Court.

12. COMMUNICATIONS: Although almost all mass media are owned and regulated by the state, some latitude is given certain of them. Press, radio, and television are the more strictly controlled, whereas control of films, book publishing, and libraries is relatively light.

13. EDUCATION: Free and compulsory through the first eight grades. Vocational training stressed over the humanities. Marxism-Leninism is backbone of the curriculum as well as of extracurricular activities.

14. ECONOMY: Development programmed in five-year plans; overall economic activity controlled by party and government. The New Economic Mechanism (NEM), attempting broad economic reform via a decentralized management system, has been in effect since 1968. Operates largely within COMECON framework; particular reliance on ties with Soviet Union.

15. LABOR: Work force in 1970 included 4.9 million wage earners from the 3.4 million males between fifteen and sixty-four years of age and the 3.3 million females between fifteen and fifty-nine. Over one-third of the work force employed in industry, about one-fourth in agriculture.

16. AGRICULTURE: Nearly three-quarters of the land is used for agriculture, and 95 percent of it is included in collective or state farms. Major crops are cereals, potatoes, sugar beets, and fodder. Livestock production inadequate; its development stressed by government. Growth of production held down by inadequate allocation of resources to the agricultural sector and generally unfavorable prices.

17. INDUSTRY: Stimulated by reforms in the New Economic Mechanism, but expansion is slowed by poor management and low productivity. Emphasis remains on capital goods industries, particularly chemicals, machinery, and electronics.

18. FINANCE: Monetary unit is nonconvertible forint. Depending on use, official exchange rates vary between 10.80 and 60 forints per US$1. Currency and foreign exchange controlled by state, administered by the Hungarian National Bank, the National Savings Bank, the State Development Bank, and the Hungarian Foreign Trade Bank.

19. FOREIGN TRADE: Essential for economic development. Annual volume equivalent to one-fifth of national income. Problems in trade expansion include noncompetitive goods for trade with West and inflexible trade agreements with COMECON neighbors.

20. RAILROADS: About 5,350 miles of track, nearly all standard gauge. About 70 percent of locomotives are steam, 20 percent diesel, 10 percent electric. System carries approximately three-quarters of

the country's freight and passenger traffic.

21. ROADS: Total network mileage is 18,400; 10,700 miles have asphalt or equivalent surfaces. Motor transport is carrying rapidly increasing percentages of short-haul traffic, both freight and passenger.

22. INLAND WATERWAYS: About 800 miles of rivers and canals considered permanently navigable, another 250 to 300 miles are of limited use. Budapest is most important of the ports on the Danube River.

23. CIVIL AVIATION: State-owned Hungarian Airlines (MALEV) eliminated domestic services in 1970, operates between Budapest and external points only.

24. ARMED FORCES: Regular military forces are included in the Hungarian People's Army, subordinate to the Ministry of Defense. Soviet Union maintains ground force and tactical aviation units in the country.

25. SECURITY: Ministry of Interior controls local civil and national security—or secret—police, regular military Frontier Guard and Internal Security Troops, various guard units, and the paramilitary Workers Militia.

HUNGARY

TABLE OF CONTENTS

LIST OF ILLUSTRATIONS

LIST OF TABLES

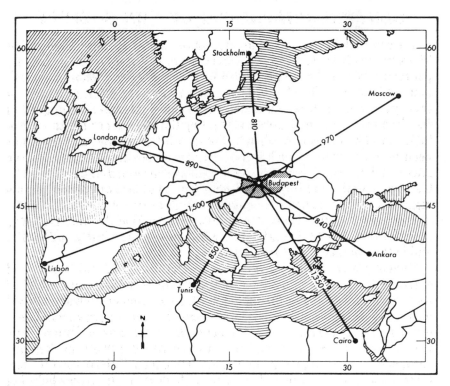

Distances in air miles.

Figure 1. Hungary

SECTION I. SOCIAL

CHAPTER 1

GENERAL CHARACTER OF THE SOCIETY

The communist party in Hungary, known as the Hungarian Socialist Workers' Party (MSZMP—see Glossary), in addition to being the only political force in the country, also directs its entire economic, social, and cultural life. The Communists seized power in 1949, proclaiming their government to be the Hungarian People's Republic; Hungary in fact had become a totalitarian state. Popular discontent led to a revolution in 1956 that was crushed by Soviet military power, and there has been no recurrence of such grave disorder. Janos Kadar has been the party leader—first secretary—since the revolution, and in early 1973, his seventeenth year in power, Kadar has no apparent opposition; his regime is stable and has even gained some measure of popular support. Soviet influence has been strong since World War II, and Hungary remains very closely tied to the Soviet Union—economically, militarily, and in the conduct of its foreign affairs.

Hungary was allied with the Axis powers during World War II and emerged from the war with a Soviet army of occupation in control of its territory. As early as December 1944, a coalition of prewar political parties, including Communists, was allowed to form a provisional government for Hungary under the auspices of the Soviet Union. This government signed an armistice with the Allied powers in January 1945, and by April fighting in Hungary had ended. Relatively free elections took place in November 1945 and, despite the overwhelming Soviet military presence in the country, the Communists won only about 17 percent of the popular vote. By prior agreement among all parties contesting the election, the coalition was to be maintained regardless of the outcome at the polls. Armed with this agreement and backed by Soviet power, the Communists insisted on retaining the Ministry of Interior, which gave them control over the police apparatus. The poor showing at the polls alerted the Hungarian Communists as well as their Soviet sponsors to their widespread unpopularity among the people, and uncontrolled elections have not again been permitted in post-World War II Hungary.

Although a republic with a freely elected government, the country after November 1945 became a political battleground between the legal government and the Communists. The struggle was heavily weighted

1

in favor of the numerically weak Communists because of the presence of Soviet troops. Matyas Rakosi, leader of what was then called the Hungarian Communist Party, gradually became the most powerful individual in the country and worked toward total communization. A new constitution, based on the Stalin Constitution of the Soviet Union, was introduced in 1949, and Rakosi, despite the small size of his party and its basic unpopularity, was in full control.

The country that Rakosi took over had more than a thousand years of history behind it, dating from the arrival of Magyar tribes in central Europe at the end of the ninth century A.D. For much of that time, the name Hungary had applied to the entire Carpathian Basin, and Hungarian territory extended as far as the shores of the Adriatic Sea. As one of the defeated powers of World War I, Hungary suffered territorially more than any other nation. By the 1920 Treaty of Trianon, Hungary was stripped of almost three-quarters of its territory and about two-thirds of its population. The basic premise of the Allies who dictated the treaty was to give self-determination to the ethnic minorities that had previously made up a large part of the population of Hungary, but in the division of territories more than 3 million ethnic Hungarians were left outside the country's new borders. Hungarians felt that the Treaty of Trianon was unnecessarily harsh and unjust, and the spirit of irredentism engendered by this treaty remained a dominant national attitude during the period between the two world wars.

As an ally of Nazi Germany, Hungary had briefly regained some of its former territories, but the Paris Peace Treaty of 1947 essentially reinstated the borders delineated by the Treaty of Trianon. Rakosi's Hungary of the post-World War II era was again the truncated version of the much larger historical kingdom of Hungary. There have been no territorial adjustments since the communist takeover, and in 1973 Hungary encompassed 35,920 square miles and had a population of about 10.4 million people. About 96 percent of the people are ethnic Hungarians; the remainder are Germans, Romanians, Serbs, Croats, and Jews. The irredentism that had been so pronounced during the interwar period supposedly had been submerged in a spirit of Marxist internationalism, but that spirit is belied by the very vocal nationalism of the peoples of Eastern Europe. The Hungarians have always been a nationalistic people and have always thought of Hungary as encompassing the entire Carpathian Basin; however, the old dreams of regaining lost territories and returning to former national boundaries are not openly advocated, probably in deference to the fraternal order that is supposed to exist among communist countries.

As leader of the new people's republic as well as leader of the party, Rakosi in the early years of the communist era ruled by terror and connivance, eliminating political opposition both outside and inside the party and, at the same time, establishing himself as the ultimate strong man; in effect, a pocket edition of the Soviet dictator, Joseph

Stalin. Rakosi's policies led eventually to the traumatic events of October through November 1956, during which the Hungarian people bid for freedom from communist domination but lost to the overwhelming military force of the Soviet Union. The regime of Janos Kadar was installed after Soviet forces had quelled the 1956 revolt.

The Soviet-sponsored Kadar regime proved to be less dogmatic than that of Rakosi. After an initial period of postrevolution repression there was a gradual lessening of the police-state atmosphere, and the Stalinist practices of the Rakosi era were not reinstituted. Even though he moderated some of the evils of the past, Kadar believed that the party should be all-powerful and took steps to ensure that such would be the case. Hungary under Kadar is a one-party state with the true sources of power resting in the party—more particularly, in the leaders of the party. The democratic text of the constitution proclaims that all power belongs to the people to be exercised through their elected representatives, but in reality facts belie the words.

Government, in effect, is the administrative structure through which the MSZMP runs the country. The central government is made up essentially of a unicameral legislature, known as the National Assembly; the Presidential Council; and the Council of Ministers. The National Assembly is constitutionally the supreme organ of state power, but it only meets for a few days each year, leaving the Presidential Council, a collective head-of-state, to exercise the legislative function. The Council of Ministers carries out the administration and supervision of the country's political, economic, social, and cultural life. It is customary for high-level party officials to hold high government office concurrently. At lower levels of government—county, district, and local—elected officials are often nonparty activists who have been carefully selected and faithfully follow the party line. At all levels there is a party apparatus paralleling the government structure.

The MSZMP itself is hierarchically structured, political power emanating from the office of the first secretary. The two top party organs are the Political Bureau (Politburo), the policymaking office, and the Secretariat, the party administrative center, both of which operate under the direction of First Secretary Kadar. The party congress, which meets every four years, is by statute the highest policymaking body; in practice, the Central Committee elected by the congress assumes overall direction of party affairs between congresses, and the Politburo and Secretariat, ostensibly elected by the Central Committee but in fact self-perpetuating, are the real centers of power. Most members of the Presidential Council and the Council of Ministers are also members of the Central Committee, and a few of the leading officials of the government are concurrently in the Politburo. The interlocking of top positions ensures total party control over all aspects of Hungarian life.

As in other countries that followed the example of the Soviet Union, the Communists in Hungary instituted strict controls, not only over the politics of the country but over the economy and the society as well. In the economic sphere, collectivization of agriculture and nationalization of industry received the greatest attention at the outset, in order to estrange the country from its past as soon as possible. A 1945 redistribution of agricultural land had given land to thousands of peasant families that had previously been landless, and in the early 1950s, when Rakosi initiated collectivization, there was great resentment and obstruction. Despite the reluctance on the part of the peasants to join collectives, the regime continued to force collectivization to the detriment of agricultural production. After Stalin's death, when Rakosi's powers were curbed to some extent, Imre Nagy became premier and began a program called the New Course, which reversed some of Rakosi's policies, including forced collectivization. Peasant families by the thousands left the collectives and began individual farming again. During the uprising of 1956 several thousand more peasants left the collectives. The freedom from collectivization was short lived, however, and in 1959 forced collectivization was again in progress. By the early 1970s, 94 percent of the arable land belonged to collective and state farms.

In the industrial sector, nationalization of existing industry (which had started under the precommunist government) and an increase in overall industrial capacity were the early goals of the Communists. Heavy industry was emphasized despite the paucity of most raw materials. Dissatisfaction among the people was rife because of chronic shortages of consumer goods and the generally low standard of living. During the brief New Course of the early 1950s, Premier Nagy promised to reorient the industrialization program to put more emphasis on light industry and the production of consumer goods, but even though some of his reforms were effected, the continuing political tug of war prevented full realization of the New Course. The people, however, had enjoyed a taste of moderation under Nagy, and when he was ousted and the hardliners again came to the fore, popular discontent eventually led to the uprising of 1956.

After the reconstruction period that followed the uprising, the Kadar regime tried to increase industrial efficiency by various means, including moderation of the emphasis on heavy industry. Despite innovations, the growth rate over the next several years was unsatisfactory, and in 1966 the party Central Committee approved a program of reform known as the New Economic Mechanism, which was put into effect on January 1, 1968. Essentially a liberalized system of management based on decentralization of control, the New Economic Mechanism in its first five years did not fulfill the demands of the lagging economy that brought it about in the first place. At the beginning of the sixth year under the new program, Hungarian leaders expressed satisfaction with the reform principles but called for greater effort in putting the principles into practice.

4

As in several other traditional societies in Europe, the social system in Hungary emerged from World War II in a state of complete disorder. The former aristocracy and gentry had been practically eliminated, much of the middle-class Jewish business community had been destroyed, land reform in 1945 had changed the status of much of the peasantry, and the wartime destruction of industry and subsequent nationalization had altered the economic base of the old social system. When the Communists took power, they instituted various policies designed, ostensibly, to create a classless society as called for in Marxist-Leninist dogma. Equalization of incomes, nationalization of industry, collectivization of agriculture, and control over education were all intended to some extent to bring about an egalitarian system. Actually, the absolute power of the communist party ensured that party leaders would replace the aristocracy as a privileged minority, party members would become a new elite, and the bulk of the population would simply be an amorphous mass. The masses did not remain amorphous for very long, however, as industrialization, urbanization, and economic reforms brought about differentiation and stratification.

In the early 1970s Hungarian society could be roughly divided into four groups or classes: the ruling elite, the white-collar employees, the workers, and the peasants. Within the groups, differentiation is based on party membership, education, occupation, and income. There is social mobility among the various groups, usually upward, resulting from the acquisition of additional education or skills. Political loyalty, though still important, is rarely the only qualification necessary for upward mobility, although it had been in the early days of the communist era. Downward mobility is most often attributable to political considerations.

The social group or class to which a person belongs largely determines his standard of living. The members of the ruling elite, of course, are in the highest income brackets, in addition to which they enjoy special privileges that place them far above everyone else in material possessions, comforts, and conveniences. For the rest of the population, income is usually the determining factor in life-styles, and the urban professional is rapidly outdistancing the lower level white-collar employees, the workers, and the peasants in affluence and standard of living. The widening gap has brought rumblings of discontent, particularly from urban blue-collar workers, whose wages have not kept pace with the cost of living.

The best means to upward social mobility, and the benefits and privileges that go along with higher status, are the acquisition of higher education or advanced technical skills. In the early communist period, special emphasis was given to the education of workers and peasants and their children—particularly as pertaining to opportunities for higher education. As the system became bureaucratized and society became stratified, however, such emphasis was played down, and in the late 1960s and early 1970s children of worker-peasant origin were underrepresented in the institutions of higher learning. Nevertheless, opportunities do exist, and many former workers and peasants do succeed in improving their social status through education. At the same time, vocational and polytechnical education was greatly expanded to meet the demands of a rapidly industrializing society. The party constantly watches over the educational system to ensure that Marxism-Leninism is not neglected in the curricula and to ensure that the educational facilities and policies fulfill the goal of producing good socialist citizens who will meet the needs of the national economy.

Before the communist takeover, Hungarian schools were heavily dominated by religious bodies in the country. The Roman Catholic Church was the most dominant influence, but Calvinist, Lutheran, and Unitarian schools were also very important in the overall educational field. Although the Communists tried vigorously to rid the educational system of religious influence, they were not wholly successful, and eventually agreements were worked out whereby some church schools continued to operate under the atheist regime. Despite the retention by religious bodies of some influence in the educational system, observers have noted a decline in the religious commitment of the people. Nevertheless, with all the factors bringing about secularization of society, the traditional Hungarian denominations continue to function, and the Communists have had to concede that religion is not yet fading from the scene. Although churches have been divested of their former landholdings, the communist government does provide subsidies for church operations. Two-thirds of the Hungarians are Roman Catholics, at least nominally; most of the remainder are divided among the Calvinists, Lutherans, and Unitarians, with some Eastern Orthodox and some Jews still remaining in the country.

In the cultural life of the country the party is in control as it is in all aspects of Hungarian life, but control of artists and intellectuals is rather subtle and covert. Historically the Hungarian people have looked to artists and authors for leadership during crises or to serve the cause of Hungarian nationalism whenever the nation was threatened. As recently as the mid-1950s, it was the writers who uttered the first cries for freedom and were in the vanguard of the movement that led to the Revolution of 1956. Well aware of the potential power of the artists and intellectuals, the authorities have carefully channeled art and literature into acceptable areas or have suppressed them. Overt censorship, a tool used often by the authorities under Rakosi, has become rare. There is freedom of expression, provided the artist or author remains within the guidelines provided by the party. With all media and all means of exposure to an audience firmly in the hands of the government, self-censorship on the part of artists and intellectuals is the most prominent form of control. In addition, artists whose work remains within the communist bounds of acceptability are subsidized, and some enjoy a life-style comparable to that of the party elite.

As far as controls on the population at large are concerned, the police, court, and penal systems usually associated with any government exist and are supplemented by uniformed internal security forces, political or secret police, a paramilitary militia, and frontier guards. The political police are no longer hated or feared by the people as they had been during the Rakosi era, but the organization still exists, even though its tactics have been modified and terror is no longer used as an instrument of control. Political trials, which in the early period were frequent and infamous, have become rare and, if held at all, are probably conducted in private rather than as show trials.

At least equally important as the police and the courts in the maintenance of public order are the mass organizations that are under the guidance and supervision of the party-dominated Patriotic People's Front. The mass organizations include the trade unions, youth groups, women's associations, and sports clubs, and through these organizations the party not only has a means of population control but also is able to mobilize literally millions of people to support its policies and programs. MSZMP control is maintained by the party members who hold leadership positions in the organizations. With all organized activity under party supervision, there is no possibility that any group or club could become a base of opposition. The mass organizations also serve as channels of information for the MSZMP whereby the party hierarchy is able to monitor popular opinions and attitudes.

Militarily, Hungary in 1973 maintained about 100,000 men in its armed forces, most of them serving in the army. Much smaller numbers served in the air and air defense forces, and a contingent of only a few hundred manned the ships of the naval force, which operates on the Danube River. All of the armed forces are administered by the Ministry of Defense, but policymaking is a prerogative of the MSZMP. Manpower for the armed forces, as well as for the frontier guards and the internal security forces, is secured through universal conscription. Hungary is a charter member of the Warsaw Treaty Organization (Warsaw Pact), and Hungarian troops participated in the 1968 invasion of Czechoslovakia despite the fact that Kadar had been publicly friendly with Alexander Dubcek, the Czechoslovak leader whose reforms brought on the invasion. Kadar had also openly opposed any move toward intervention in Czechoslovakia but, when called upon by the Soviet leadership, he fell into line along with the other Warsaw Pact members; the sole exception was Romania, whose leaders refused to participate.

CHAPTER 2

HISTORICAL SETTING

For long periods in their history the Hungarians have been an oppressed people trying to escape imperial power and foreign control. On the other hand, their efforts to control the Carpathian Basin have expressed a determination to impose a type of Hungarian imperial control. The Hungarians have been ethnically and linguistically isolated in a region coveted by more powerful peoples, often in conflict with one another. Before World War II the most serious and concrete political, cultural, and military threat was posed by the Germans, but fear of Soviet ambitions led to an accommodation to German ambitions. Since World War II Hungarian national interests have been affected by the Soviet military presence and the strong Soviet influence throughout Eastern Europe.

Ever since the Hungarians came from the east to the Carpathian Basin roughly 1,100 years ago, some tension has existed between the original Eastern cultural heritage and the new Western cultural accretions. The Eastern heritage is seen most clearly in the national folklore, in the special ways and means of maintaining life among the rural people, and in the structure of local communities. The Hungarian amalgam of Eastern and Western traditions and cultures showed a powerful capacity to bring new peoples into the Hungarian fold until the rise of counternationalism in the late nineteenth century.

The problem of national groups or minorities has been a recurrent factor, especially since the latter part of the nineteenth century. During much of the past, other peoples had been assimilated into Magyar culture, but in recent decades the ambition of the Magyars to continue this process in the face of competing nationalisms has been labeled "chauvinism" or "irredentism." Under the Communists, efforts have been made to counter such nationalism in the interest of safeguarding a status quo patterned according to their own concepts and interests.

Long periods of the nation's history have been marked by religious conflict. The politics of the very early period revolved around the conflict of the original paganism and the acquired Christianity. Paganism was defeated, but its remnants were preserved in local culture. Later, after the emergence of Protestantism during the Reformation, a conflict between the Roman Catholic Church and the new, more national Christianity also developed. The struggle quickly took on political implications. Since World War II the conflict has been between the teachings of Christianity and those of communism.

EARLY HISTORY

The Hungarians, or Magyars, arrived in the Carpathian Basin, that is, the general area of modern Hungary, at the end of the ninth century A.D. The date usually ascribed by historians to this migration is 896, but it is likely that Magyar raiding parties were already familiar with the region from previous incursions. Before moving into the area that eventually became their new homeland, the Magyars had lived in the Khazar state, north of the Black Sea, to which they had earlier migrated, probably from the region between the great bend of the Volga River and the Ural Mountains. Little is known about the Magyars before they began the migration that took them south to the Black Sea and eventually west to the middle Danube River. Their language, which became modern Hungarian, is of the Finno-Ugric language group and has strong influences from the Turkic languages with which it came in contact during the Magyars' indeterminate stay in the Black Sea area. These early Magyars were a seminomadic pastoral people, who associated in a loose tribal confederation for offense as well as defense.

The Finno-Ugric family of languages had over 19 million speakers in 1970, the majority of whom—over 13 million—were Hungarian. Although Finnish is a very distant relative of Hungarian, the two languages are not mutually understandable; neither are the nearest Ugric relatives, such as Vogul (Mansi) and Ostyak (Khanty), which are spoken by a few thousand herdsmen and fishermen living in Siberia. During the migrations of the early Magyars, their language was influenced by contacts with Turkic peoples and later incorporated loanwords from the Slavic, Germanic, and Romance languages.

The Magyars were merely one among many of the warlike, nomadic hordes that swept into Europe from the East, bent on conquest and plunder. Their warriors were as competent at fighting from horseback as were the Huns who preceded them or the Mongols who came later; but the Magyars were not as numerous as these other hordes nor, it would seem, did their leaders entertain the grandiose schemes of conquest that motivated such men as Attila the Hun or Genghis Khan. The seven tribes that easily and rapidly defeated the Slavs and other peoples living around the middle course of the Danube River in A.D. 896 were led by Arpad, an elected chieftain. Although Arpad was a tribal chieftain rather than a king, his successors later became kings of Hungary, and the Arpad dynasty lasted until the male line died out at the beginning of the fourteenth century.

For the first few decades after settling along the Danube, the Hungarian tribes seemed to consider the area more as a base of operations than a new homeland. The majority of the people maintained the seminomadic existence they had known in the East—moving with their herds from mountain pastures in summer to milder lowlands in winter. In the meantime, marauding armies of the tribes swept from Constantinople to the North Sea and from southern Italy to the Pyrenees Mountains, returning with booty and slaves but instilling fear and incurring wrath in the countries they invaded. Finally, the Hungarians suffered a catastrophic defeat by a coalition of forces of the Holy Roman Empire. The defeat at Augsburg proved to be a turning point in Hungarian history as the tribes ceased their depredations and became more sedentary along the waterways of the Carpathian Basin. After giving up their incursions into the territories of other peoples, the Hungarians themselves endured centuries of invasions and incursions as their adopted land proved to be a crossroads for Eastern hordes moving into Europe as well as for Germanic forces raiding the Balkans.

In A.D. 972 Prince Geza, great-grandson of Arpad, became the leader of the entire Hungarian confederation and succeeded in curbing the power of the individual tribal chieftains. Geza, recognizing that a pagan nation surrounded by the Eastern and Western forms of Christianity would be in constant danger and fearing domination from the East, admitted missionaries from the West and permitted his son, Istvan (Stephen), to be baptized a Roman Catholic. Stephen's later marriage to a Bavarian princess, the conversion to Roman Catholicism of the Hungarian people, and the development of a Latin alphabet for the Magyar language solidified the Western orientation of the country.

When Geza died, Stephen became ruling chieftain and worked strenuously to erase paganism among his people, to convert them to Roman Catholicism, and to resist any encroachment by the Eastern Orthodox Church. As a reward Stephen received a crown from the pope (a story doubted by some modern historians but indelibly inscribed in Hungarian tradition) and, about the year A.D. 1000, became the first king of Hungary. Stephen was later canonized by the Roman Catholic Church and, as Saint Stephen, became the most famous king in Hungarian history. Stephen's crown was revered as the symbol of Hungarian nationhood until World War II.

King Stephen asserted the unity of the state, the supremacy of the royal authority, and the need for the unquestioning obedience of the people. Under Stephen much of the country became crown land, personal domains of the monarch from which he could derive revenue as well as manpower for military service. The crown lands remained a foundation of power for many of Stephen's successors. It was also during Stephen's reign that the vast territory of Transylvania was brought under Hungarian hegemony.

In addition to the vast domains he already possessed, Stephen occupied large tracts of uninhabited territories lying between existing settlements and added land to the royal domain. In these areas, he fortified strategic points and, in time, towns grew up around the fortresses. The king appointed administrators to guide the affairs of the fortified areas and towns, which were embryos of future counties, thus facilitating the development of the medieval state.

In the three centuries from the coronation of Stephen until the death of the last Arpad king in 1301, the kingdom acquired vast new territories and assumed a multinational, multilingual character. In addition to the indigenous peoples who were brought under Hungarian control, foreign colonists were invited in great numbers to occupy the uninhabited lands of the kingdom. Many of the peoples, particularly those from the East, were absorbed and became completely magyarized. Others, such as the Germans (called Saxons) who colonized Transylvania for the Arpads in the early thirteenth century, retained their own cultures and languages and never were assimilated.

One of the most important developments in Hungarian constitutional history occurred in 1222 when the people compelled the king to sign the Golden Bull. The Golden Bull has often been compared to the English Magna Carta in that both documents placed limitations upon the crown. The Golden Bull, unlike the Magna Carta, however, was realized through the pressures of small landholders, the so-called freemen, rather than barons. The Golden Bull set limits on the king, but it also had the unfortunate effect of further isolating the landless peasants, as they had no voice in its establishment.

Despite the Golden Bull, the thirteenth century was a century of trouble for the country. In 1241 the Mongols invaded Hungary, eventually gaining control of territory to the east and north of the Danube. This was Hungary's first experience as a buffer state between East and West, but it was a costly experience in that the western monarchs allowed the Hungarians to bear the brunt of the Mongol onslaught, which actually endangered all of Europe. Hungary stood alone, and her forces were not equal to the task presented by the overpowering Golden Horde of the Mongols. Although the Mongol invasion lasted only until 1242, the country was devastated and depopulated. The Mongols withdrew to the Russian steppes, from which they still presented a threat. Twice during the next twenty years the Mongols offered to join the Hungarians as allies, but both offers were refused as Hungary chose to retain its strongly developed Western orientation.

The death of Endre III, the last Arpad in the direct male line, initiated a period of crisis that lasted for over 200 years. The crises were created by growing Turkish pressure upon Europe, in which Hungary again became a buffer between East and West; the Habsburg ambition to absorb Hungary into its empire; the political and social power of the great nobles who placed their personal welfare before that of the kingdom; and the periodic lack of effective rulers. Hungarian feudalism reached its fullest development during this period, and the serfs suffered as the nobles gained power.

During the more than two centuries from the end of the Arpad dynasty until the Turkish conquest, Hungary suffered from a seemingly endless power struggle, during which various royal houses of Europe vied for the crown of Saint Stephen. A Bohemian king rapidly gave way to a Bavarian who, in turn, was succeeded by Charles Robert of the house of Anjou. Charles Robert gradually brought some stability to the court while maintaining peace and a measure of prosperity in the country. Under his son, Louis the Great, Hungary extended its influence into the Balkans and into Poland (the throne of which Louis also held).

A tight rein was maintained on the nobility. A new military system was organized in which royal forces were supported by the militia of the magnates (leading nobles) and the county forces of the lesser nobility. Financial reforms, through which the state treasury became independent of the large estates, were accomplished. The maintenance of the royal fortified areas was based on the crown lands and the original counties, which became autonomous under officials appointed by the king. New sources of revenue were tapped in the form of customs duties, direct taxes, and a monopoly on precious metals.

Commercial transactions with other countries were improved, and by the end of the fourteenth century the country had achieved an enviable measure of prosperity. As a result of a growing number of villages and towns, a viable economy, and a flourishing of the arts and sciences, Louis enjoyed a successful reign; moreover, his reissuing of the Golden Bull in 1351 helped to stabilize the social order.

Sigismund of Luxembourg followed the Anjous on the Hungarian throne but, because he also became the Holy Roman emperor, his interests were diffused to the detriment of Hungary. At the same time, the Ottoman Turks were becoming more menacing around the fringes of the vast Hungarian domains. Janos Hunyadi, one of Hungary's greatest heroes, came to power as a regent and initiated a long overdue policy of defense against the Turks. He defeated them decisively at Belgrade in 1456, delaying their advance into Europe for seventy years. After Hunyadi's death, his son Matyas was elected king and brought to the country significant talents for administration, social justice, cultural development, and military operations at a time of great need.

Matyas Hunyadi (known to history as Corvinus Matthias), ruling from 1458 until 1490, gave Hungary a period of prosperity and national glory. He fought the country's enemies and established a standing army of mercenaries, which he used as quickly against dissenting magnates as against foreign enemies. Matyas restored the public finance and improved the system of taxation so that the nobility's traditional exemption was eliminated, and he reduced the power of masters over serfs. In foreign affairs he succeeded in becoming ruler of Bohemia, Silesia, Moravia, Lower Austria, and other principalities. He maintained defenses against the Turks but also recognized the fundamental nature of the struggle with the growing power of the Habsburgs. Matyas also found time to become a great patron of the arts and of learning in general.

After the sudden death of Matyas, the inevitable power struggle eventually culminated in the election of a weak king, whom the magnates could manipulate. Many of the foreign territories that Matyas had incorporated broke away immediately and, internally, most of the curbs that he had effected against the nobles were cast aside. New law codes widened the cleavage between the nobility and the peasantry and weakened the power of the monarchy. Internal conditions deteriorated to the point that, in 1514, a serious serf uprising occurred. The uprising was suppressed with great loss of life and bloodshed, but the reprisals that followed were even more debilitating to the country as a whole. Tens of thousands of serfs were executed because of their participation in the rebellion, and the conditions against which the serfs had rebelled became more burdensome than ever before. Twelve years later, the Turkish and Hungarian armies met in the Battle of Mohacs, which proved to be utterly disastrous for the Hungarians and which initiated 150 years of Turkish rule. Hungary never regained unqualified control of the Carpathian Basin homeland that the original Magyars had secured over six centuries earlier.

After the defeat at Mohacs and a period of internecine strife, Hungary was partitioned; the western and northern section was drawn into the Habsburg domains, the central area was under direct Turkish control, and Transylvania was governed by Hungarian princes under Turkish suzerainty. The three-way partition lasted for almost 150 years and finally ended in Habsburg domination rather than in independence. Hungarian nationalists were active at all times during the long occupation; various leaders arose to champion the cause of self-determination and, although they fought valiantly against Turks and Austrians alike, the Hungarians could not match the power of the Ottomans and the Habsburgs. When the Turks were finally forced to withdraw from Hungary, the Habsburgs were in control and forced the Hungarians to accept Austrian succession to the Hungarian crown.

The area of western and northern Hungary, ruled by the Habsburgs during most of the Turkish period, witnessed the original outbreak of the conflict between the Habsburg loyalists and the Hungarian nationalists, although the nationalists later became associated with Transylvania. As a result of the Habsburg success, the Kingdom of Hungary began to experience a type of absolutism that came to stand for foreign interference or intervention.

The feudal bases of the nobility's position were becoming weaker, and their ability to resist was weakened as well. The Hungarian administrative apparatus declined, and the chief organs of government were almost totally staffed by non-Hungarians. Public finance, foreign affairs, and defense of the kingdom were made subordinate to those of

Austria. Foreign troops were stationed in the country, and their commanders were always foreigners. The Diet was ineffectual and was largely reduced to registering protests.

The chief aim of Turkish officials had been to take as much as possible from the country in the shortest possible time. The Hungarian population was sharply reduced, and the people who survived were in a condition of servitude. For defense purposes many left their individual farms and joined large cooperative farms, which incorporated the lands of outlying farms and villages and formed the basis of new kinds of towns. Many of the former towns almost disappeared. The people in outlying regions often paid taxes not only to Turkish authorities but also to Hungarian nobles.

Transylvania was able to maintain a semi-independent status, usually balancing the power of the Turkish sultan against that of the Habsburg emperor. The maintenance of Hungarian culture and national independence was promoted by a line of able princes and statesmen, such as Gabor Bethlen and Gyorgy Martinuzzi. Their internal policies brought about a measure of religious tolerance that was unique in Europe at that time. The Transylvanian princes also broadened the base of the privileged classes, but they did not go as far as to eliminate serfdom. Probably the Turks did not take over the principality because the gold coming from it—the richest source of the precious metal in Europe—was important to them, and they no doubt believed that its uninterrupted production and receipt by the sultan's government were more certain under conditions of semi-independence than under absolute control. Transylvania remained as a symbol of the survival of the Hungarian potential for independence, from both the Turks and Habsburgs, as well as of the ideal of east-central European cooperation.

THE HABSBURG ERA

The final expulsion of the Turks and the confirmation of Habsburg rule initiated a long struggle between the absolutist empire and a reviving country. In 1711 conditions were desperate. In the central areas, depopulated under Turkish rule, the Austrian government introduced alien and more docile groups to weaken the unruly Magyar element. Much of the land was parceled out to foreign beneficiaries of the monarch's favor, who were recipients of political and social power, and some parts of the country were exempted from the jurisdiction of the Diet, especially the military frontier district of the south. The state apparatus on the whole was Hungarian, although for long periods the sovereign ruled by executive fiat rather than through traditional constitutional procedures. A discriminatory tariff policy was used to keep the country economically repressed in order to maintain it as a source of cheap raw materials and food supplies. Peasants lived miserably, and the agricultural enterprise of the countryside was hampered by outmoded systems of land tenure.

Nevertheless, the Hungarian will to independence survived, and forces of national revival emerged. Their origin was essentially the persistence and determination at this time of the lesser nobility and small farmers in defending the traditional rights of Hungary and Hungarians. Their activities were effective mainly on the level of county government, where many officials continued to be locally elected and within whose assemblies national interest could be maintained. At this level the effectiveness of the lesser nobility and a measure of democracy could be maintained.

Toward the end of the eighteenth century a national renaissance, notably in general literature and political theory, began in Hungary. Much influenced by the French, the movement opposed intolerance and fostered the nobility's opposition to the Austrian monarchy. A significant aspect of the literature was its nativistic emphasis upon the contribution of the pagan Magyars to the mainstream of Hungarian culture. More importantly, a large group of academicians, lawyers, writers, and other professionals strove for the abolition of feudal privileges and emphasized the peasantry as the foundation of the nation. The group's activities culminated in a conspiracy in 1795; the conspiracy was discovered, and many of those involved were executed or imprisoned. The development, however, became evidence of the need for reform. Also at this time the issue of the right of the Hungarian people to employ their own language, especially in contact with officialdom, was expanding in importance.

During the reigns of Charles III and Maria Theresa the Habsburgs had such a diversity of interests that it was important for them to preserve peace in the east. Under Charles III a permanent army was stationed in Hungary, administered by a war council and supported by a general war tax. Although Hungarian troops served in the army, no Hungarian could reach the higher ranks. The Royal Court Chancery and the Hungarian Deputy Council were entirely dependent on the king. The Austrians often retained control over the subordinate nationalities, and under this administration Transylvania and Croatia were administered separately.

After a long period of political quiescence, Hungarians again opposed Austrian absolutism, and a great reform movement began about 1830. Count Istvan Szechenyi, a wealthy aristocrat, became a leader of the second Hungarian renaissance and led the forces of the lesser nobility supporting evolutionary reform. More importantly, he became, in effect, a national educator defining the situation and necessities of Hungary. Szechenyi, filled with religious devotion and sensitive to the forces moving about him, called especially for the nation to turn its attentions to its own weaknesses. He analyzed the faults of the nobility, attacked their special privileges, and strove to incite them to enthusiasm for national reform. Some of his followers were conservative and evolutionary in their thinking and willing to work under the authority of the Habsburgs, but he also inspired those who believed that reform could be accomplished only by a disestablishment of the existing political regime, an idea to which he was opposed. Szechenyi called for cultural, economic, and social reforms under the rule of the Habsburgs rather than a revolution to overthrow the alien rule.

Whereas Szechenyi counseled economic and social improvement, Lajos Kossuth, a landless noble, advocated political revolution and independence. Szechenyi called for a revolution from the top, but Kossuth wanted an uprising of the common people. The one desired the mass educated; the other, the mass unleashed. The one counseled looking inward for the assessment of the nation's problems; the other prescribed looking abroad for the national enemy and found him in Vienna. The one's sternest lesson was hard, critical realism; the other's message was nationalist idealism. Szechenyi's evolutionary approach was enhanced by his great respect for Great Britain and its culture and civilization. Kossuth's revolutionary position was the product of a more active French influence. In effect, these two leaders became opposite poles of the Hungarian response to the revolutionary influences of the nineteenth century.

Repression followed every demand for reform, and each repression made each future demand more violent. Szechenyi's reform plans, which would have preserved the legal framework of evolutionary change, were not enough. Kossuth assumed leadership; his prestige was only enhanced by imprisonment between 1837 and 1840 for the political offense, among others, of publishing the proceedings of the county assemblies. Greatly influenced by French literary and political figures and French and American revolutionary events, Kossuth transformed a journalistic career into a career of national political leadership and gained renown through his slogans calling for a free people and a free fatherland.

The Diet, which opened in November 1847, was presented a program of conservative reform proposing the establishment of responsible government in Hungary (as opposed to Vienna) and an elected legislature, a system of uniform and general taxation, freedom of the press, and reinclusion of Transylvania in Hungary. Kossuth, however, soon demonstrated his control over the Diet, which went through a period of unproductive controversy until news of the revolution in Paris was received. Realizing the opportunity to initiate events and force change, Kossuth demanded the abolition of serfdom, popular representation, and the replacement of control from Vienna by control in a Hungarian government. These demands were presented to King Ferdinand, who responded favorably by appointing Count Lajos Batthyany as president of a Hungarian council.

Following the model of the Belgian constitution, the king was to exercise his power and prerogative through responsible ministers, whose countersignatures were required to give validity to his acts. The

Diet, established as a bicameral legislature (the Chamber of Deputies and the Chamber of Magnates), was to be elected for three years. Representation was related to the payment of taxes, educational qualifications, and knowledge of the Hungarian language. Several aspects of the new constitutional laws revealed the implicit radical Hungarian assumption, found also among the conservatives, that the ethnic minorities could be included within the Hungarian state without regard to their own national aspirations.

Certain aspects of relations with Austria remained vague, and control over such matters of common concern as public finance, defense, and foreign affairs was left in doubt. Austrian reactionaries and Hungarian counterrevolutionaries tried to undo what had been accomplished; in 1848 they contrived to set the national minorities against the Hungarians, at first covertly and then openly. King Ferdinand, who had granted the concessions in March 1848, was forced to abdicate in favor of Francis Joseph, who stated that he was not bound by the concessions made by his predecessor. The Austrians then moved with direct military force against the Hungarians; in 1849, when their efforts fell short, the Austrians asked the Russians for military assistance. The national minorities aroused to anti-Hungarian activity were Croats, Serbs, Romanians, Ruthenians, and Slovaks. The sporadic outbreaks of violence in Transylvania between Romanians and Hungarians in 1848 and 1849 were especially bloody.

Despite the bravery and skill of the Hungarians, the imperial Austrian and Russian forces defeated them. This defeat was hastened by internecine strife, and the head of the revolutionary government, Kossuth, was not above reproach in his role in such internal controversy. The Declaration of Independence of April 14, 1849, which had been insisted upon by Kossuth, proved to be a tactical blunder. It confirmed the worst suspicions of the Vienna reactionaries—that Kossuth was intellectually unprepared to remain in a moderate position. It created difficulties for the national forces in that it required a violation of the oath of loyalty to the king. The declaration made even more determined the efforts of the imperial and Russian armies to put down the Hungarian revolution, just as it doubtless increased the fears of the British and the French. Although they generally supported the development of constitutional monarchy, the British and the French could not but be alarmed at the prospect of the dissolution of the Habsburgs, whom they considered necessary to the European balance of power.

The decision of the government in Vienna was to make use of Hungary's defeat to destroy it as a state and to incorporate it into the empire as a province; some of its historic lands, such as Croatia and Transylvania, were separated from it in order to reduce its unity and strength. The new emperor, Francis Joseph I, had assumed the direction of the monarchy upon the abdication of Ferdinand. The first

18

seventeen years of his rule were characterized by the last attempt at absolute rule under the monarchy. The national minorities, which had been used against the Hungarians during the revolution, fared equally badly during the period of reaction and came to detest Austria as much as did the Hungarians.

Although the regime was soon changed from a military into a civil administration, no amelioration of the situation took place. A gigantic and corrupt state bureaucracy and system of political police imposed persecution and repression at great expense. For years it was controlled by Alexander von Bach, minister of internal affairs and revolutionary agitator turned tool of absolutism. Austrian, Galician, and Czech officials dominated the Hungarian administration, through which the emperor ruled by decree—entirely without reference to a constitution. Kossuth was forced into exile.

The general reaction was the development of a more intense national patriotism accompanied, at least among moderate and radical groups, by a hatred of everything German or Austrian. Many significant groups—their educational function for the time neglected—retired into political inactivity. Formal education itself declined in quality; much of it remained adequate only to train those who could fit into the bureaucracy.

The remaining political groups were all united in the view that historic Hungary had not lost its continuity and rejected the Austrian view that by reason of rebellion the Hungarians had forfeited the right to independence. They nevertheless were divided with respect to the type of reform they supported. The old conservatives called for a return to the constitutional arrangement of 1847, which presupposed Hungarian autonomy under a general monarchy. They also desired the reestablishment of county autonomy. In addition to desiring the maintenance of traditional relations with Austria, this group strove for some modernization. They were more politically passive than some other groups, but they became more active in general cultural affairs.

Another general group followed the leadership of Ferenc Deak, a conservative reformer, in demanding a return to the laws of April 1848, which the group declared to have an organic relationship with the traditional constitution. A third group, made up primarily of émigrés who had fled the country, insisted upon the principles of the April 1849 Declaration of Independence. The leader of the group was Kossuth, who over decades of exile never wavered from this position. On two occasions during the period they were able to continue the fight against the Habsburgs: the Italo-French war against Austria in 1859, as a result of which Austria lost Lombardy; and the war with Prussia in 1866, which removed Austria from any pretense of control in Germany.

The group led by Deak proved to have a compromise solution between the unitary concept of the Habsburgs and the complete independence of the radicals. Defeat in war and diplomatic isolation, especially from Russia, whose ambitions in the Balkans were causing a breach with that power, stimulated the emperor to choose the compromise position. His decision was supported by the official British desire to see the monarchy maintained as a bulwark against the Russian drive toward the Balkans and the Dardanelles.

Before the compromise advocated by Deak and his followers was passed by the Diet and accepted by Francis Joseph, Count Gyula Andrassy had been appointed as the responsible head of a Hungarian ministry, and Transylvania was brought again into union with Hungary. Thus, although the Revolution of 1848 had proved abortive, it in effect produced the compromise establishing the Dual Monarchy, finally adopted in 1867, which provided a workable arrangement between Austria and Hungary for fifty years.

THE DUAL MONARCHY

The Compromise of 1867 established a mode of relationship with Austria and the Habsburgs. It set forth the details of control over matters of common concern to the two countries—defense, finance, and foreign affairs. Failure to deal with them in 1848 had aroused the suspicions of court circles that the Hungarians were seeking complete independence. The arrangement of 1867 established a legal link between the two states.

A common monarch and the obligation to render mutual support on matters of general concern were accepted. Parliamentary bodies were to function in both states, and any suggestion of a general legislature was abandoned as an affront to Hungarian autonomy. The ministers involved with the matters of common concern were responsible to equal delegations from the two parliaments sitting alternately in the two capitals. The delegations fixed the budget for the matters of common concern, and a special committee periodically determined the relative financial contributions of the two countries. The army was made subject to the king with respect to its leadership and internal organization and to the Hungarian parliament on matters of the draft, recruitment, and the general system of defense. Agreements concerning commerce and the customs were made subject to periodic review every ten years.

The politics of the period from the compromise to World War I were almost entirely dominated by the issue of relations with Austria. Every Hungarian government was caught between unpopularity at home and an obstructive Austrian officialdom that remained adamant about the idea of a centralized monarchy, although Emperor Francis Joseph was consistently loyal to the 1867 arrangement. The dominating role of the question of public law tended to prevent concentration by the government upon the solution of social and economic problems.

The problem of minorities loomed ever larger. The one involving the

Croats was the most critical and, perhaps, the most revealing. The Croats received considerable autonomy, especially in local administration, education, and justice. It was provided that their language would be employed in matters connected with civil administration and justice and in education below the higher levels. They were made responsible to the Hungarian government through the governor and were empowered to send forty deputies to the Hungarian parliament. Despite such concessions, the Croats and other ethnic groups were no more satisfied with their status than were the Hungarians with dualism.

At the outbreak of World War I, after the assassination of Archduke Francis Ferdinand, the Hungarian government faced a dilemma. If the Hungarians failed to support the imperial government, minorities in the empire and the governments of peoples of similar ethnic background would exert pressure for the independence of those minorities on the assumption that the Dual Monarchy could not survive. On the other hand, a victory for the Central Powers might result in the inclusion of a larger number of Slavs in the Dual Monarchy. The situation forced the Hungarian leaders to accept the decisions already taken. The Hungarian decision was made easier by the fact that the killing of the wife of the archduke had turned political assassination into an even more heinous type of murder. The war policy could be supported, or rationalized as necessary, in order to withstand Russian imperial aggression. On this basis most parties in the country, including the Social Democratic Party, were able to bring some enthusiasm to the prosecution of the war.

Before Emperor Francis Joseph died in the fall of 1916, he recognized the need for peace if the Dual Monarchy was to be preserved. The Serbs were the only minority that had actively attempted to obstruct entry into the war, but it became increasingly difficult to use troop units made up of minorities at critical points on the war front; more and more the strain on Hungarian contingents became disproportionate to their number. Economic conditions deteriorated; hunger and privation became widespread. Despite the relatively large production of foodstuffs in the country, the drain imposed by the requirements of the Central Powers found production unequal to demand.

The successive failures of Russian military campaigns and the subsequent appearance of revolution in Russia encouraged Germany and Austria-Hungary to believe that they could win the war. The decision of the German high command to carry through offensives on the western front made it difficult to entertain the idea of a negotiated peace. Moreover, Germany's unrestricted submarine warfare raised an issue that ruled out any result except the unquestionable victory of one side or the other. Finally, the entry of the United States into the war made the Hungarians believe that their Hungarian national state could be preserved only if they persisted in the fight long enough to make unreasonably high the price the Allies would have to pay to destroy it. At the same time the minorities became more confident of an independent future, and the chance that conciliation could make them accept a status within the Hungarian state became more remote.

In October 1918 Count Mihaly Karolyi, a leader of the left wing of the Party of Independence, was appointed premier and formed a cabinet made up of Social Democrats, radicals, and members of his own group. In November this government declared Hungary a republic. Karolyi believed that a new policy of toleration toward the minorities and an orientation toward the Triple Entente could preserve a larger Hungary. The Allies, however, accepted Italian, South Slav, Romanian, and Czech demands. Serbian, Romanian, and Czech army units then established areas of occupation on Hungarian territory.

Gradually, the Karolyi government was infiltrated at all levels and at key points by Communists, who had in many cases returned from Russian prisoner of war camps where they had been influenced by the followers of Lenin. The Hungarian military forces on their return from the front had been disarmed before the security of the state had been established, and the Social Democrats proved incapable of withstanding pressure from the Left. In March 1919 the leftist group formed a bloc with the Communists. After Karolyi's resignation the communist leader, Bela Kun, formed a cabinet and, although technically not the head of government, reserved to himself full powers, including those over foreign affairs. A reign of terror was conducted by Bela Kun; its memory was a powerful factor in Hungarian resistance to communism and Russian influence. Bela Kun defended the country against the Czechs but, defeated by the Romanians, was forced to resign after five months in power.

The leader of the new counterrevolutionary regime was Admiral Miklos Horthy, commander in chief of the armed forces that entered Budapest in November 1919. In the absence of any possibility of a return of the Habsburgs, Admiral Horthy was elected regent of Hungary by the parliament in 1920. The government he headed was one of reaction and initially one of terror, and it carried out stringent reprisals against many who could be identified with the Bela Kun and Karolyi regimes, especially Jews.

The National Assembly on March 1, 1920, confirmed the selection of Horthy as regent. It also abolished the legislation of 1867 that had established the Dual Monarchy arrangement, but it did not finally settle whether the Habsburgs retained the right of succession. Even after two attempts by Charles IV to resume the throne in 1921 caused pressure to be applied on the legislature to declare the Habsburg succession revoked, there remained a division in Hungarian political thought on this subject. Horthy was most instrumental in bringing about the expulsion of Charles from Hungary. As regent, he symbolized a certain constitutional continuity in that he occupied a position previously held by Janos Hunyadi and Kossuth.

Hungary was forced to accept a dictated war settlement embodied in the Treaty of Trianon, signed on June 4, 1920, which most Hungarians considered underserved, unjust, and savage. Hungary lost 72 percent of its territory and 64 percent of its population to the so-called Successor States of the Dual Monarchy.

The frontiers of historic Hungary, which had been relatively stabilized for centuries and closely related to the Carpathian Basin as a natural geographic unit, were drastically altered. Three new states, made up of several ethnic groups, not all of which had been consulted about their desires for new political affiliations, were created as successors to Austria and Hungary. Many inhabitants of the new states had settled there during the Turkish period or shortly afterward as instruments of Habsburg policy against the Hungarians. In some areas of the new states, Hungarians averaged one-third of the population.

The regency was a period of reaction and attempted to return to traditional political and social institutions. The first ten years, largely under the premiership of Count Istvan Bethlen, was a period of conservative reconstruction and consolidation, with only unavoidable concessions to the various pressures for reform. The 1930s were characterized by ferment and unrest growing out of the effects of the world economic depression and the influence of the Nazi regime in Germany. Many events were affected by the domination of rightist radicals or extremist sympathizers with national socialism, whose prominent role was made possible by the Hungarian obsession with the injustices of the Trianon settlement.

The premiership of Count Bethlen was based on a majority in parliament of the Party of Unity, which was made up of members of the former Christian National Party and the Small Landowners' Party. Istvan Nagyatadi-Szabo, the leader of the Small Landowners' Party and a man of simple peasant background, was prevailed upon, in the name of patriotism, to collaborate with the Bethlen party. In return, he received assurances that some agrarian reform would be undertaken and that Bethlen would not hold fast to the legitimist (pro-Habsburg) position. Bethlen's agreement on legitimism cost him support in his own group, and for a time his position mainly depended on the support of members of the Small Landowners' Party. The Party of Unity won majorities in 1922 and 1926.

The premier's policy of conservative consolidation succeeded in reestablishing the old order, despite some concessions to change. Among these was a land-reform program, which was important in itself and also in providing a precedent for the future. Out of 1,785,000 acres requisitioned, 987,000 were reserved for small holdings, and 259,000 home sites were provided. The drive against inflation was pursued vigorously, and a reorganization of public finances was accomplished. The national economy was bolstered by the receipt of about

US$50 million from the League of Nations.

The country experienced a cultural revival, sponsored by both official and unofficial quarters. Important advances were made in the organization and improvement of the educational establishment (see ch. 6). The premier's policy was designed to recreate a position of prestige for the country, reflecting internal stability and soundness so that advantage might be taken of every opportunity to justify a restoration of historic Hungary.

The main immediate obstacle to this design was the policy of the Little Entente, made up of Czechoslovakia, Romania, and Yugoslavia, which was determined to preserve the advantages gained under the peace treaties. A possible solution to the problem of regional relations appeared to many non-Hungarians to be schemes of economic cooperation. The Hungarians were not at all disposed, however, to accept such schemes as a substitute for the rectification of what they considered political injustice. The foreign policy of the country sought alignments that would advance its power and prestige. The Bethlen government's first major step along these lines was the Friendship Agreement of 1927 with Italy, which, although it had fought on the winning side, was dissatisfied with the fruits of victory.

The effects of world economic depression led to more extreme leadership. Blamed for deteriorating economic circumstances, Bethlen resigned. After Count Gyula Karolyi held office briefly, General Gyula Gombos became premier in the fall of 1932. He had the advantage of close association with the regent—having been responsible for the regent's appointment as commander in chief of the forces that had established the interwar government—and he was the leader of strong rightist radical groups. Passionately obsessive in his nationalism, he not only continued the pro-Italian policy but also made an agreement with Austria and favored friendship with Nazi Germany.

Gombos was anti-Semitic, but not in the vicious form that prevailed in Germany. Most of the leading Hungarian statesmen were seriously preoccupied with what they called the Jewish problem. Anti-Semitic concepts ranged from the view that the Jews could not be well enough assimilated culturally to avoid their posing a threat to the integrity of the Hungarian nation and its culture to the view that they were inherently inferior. The rank-and-file frequently were anti-Semitic because many Jews had been associated with the regime of Bela Kun.

National socialist ideas spread widely during the mid-1930s, accompanied by an increase in anti-Jewish sentiment. The Arrow Cross parties, a collection of rightist groups, became more important and active and were helped especially by strong support from military leaders. A measure was proposed in the legislature to limit the participation of Jews in industrial, commercial, and intellectual activity to 20 percent of the total number in such activities.

The two premiers who served just before the outbreak of war were

Bela Imredy (May 1938-February 1939) and Count Pal Teleki (February 1939-April 1941). During Imredy's tenure dramatic events abroad made it certain that Hungary would be drawn into the international crisis, if only because of its determination to achieve its revisionist ambitions. In March 1938 Hitler annexed Austria, thus making Germany a direct neighbor of Hungary. By the first so-called Vienna Award, Germany and Italy gave Hungary 4,600 square miles of Czechoslovak territory, north of the Trianon frontier. Thus, Hungary received lost territory as a byproduct of German aggression. Although Premier Teleki was determinedly anti-German, Hungary received 16,000 square miles and 2.5 million people of northern Transylvania under his administration by the second Vienna Award in late 1940.

Teleki's tenure represented a growing fear of German encroachment and a determination to resist extremist pressure from the Right. Against the groups who proposed autocratic reform government and almost total exclusion of the Jews from national life, Teleki represented constitutionalism and determination to preserve 'national independence. The reforms he proposed were to be constitutionally accomplished and administered, but the outbreak of war in September 1939 produced conditions that destroyed almost the last vestiges of the country's freedom of choice.

WORLD WAR II AND ITS AFTERMATH

The start of the war preceded by several years the end of the regency, but the war initiated a period of crumbling independence. Count Teleki and his successors, especially Miklos Kallay, were unable to keep the country from becoming a Nazi satellite, although it was for a time freer than any other country in the German orbit. A measure of the extent of German control was the decision to abandon neutrality and to adhere to the Axis side of the war. Another indication was the requirement imposed on the country to assist Hitler by allowing the passage of German troops for an attack on Yugoslavia, despite an agreement of eternal friendship that Teleki had made with the Yugoslavs shortly before. Although acquiescence to the Nazi demands was the only way to avoid German occupation of the country, Teleki's own position was made untenable by negotiations carried on without his knowledge between the Hungarian general staff and the German high command. These developments drove Teleki to suicide.

The next premier was Laszlo Bardossy. During his tenure close military cooperation was developed with the Nazis and Hungary joined Germany in the invasion of the Soviet Union in June 1941. By the end of the year Hungary was also at war with the United Kingdom and the United States. Bardossy's declaration of war against the United States after the Japanese attack on Pearl Harbor was made without prior consultation with Horthy or the parliament. A short time later Horthy relieved Bardossy and appointed Miklos Kallay to the premiership.

Kallay, unlike Bardossy, had no sympathy for the Nazi cause, nor did he want Hungary overrun by Communists. He tried on several occasions to negotiate secretly with the Western Allies in the hope of extricating his country from the war. Through Kallay's efforts, Hungary occupied a special position in that it did not suffer from Allied aerial attacks. Eventually, Hitler became exasperated with his nominal ally and called Horthy to Germany. He informed Horthy that German troops would occupy Hungary, that Kallay would be dismissed, and that no further dealing with the Allies would be tolerated. Dome Sztojay, a Nazi sympathizer, was named premier, and a reign of terror, aimed primarily at Hungarian Jews, ensued. Horthy, still the nominal regent, managed to curtail some of the deportations of Jews to the extermination camps, but by the end of the war about two-thirds of Hungary's Jews—approximately 600,000 people—had been murdered.

In October 1944 Horthy arranged an armistice and broke off the alliance with Nazi Germany, for which he was subsequently arrested and imprisoned in Germany. The country, which had been under German occupation since early spring, was now a theater of war; Soviet armies were advancing from the east, and right-wing Nazi sympathizers were in control of the govermment. By Christmas Eve the Soviets had entered Budapest, which had been devastated by the retreating Nazis, as had the rest of the country. The last German troops were not driven out of Hungary until April 1945, but a Soviet-sponsored Hungarian government had already been in existence for several months.

The provisional government was nominally a coalition of the non-fascist parties, but the overriding political fact of life in postwar Hungary was the occupation by Soviet forces. The Allied Control Commission, made up of American, British, and Soviet representatives, was chaired by a Soviet marshal and was dominated by Soviet policy. Russian troops were in control of the territory, and it was not difficult for the Russian leadership to exert its authority while effectively blocking American and British initiatives. President Harry S. Truman of the United States and Prime Minister Clement Attlee of the United Kingdom complained that the Allied Control Commission was thwarted in its tripartite functions because of Soviet high-handedness and intransigence, and, further, that the provisional government was not truly representative of the Hungarian people. The Allied complaints did not affect Premier Joseph Stalin of the Soviet Union, however, who saw Eastern Europe as necessarily subject to Soviet control. In the meantime, noncommunist Hungarian politicians were trying to establish an independent sovereign state, but their efforts could not block the communization of Hungary as the Soviet Union, working through indigenous Communists as well as through Soviet military power, pushed the country inexorably toward the status of a Soviet satellite.

In November 1945 the Soviets allowed relatively free elections, in which the Smallholders' Party won 57 percent of the seats in the legislature and the Hungarian Communists won only 17 percent. The Smallholders' held the office of premier until 1952, but uncontrolled elections were not again permitted, and actual political power was drawn into the hands of the Communists by undercutting the political bases and the programs of all other parties. The Ministry of Interior, which was the key to power, was in communist hands, and the leader of the Hungarian Communist Party, Matyas Rakosi, became the real ruler of the country. Rakosi became well known for his so-called salami tactics by which, in his definition, he sliced off from the body politic all opposition parties and opposition factions within his own party. Rakosi, in attaining power and destroying opposition, was backed by the Soviet military and the newly organized Hungarian political police, the State Security Department (Allamvedelmi Osztaly—AVO).

Although elections in the summer of 1947 gave considerable strength to the opposition and a government representing the Smallholders' Party was continued in office nominally under Premier Lajos Dinnyes, the domination of the Communists was complete, if not formal, by this time. Such absolute control was made formal in 1949 with the adoption of a new constitution establishing a single-party government. Meanwhile, the process of destroying the political opposition continued, and the result was a foregone conclusion—in a short time the Communists had no real political competition. The single remaining source of popular resistance, the Roman Catholic Church, was also gradually weakened.

To Rakosi, who emulated Stalin in his approach to governing, the fact that more than 60 percent of the people were nominal Roman Catholics presented a challenge, which he chose to meet by attacking the hierarchy of the Hungarian church. He had openly criticized the communist leadership in Poland for being too lenient in dealing with the religious problem and, to back up his expressed ideas, he ordered the arrest of Jozsef Cardinal Mindszenty, Roman Catholic primate of Hungary. Brought to trial, Mindszenty was charged with a variety of crimes against the state—to which he confessed his guilt; however, to Hungarian Catholics who were aware that the cardinal had stated earlier that any confession he might make would be made under duress, Mindszenty became a martyr. The cardinal's sentence of life imprisonment enraged and emboldened the people, who reacted by attending religious services more than they had before the persecutions began. The Rakosi regime, however, did not retreat in the face of adverse public reaction but increased its antireligious activities and enlarged them to include Protestants and Jews.

Rakosi, after achieving full power, set about to transform Hungary into a miniature Soviet Union. His strength was based on control of the communist party, the secret police, and the armed forces. A three-year economic plan, inaugurated in 1947, was designed to nationalize industry and collectivize agriculture; great emphasis was placed on heavy industry, and other aspects of the economy suffered accordingly. Peasants, most of whom had owned land only since 1945, resisted collectivization and compulsory deliveries of their products to the state. Resentment on the part of the peasants and general underinvestment in agriculture by the state caused great economic difficulties in the early 1950s. Agriculture and all other sectors of Hungary's economy suffered from the early economic policies of the Communists. Rakosi, meanwhile, had made himself premier, thus occupying the top position in the government as well as in the party.

Rakosi patterned his regime on that of Stalin in the Soviet Union, building around himself a so-called cult of personality and running the country by means of force and terror. The secret police, which had been renamed the State Security Authority (Allamvedelmi Hatosag—AVH), had become a dreaded force, and Hungarian prisons were overflowing with political prisoners. (The Hungarian people continued to use the acronym AVO as a derogatory epithet). Discontent was rife among all segments of the population, and the discrepancies between the claims of official propaganda and actual conditions placed an intolerable strain on popular credulity. Stalin's death in March 1953 began a period of decline in the power held by Rakosi. Apparently Stalin's successors did not appreciate the concentration of power in the hands of a single individual in their Hungarian satellite; Rakosi was summoned to Moscow in May 1953 and, upon his return, he divested himself of some of his power and personally condemned the cult of personality, the development of which he had so assiduously nurtured earlier. Imre Nagy was named premier and instituted the so-called New Course, which was supposed to eradicate the ills of the past and set the country on the proper path toward socialism.

Nagy's New Course brought almost immediate change to the country. Living conditions improved; concentration camps were abolished, and prisoners were released; curbs were placed on the power of the AVH; and about half of the peasants who had been forced into collectives left them. Although his reforms met with popular approval, Nagy still faced strong opposition within the party, where Rakosi continued to wield great influence. Nagy himself had impeccable communist credentials, but his reform methods did not appeal to the old-line Stalinists led by Rakosi. A power struggle within the party and government continued until early 1955, when Rakosi gained the upper hand and Nagy was ousted from both party and government.

The taste of freedom that the Hungarian people enjoyed under Nagy left them with a great desire to seek more. Although Rakosi was back in power, his position was not nearly as secure as it had been during his early years. Rakosi was unable to reestablish his authoritarianism and, after several hectic months, he was replaced by Erno Gero, apparently on orders from Soviet Premier Nikita Khrushchev. Gero, a former Rakosi henchman, was unable to stem the rising tide of public dissatisfaction, and the people openly demonstrated for independence and the return of Nagy. On October 23, 1956, a large group of demonstrators tried to seize the radio station in Budapest in order to broadcast their grievances. The AVH forces defending the radio station opened fire, killing many of the demonstrators. Word of the massacre spread rapidly and, within hours, a full-scale uprising was in progress.

After several days of intense fighting, Russian tank forces managed to quell the revolt and extinguish the flame of freedom, which had burned fiercely for a short time. Nagy emerged as the national leader during the short revolution but, betrayed by a false promise of safe conduct, he fell into Soviet hands and was later executed. Cardinal Mindszenty was among the thousands of political prisoners released by the revolutionaries; however, when Soviet forces retook the country from the insurgents, the cardinal asked for and received asylum in the American legation.

Fighting continued in some regions for several weeks but, after the Soviet troops had eliminated all traces of rebellion, Hungary was more of a puppet state than at any other time. Janos Kadar was named to the position of party first secretary with Soviet approval. The party, now known as the Hungarian Socialist Workers' Party, was once again in sole power, and foreign policies were completely aligned with those of Moscow. Kadar, however, after a period of repression, gradually began to soften his regime by granting amnesty to political prisoners and by curbing the power of the political police. In an oft-quoted statement Kadar said, "Those who are not against us are with us," and this summed up the pragmatic attitude of his government during the 1960s. In accord with the new pragmatism, Kadar inaugurated the so-called New Economic Mechanism in 1968, which was intended to bolster the country's economy by introducing as many aspects of a free-market economy as could be consistent with the control of the party.

CHAPTER 3

PHYSICAL ENVIRONMENT AND POPULATION

Hungary is a landlocked country of east-central Europe that has access to the Black Sea via the Danube River. Its central location places the capital city, Budapest, within 1,500 miles of all other European and North African capitals (see fig. 1). The country is approximately 325 miles from east to west and 155 miles from north to south and has an area of about 35,920 square miles. According to a 1972 estimate Hungary's population was 10.4 million. Austria is the only noncommunist country with which Hungary shares borders.

The 1972 boundaries were nearly the same as those drawn for the country in 1920, when the Treaty of Trianon attempted to limit its area to that predominantly occupied by the Hungarian, or Magyar, people. In so doing, a great part of the traditional Kingdom of Hungary was divided among neighboring states, and its population was reduced by nearly 40 percent, including approximately 3.4 million Magyars. As Germany's ally during World War II major portions of the old kingdom were briefly restored, but settlements after the war returned the state to within about fifty square miles of its prewar size and to nearly its identical earlier boundaries.

About two-thirds of the land has an elevation of less than 650 feet, and the highest mountain point is only a little more than 3,300 feet. Of the lower land, plains country predominates, but there is much low, gently undulating hilly ground. The southeastern section of the country and the extreme northwest are generally flat; low hills prevail over the major part of the land west of the Danube River, which roughly bisects the country from north to south. Low mountains extend in a roughly straight line northeast from the Austrian border. East of the Danube the mountains intercept the Czechoslovak border and follow it to the northernmost points in the country. Lower elevations have great expanses of fertile soils.

The largely Magyar population is descended from the tribes that migrated into and settled this region in the ninth century. Minorities constituted less than 5 percent of the total population in 1972. People have been gravitating to the towns since the mid-nineteenth century and in increasing numbers since World War II. The country remains more rural than urban, however, and Budapest is the only large city. A few others are medium-sized industrial and cultural centers, but typical towns are small market centers.

NATURAL FEATURES

Topography

Although the area is small and the whole of it is within the middle-Danube, or Carpathian, basin, the country is usually divided into four major topographic regions (see fig. 2). The Great Hungarian Plain

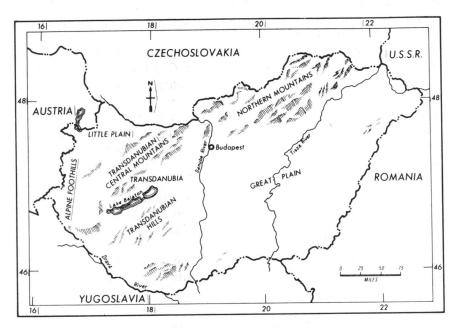

Figure 2. Topography of Hungary

(Nagy Magyar Alfold), more commonly called the Great Plain, accounts for about one-half of the total area and comprises the lowlands east of the Danube River. Transdanubia (Dunantul), the hillier region west of the Danube, is approximately two-thirds the size of the Great Plain. The remainder of the country is accounted for in the Little Plain (Kisalfold) in the extreme northwest and the low Northern Mountains that range along the Czechoslovak border east of the Danube and north of the Great Plain.

The Great Plain has a mean elevation of a little more than 300 feet. Except for its river valleys, its landscape is relieved largely by hillocks and sand dunes. The largest deviations from the average elevation occur on a plateau between the Danube and Tisza rivers and in an area in the northeast along the Romanian border. The plateau is from 100 to 150 feet higher than the floodplains of the rivers, and the gentle northeastern hills reach approximately 600 feet.

Dunaı tul, the Hungarian name for Transdanubia, means the land beyond the Danube. It consists of approximately 12,500 square miles of rolling country. Its flatter lands are less monotonous than those of the Great Plain and occupy less of the region than do its hilly and low mountainous sections. The uplands in the west are foothills of the Alps.

Lake Balaton, the last remnant of the ancient Pannonian Sea, is roughly in the center of the region. To its east, and extending to the Danube River, is the Mezofold, a lowland similar in many respects to the Great Plain. The higher lands immediately south of the lake are the Transdanubian Hills, or the Somogy Hills. Farther south are the coal-bearing and uranium-rich Mecsek and Villany mountains.

Most elevations in the alpine foothills to the west of the lake are below 1,000 feet, but a few isolated spots on the Austrian border rise to nearly 3,000 feet. The Transdanubian Central Mountains extend along the northern side of the lake and continue northeastward into the residential areas of Budapest and into the Danube Nook (Dunazug). The chain consists of several minor ranges, many of them having much relatively unspoiled beauty. The scenery is not of the rugged mountain type; most of the hillcrests are rounded, and elevations range from about 700 to less than 2,500 feet.

The Little Plain, an area of about 2,300 square miles, is so small that it is sometimes considered a part of Transdanubia. Its mean elevation is approximately 100 feet higher than that of the Great Plain. Most of this region consists of rich agricultural land, but swampland is also prevalent.

The Northern Mountains constitute the remaining 3,100 miles of the country's area. They are the lower volcanic fringe of the Carpathian Mountains, the only uplands in the country that are part of the Carpathian system.

The individual ranges in the group extend northeastward from the gorge of the Danube River near Esztergom for about 140 miles. Although the highest point in the mountains—Mount Kekes in the Matra range—is only about 3,330 feet above sea level, many of the slopes in the area are steep and give a false impression of their height. Points at the upper elevations are sunny, have many springs and small streams, and are popular resort areas.

Drainage

The entire country is located in the middle-Danube basin. The drainage pattern follows the Danube River, which eventually flows into the Black Sea. Local streams in northern Transdanubia and the Little Plain flow to the Danube within Hungary, but those in larger portions of the country, including southern Transdanubia and most of the Great Plain, drain to its tributaries—the Drava and Tisza—and join the Danube in Yugoslavia.

The middle course of the Danube stretches for 600 miles between the Deveny Gate (just above Bratislava, Czechoslovakia) and the Iron Gate on the boundary between Yugoslavia and Romania. About 240 miles of the middle river is in, or borders, Hungary. Although it is a great stream as it flows through Budapest and continues southward through Hungary, its size within this portion is only about 35 percent of that which it attains by the time it enters the Black Sea. Its flow averages 3,050 cubic yards per second at Budapest, as compared with 8,420 cubic yards per second at its exit into the Black Sea.

As it flows through Hungary, the Danube falls very little. It is about 440 feet above sea level as it reaches Hungary and about 280 feet above sea level as it leaves the country, but by far the greater portion of the fall is along the Czechoslovak border and in the gorge of the river north of Budapest. In the Great Plain between the capital and the Yugoslav border it falls only about fifty feet, or less than six inches per mile.

The slight fall and irregular waterflow account for the devastation that the river has periodically inflicted upon the river cities and the adjacent plains. Floodwaters are expected twice during each normal year. The first, its white flood, occurs in April or May when snow melts at lower elevations up the river and its ice breaks up. The water released in the white flood is usually not its most dangerous factor. Ice plugs can develop, and the backed-up water and ice then can be much more destructive than the high water alone. An ice plug during the white flood of 1838, for example, destroyed the cities of Obuda, Pest, and much of Buda.

The second, or green flood, usually occurs in June. Most of the up-river tributaries are fed by heavy rains during the late spring, and much of the snow at higher elevations melts at about the same time; the result is usually higher water levels than are experienced during the early flood. At Budapest the river may rise twenty-five feet or more above its normal level during the green flood. Devastation from the ice-free water is usually less, however, because the flood stages are more predictable and flood controls are more effective.

The Tisza and Drava are also major rivers, although they are not in the same class with the Danube. The Tisza is the Danube's second largest tributary. Similar to the Danube, during the seasons when its flow is low or moderate, it meanders slowly across the Great Plain but, in contrast to the Danube, its streambed is flat, and it has little or no valley. Its flow is highly irregular, and during early and late spring floods it may carry fifty times as much water as it does during the summer. Like the Drava it may also have a lesser flood in October, but in most respects it is more similar to the Danube, and its highest waters usually occur during the second, or June, flood. The earlier one may also be its more dangerous but for different reasons. The Tisza's ice melts first in the south and does not accumulate in increasing quantities downstream; consequently, it has had no serious ice plugs in recent history. Its high water, however, may concur with that of the Danube. When this happens, the swollen Danube cannot accept the Tisza's waters, and they back up for the river's entire length in Yugoslavia and into vast areas of Hungary's Great Plain. It was such a flood in

1879 that devastated the city of Szeged, which is located about ten miles north of the Hungarian-Yugoslav border.

The Tisza's early summer and greater flood usually does not concur with that of the Danube. Caused almost exclusively by heavy seasonal precipitation, the greater part of which falls in the Carpathians, this flood is most severe in northern areas and diminishes in the south. The southern tributaries, fed from less extreme amounts of rainfall, are relatively less swollen.

The Drava is smaller than the Tisza by only a slight margin. It accumulates most of its volume in Austria, flows across the northern tip of Yugoslavia, forms a part of the Hungarian-Yugoslav border for about eighty miles, and turns back into Yugoslavia again for about forty miles before joining the Danube. It may have three annual floods—the third in early autumn—but it flows adjacent to higher terrain on its northern shore and is a significant feature in the life of far fewer Hungarians than are the Danube and Tisza.

Both the Danube and Tisza rivers have been controlled since the mid-nineteenth century. The Tisza had been an especially capricious stream. It frequently had inundated enough territory to make its valley resemble an inland sea, and it had changed channels often and unpredictably. Control measures are not completely effective, but they have permitted the populating of several millions of acres of hitherto worthless land. In addition to maintaining river channels, irrigation water has been made available, swamps have been drained, and all-season roads have been built where transport was formerly paralyzed for much of the year.

Lake Balaton, seventy-five miles southwest of Budapest, is about forty-five miles long; its width varies, never reaching more than eight miles. It averages a little more than ten feet in depth, and its deepest point is only about thirty-five feet. The deeper northern end drops off steeply from the shore, providing excellent fishing but few good beaches for bathing. In the south there are beaches with fine sand and water depths that increase gradually. In some places bathers may wade on soft sand for half a mile or more from shore.

Lake Ferto (Neusiedler See in German) on the northwestern border is shared with Austria, but Hungary's portion is only about one-fourth of the total. Although its depth varies, the lake averages only approximately three feet. The shallow lake frequently freezes entirely and is unsuitable for recreational purposes and fish-breeding. Reeds grown in and around it have some commercial value, however, and it provides a haven for many species and great numbers of waterfowl.

Lake Velence, between Lake Balaton and Budapest, is worked artificially to maintain water depths of from three to six feet and to keep it suitable for holiday bathing, even though it does not have good natural beaches. It is excellent for fishing and is stocked largely with sporting varieties for anglers. Marshes on the southwestern end of the lake have been drained, and the reeds have been cleared from about half of its surface.

Climate

A high percentage of clear, sunny days—in addition to the characteristically cold winters, hot summers, and well defined four seasons—gives the impression that the country's climate is continental. In fact, Atlantic and Mediterranean systems are also influential, but their effects are less obvious. Continental and polar airmasses dominate the weather about 65 percent of the time during the winter months but only about 20 percent of the time in the summer. Maritime weather prevails about 30 percent of the time in winter and about 65 percent of the time in the summer. Subtropical Mediterranean systems are dominant for the remainder of the time—about 5 percent in winter and 15 percent in summer.

Geography and topographic relief account for the lesser influence from maritime and Mediterranean systems. The country is more than 700 miles from the Atlantic Ocean and is separated from it by the Alps. It is nearer the Mediterranean but is separated from it by high terrain. Both the maritime and Mediterranean systems have a large proportion of low-pressure airmasses, but their clouds dissipate when they lose their moisture upon encountering high elevations en route to Hungary.

Clear, dry air from the high-pressure polar and continental airmasses that have clockwise circulation enters the country from the eastern quadrants. The low hills of the eastern Carpathians provide little resistance to its entry into the basin but, once there, it tends to be trapped. Stagnant high-pressure air settles in the mountain-surrounded basin and is difficult to dislodge. Nonetheless, the weather that reaches the country from the Atlantic and the Mediterranean is moderating and brings in a great portion of its precipitation. At the same time, because neither of the moderating systems bear on the country directly, their effects are irregular and undependable. This accounts for a distribution of rainfall that is not the most advantageous for vegetation and that results in overfrequent seasons of drought or serious flooding.

Rainfall averages approximately twenty-eight inches per year in the western part of the country and approximately twenty-two inches in the eastern part. Even the most arid portions of the Great Plain receive a little less than twenty inches.

The total amount of precipitation, and its normal seasonal distribution, would appear to be highly favorable for agricultural production. The statistics are misleading in this case, however, and in many individual seasons the quantities or distribution, or both, may deviate widely from the norm. There are usually two or three years of each decade when total precipitation is six inches or more below normal, and it may then fall at the wrong time for agricultural purposes. There are also two or three years during each decade in which average precipitation is higher by about the same amount. If the extra precipitation is received at the wrong time, flooding can be as disastrous as drought.

Mean average temperature for the country is about 50°F. Budapest, in which the city buildup retains or generates extra heat, and the extreme southeast regions average about 2°F warmer than the mean for the country. Higher elevations average up to 4°F cooler. July, which averages about 70°F, is the warmest month; January, averaging about 29°F, is the coldest. Although the year-round averages are nearly the same in the various regions, the winters are warmer and the summers are cooler in Transdanubia than they are in the Great Plain. The highest temperature recorded over a 175-year period occurred in 1950, when it reached 106°F in the city of Pecs in southern Transdanubia. The lowest reading during that period was -29°F in 1942. Typical yearly extremes are about -15°F and 95°F.

Prevailing surface winds are influenced in large degree by the local terrain. This is particularly true in a basin situation, such as Hungary's, where the surrounding mountains reduce the surface effects of the airmasses that are dominant in the general area. Over the greater part of the country, including most of Transdanubia and the Great Plain west of the Tisza River, the winds are most frequently from the north and northwest. East of the Tisza and in the eastern portion of the Northern Mountains, they are most often from the northeast.

Based on fifty years of local records, the sun shines in Budapest approximately 2,000 hours a year, or nearly 5½ hours a day, which is near the average for the country. December is a dark, overcast month, however, and has only an hour and fifteen minutes of sunshine daily. August has the most of any month, averaging approximately nine hours and forty minutes per day. In general, western regions are slightly less sunny than those in the east, but the plateau between the Danube and Tisza rivers experiences the most sunshine. The excellent orchards and vineyards are attributable to the high country averages.

Soils

Soils vary from nearly worthless to among the finest in Europe. The poorer types include alluvial, swamp, leached podzols, and sandy soils that have high salt content. Fortunately for the country many of the poor varieties at low elevations respond to flood control, drainage, and soil treatment and can be made productive. The podzols occur in forested areas at higher elevations that will probably be retained as forest land.

The alluvial, heavily saline, and swampy soils of the lowlands have resulted from the Danube and Tisza river sedimentation. All of it was initially alluvial. Where the grades of the rivers were slight and the bases relatively nonporous, clayey swamp soils have formed. Where the rivers' grades were slightly greater, deposits were more coarse and, if the bases drained quickly and flooding was regular, there was little chance for vegetation to take hold. As humus developed slowly, the soil remained sandy. Danube sediment is alkaline; the Tisza's is high in some minerals but deficient in lime. Where the mineral contents are concentrated, the soils support only limited and specialized plantlife.

Flood controls along major rivers have been effective for about a century, and both natural processes and artificial practices are gradually showing favorable results. The swampy soils are usually fertile, and most of them are friable when they are dry. The looser alluvial types develop humus more rapidly when they are free from excessive flooding and as more vegetation is developed on them. Irrigation has helped where precipitation has been inadequate or irregular. Areas of free-blowing, shifting sands have been reduced considerably.

Intermediate grades of dense soils are usually called meadow soils because they are difficult to till and are most advantageously retained as hayfields or pastureland. These soils are most prevalent at low elevations, where they were frequently flooded and covered for long periods by stagnant water. There was much of this type of terrain adjacent to and between the Danube and Tisza before the rivers were controlled.

Finer soils also occur in several varieties and prevail over greater areas. On the Great Plain, at elevations generally above flood level, humus developed, loess deposits were not washed away, and even the alluvium acted beneficially when it was deposited in small quantities. Top soils are thick, some having loess deposits that are up to sixty yards thick. In the steppe area of the southeast, where the finest soil in the country is found, brown humus is mixed with the loess for average depths of 1½ to two yards.

Transdanubia has also received heavy loess deposits, and its slightly higher elevations have been flood free and heavily vegetated for centuries. The result has been thick, fertile, dark brown and black earth. Lower levels, as in the Great Plain, have alluvial sands and meadow clays.

Soils of the Little Plain resemble those of the Great Plain, but larger areas in proportion to its size have not been drained. Land that can be worked yields excellent crops because precipitation in that area is more abundant and dependable.

Vegetation

Although local weather and, especially, temperature ranges are more closely associated with a continental climate, maritime and Mediterranean weather systems have had, and continue to have, a surprising amount of influence on the area's vegetation. Some sheltering from severe winds and low temperatures results from the wreath of mountains surrounding the mid-Danubian basin, and remnants of subtropical plant species have been able to survive on lower slopes that have southern exposures.

Before the greater part of the land was cleared for cultivated crops, natural vegetation in most of Transdanubia and on nearly all of the land at higher elevations was forest. The southeastern portion of the Great Plain was a continuation of the Russian steppe. Depending upon the soils—which might be sandy, swampy, or alkaline—typical vegetation consisted of high grasses and low shrubs, reeds and coarse swamp grasses, or sparse scrub bushes, respectively. The steppe influence declined in the western plains, the land became more heavily wooded, and individual trees grew to larger sizes.

Forests throughout Transdanubia were predominantly deciduous. Conifers were spotted at isolated places in the extreme western and northern upland regions. Oaks and willows, which tolerate ground moisture and periodic inundation better than most species, were most widespread in lower areas. Beech, which prefer cool, moist weather and a little elevation, proliferated in most of the uplands of northern Transdanubia and in the Northern Mountains. Beech provided the most and best quality timber during the years that the original forests were being exploited.

Since most of the land has been put to man's use and most of the natural vegetation has been replaced, a little more than 55 percent of the land has come under cultivation for annual crops. Forests, many of them with their original trees replaced by more rapidly growing species, remain on only approximately 14 percent of the land. Orchards and vineyards occupy another 4 percent; most of them are on the southern slopes of hilly regions and on the reclaimed sandy lands of the Great Plain. Meadows and pastures account for 15 percent, including much of the land that is difficult to drain and too heavy to till easily. The remaining land is urban area or for some other reason cannot be used for agricultural production (see ch. 13).

The high percentage of sunny hours favors wine-producing grapes. During the nineteenth century vineyards on most mountain slopes were destroyed by plant lice, but the sandy soils of the Great Plain proved to be immune to the pest and now produce most of the country's wine.

Fruit also grows in profusion. Apple varieties, each adapted to a different section of the country, produce the greatest yields. Peaches, plums, pears, cherries, and apricots also do well. Nut crops include walnuts, almonds, chestnuts, and hazelnuts.

Wildlife

Undisturbed land on which large wild animals can breed or find natural food and shelter has been steadily decreasing. A few wolves and lynx remain; and game animals, such as the wild boar and a few species of deer, are protected. The Hortobagy region in the northeastern part of the Great Plain, formerly a colorful land of wild and semiwild horses, is now largely cultivated.

The shallow lakes, particularly Lake Balaton and Lake Ferto, provide shelter for many species of waterfowl and other birdlife. The country's largest wildlife refuge, the Kis Balaton bird sanctuary, is at the shallow southwestern end of the lake. Large birds that prefer a drier habitat—including black storks, great bustards, and little bustards—are found on the Great Plain.

Several fish species—including European carp, perch, pike, and sheatfish—are plentiful in several of the rivers and lakes, but about 70 percent of those sold commercially are spawned and developed in fish hatcheries. Carp is the species most often bred. Since irrigation water has enabled rice cultivation in some areas, fish farming has also become possible. This farming performs a dual function; in addition to the fish harvest, it provides a naturally fertilized soil for the rice crops.

Mineral Resources

Significant quantities of bauxite and some uranium, coal, oil, and natural gas are available. Iron, manganese, copper, and lead occur in lesser quantities, but all of them are being mined. Some gold appears in the local copper ores, and small deposits of silver are found in the same vicinities. Of the nonmetallic ores, sulfur and arsenic are the most important. The local population also considers that the country's mineral and medicinal waters are important mineral resources; there are hundreds of such springs that have several differing varieties of chemical content.

Bauxite reserves exceed those of the Soviet Union, are second in Europe only to those of France, and constitute 9 percent of those known to exist throughout the world. The ore is found at several places in the Transdanubian Central Mountains southwest of Budapest. It is of high quality and may be surface mined. The ore contains between 50 and 63 percent aluminum oxide, and some of it also contains 15 to 23 percent iron oxide in addition to the aluminum.

Uranium is found in two areas of the Mecsek Mountains in southern Transdanubia. Discovered in 1954, the mines have been developed by the Soviet Union, and the ores have not received final processing in the country.

Black anthracite coal is also mined in small quantities in the Mecsek Mountains. It is good quality in certain respects, but it makes a brittle coke that is not ideal for production of iron and steel, and some better grades must be imported.

Lignites and brown coals are much more plentiful. The better quality brown coals are most abundant in the Transdanubian Central Mountains west of Budapest. The largest quantities of lignite are found in the southern part of the Northern Mountains, but there are smaller deposits in all of the other upland areas of the country.

Known reserves of oil will allow some further exploitation, but crude oil must also be imported. Natural gas occurs in quantities that could serve local requirements, although it is cheaper to import gas from Romania for some of the eastern areas. The major oilfields are located in the Alpine foothills in the western county of Zala; minor quantities have been discovered on the Great Plain. Natural gas is more widely distributed and is piped to many of the larger cities and towns, but the gas pipelines appear to converge on Budapest, as the demand for it is heaviest in that vicinity.

BOUNDARIES AND POLITICAL SUBDIVISIONS

Boundaries

The total boundary of Hungary is about 1,400 miles long. About 222 miles are shared with Austria to the west, 448 with Czechoslovakia to the north, sixty-six with the Soviet Union to the northeast, 270 with Romania to the east, and 394 with Yugoslavia to the south. The Danube and Ipoly rivers delineate the western portion of the northern border; the Drava and Mura rivers delineate a considerable portion of the southwestern border; and some ten miles of the northern boundary line crosses Lake Ferto. Elsewhere, terrain features are not sufficiently salient to serve as natural borders.

The 1972 boundaries are close to those established for the country in 1920 by the Treaty of Trianon. After the country's defeat in World War 1, the treaty stripped 71.4 percent of its territory from the old kingdom. Areas removed were major contributions to the formation of Czechoslovakia and Yugoslavia and increased the size of Romania by roughly 50 percent. Some Hungarian geographers have argued that the treaty destroyed most of the former natural boundaries and that the smaller state was no longer the viable economic and geographic unit that had existed before. From a physical standpoint the old boundaries encompassed the middle-Danube basin, which was a territorial entity wreathed naturally by the Carpathian Mountains in the north and east, by the Alps in the west, and by the Dinaric Alps in the south.

Political Subdivisions

The major administrative areas for local government are the nineteen counties and five towns of county rank (see fig. 3). The counties range in size from 870 to 3,230 square miles and in population from about 240,000 to 860,000. County boundaries have not adhered to those of the topographic regions; most of Pest County, for example, is in the Great Plain, but some of its western and northern sections are in Transdanubia and the Northern Mountains. In general, there are three counties in the Northern Mountains, seven in the Great Plain, and eight in Transdanubia. Gyor-Sopron County encompasses most of the Little Plain.

Of the cities having county rank, Budapest stands alone in population

41

with nearly 2 million inhabitants. The other four average approximately 150,000 each. Miskolc, a mining and industrial town, is located in the northeast in the foothills of the Northern Mountains. Debrecen is a cultural and university city with a rich tradition and is located in the easternmost part of the country. Szeged, on the Tisza River near the southern border, is a frontier and commercial town, but it is also the major cultural center for the southern portion of the Great Plain. Most buildings in the city have been built since 1879 because only a few of the most substantial ones survived the great flood of that year. Pecs, on the southern slopes of the Mecsek Mountains in southern Transdanubia, is an old city with much history and tradition, and it has also become the commerical and industrial center for its section of the country.

There are two administrative levels of local government below that of the counties and the cities of county rank. The intermediate group consists of districts and towns of district rank. The lowest level consists of small towns, villages, cooperatives, and others. From the administrative standpoint, the classifications of village and town denote little, except whether or not the settlement is to be considered rural or urban.

If they are not built around some nonagricultural enterprise, all settlements or areas having populations of less than 5,000 are considered villages. Of the settlements or areas having between 5,000 and 20,000 inhabitants, 205 are considered villages, and twenty-five are considered towns. Of those having populations greater than 20,000, only two of the fifty-three are classified as villages.

SETTLEMENT PATTERNS

The seven Magyar tribes that settled Hungary in the late ninth century were nomads, horsemen, and raiders. Before their arrival in the middle-Danube basin, they had been so constantly in movement that their ethnic identification from earlier days was inconclusive (see ch. 2).

At the time of their appearance, the Great Plain was a no man's land between German states and the Byzantine empire. It was ideal horse country, and the surrounding mountains provided shelter for the tribes if they were pursued after raiding sorties into neighboring territories. In A.D. 955 the Magyars settled down on the Great Plain—after suffering a decisive defeat. Later they occupied Transdanubia, the land across the Danube. The extent of the land they have occupied has been subject to compression by neighboring ethnic groups, but the Magyars have at times exerted outward pressures.

The country is usually depicted as one characterized by its villages and towns—most of them small, a few medium-sized. Only Budapest and four other cities have populations greater than 100,000. The sizes of villages and towns overlap; the determination between them is based mostly on size but also upon whether the inhabitants should be termed urban or rural. According to the 1970 census, 5.7 million persons were villagers, and they comprised the entire 55 percent of the population classified as rural. The term *village* is not used in its generally accepted sense to describe the small cluster of houses and shops at the center of a rural area; a Hungarian village encompasses the entire area. The 3,135 villages, therefore, account for 88 percent of the country's total area, and the seventy-six towns, for the remaining 12 percent. Of the settlements classified as villages, about 1,500 have fewer than 1,000 persons, and another 1,500 have between 1,000 and 5,000. Of the remaining 210 larger villages, two have more than 20,000 inhabitants (see table 1).

Table 1. Urban-Rural Population of Hungary, 1970 Census

Settlement Size (population)	Number of		Populations (in thousands)	
	Villages	Towns	Villages	Towns
Less than 500	664	0	213	0
500–1,000	814	0	596	0
1,000–1,500	500	0	616	0
1,500–2,000	329	0	571	0
2,000–3,000	340	0	834	0
3,000–5,000	281	0	1,066	0
5,000–10,000	151	2	1,041	16
10,000–20,000	54	23	678	336
20,000 and over	2	51	52	4,296
Total	3,135	76	5,667	4,648

Source: Adapted from *Statistical Pocket Book of Hungary, 1971*, Budapest, 1971.

A village describes a rural territorial area, which may comprise one or more nucleated settlements, or possibly elongated or street settlements, plus the isolated farmsteads surrounding them. In the Great Plain and in parts of Transdanubia the portion of the village population living in isolated homes is significant. Farmland collectivization— which was largely completed by 1961—is reducing their numbers gradually.

The feature of towns and cities that distinguishes them from villages and categorizes their inhabitants as urban, as opposed to rural, is that they are not oriented primarily toward agriculture. Most have commercial or industrial enterprises and have attracted cultural and educational institutions and the businesses necessary to provide for the needs of the local people. Those close to an exploitable natural resource or having an industrial enterprise have grown rapidly since about 1880, and their growth has accelerated since 1945.

Budapest, capital of the country and center of its administration, industry, culture, and commerce, dwarfs all other cities and towns in size and importance. The city acquired its name and took the major step toward its present status in 1873, when three cities—Obuda, Buda, and Pest—clustered at its excellent Danube-crossing point were combined into one. Obuda (Old Buda) was a city of 50,000 inhabitants when it was the Roman city of Aquincum, capital of the old Roman province of Pannonia. Buda was built on Castle Hill, just south of the old city. It was constructed after the Mongols withdrew from the area in the early thirteenth century, and it was built on more easily defended terrain. Originally a walled city, Buda has been the Hungarian capital since 1242. Pest was the plains city on the eastern bank of the river. It developed first as a commercial town and has become the industrial center of the city complex and of the country. It also houses the administrative sections of the central government, leaving Buda to become more characteristically residential. In 1949 several suburban towns were added, increasing the size of the greater city from fifteen to twenty-two districts. As of 1972 it has retained that size.

The city has had an interesting and turbulent existence. It languished under Turkish rule for about 150 years before liberation in 1686, and only a few hundred of its inhabitants survived the siege of the city that year. Nearly all of Obuda, Pest, and much of Buda were destroyed by the Danube flood of 1838. Since that time its growth has only occasionally been interrupted. Its claim to being the country's focal point for industry and culture is substantiated by the facts that, in 1970, 47 percent of the country's industrial work force worked in Budapest and 55 percent of the country's undergraduate students were resident at its seventeen universities and colleges.

Several smaller cities are old and boast colorful traditions. Miskolc, Debrecen, Szeged, and Pecs—in that order—are the four that follow Budapest in size, but all are dwarfed in comparison. Most such towns originated along waterways or overland communication routes and developed as trading centers and market towns for their various regions. As they grew they became local cultural centers and acquired educational or artistic institutions. During the past century or so, growth was greatest in those with local industrial enterprises, particularly if they were near mineral resources.

POPULATION

Structure

Of the population, estimated at 10,447,000 in 1972, 20.2 percent was under fifteen years of age, 62.2 percent was between the ages of fifteen and fifty-nine, and 17.6 percent was sixty years or over (see table 2). Lower than normal percentages in certain age brackets show the effects of casualties and difficult conditions during the recent great wars. The effects of World War II show in the below-normal numbers in the twenty-five to thirty-four age groups; and the effects of World War I, in the fifty to fifty-nine age groups. The very low numbers under fifteen years of age reflect a low birth rate since the middle 1950s, brought about in large part by the prevalent practice of abortion during that period.

Males outnumber females in all brackets below the age of thirty. The longer life expectancy of females is reflected increasingly in the more advanced age groups.

Minority ethnic groups are small. About 4 percent of the population is non-Magyar, but about half of them are almost entirely integrated into the population—to the point, for example, that Hungarian is their primary language. Of the other nationalities, about two-thirds are German. All but a few of the remainder are Slovaks, Romanians, Ruthenians, and Serbo-Croats.

Table 2. Population of Hungary, by Age and Sex, 1972 Estimate

Age Group	Number of People in Age Group[1]	Percentage of Total Population	Females per 100 Males
0–4	746	7.2	94
5–9	633	6.1	95
10–14	720	6.9	96
15–19	935	9.0	96
20–24	843	8.1	97
25–29	737	7.1	99
30–34	690	6.6	104
35–39	684	6.6	106
40–44	724	7.0	105
45–49	735	7.1	110
50–54	551	5.3	115
55–59	560	5.4	118
60–64	604	5.8	118
65–69	484	4.6	122
70–74	374	3.6	131
75 years and over	372	3.6	160
Total	10,392	100.0	106[2]

[1] In thousands.
[2] Overall ratio for total population.

Source: Adapted from Godfrey Baldwin (ed.), *International Population Reports* (U.S. Department of Commerce, Series P–91, No. 18), Washington, 1969.

About 45 percent of the population is urban, and 55 percent is rural. The percentages are affected to an unusual degree by the prominence of the city of Budapest. At the time of the 1970 census the capital city had 1.94 million persons, or 42 percent of the 4.65 million total urban population. The seventy-five towns that contained the remainder, therefore, averaged only approximately 27,000 persons each. Inasmuch as four of them were in the range between 100,000 and 200,000, typical towns are considerably smaller than the average, more accurately reflecting the rural and small town character of much of the land.

The average density is about 290 persons per square mile. Budapest and its environs—the industrial, administrative, and cultural center of the country—comprise the largest area of high density, having about 390 persons per square mile. In other regions the density is linked directly with industry, natural resources, or good agricultural land. The mining and industrial region in the north and northeast has densities close to that of Budapest's area. Smaller pockets of high density occur in the south and southeastern Great Plain, in southern Transdanubia and, less frequently, scattered throughout Transdanubia and the central Great Plain. The largest areas of low density occur in the southwestern and northwestern parts of Transdanubia, and in the north-central and southwestern Great Plain. Areas having poor soils, poor drainage, and no mineral resources support the fewest people. There is no large section where the terrain is rugged enough to inhibit settlement.

Dynamics

With the exception of the period between 1941 and 1948, when it was affected by World War II and its aftermath, and for an occasional year when it has been influenced by temporary factors, the 1971 rate of growth was the lowest it has been for more than a century. In 1840 there were about 4 million inhabitants in the area that is within the present boundaries. Growth was moderate for the next forty years, but it accelerated between about 1880 and 1910, when it was stimulated by the industrial revolution that was then occurring in that part of Europe. With interruptions to the norm during the world war periods, the rate remained moderate until about 1960, since which time it has slowed markedly.

During 1971 the birth and death rates were 14.7 and 11.7 per 1,000 of the population, respectively. The rate of growth, at 0.3 percent, is less than one-half of the 0.7 percent characteristic of both Eastern Europe and Europe as a whole.

Except for great progress in reducing infant mortality during the past half century, that factor would have had a far greater impact on the rate of growth. During the 1920s, 180 of every 1,000 babies born alive failed to survive their first year. In 1971 the comparable statistic had been reduced to about thirty-six, which was still higher than most East European countries. Life expectancy increased by about 67 percent, from forty-two years in the 1920s to about seventy in 1971. Females can expect to outlive males by approximately five years. Except for short periods, such as after the 1956 revolution, there has been little migration into or out of the country.

Internal migration has consisted mainly of the movement from rural areas to the towns. Most of the people involved have been attracted to new industries. The country remains less industrial than agricultural, however, and the movement to the cities has been less rapid than average throughout Europe.

Working Force

The working force includes males aged fifteen through sixty-four and females aged fifteen through fifty-nine. There are 3.4 million males and 3.3 million females, a total of 6.7 million persons in the age groups. About 4.9 million are active wage earners. The 1.8 million of working age who are not wage earners include students, women who are occupied full time in care of their homes and families, and small numbers of others who are unemployable for a variety of reasons.

Although the rural population is greater than the urban, only about one-fourth of the working force is employed in agriculture; a little more than one-third of the labor force is employed in industry. About 6 to 7 percent—in each of the fields—are employed in constructic trade, and transportation. Dependents and inactive workers comprise approximately 53 percent of the population, although some of them work part time.

TRANSPORTATION

Railroads are still important for long-distance hauling but are losing local freight and passenger traffic to trucks, buses, and private automobiles. The importance of waterway shipping has decreased, and that of the airways and pipelines has increased considerably (see table 3; fig. 4).

Table 3. Use of Transportation Facilities in Hungary, 1960 and 1970

Cargo Traffic	Total Freight (in million tons)		Ton Miles (in millions)	
	1960	1970	1960	1970
Railroads	92.9	116.2	8,300	12,400
Motor transport	70.6	146.2	560	1,780
Waterways	2.4	3.2	820	1,700
Pipelines	1.2	9.2	45	650

Passenger Traffic	Total Passengers (in millions)		Passenger Miles (in millions)	
	1960	1970	1960	1970
Railroads	478.9	536.4	8,900	10,300
Buses	236.2	474.2	2,250	4,500
Ships	4.0	3.4	50	40

Source: Adapted from *Statistical Pocket Book of Hungary, 1971*, Budapest, 1971.

Although nearly three-quarters of all freight and passenger traffic was carried by rail as late as 1970, trucks and buses were accounting for increasing amounts of the short-haul business in both categories.

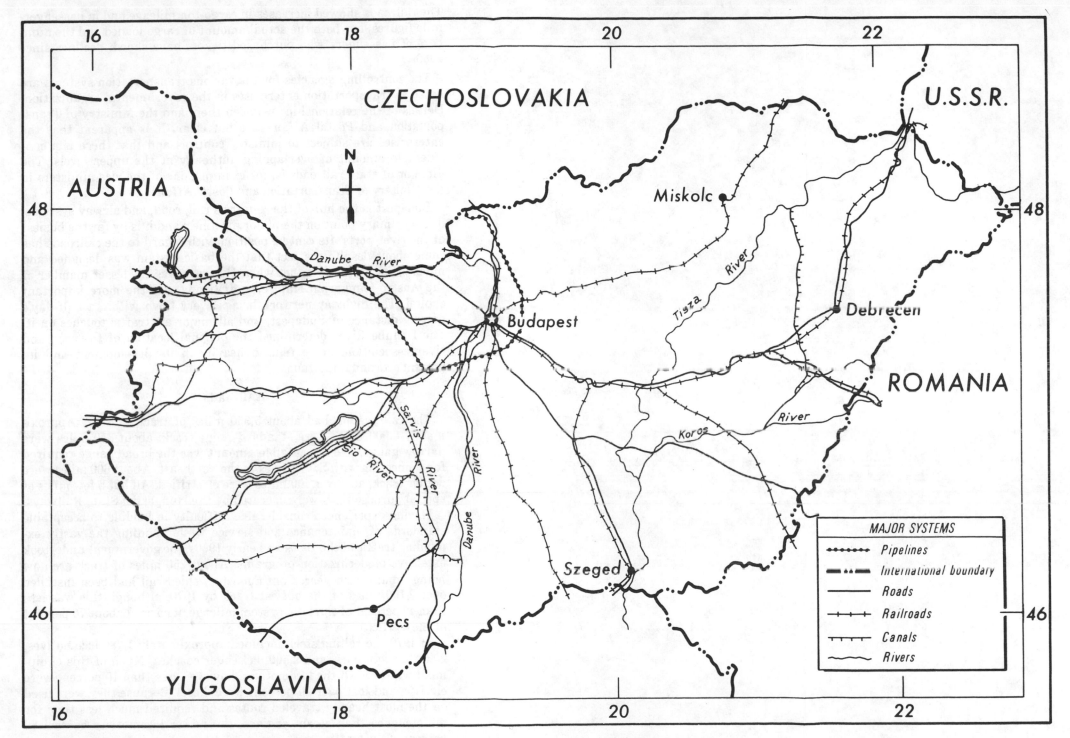

CZECHOSLOVAKIA

U.S.S.R.

AUSTRIA

N

48

Miskolc

Danube River

Tisza River

Debrecen

Budapest

ROMANIA

Sárvíz River

Sió River

Danube River

Koros River

River

MAJOR SYSTEMS

Szeged

46

Pecs

••••••• Pipelines
══•══ International boundary
───── Roads
─┼─┼─ Railroads
─┴─┴─ Canals
───── Rivers

YUGOSLAVIA

Figure 4. Communication Systems in Hungary, 1972

The railroads showed increases in cargo-ton mileage and in passenger-mile figures, but both the actual amount of cargo loaded and the numbers of passengers who purchased tickets have shown declines since 1960.

The controlling agencies for the various transportation systems are listed as transportation enterprises in the governmental organization. Details of the relationships between them and the Ministry of Transportation and Postal Affairs are not clear. It is apparent that the enterprises are subject to ministry controls and that there is a considerable amount of overlapping authority at the upper levels. The director of state railroads is, for example, one of the vice ministers in the Ministry of Transportation and Postal Affairs.

Budapest is the hub of the country's rail, road, and airway systems; it is a primary point on the major pipelines; and it is by far the busiest of the river ports. Its central position with regard to the railroads has come about despite the fact that the basic system was designed and much of its pattern was set when Hungary was the lesser member of the Austro-Hungarian empire, and Vienna was the more important capital. The highway network brings every town within a half-day's driving distance of Budapest, and all major air traffic touches on it. The Danube River determined the original location of the city, and river associations have figured heavily in its development and its present size and importance.

Railroads

The rail system had about 5,350 miles of track in 1972. Approximately 5,000 miles were standard-gauge track; about 340 miles were narrow gauge, and a negligible amount was the broad gauge required for connecting with Soviet lines in the northeast. About 600 miles were double track, and over 400 miles were electrified. All but a few miles of special purpose lines were operated by the Hungarian State Railways.

Having experienced considerable difficulty in holding to acceptable standards of maintenance and service while handling the vastly expanding traffic of the 1950s and early 1960s, the government undertook extensive modernization programs. About 250 miles of track are now being rebuilt each year. Continuously welded rail had been installed over 2,100 miles of the busiest track by 1970; although this was less than 40 percent of the total system mileage, it carried about 70 percent of the traffic.

In 1970 the rolling stock included approximately 1,780 locomotives, 20,000 freight cars, and 2,500 passenger coaches. Much of this equipment was new. Of the locomotives, however, less than 10 percent were electric, and just over 20 percent were diesel. Because they were used on the most heavily traveled routes and required much less time for maintenance than steam engines, the newer locomotives carried 80 percent of the traffic.

Roads

There were approximately 18,400 miles of public roads in 1970, of which all but about 750 miles, or 4 percent, were paved or had some surface improvement enabling them to be classified as dust free. Of the approximately 10,700 miles that are rated as better roads, about 90 percent had asphalt pavement, 7 percent were concrete, and 3 percent were cobblestone or brick. The 6,950 miles of secondary, but dust-free, roads had some macadamized treatment to their surfaces.

The mileage of the road network is extensive enough to serve the country's needs, and less than 250 miles of additional roads have been added since 1960. Most road construction since 1960 has consisted of improvements to existing roads. Less than 30 percent of the road network was considered dust free in 1960, although many roads that were not dust free had some crushed stone, gravel, or other form of surface hardening. During the 1960s the length of roadway with asphalt pavement was increased by nearly 6,000 miles, and most of the remaining secondary roads received some form of dust-inhibiting treatment.

Intercity bus routes total about 15,000 miles and carry nearly 50 percent of the long-distance passenger traffic. They provide nearly all towns and villages with public transport. In addition, there are about 2,000 miles of urban bus and tram routes. Buslines outdistance those for trams by ten to one, but the trams travel the busiest streets and carry more passengers than do city buses.

Per capita tram traffic in Budapest remains among the highest in the world, despite increased numbers of automobiles, which have made it necessary to remove tracks from narrower streets. Extension of the old subway system began in 1953, but work was interrupted for several years. New sections were completed in 1970, and others are being opened as financial and technical difficulties are overcome.

The use of privately owned automobiles has increased rapidly, but official statistics do not estimate the degree to which they have taken passengers from public conveyances. Private cars increased from about 18,000 in 1960 to over 200,000 in 1970, but motorcycles still outnumbered cars by a factor of nearly three. Of the private automobiles, 92 percent were manufactured in the Soviet Union or in Eastern Europe.

Waterways

About 800 miles of rivers and canals are considered permanently navigable, and another 250 to 300 miles are navigable for limited use at certain times of the year. Of the so-called permanently navigable, however, even the Danube may be frozen over for a month or so during severe winter seasons.

Significant quantities of freight are carried on the waterways, but several factors, in addition to ice, make them less important than the length of the routes would indicate. Seasonal waterflow variations are large in all rivers and affect navigability even in some of the interconnecting canals. Both of the most important rivers, the Danube and the Tisza, flow north to south, and by far the greater portion of the cargo must be moved in the upstream direction. The third-largest stream, the Drava River, flows along the relatively sparsely settled southwestern border. Also, there is no interconnection within the country between the major rivers. Cargo destined for Budapest, for example, from points on either the Tisza or the Drava must take long detours into Yugoslavia before those streams join the Danube.

The Danube is navigable for its entire course in and bordering the country. The main river, from the point where it touches the country east of Vienna to its exit at the southern border, is 260 miles long. Alternate channels provide another sixty-five miles of navigable water. The Tisza is navigable for 275 miles. Portions of the Koros and Drava rivers, the Sio Canal, and the canalized Sarvis and Zala rivers make up most of the remaining mileage. The Koros is a tributary of the Tisza that flows to it from the eastern Great Plain. The Sio Canal and the Sarvis River connect Lake Balaton and the plain east of the lake to the Danube River. The Drava and its tributaries are less important because they cannot serve their region well from an economic standpoint.

The Danube was enabled to take large river ships between its middle and lower courses and was opened to smaller seagoing vessels in 1896, when a canal bypassing the Iron Gate cataracts was completed. Danube shipping is reasonably dependable. Channels are deep enough so that low water is seldom a problem, but ice and floods do halt traffic at times. The Tisza is less dependable. It freezes for longer periods than the Danube, its channels are shallower, and the extremes of its water-flow and of its flooding are greater. The river controls undertaken since the mid-nineteenth century, however, have eliminated over 100 curves from the old course, shortened it by about 290 miles, and established a channel that can ordinarily be maintained at adequate depths.

Waterway cargo—the larger portion of it consisting of bulk shipments of coal, ores, and other minerals—amounted to approximately 3.2 million tons in 1970. Although this represented an increase of about one-third in a ten-year period, the other means of transportation, especially highways and pipelines, were increasing their capacities at even faster rates. Among the major carriers, the waterways remained a poor fourth; their share of total cargo carried and ton-mileages constituted approximately 1 percent and were declining slightly.

Oceangoing vessels carry a minor portion of the middle-river traffic; barges carry far more weight with their shallower draft. Most of the barges are pushed or towed by tugboats but, since diesel engines have become more plentiful and economical, more of the newly constructed barges are self-propelled.

The portion of the Danube in Hungary is relatively short, but because both the upper and lower courses of the river can be used to less advantage, over 40 percent of the total Danube shipping is Hungarian.

52

That 40 percent, however, comprises exports from or imports to Hungary or internal Hungarian cargo. Of the cargo that stops at Hungarian ports, a small percentage is purely internal, and another small percentage is purely transit—that is, having origin and destination outside the country. Between 85 and 90 percent consists of external Hungarian trade. Passenger traffic on the waterways is negligible except for a few remaining ferries and some tourist and holiday runs.

Pipelines

In 1970 there were about 1,090 miles of pipeline for natural gas and about 380 miles for liquid petroleum. Extensions of the liquid lines, scheduled for completion in 1973, were under construction. The earliest lines were laid just before World War II to transport crude oil from the newly discovered oilfields in western Transdanubia to refineries in the Budapest area. Other local lines transport natural gas, which was discovered with the oil in Transdanubia and at several points on the Great Plain, to the larger towns and cities.

A section of the Council for Mutual Economic Assistance (COMECON) Friendship Pipeline branches off from its east-west line crossing Czechoslovakia. It brings crude oil from the Soviet Union to a refinery and power station in Szazhalombatta, southwest of Budapest. A second international pipeline brings natural gas from Romania. Most of the Romanian gas is directed toward Miskolc for use in iron smelters in that vicinity.

The relatively short lengths of liquid-carrying pipe transports practically all the pipeline tonnage. By 1970 liquid pipelines carried 9.2 million tons of fuel, or 3.3 percent of the country's total freight, and nearly 4 percent of the total ton-mileage.

Airlines

Commercial aviation is controlled and operated by Hungarian Airlines, invariably known by its abbreviated title MALEV. The line operated between local airports during the early 1960s but with steadily diminishing traffic until, by 1970, it had eliminated regularly scheduled domestic flights.

External traffic, on the other hand, has increased steadily. In 1970 MALEV had routes totaling about 25,000 miles. It connected Budapest with about twenty cities in Western Europe and the Middle East and with about a dozen cities in the neighboring East European countries and the Soviet Union. Almost 360,000 passengers were carried on foreign flights in 1970, up from only about 60,000 in 1960. The 1970 figure represents between 35 and 40 percent of the air passenger traffic that entered Hungary and departed from it, although about fifteen foreign airlines had service into Budapest. Ferihegy Airport, on the southeastern outskirts of the city, is the international airport of entry.

Merchant Marine

Landlocked Hungary, rather surprisingly, has figured for many years in a seafaring role. Since the building of a free port on Csepel Island in the city, Budapest has been the most important of the inland Danube ports, and it has been the transfer point between upriver shipping and Danube-to-sea oceangoing ships.

There is a shipyard north of Csepel Island in addition to the docks on the island, and most of the country's shipbuilding is done there. Other than tugs and barges, the merchant marine consists of about a dozen river ships and about a dozen that are classified as river and oceangoing. Most are in the 1,000-deadweight-ton class, but a few larger vessels have been built for Hungary in Bulgarian ports.

CHAPTER 4

SOCIAL SYSTEMS

Since the Communists took power in the late 1940s, Hungarian society has been in flux. The aim of communist social and economic policies has been to destroy the old order and replace it with a new one that will reflect communist ideology. The resulting changes have been far reaching, but traditional institutions, such as the family and the churches, often act as brakes on drastic change and provide some continuity between the old and the new.

The pace of change has been slowing down since the early 1960s as the government gradually reduced its efforts at social engineering. By the early 1970s the society was settling into a discernible pattern in which some aspects of the old social order were beginning to reemerge. Changes that continued to affect the social system resulted from economic growth and urbanization rather than from the efforts of communist social planners.

Because of the territorial adjustments and population exchanges that followed World War II, Hungary has been ethnically homogeneous and free of ethnic conflict. A tradition of religious tolerance dating from the Protestant Reformation has limited denominational friction, despite religious diversity. Anti-Semitism on the part of the government and the people was widespread between the two world wars, but Hungarian Jews escaped the outbursts of anti-Semitism that erupted in other communist countries after the Arab-Israeli Six-Day War of 1967 (see ch. 2).

ETHNIC AND RELIGIOUS COMPOSITION

About 96 percent of the population in 1972 was Hungarian, or Magyar. In the Hungarian language the term *Magyar* applies equally to persons whose ancestors are of that ethnic group and to persons descended from non-Magyar groups but who have been assimilated to the point of claiming Hungarian as their mother tongue and abandoning all other cultural distinctions. Four percent of the population in 1972 were considered members of national minorities whose mother tongue was not Hungarian and who wished to preserve their own distinct culture. The majority of them also spoke Hungarian.

Officially recognized minorities included over 400,000 Germans, over 200,000 Slovaks, about 100,000 Serbs and Croats, about 25,000 Romanians, and some Ruthenians. Gypsies, estimated by one source to number about 26,000, were not considered an ethnic minority by the state, although they considered themselves as such. Under the constitution, ethnic minorities are guaranteed equal rights as citizens, protected against discrimination, assured the possibility of education in their own languages, and assured promotion of their national cultures.

Over two-thirds of each of the minorities are peasants residing in villages dispersed across the country. Their attachment to rural life is often greater than that of the Hungarians around them because the village offers a better climate for the preservation of distinct cultural heritage than would be possible in an urban setting. Those who have moved to the cities are usually completely integrated into Hungarian society.

There has been little evidence of interethnic friction, although the press occasionally carries reports indicating that the constitutional guarantees are not being fully implemented. The government has found it difficult to recruit bilingual teachers to provide education in the mother tongue and to find bilingual officials to staff the courts and local government offices in towns and villages with members of minority populations.

Long-established prejudice persists, however, and is particularly strong against the Gypsies, according to a survey by the Hungarian Academy of Sciences. Because of their nomadic life-style and values that differ considerably from those of the rest of the population, Gypsies have been the object of prejudice throughout history. A growing number of them are becoming settled and integrated into national life, but prejudice against them continues among all segments of the society.

No census of religious affiliation has been taken since the Communists took power. As a result, only an approximate picture of the religious composition of the population is available, based on estimates of membership by the various churches involved. Roughly two-thirds of Hungarians are at least nominally Roman Catholic; and one-third, Protestant. Of the Protestants, about two-thirds are Calvinists, and the majority of the rest are Lutherans. An estimated 60,000 Jews remained in the country in 1970 after the exterminations and deportations of World War II and migrations since the late 1930s. Some 60,000 followers of the Eastern Orthodox Church and an undetermined number of Unitarians are also found among the population.

Most observers comment on a notable decline in the religious commitment of what has been a strongly Christian people. The outlook and values of the majority of Hungarians are becoming increasingly secular, more so than those of other European societies with a comparable level of industrialization and urbanization. The churches, however, continue to exert enough influence that the government has found it necessary to reach an accommodation with them. This has been particularly true of the Roman Catholic Church which, through its identification with the crown of Saint Stephen, has become a symbol of Hungarian nationalism and a channel for expression of disapproval of the regime and its policies. Attendance at mass is often a barometer of popular sentiment concerning political issues.

Freedom of religion is guaranteed by the constitution, and only outspoken priests and church officials have been persecuted directly. All churches have been deprived of their landholdings, which had been their main source of income, but the government provides them with a subsidy for operating expenses. The State Office of Church Affairs supervises the activities of the churches and confirms all clerical appointments. The formerly substantial education and welfare activities of the churches have been drastically curtailed (see ch. 6; ch. 5). All denominations, however, continue to operate seminaries and other training facilities, which assure a continuous flow of new priests and ministers.

SOCIAL STRATIFICATION

Until World War II stratification in Hungary was marked by pronounced inequality in the distribution of wealth, power, privilege, and opportunity and by certain differences in codes of behavior, dress, speech, and manners. Social distinctions were conceived not in terms of large classes but in terms of small strata reflecting intricate gradations. Some of the strata at the middle and upper levels of society were based entirely upon birth; and some, on the holding of certain occupations. Among the agricultural population, which comprised the majority of the people, internal subdivisions were based, according to local tradition, on such factors as family reputation; the size of landholding; and whether the family owned its land and hired help to work it, owned and worked the land itself, or worked for others.

An individual's social status was in large part determined by his family. A pronounced change in status on an individual basis was possible but unusual. Family connections played a prominent role in obtaining jobs among individuals in the middle and upper strata. In the life of the peasant, family reputation was of great importance, and his social code stressed the value of bringing honor to his relatives. The characteristics that defined a good family varied in different sections of society, but family standing was generally given more weight than was wealth. Upward or downward mobility tended to be a function of the larger family rather than of the individual, thus taking several generations and involving a change in educational level, behavior, and life-style as well as occupation or wealth.

The uneven distribution of wealth made it a more important factor of status among some strata than among others. Gradations in rank among the lower middle urban classes and the peasantry were often based largely on financial status. In the upper classes, however, and in the society as a whole, higher status was associated with wealth but not created by it. Distinction was made also according to the source of wealth; landed wealth was considered to be much more respectable than that derived from trade or banking.

Location of residence was also a factor in determining status. The active cultural and social life of the towns and cities made urban residence more prestigious than dull, relatively cultureless rural life. A wealthy landowner was likely to establish urban residence.

Social status was reflected in an intricate system of ranks and titles. Hereditary titles designated the aristocracy and the gentry. Nonhereditary titles were accorded by the state to persons who had achieved positions of importance, whether or not they were of noble birth. The gradations of rank derived from titles had great significance in social intercourse and in the relations between individual and state. In practice, even the nonhereditary titles became almost hereditary because their status was imputed to the bearer's family in succeeding generations.

The small social strata reflecting the gradations of status could arbitrarily be grouped into three major divisions: the upper classes, the middle classes, and the lower classes. An important dividing line was between persons who engaged in manual labor and those who did not, coinciding roughly with the line between the lower classes and the majority of the other classes.

By the time the Communists came to power, most of the old society had been weakened or eliminated. The devastation from the 1944–45 fighting, the disappearance of much of the Jewish business community because of deportation by the Nazis and emigration, the land reforms of 1945, and the nationalization of commerce and industry destroyed the economic base of the old social system. In addition, a feeling of common privation during the war and of national identity under German and Soviet occupation erased many class distinctions. During the first decade or more of communist rule a classless society was consciously being constructed through such policies as equalization of incomes, collectivization of agriculture, expropriation of property, and tight control over educational opportunities. The society was divided into two groups: a privileged ruling elite of the Hungarian Socialist Workers' Party (MSZMP—see Glossary) functionaries combined with elements of the prewar elite who were willing to lend their power and prestige to the communist cause; and the rest of the population, who formed a large heterogeneous mass.

Under the influence of extensive industrialization, urbanization, and the economic reforms introduced in the 1960s, however, rather than becoming classless, the society again became differentiated into stratified groups. In order to reconcile these realities with ideology, communist theoreticians have been developing modifications of Marxist theory. The idea of a classless society has been either abandoned or pushed into the distant future by modern theoreticians in Hungary and elsewhere. They argue that a complex industrial society must be differentiated by skill and occupation and those individuals with greater skill and more responsibility must receive greater rewards than others. The fact that social stratification in communist countries is based on occupation and skill rather than on the possession of property, these theoreticians claim, makes it qualitatively different from stratification in capitalist countries and, therefore, acceptable in Marxist terms.

Stratification in contemporary Hungarian society is based on party affiliation, occupation, income, and education. The difference in prestige between rural and urban residence continues to affect social status as it did in precommunist society. Based on these criteria, society in the early 1970s could be broadly divided into four groups or classes forming a hierarchical system: the ruling elite; the middle class; the working class; and the peasantry. Each group was internally differentiated by education, specific occupational skill, and location of employment or residence. These, in turn, affected income and prestige.

Earning power was closely tied to class standing in that the salary levels of professionals and managers in the middle class were about double that of skilled workers. The wages of skilled workers, in turn, were almost double the earnings of unskilled workers and peasants.

The Ruling Elite

The ruling elite is composed of the top communist leadership in the party, government, security forces, mass organizations, and various branches of the economy. It also includes members of the cultural and intellectual elite who, by virtue of their political loyalty and willingness to serve the regime, share in the power and privileges reserved for the top communist leadership. By lending their talents to the communist cause, however, these individuals often lose some of the prestige and deference traditionally enjoyed by the intellectual elite. In the late 1960s the ruling elite was estimated to constitute about 3 percent of the population.

The main criterion for membership in the ruling elite is power derived from approved ideological and political orientation. Most members came from peasant or worker families and were veterans of the communist movement in the interwar period.

The privileges of the elite include high incomes derived not only from salary or wages but also from special bonuses, premiums, and tax exemptions; allocation of the best housing; use of official cars; and travel privileges at home and abroad. Membership in the ruling elite, however, is accompanied by considerable insecurity because it is highly dependent on political loyalty and the correct interpretation of ideology. A change in official policy can deprive a member of his status and all privileges.

The Middle Class

The middle class encompasses all persons in nonmanual occupations who are not members of the ruling elite. It includes administrators, managers, professionals, technicians, and all categories of white-collar personnel. Next to the working class, this has been the fastest growing social group in postwar Hungary. As a result, most of its members are relatively young. Their social origins represent the entire spectrum of precommunist society, but some 40 percent of them are of peasant or worker background.

Within the middle class, further differentiation is made in terms of income and prestige between persons in the upper levels of management and the professions who have a higher education and those in the lower levels of technical and white-collar employment who have only a secondary education. The group as a whole was estimated to constitute about 15 percent of the population in the late 1960s. The relative size of the upper and lower levels was not known, although the lower level was probably the larger.

The power and importance of those with higher education, who are frequently referred to as the intelligentsia or the managerial-technical elite, have grown considerably as a result of the relaxation of central control in the 1960s. As the managers and technicians whose skills and talents are needed to run the society, they have come to play a major role in decisionmaking and are reaping commensurably high rewards in terms of salaries and privileges. As a group, the managerial-technical elite is nominally communist but individualistic in its values (see Social Values, this ch.). Because major policy decisions, however, continue to be the monopoly of the MSZMP, a high percentage of the group belongs to the party for practical reasons. In addition to opening the doors to the highest policymaking levels, membership in the MSZMP also provides access to a network of informal contacts within the power and control structure that can win many personal favors.

The lower level of the middle class is composed of the mass of bureaucrats required in a centrally planned and administered society. Their material well-being and prestige differ considerably from that of the upper level to which they aspire. Some are able to move into the upper middle class by obtaining a higher education.

The Working Class

In Marxist ideology, the workers form a self-conscious social class that is the least privileged class in a capitalist system but the foundation of society in a socialist system. This privileged position in orthodox communist ideology has benefited the working class primarily by enhancing its standing in society and by opening channels of education that allowed members of the class to move into higher social strata.

An estimation of the size of the working class is made difficult by the tendency of many communist writers to define as workers anyone employed in the productive sector of the economy, including managers, clerks, and assembly-line workers. Under this definition, persons engaged in manual labor in the nonproductive section of the economy (as in services) are not counted as workers.

Another factor affecting the definition and size of the working class is the growing number of peasants who commute regularly to part-time or full-time jobs in industry or construction. On the basis of their income and occupation, they should be counted as workers but, because they continue to reside in the village and to cultivate their small private plots, they are usually classified as peasants. In fact, they form a separate social group that participates in two economic and social systems at the same time, bridging the division between urban and rural cultures and between the peasantry and the working class.

By defining the working class as that group whose livelihood is derived from manual work outside of agriculture, the class was estimated to constitute about 40 percent of the population in the late 1960s. As a result of the industrialization program, it has been the most rapidly growing class in postwar Hungary.

Within the working class, further differentiation is made according to education and skill, which is reflected in income and prestige. Although they represented slightly over one-third of the workers in 1970, skilled workers are still in relatively short supply; therefore, they command considerably higher wages and are likely to receive special housing and other privileges as incentives from employers. The higher standard of living that these material advantages can provide and the higher level of education required to be a skilled worker enhance his prestige in relation to the semiskilled and unskilled worker.

The semiskilled workers constitute another one-third of the working class. They generally share the life-style of the skilled worker, although on a more modest scale, in line with their lower material rewards.

Unskilled workers, who together with apprentices constitute the remainder of the working class, share with the majority of peasants the poverty and the lack of prestige of the bottom of the social scale. A large proportion of unskilled workers are commuters between village and industry whose life-style and outlook are a mixture of long-established rural traditions and newly adopted urban models. Most unskilled workers, in fact, are just one step removed from the village, whether their permanent residences are urban or rural. Even those who have lived and worked in town or city for years have usually grown up in the village and retain much of the rural life-style and values. This, as well as their lower income, sets them apart from the semiskilled and skilled workers, who are usually completely urban in their outlook and way of life.

The Peasantry

The peasantry constituted about 34 percent of the population in the late 1960s. The group included farm workers on state farms, members of farm cooperatives, and a small remnant of independent farmers (see ch. 13). Formerly by far the largest group in society, the peasantry has been shrinking in size as industrialization and urbanization lure younger members away from the land. At the same time there has been a steady increase in the average age of the group, particularly among members of farm cooperatives—over 40 percent of whom were over sixty years of age in the mid-1960s.

Despite considerable mechanization, agriculture continues to be a strenuous and time-consuming occupation, and agricultural wages are often low and irregular. In contrast, the eight-hour workday and the regular and higher wages of nonagricultural occupations look very attractive. Other attractions are the educational and welfare benefits available to nonagricultural workers and the greater excitement of urban life as compared to rural life (see ch. 5).

These are the factors that prompt young peasants to either adopt a semiurban commuting life or migrate to the city altogether. A survey of rural youth between the ages of twenty and twenty-three conducted in eight counties in the mid-1960s found that 44 percent of them commuted to towns for work or study and almost 22 percent of them have moved to town permanently.

During the same period it was estimated that almost one-half of peasant families derived their income from a combination of agricultural and other pursuits. In fact, several observers have indicated that very few villages continue to depend entirely on agriculture as the source of income. This diversification of the source of income for peasants has expanded their horizons and created demands that have affected their life-style and values. As a result, the former differences in the thinking and behavior patterns of the rural and the urban population are diminishing.

Social Mobility

The social and economic changes that have taken place in Hungary since World War II have permitted, even encouraged, a great deal of social mobility. With expanding industrialization, large numbers of peasants entered the industrial labor force, and the bureaucracy, which developed as a result of centralized planning, attracted large numbers of persons from all social groups into white-collar jobs. The extent and nature of social mobility were the subject of considerable research by Hungarian sociologists in the 1960s. One such study found that two out of three gainfully employed Hungarians started life in different social strata from those occupied at the time of the study. Some of them had changed their social position through their own efforts, whereas others changed status in childhood because their parents had moved from one class to another.

Most of the movement was up the social ladder, although some downward movement also occurred. The most notable instance of the latter was the decline of the precommunist ruling elite, members of which lost property and political power and were forced into the middle class or lower. A large percentage of that group left the country, and some members were absorbed by the new ruling elite.

The principal avenues for mobility are the acquisition of education or skill. Emphasis on formal educational qualifications, however, limits the possibility of working oneself up the ladder through skill alone. Membership in the MSZMP can sometimes override educational qualifications as a means of upward mobility, but to a lesser degree than in the early years of communist rule. The highest levels of decisionmaking are occupied largely by persons with limited formal education who have risen from peasant or worker background through continuous loyalty and work for the MSZMP. In the early 1970s, however, political loyalty alone could no longer act as a force for upward mobility among workers and peasants; it had to be supplemented by appropriate education or skill. Only in access to the ruling elite did political considerations remain paramount.

The high rate of individual mobility brought about by the political and economic changes that have taken place in the decades since World War II has affected the distance between the social classes. In the former rigidly stratified society, membership in a class dictated an individual's life-style, values, and mores. The resulting differences firmly identified the individual with his class and reinforced class divisions. In a situation where two out of three adults have changed their class status in their lifetime, individual values and mores, if not life-styles, are no longer so closely identifiable with class status. Thus, class-based differences are reduced, and the whole society becomes more uniform.

A high rate of individual mobility in an open society has raised the expectations of all individuals for a better future. In the relatively static prewar society, most Hungarians accepted their station in life because there was little possibility for changing it. Since the war, most peasants and workers have dreamed of moving up the social ladder— the peasant by moving to the city and becoming a skilled worker and the worker by improving his skill and becoming a white-collar supervisor. All parents hope that their children will become white-collar workers and will not have to exert themselves physically or perform manual labor. As the rate of industrialization and bureaucratization slows down, however, the possibilities for upward mobility will be reduced, and many expectations will remain unfulfilled, creating a potential source of unrest.

Most observers see such a situation developing in Hungary, as well as in other East European countries. The economic and social changes that have produced the high level of social mobility are losing momentum as the communist architects of these changes achieve their goals or abandon them. Hungarian society, therefore, is stabilizing into a new mold in which the hierarchical social divisions are becoming settled into self-perpetuating groups. Evidence for this is found in a growing interrelation of class standing and educational opportunities. After the special admission privileges to secondary and higher education were revoked for children of peasant and worker origin in 1963, the percentage of such children among students dropped drastically (see ch. 6). As in other countries, children from culturally and intellectually deprived families on the lower levels of the income and prestige scales do not have the background and preparation needed to meet the demands of higher education. They frequently cannot meet the usually high standards of admission and have a high dropout rate in comparison to those from middle class families. Consequently, a middle class child has about twenty times more chance of completing higher education than one from a peasant or worker family. Given education as a main channel for mobility, a reduction in educational opportunities means a reduction in opportunities for upward mobility.

THE FAMILY

Traditionally the family has been the basic social unit and has given security and identity to the individual and furthered the values of society. In rural areas it was also the basic economic unit, in which all members worked together for the material well-being of the whole family. As a result, family cohesion was great, and close relations were maintained with parents, brothers and sisters, uncles and aunts, and first cousins. Three-generation families, having the oldest male as the head and decisionmaker, were the rule in rural areas. Urban families were more likely to be nuclear, but the physical proximity of most extended-family members allowed constant and close contact.

Increased geographic mobility and changing patterns of family life are loosening family cohesion. Many of the younger peasants leave agriculture for industrial or other jobs in the cities, some commuting long distances from work to home; others combine work and study or work at more than one job in order to improve the family standard of living; a growing number of women work outside the home; and children spend most of their time in school or in youth organization activities. Thus, members of the family spend less time together, and emphasis in daily life has shifted from the family to the outside world. Most members of the extended family get together only for important ceremonies, such as weddings or funerals, and other special occasions.

As a consequence of these changes, the traditional roles of family members have been altered. The dominance of the head of the family has given way to a greater distribution of decisionmaking and a greater independence on the part of other family members. The role of women has changed most notably. In 1970 over 60 percent of the working-age women were gainfully employed. Even the peasant woman has become a wage earner on the collective farm. This fact has altered women's status in the family and in the community. By taking on part of her husband's function as breadwinner, she has had to relinquish some of her traditional functions as housewife and mother. These functions have been taken over in part by the husband and children, who help with household chores more than they did before, and in part by outside institutions such as schools and nurseries.

Since World War II urban families have tended to be small, having one or two children at most. Rural families are often larger, a carryover from the times when children were a needed source of labor on the farm. After reaching a postwar high in 1954 of twenty-three live births per 1,000 population, the birth rate declined sharply until 1962, when it reached a low of just over thirteen per 1,000. Hungarian authorities attributed the declining birth rate to the prevalence of working women, who want few—if any—children, and passed a program of maternity benefits to counter the trend (see ch. 5; ch. 3). Partly as a result of these benefits, the birth rate rose to around fifteen per 1,000 in the late 1960s. Some observers have attributed the low birth rate to the high number of abortions, which were legalized in 1956. The sharp decline in the number of live births, however, began before abortions became readily available to women. The main causes of the drop in birth rate and the reduction in family size have probably been the insecurity of a changing society; low wages; and crowded and inadequate housing, particularly in the rapidly growing cities. On the basis of experience in other societies, however, extensive upward mobility may also have been a factor.

In the eyes of the state, marriage was a secular matter governed by civil law. Religious ceremonies were permitted but had to be preceded by a civil marriage. The minimum age for marriage without parental consent was fourteen for both men and women. Men generally married between the ages of twenty and thirty, and women, between the ages of fifteen and twenty-five. The law assigned equal rights and obligations to both partners in a marriage. Divorce was easily obtained, and the divorce rate in the 1960s was the highest in Europe.

Despite changing patterns of family life, most observers find that the cohesive force of the family continues to be strong. The pressures of change and the burdens of daily life hold families together. The traditional sense of family loyalty and responsibility also seems to survive. Family members continue to help each other in finding jobs or housing, in gaining admission to schools, and in providing for each other in times of need.

OTHER GROUPS

Small Informal Groups

Small groups of close friends and relatives are the most important and most influential social grouping in Hungary. They are the framework for intimate human relations, which cannot find fulfillment in an increasingly mechanized and planned society. Getting together over a cup of coffee or a glass of wine, members of such groups discuss their hopes and yearnings, their doubts and disappointments. In such discussions, traditional values and mores are preserved and reinforced, and new values are developed.

Because they lack formal organization and are based entirely on face-to-face interaction, these groups are difficult to control from the outside. For this reason they are of particular importance in a centrally directed society such as that of Hungary. Experience has shown that such groups tend to maintain traditional norms and values and thereby act as a check on imposed institutional changes.

Formal Groups

In order to facilitate the control and direction of society by the government and the MSZMP, the Hungarian regime, like other communist regimes, has created a variety of formal organizations designed to serve specific interest groups (see ch. 9; ch. 15). Most prominent of these on a national scale are the trade unions and the youth organizations. Others, usually organized on a community or enterprise basis, are sports clubs, discussion groups, and cultural clubs of various kinds.

By catering to specific interests of individuals, these groups attempt to attract a large percentage of the population into formal organizations that can be used to promote desired norms and values or undertake specific activities. Their covert political purpose, however, makes them unattractive to most Hungarians, and membership in most has been far below desired levels. Trade unions and youth organizations are frequently joined only pro forma—because a membership card is required to obtain a job or to be admitted to a school.

Many of these formal organizations, particularly those of a cultural nature, predate the communist regime and have been incorporated into the system of mass organizations with little or no structural change. Other precommunist organizations, notably the important and powerful Roman Catholic professional and cultural associations, were disbanded in the late 1940s because they could not or would not adapt themselves to the purposes of the new regime.

SOCIAL VALUES

Most observers characterize the value system as dominated by strong materialism and growing individualization. Acute feelings of frustration and impotence in the determining of one's life and future have led to cynicism and alienation of the individual from society. This, in turn, has resulted in a decline in public morality, manifested in a lack of respect for public property.

In the traditional Hungarian value system the possession of land or some other form of real estate was seen as the most dependable means of providing for the well-being and security of the individual and his family. Therefore, it ranked extremely high on the value scale. The amount of land owned determined a family's wealth and social standing. With the restrictions on private ownership imposed by the communist regime, this value was modified by substituting the accumulation of money in the form of income or savings and of consumer goods as the basis for security and social standing. To peasant and townsman alike, owning a house is of high priority, followed by possession of good furniture, a car or motorcycle, a television, a refrigerator, and other modern appliances. The long years of deprivation when consumer goods of any kind were available only to the privileged few have stimulated a strong appetite for them. In comparison, formerly highly valued cultural and intellectual activities, which are now widely accessible at very low cost, have lost some of their importance.

Government policies and ideology were intended to foster a collectivist social spirit in the people, imbuing them with the desire to place the interests of society over and above their own, but the people retain individualistic attitudes. Although the population has readily accepted the benefits of the welfare state, it has not accepted the ideological base. This has led to both collective and individual alienation, which has drawn the attention of Hungarian writers and other intellectuals. Peter Veres, in particular, has been outspoken about the problems of working in a system that provides little means of participation in the decisionmaking process if one lacks ideological conviction (see ch. 7).

Alienation resulting from a lack of purpose has produced widespread disregard for public property. Petty theft, misuse of property and funds, absenteeism, and using one's time on the job for private purposes are widespread practices. They are directed only against social property, however. Cartoons in the Hungarian press frequently show a group of persons about to damage or destroy something who are stopped when the owner identifies it as his own. Private property continues to be respected by all social classes and all age groups. Most Hungarians proudly point out that there was no looting anywhere in the country during the Revolution of 1956.

Interspersed in the contemporary value system are several traditional Hungarian values. Prominent among them is patriotism, which continues to be a powerful integrating force. The government and the party have tried to utilize this feeling to gain acceptance for their ideology and their policies, but they are hampered in this by the traditional identification of Hungarian nationalism with irredentist territorial claims against neighboring countries and its more recent identification with anti-Soviet sentiment. Any official expression or support of patriotic feeling must be balanced with equal expressions of internationalism and communist solidarity.

Because the state cannot give expression to the nationalism of the people without risking loss of its independence, the people have turned to the Roman Catholic Church as a symbol of their national aspirations. The Roman Catholic Church has been identified with the Hungarian nation since the beginning of the eleventh century when King Stephen converted the inhabitants of his extensive kingdom to Christianity. Stephen was canonized for this accomplishment, and his crown has been the symbol of Christianity and nationhood to Hungarians through the ages. The lands that constituted Stephen's kingdom are still seen as the rightful domain of the Hungarian nation (see ch. 2).

In addition to survival of traditional patriotism, habitual patterns of religious practice continue to be widely followed, despite the regime's efforts to supplant them with secular counterparts. They are motivated, however, not so much by deep religious belief as by a need to uphold tradition as a source of stability in a rapidly changing world and by a desire to show unwillingness to submit to the ideological principles of the communist regime.

CHAPTER 5

LIVING CONDITIONS

The physical well-being of most Hungarians has been improving steadily since the end of World War II. The rate of disease has decreased noticeably; the drop in the overall death rate and the infant mortality rate have resulted in a dramatic increase in life expectancy. After a period of postwar austerity, during which consumer needs were neglected in favor of rapid industrialization, the standard of living began to improve in the 1960s as economic reforms made more goods and services available to the population.

A marked difference in the quality of life between urban and rural areas persists, however. Medical care, education, and many modern conveniences are not as readily available in the countryside, particularly in the more remote areas of the Great Plain. A growing difference in the quality of life was also apparent among the various income groups. The increasing affluence of urban professionals and higher white-collar employees is manifested in their fashionable clothes, their privately owned housing with modern appliances, their cars, and their general life-style, which stresses comfort, leisure, and pleasure. In comparison, the standard of living of most blue-collar workers has been declining as their wages lag behind the rising cost of living (see ch. 12). In rural areas a marked difference can be seen in the quality of life between families that depend entirely on agriculture for their livelihood and those that derive income from both agricultural and nonagricultural pursuits. The latter are found mostly in areas that are within reasonable commuting distance from a town or industrial complex that can provide employment to some members of the family. Not only do the dual-income families have a larger income at their disposal, but they also have contact with the urban amenities that can make life easier and more pleasurable.

Until the mid-1960s the cost of living was kept artificially low by government control of prices. With the introduction of a more flexible pricing system, however, rising prices have raised the cost of living and brought serious hardships to persons having fixed incomes and to those whose incomes have risen at a slower rate.

Ninety-seven percent of the population is eligible for free or low-cost health care and for an extensive system of social benefits. Inequalities in the treatment of state employees and peasants living in cooperatives are gradually being eliminated as peasants become eligible for more of the benefits available to workers. Benefit payments, however, continue to be higher for workers than for peasants. Self-employed individuals are discriminated against in that they are not eligible for any benefits.

HEALTH

Death and Disease

In the late 1960s life expectancy at birth was about sixty-six years for males and seventy-two years for females. This was a dramatic increase from comparable figures in the 1920s. The increase was brought about by a drop in the death rate from about twenty per 1,000 population in the mid-1920s to about eleven in 1970 and by a drop in the infant mortality rate from about 180 per 1,000 live births to about thirty-six during the same period. Despite the fact that almost all births take place under professional supervision and that over 80 percent of babies receive regular monthly checkups during the first year of life, injuries at birth and infectious diseases are by far the greatest cause of infant mortality.

The major cause of death since World War II has been diseases of the heart and circulatory system, which accounted for 53 percent of the deaths in 1970. Cancer, the second-largest cause of death in that year, accounted for 19 percent of the deaths, and accidents and violent acts accounted for almost 8 percent of deaths. Hungary has long had one of the highest suicide rates in the world. Suicide usually ranks as the fourth or fifth most important cause of death in the population at large and as the single most important cause of death among youths between ages fifteen and twenty.

Before World War II Hungary, of all European countries, had the highest mortality rate from tuberculosis. After the war, therefore, high priority was given to fighting this disease. Facilities were established to enable the whole population to be screened for tuberculosis every two years by means of X-rays and other tests, and all persons under the age of twenty are vaccinated every three years. Tuberculosis patients receive free treatment and medication whether or not they qualify for free medical service. They also receive sick pay for a longer period than others.

As a result of these programs, the mortality rate from tuberculosis in the 1960s was one-fifth of the prewar rate. The number of new cases has dropped from forty-nine per 10,000 inhabitants in 1950 to ten in 1970. Nevertheless, tuberculosis is still the most widespread infectious disease.

Such diseases as malaria, syphyllis, and typhoid, which were once widespread, have either been brought under control or eradicated completely. In 1970 the greatest incidence was reported for contagious hepatitis, dysentery, measles, and scarlet fever.

The law requires that all cases of contagious disease be registered with the public health service. It also requires immunization of all children against smallpox, diphtheria, tetanus, whooping cough, tuberculosis, poliomyelitis, and measles. Inoculation against other contagious diseases is required if an epidemic threatens.

The National Health Service

The national health service is administered and financed by the central government. It is based on the premise that the state has the responsibility of providing free health care for the population and that such care should be uniform and readily available. In 1972, however, serious discrepancies existed in the quality and availability of health care in different parts of the country, particularly between urban and rural areas.

Wage earners in state enterprises and their dependents are entitled to free medical and dental care, including hospitalization. Cooperative farmers and their dependents are entitled to the same service if they subscribe to it by paying a small monthly fee. Self-employed persons and their dependents must pay the full cost of medical services received.

The cornerstone of the health service is the district physician, who acts as the family physician for the inhabitants of his area. The geographical area covered by a district physician varies considerably in different parts of the country. In 1971 a district physician was responsible for an average of 2,800 people. In most urban areas, and in densely populated rural regions, the district physician treats only persons over the age of fourteen. The health needs of children up to that age are the responsibility of district pediatricians.

Most district physicians are assisted by a staff consisting of a secretary, who takes care of the administrative work; a nurse, who assists the doctor and takes care of such routine functions as giving injections and dressing minor wounds; and a health visitor, who is responsible for routine maternity and child care. In urban areas, where specialized physicians and other specialized services are readily available, the district physician is a specialist in internal medicine. In rural areas, however, he is a general practitioner required to treat a broad range of problems.

At the next level in the health service is the polyclinic, which provides outpatient services in specialized fields, such as pediatrics, obstetrics, gynecology, surgery, dentistry, neurology, ophthalmology, orthopedics, and others. It also provides X-ray facilities and clinical laboratories for the physicians on its staff and the district physicians in its area. Ideally, there is to be one polyclinic in each district center, but the shortage of staff and other drawbacks had left this aim unfulfilled in the early 1970s. Not all polyclinics provide services in all the specialized fields of medicine. The minimum requirements are that each have departments of internal medicine, surgery, gynecology, pediatrics, and dentistry, together with the necessary laboratory facilities In order to reduce the workload at polyclinics, continuous care for such ailments as tuberculosis, venereal disease, and skin disease is provided at special district dispensaries.

The services provided by the district physician and the polyclinic are often supplemented by factory health services in the larger industrial enterprises. These services supervise the sanitary and health conditions in the factories, provide first-aid and emergency assistance, and often cater to the regular health needs of the workers. Many also provide eye care and dental care for the employees. The law requires that all factories employing 500 to 1,800 workers must have part-time physicians on their staffs. Plants with 1,800 to 2,000 employees must have one full-time physician, and larger plants must have more than one.

A hospital network rounds out the health service by providing the needed inpatient facilities. The senior staffs at hospitals are also charged with directing and supervising the work of the outpatient facilities in their area. In addition, hospitals serve as training facilities for physicians and auxiliary medical personnel. The hospital network itself is hierarchically organized in terms of medical competence and authority. The lowest unit is the district or municipal hospital, followed by the county hospital and by specialized national institutes, such as the National Institute of Oncology, the National Institute of Cardiology, and others.

District hospitals have a capacity of 100 to 600 beds. The goal is to provide each district with a 500-bed hospital that has departments for internal medicine; surgery; obstetrics and gynecology; pediatrics; ophthalmology; ear, nose, and throat; infectious diseases; and diagnostic X-rays.

County hospitals have a 600- to 1,000-bed capacity and are equipped to handle all except the most unusual medical problems. Their facilities include therapeutic as well as diagnostic and clinical capabilities. Most of them have nursing schools attached. In the late 1960s each county had a county hospital, although not all of them met the desired standards.

The total number of hospital beds in 1971 was 84,818, or 81.9 for each 10,000 inhabitants. Distribution, however, was very uneven, and Budapest had twice as many beds per 10,000 inhabitants as the rest of the country. A shortage of medical personnel has resulted in continuous understaffing of most hospitals. Many of the district hospitals are plagued by old and deteriorating plants and by obsolete equipment. Although a program of systematic renovation of hospitals has been in existence since 1957, the funds and materials allocated for it have not been adequate, and the pace of renovation has been very slow.

The general hospital network is supplemented by extended care facilities for patients suffering from tuberculosis, cardiac diseases, gastric and intestinal diseases, and other chronic ailments. An extensive network of maternity homes also supplements hospital facilities.

Other specialized facilities of the health service include medical baths, which have traditionally played an important role in the health care of Hungarians. The chemical composition of some of the Hungarian spas is reputed to be particularly effective and attracts visitors from all parts of Europe. Hot-spring baths are used extensively in the treatment of rheumatism and arthritis.

In theory, the national health service is as concerned with the prevention of disease as with its cure. Considerable emphasis has been placed on educating the population about good health and sanitary practices and on encouraging regular health checkups for early detection of any problems. All school children are given biannual examinations including eye tests and dental examinations. Factory workers are also required to undergo periodic checkups by the factory health service. Mobile chest X-ray units and other specialized mobile units periodically screen the rural population for disease. The shortage of personnel and facilities, however, has prevented as systematic and regular an effort in disease prevention as that desired by the government and by medical authorities. Most doctors and medical facilities are too burdened with curing illness to have much time and space for prevention.

In 1971 the country had a total of 24,310 physicians—23.5 for every 10,000 inhabitants. Almost 40 percent of the physicians were practicing in Budapest, giving that city a ratio of 46.8 physicians per 10,000 inhabitants. Approximately two-thirds of the physicians had specialized training; approximately one-third of the physicians were women. The number of physicians had more than doubled in the twenty years since 1950; most of them, therefore, were between the ages of twenty-five and forty-five.

The auxiliary medical personnel has expanded along the same lines. In 1970 there were 32,053 general nurses, of which almost 90 percent were male; 8,228 nurses specializing in child care, all of whom were female; 1,897 midwives; 3,924 pharmacists; and 15,728 medical assistants of various kinds.

Physicians and auxiliary medical personnel are all employed by the state in the national health service. Physicians are allowed to see private patients during their free time, and many of them have very lucrative private practices. Persons in upper income groups, who can afford the high price of private medical care, prefer to use the services of a physician of their own choosing rather than one assigned to them by the health service. The care given by private physicians is frequently better and always more personal than that given by the health service.

DIET AND NUTRITION

The diet and nutrition of most Hungarians are generally considered adequate, although great variation can be found among regions and between rural and urban populations. Long-established habits and preferences rather than nutritional considerations continue to influence dietary patterns, despite long-standing efforts by the government and other agencies to increase awareness of nutritional needs. The per capita daily caloric intake in 1969 was 3,164 calories; a 10-percent increase from 1950. The diet, however, was high in carbohydrates and fats and low in fresh fruits and vegetables. Daily consumption of protein was 97 grams; less than half of which were of animal origin.

The staple food in most diets is bread; it is consumed in large quantities at each meal. Bread is generally made from wheat flour blended with rye, corn, or potato flour. The proportions of the mixture vary with the price and availability of wheat flour and the economic circumstances of the household.

The other major dietary item is soup, which takes a myriad of guises and attests to the cooking skill of the person preparing it. The widely known goulash (*gyulas*) is a heavy soup rather than a stew, well-seasoned with paprika, which is believed by Hungarians to have high nutritional value. Goulash is made from pork, sausages, potatoes, and many other ingredients besides beef and is probably the most popular form of soup.

Meat consumption in the late 1960s compared favorably with the other communist countries but was considerably lower than that in most of Western Europe. Press reports and speeches by Hungarian officials have indicated that the supply of meat is irregular and does not meet the demands of the population. Pork is the most widely consumed meat followed, in order, by poultry and beef. The most popular method of preparing meat is in a rich, well-seasoned sauce, served with noodles, small dumplings, or potatoes.

Fish consumption is quite low, although it has increased almost fourfold between 1950 and 1970. The consumption of eggs and dairy foods has also increased considerably in the same period, resulting in a higher intake of proteins and a more balanced diet. Fresh milk is seldom consumed, even by children. Such milk products as cheese and sour cream are widely used, however. Milk is used in considerable quantities with coffee, which is often mixed in the proportion of one part coffee to four or five parts milk.

Consumption of fruits and vegetables varies a great deal with the season. It is generally lower than is considered adequate by nutritionists for a balanced diet. Fruits and vegetables are a primary export item, and the domestic consumer often suffers in favor of the export market. In times of short supply, prices rise beyond the reach of large segments of the population. A high percentage of vegetables and fruits is grown by peasants on their private plots and sold in the city for whatever the market will bear. Because demand is usually high, peasants tend to sell their production rather than consume it themselves. Thus, urban residents usually eat more fruits and vegetables than do the peasants.

Wine and beer are the most popular beverages. Consumption of beer has increased sharply since the early 1950s when the government imposed a high tax on wine. The increased consumption of beer and other alcoholic beverages has alarmed the government because of the growing number of accidents and other social ills attributable to alcoholism.

The standard eating pattern consists of three meals a day. Traditionally the main meal was eaten at mid-day, but changing life-styles are shifting the main meal to the evening. Breakfast usually consists of coffee with milk and bread with butter, lard, or jam. Lunch may be a bowl of soup or a piece of sausage or smoked bacon with bread and a cup of black coffee or a glass of beer or wine.

CLOTHING

Hungary has been known for the colorful and distinct costumes worn by the peasants in different regions. Many peasants still wear these costumes daily. Most of them, however, have adopted standard Western dress as everyday clothing and wear the costumes on special occasions only. Western clothing had been common in the towns and cities even before the beginning of the twentieth century, and Budapest women have enjoyed a reputation of being extremely well-dressed and fashionable.

Before World War II most of the fabrics, clothing, and footwear used by peasants were manufactured at home. Inhabitants of towns and cities and members of the rural upper class purchased their footwear and purchased fabrics that were made into clothes either at home or by seamstresses or tailors. Manufactured clothing did not come into widespread use until the war.

In 1970 about 40 percent of the money expended on dresses, skirts and suits by urban women and 50 percent of that expended by rural women was used to purchase fabrics rather than readymade garments. Clothing, such as coats and other outerwear, men's suits, and underwear were mostly purchased ready made.

Between the end of World War II and the mid-1960s wearing apparel and clothing materials were in short supply and relatively expensive— a reflection of the low priority ascribed by the government to consumer goods. Since the introduction of economic reforms in 1968, clothing has become more readily available, and Western travelers have commented on the well-dressed and fashionable appearance of many Hungarians. On the other hand, there were indications in the Hungarian press and elsewhere that neither the quantity nor the quality of the available clothing is satisfactory to most Hungarians. One reporter from Yugoslavia commented on the eagerness with which Hungarian tourists buy Yugoslav clothing, even those items that are considered less desirable in quality or style by the Yugoslavs.

HOUSING

In common with other Eastern European countries, Hungary has suffered a serious housing shortage since World War II, particularly in urban housing. Construction of housing has not kept pace with urban industrial expansion, which has attracted large numbers of workers from the village into the cities. During the early years of communist rule, priority in the allocation of scarce building materials and funds was given to the building of new plants and other industrial installations rather than to new housing. In the 1960s approximately 15 percent of the national income was invested in housing construction as compared to 20 percent or more in most Western European countries.

Although investment in housing construction increased in the 1960s and more materials and labor were made available for that purpose, the stock of housing units has risen slowly. A study published by the Institute of Sociology of the Hungarian Academy of Sciences complained that the supply of housing and communal services in 1970 was only 30 percent of what Hungary's general development would justify. Another Hungarian source states that even if the housing plan for the 1970–75 period were fulfilled, 200,000 families would be without their own housing.

Aggravating the housing shortage in the early 1970s was the accelerating deterioration of old buildings, many of which should be demolished. Money and materials for maintenance of existing structures have been even harder to come by than for new construction. In addition, many of the postwar apartment buildings were put up hastily, using inferior materials and workmanship, and soon turned into crumbling slums.

To keep overcrowding to a minimum, Budapest and some other cities issue residence permits to rural migrants only if they have jobs. Because many would-be migrants cannot commute daily from their villages while they are looking for work, they settle in makeshift quarters on the outskirts of such cities, giving rise to shantytowns. Employed migrants who cannot find housing in the city often join their friends in the shantytowns instead of spending many hours commuting from home.

In order to spur housing construction without imposing too great a burden on the state budget, the government was forced to abandon its intention of providing low-rent apartments for everyone. Instead, it has encouraged the population to invest in its own housing and has made available low-interest loans for the construction of cooperative apartment buildings and private homes. In 1971 such combined state and private investment accounted for 57 percent of the total investment in new housing construction. The five-year plan for the 1970–75 period envisages at least 50 percent of the housing construction to be financed by private funds.

The increasing reliance on tenant-financed cooperative housing is helping to reduce the overall housing shortage, but it has meant that most new housing units are built for the higher income groups. Co-operative housing requires a substantial initial investment and the assumption of a twenty- to thirty-year mortgage, which are beyond the means of most blue-collar and lower level white-collar workers. These groups continue to rely on state-financed or industry-financed low-rent housing, for which there are usually long waiting lists of prospective tenants.

The average number of occupants per room in 1972 was 1.8 in Buda-pest, two in other urban areas, and 1.9 in rural areas. Forty-three per-cent of the housing units consisted only of one room for living and sleeping, and 46 percent consisted of two rooms. Eleven percent had three or more rooms. Kitchens, bathrooms, and other utility rooms were not counted. The size of the average housing unit has increased since 1960, when 61 percent had only one room. About two-thirds of the units constructed since that year had two rooms, and a growing num-ber had three or more rooms. Sixty-five percent of all units in 1970, however, had only a kitchen and some storage space in addition to the living and sleeping rooms. Only 25 percent had bathrooms; bathrooms were often shared among several units.

In 1970 approximately 12 percent of the housing units were not equipped with any utilities. Of those with utilities, 27 percent had private indoor toilets, 92 percent had electricity, 44 percent had access to running water, and 51 percent had gas. Toilets, like bathrooms, are often shared. In 8 percent of the units running water was available from a nearby source outside the unit itself.

PERSONAL INCOME AND EXPENDITURES

Cost of Living

Until price controls were lifted in the late 1960s as part of the economic reforms, the cost of living was relatively stable. Consumer goods were scarce, and periodic food shortages forced a comparatively low standard of living on the population, but real incomes generally exceeded the cost of living. Forced saving was imposed on much of the population by the absence of goods and services for which incomes could be spent.

The economic reforms introduced a flexible pricing policy that re-sulted in a rising cost of living. Wages have increased, but not uni-formly for all segments of the population. Wages of industrial workers in large enterprises have risen little compared to other wages and peasant incomes because industrial enterprises are caught in a squeeze between rising costs of raw materials and fixed prices for their products (see ch. 12). The wages of over 40 percent of industrial workers in 1970 were not sufficient to meet the basic needs of a family with only one wage earner, and families with many dependents and persons on fixed incomes, such as pensioners, were affected the most. The Hungarian press has indicated growing dissatisfaction among the workers and latent social tension between them and the increasingly affluent white-collar group, which openly displays its new affluence.

Consumption

According to official figures, per capita consumption has grown steadily since the 1950s. The economic reforms of the 1960s put greater emphasis on the production of consumer goods, making them more readily available than before. This encouraged consumption, and a greater percentage of expenditures was being devoted to the purchase of consumer goods. By the early 1970s demand for such durable goods as appliances and vehicles had increased to the point where production could not meet demand. At the end of 1970, 31 percent of households had an electric refrigerator; 50 percent had an electric washing machine; 30 percent had a vacuum cleaner; 7 percent had a private car; 18 percent had a motorcycle, motorbike, or scooter; 72 percent had a radio; and 53 percent had a television set.

In September 1972 there were 105,000 names on a waiting list to purchase private automobiles. The waiting period for the cheaper models of cars was two to three years. The rapid growth in automobile use has put a serious strain on the existing road network and parking facilities and on service stations and repair shops.

In the early 1970s the supply and quality of consumer goods compared favorably with other communist countries but did not meet the levels of Western Europe or the demands of the population. Some items, such as meat and building materials, are in chronic short supply because of inadequate production capacity and because of export priorities. Other items are in short supply from time to time, usually as a result of poor planning and inefficient distribution.

The domestic trade network is too small and too inefficient to adequately serve the needs of the population. Retail outlets are state owned and have received very low priority in the allocation of funds. As a result, they are too few in number and are seriously understaffed, making shopping a time-consuming and frustrating activity. Travelers report that it is often necessary to stand in three different lines to purchase one item—first to select the item, then to pay for it, and finally to have it wrapped. The selection of goods has been improving but still lacks the variety found in most Western countries. Stores are reluctant to stock new styles in response to consumer demands until their old stocks have been almost depleted. High quality and special items are usually available only from private craftsmen who, because they satisfy a great demand, can charge high prices.

Private craftsmen and artisans provide virtually the only service network in the country. The service industry has been considered as nonessential and therefore has been neglected by the state (see ch. 12). The gap thus created has been filled by craftsmen and artisans working on their own account. Many of these are regularly employed in industry and provide specialized services during their spare time. Because they are in great demand, they can set their own prices, and many are in the highest income groups. The government has attempted to keep their earnings under control by taxes but has made no effort to eliminate their services. On the contrary, licensing and other regulations have been adjusted to encourage moonlighters and retired persons to enter the service network in order to satisfy an ever-growing demand.

The largest share of consumer expenditures in 1970 went for food; ranging from 50 percent of total expenditures for peasants to 38 percent of total expenditures for white-collar workers (see table 4). In calculating expenditures for food, the value of food produced for personal consumption was included.

Table 4. Hungary, Percentage Distribution of Net Expenditure by Population Group, 1970

Item	White Collar	Blue Collar	Peasant	Dual Income*
Food, beverage, and tobacco	38.4	44.3	50.3	45.6
Clothing	14.7	14.8	12.4	14.8
Housing, including utilities	12.8	13.0	14.3	14.2
Household furnishings	8.9	9.3	8.6	9.3
Health and hygiene	3.0	2.3	1.6	1.5
Transportation and communication	8.3	5.0	3.6	6.2
Education and entertainment	6.6	5.5	3.6	4.0
Other	7.3	5.8	5.6	4.4
Total	100.0	100.0	100.0	100.0

*Households deriving income from both agricultural and nonagricultural pursuits.

Source: Adapted from U.S. Department of Commerce, Office of Technical Services, Joint Publications Research Service—JPRS (Washington), *Translations on Eastern Europe: Political, Sociological, and Military Affairs, Hungarian Statistical Yearbook, 1970*, Part II, Budapest, August 16, 1972 (JPRS 56,789, 1972), pp. 418, 423.

The proportion of expenditures for clothing was rather uniform. The exceptions were the peasants who spent proportionately less on clothing than families influenced by urban life-styles. Housing, including utilities, also accounted for roughly the same proportion of total expenditures for all groups.

The greatest variation in consumption patterns among the different population groups was in the proportion of expenditures devoted to health and hygiene, transportation and communication, and education and entertainment (see table 5). Although peasant households and

Table 5. Hungary, Income and Expenditure of Representative Households, 1970
(in forints)[1]

	White Collar	Blue Collar	Peasant	Dual Income[2]
Average number of persons in household	3.15	3.25	2.67	3.92
Average Yearly Income (per capita):				
Wages and cash receipts from sales ..	16,868	12,365	12,228	13,433
Sick pay	253	232	160	201
Pensions	854	586	975	365
Family allowance and other grants ..	568	598	290	369
Overtime, moonlighting, and other ..	2,629	2,012	1,075	888
Net income from household plot[3]	230	513	2,581	2,382
Value of products received in kind	512	290		
Gross income	21,914	16,596	17,309	17,638
Taxes and similar expenses	1,092	673	724	779
NET INCOME	20,820	15,923	16,585	16,859
Yearly Net Expenditure (per capita):				
Food, beverages, and tobacco	7,754[3]	6,858[3]	7,784[3]	7,224[3]
Clothing	2,977	2,305	1,913	2,353
Housing, including utilities	2,576	2,013	2,208	2,250
Household furnishings	1,787	1,437	1,335	1,479
Health and hygiene	611	352	241	232
Transportation and communication..	1,675	775	568	991
Education and entertainment	1,337	853	561	642
Other	1,472	896	872	694
NET EXPENDITURE	20,189	15,489	15,482	15,865

[1] For value of forint—see Glossary.
[2] Households deriving income from both agricultural and nonagricultural pursuits.
[3] Including value of food produced for own consumption.

Source: Adapted from U.S. Department of Commerce, Office of Technical Services, Joint Publications Research Service—JPRS (Washington), *Translations on Eastern Europe: Political, Sociological, and Military Affairs, Hungarian Statistical Yearbook 1970*, Part II, Budapest, August 16, 1972 (JPRS 56,789, 1972), pp. 418, 423.

those with a dual source of income must pay partly for their health care, they devoted a smaller portion of their expenditures for that purpose than blue-collar and white-collar workers, who are entitled to free medical care. The high expenditure for health and hygiene on the part of white-collar workers is accounted for by the fact that the higher income groups prefer to forego the inconveniences and bureaucratic red tape that accompany free health care and instead often consult private physicians who set their own rates.

The relatively high proportion of expenditures devoted to transportation and communication by white-collar households is a reflection of their higher standard of living. These are the families whose income allows them to own private cars and television sets, which are expensive to purchase and to maintain. The high proportion of income spent on transportation by dual-income households is generally a consequence of their having to commute great distances between village and town.

The proportion of expenditures devoted to education and entertainment reflects the differences .between urban and rural life-styles. Those exposed to movies, theaters, concerts, and other entertainment facilities in the towns spend a greater proportion of their income on such recreation. The differences also reflect the relative value placed on cultural pursuits by the various segments of the population.

SOCIAL INSURANCE

In addition to receiving complete or partial free medical care, 97 percent of the population is covered by social insurance, which includes sickness and disability benefits, pensions, maternity benefits, and family allowances. Eligibility requirements and payments differ for wage and salary earners and for members of agricultural or craft cooperatives. Self-employed entrepreneurs have no coverage at all.

Sickness and disability benefits are paid to salaried and wage workers during periods of incapacity up to one year. Benefits vary according to length of service, number of dependents, and whether the recipient is hospitalized or not. Members of cooperatives are not entitled to such benefits but often receive some sort of assistance from the cooperative. Prolonged or permanent disability entitles an individual to a pension.

Pension payments vary a great deal depending on when the individual retired and the kind and duration of former employment. Payments to retired wage earners are considerably higher than those to retired cooperative members, but the latter receive a supplement in kind. Men are pensionable at age sixty and women at age fifty-five. The number of pensioners has been growing very rapidly since the end of World War II as a result of longer life expectancy and expanding pension coverage of the population. This has put a heavy burden on the government, which is the main source of pension funds. Even so, the vast majority of pensioners barely subsists on pension payments because these have not kept up with the rising cost of living. Calls for pension reform are a frequent subject in the Hungarian press; special stress has been laid on the need to adjust the rates of those individuals whose pensions are based on prewar wages and costs of living.

Employed women are entitled to twenty-six weeks of fully paid maternity leave and up to three years extended maternity leave of absence from their job with a set monthly allowance. All women covered by social insurance, whether in their own right or as dependents, receive a lump sum payment and a complete layette at the birth of each child. The extended maternity leave and child payments were instituted in 1967 to encourage a higher birth rate. They accomplished their aim for a short time, but by 1972 the birth rate was again declining. The Hungarian press has indicated that the attraction of these inducements has diminished with the rising cost of living. The monthly payment during maternity leave is no longer sufficient to support a child during the first three years of life, but the mother is not allowed to earn any other income. In addition, the shortage of child-care facilities often prevents a mother from returning to work when her three years of leave are over.

Another inducement for larger families is the system of family allowances, which is also intended to keep children from lower income families in school longer than they might otherwise be. Manual and clerical workers, members of farm and craft cooperatives, and students are eligible for a monthly allowance for each child beyond the second if the child is in school and has not reached his nineteenth birthday. The payment scale favors three or more children. Payments to cooperative members are about one-third lower than those to wage earners and students. Single and handicapped parents receive an allowance for the first child also and receive higher payments than other families. A supplement is also paid for handicapped children.

Social insurance is administered by the trade unions through their local branches. It is financed by the central government and by contributions from employers based on a percentage of gross salaries and wages paid. Only the pension fund receives contributions from the insured in the form of a percentage assessment on salaries and wages or on the earnings of members of cooperatives.

The social insurance programs, which are national in scope, are supplemented by a variety of social aid programs undertaken by local governments. Most of those involve short-term emergency assistance and aid to indigents. Other welfare activity undertaken by both the national and local governments include, among others, the maintenance of orphanages and homes for the aged and disaster relief.

WORK AND LEISURE

The forty-hour work week was gradually adopted during the 1960s and had become well established by 1972. This provided the employed Hungarian with more time at his disposal than he was accustomed to having. A large number of them use this time for engaging in secondary occupations or for cultivating private plots of land, both of which can add considerably to their incomes. Collective farmers must work a minimum number of hours per season for the collective in order to qualify for private plots. The required minimum is small enough to allow members of peasant families to spend most of their effort on cultivating their private plots or on working in nonagricultural jobs.

Given the widespread practice of moonlighting and the increasing amount of time that is taken up by commuting, many Hungarians have little time for leisure. The criticism is frequently voiced in the

Hungarian press that the materialistic striving for higher incomes and better possessions allows time only for work and sleep.

The favorite way to spend leisure time is with friends. A popular meeting place is the café, where friends gather after work in the evening or whenever there is nothing specific to do. Hungarians of all walks of life have their favorite cafés where they sit for hours over coffee or wine, talking, reading, or simply doing nothing.

Various cultural pursuits, such as reading, music, and theater, are also popular leisure time activities, particularly among the urban intelligentsia. These people consider regular attendance at concerts, plays, opera, or art exhibits not only as relaxation and entertainment but also as a necessary educational experience. Television viewing is gradually becoming an important leisure time activity as more and more households acquire television sets.

Soccer is the national sport and arouses great enthusiasm among participants and spectators alike. Soccer clubs are found throughout the country, and well-known teams have a national following. Hungarian soccer teams have won many international honors.

Fencing is another popular sport that has earned Hungary international honors. Swimming and winter sports also rank high as popular competitive sports and as leisure activities. Hunting and fishing are traditional leisure pastimes. Although most species of wildlife are protected, hunting is allowed under specific conditions.

Participation in sports has been encouraged by the authorities as a means to channel the physical energies of youth in constructive ways and to promote physical fitness among the population.

CHAPTER 6

EDUCATION

Although the educational system in Hungary under the Communists differs substantially from the pre-World War II system, broadly speaking, the changes are more a matter of degree and emphasis than of kind. The Communists used the structure of the old system as a foundation on which to build and develop a system suited to their own needs. Religion was a dominant influence in prewar Hungarian education. Although the Communists undertook a vigorous campaign to rid the educational system of this influence, over a period of time agreements have been made between church and state. As a result, church schools still continue to exist in Hungary. Similarly, prewar education above the elementary level was generally limited to the social elite of the country. The Communists, in their attempts to dispel the concept that education was only for the wealthy and to make the system more universally accessible, actively promoted the educational advancement of persons of worker-peasant origin. Ultimately, however, this policy was played down. In 1972 these students, at the secondary and higher educational levels, constituted a vastly smaller proportion of the total worker-peasant population than before. Also, in prewar education, the emphasis was on the humanities or liberal arts rather than technical or vocational specializations. Although the communist objective of reorienting the educational system toward the technical and vocational fields has been partially realized, there is still a great demand on the part of students, particularly in higher education, for courses in the humanities.

Hungarian education, however, has undergone a rather sweeping transformation in other respects. In many cases, the regime has set objectives for the educational system that have proved to be—as yet—unattainable. In other cases, the system has fulfilled many of the early goals. A major objective of education was to produce the ideal Communist who would serve and promote the Hungarian state. This objective was to be achieved through the formal educational system, which includes Marxism-Leninism in the curriculum from kindergarten through the university, and through extracurricular activities that are both highly centralized and closely related to the party. Although it is difficult to speculate on the success of this objective, there can be little doubt that the system is so constructed as to maximize the possibility of its achievement (see ch. 9).

Another objective of the Communists was to make education available to the entire population and to stress certain areas that were deemed important to the society. Although the base for such a plan existed in prewar Hungary—in terms of supposedly compulsory education at the elementary level, adult education, education for the handicapped, and so forth—the Communists have made the system more comprehensive. Enforcement of compulsory attendance in the general, or elementary, school has made education more universal. At the same time, vocational and polytechnical schools, which did exist in prewar Hungary, were greatly developed and emphasized by the communist system. This development was a response to the demands of the newly industrialized society for technical specialists, a need that barely existed in prewar, largely agrarian, Hungary.

The communist system of education, however, like the prewar system, has had its share of difficulties. Major problems in recent years have been in the areas of secondary and higher education—areas that also experienced problems before the war. Although the number of both institutions and students has increased significantly on every level, the percentage of the population of school-age children attending institutions of secondary and higher education is still disproportionately low. At the university level the problem of shortage of places is acute. As a result many eager Hungarian secondary school graduates are either driven away from higher education altogether or forced to enroll in more accessible universities in foreign countries.

HISTORY OF EDUCATION IN HUNGARY

Hungarians have displayed a keen interest in education since the Middle Ages. The communist regime has actively encouraged this love of education while imposing new patterns and directions on the precommunist system.

Before 1949 elementary education was tuition free, but secondary and higher education were generally the exclusive domain of the middle and upper classes; students of worker and peasant background constituted only 3 to 4 percent of the student bodies at these levels. Exclusiveness reached an extreme point in the era of Miklos Horthy after World War I when the anti-Jewish laws of 1920 and 1928 restricted the number of Jewish students in universities and colleges.

Hungarian schools were based primarily on the West European model, heavy emphasis being placed on a broad education and little value being attached to technical specialization, except in the case of such professions as law and medicine. The Roman Catholic Church was the dominant influence in the schools, and other Christian churches also played major roles. Of the church-dominated European school systems, Hungary's was considered to be the most deeply permeated with religious influence. Much of secondary and higher education was under Roman Catholic, Calvinist, Lutheran, and Unitarian sponsorship. One manifestation of this religious dominance was the administration of education, until the communist takeover, by the Ministry of Religion and Education.

The literacy level just preceding the communist reforms of 1948 and 1949 was relatively high. Until the 1860s illiteracy had been virtually unchecked because elementary schools had been neglected. When elementary education became compulsory in 1868, however, this problem was slowly eradicated. By 1920, 86.6 percent of the population was literate; by 1930, 90.0 percent; by 1941, 94 percent; and by 1949, 95.3 percent.

GOALS OF COMMUNIST EDUCATION

The educational philosophy and ideals of the communist regime in Hungary have been articulated in various pronouncements surrounding major legislation on education. The major education acts were passed in 1949, 1954, and 1961, the first and last involving the most sweeping reforms. Generally, the goals expressed in these statements have been flexibly formulated and have been modified when they proved to be unattainable or unrealistic.

The major objective of communist education is to produce citizens who will benefit Hungarian socialist society. This goal is to be achieved through a total communist education both within and outside the school framework. Such an education includes a complete comprehension of Marxism-Leninism, which permeates the curriculum at all levels of the school system, and a thorough understanding of the Hungarian Socialist Workers' Party (MSZMP—see Glossary), which is encouraged by youth organizations functioning outside the formal educational process.

Although this objective was defined from the outset, it was expressed most recently, in 1972, by Janos Kadar, first secretary of the MSZMP. He stated: "Of course, what would please me, as a Communist, would be for secondary schools and higher educational institutes to produce perfect Communists. Of course, this is impossible. It is a fair demand, however, that young people be taught a sense of duty to the people bent on socialist construction." The ideal of the perfect Communist—ideally based on the Soviet model—has been modified, through the process of adapting to the local situation, to produce the perfect Hungarian socialist citizen. In 1954 it was stated that Hungarian "national culture" and "patriotic education" were to be stressed. In 1972 this goal was still more liberally interpreted when it was conceded that it was acceptable to learn not only from other socialist countries but also from Western models.

The second objective of communist education is to produce technical specialists who will meet the needs of the national economy. In 1949 the minister of education explicitly stated: "In the interest of promoting the success of the economic Five Year Plan, it is necessary to improve the economic and technical professional training on a high level; of training an adequate number of technicians, adjusted to the necessities of individual fields primarily of economic life, who are entirely familiar with the different specific trades and will be suited to fill leading positions." Thus, education played a part in the supply and demand process by selecting the necessary numbers of students and training them for specific functions in the economy. This objective, however, has also been modified, partly as a result of relative success in industrialization and partly because of the awareness of the qualitative shortcomings resulting from this policy. In 1972, at a conference of educators, one of the stated goals was the achievement of the proper balance between the arts and sciences.

The third objective of the communist government was to raise the educational level of workers and peasants who had been deprived under the prewar regime. Like the other objectives, however, the goals of the policy had to be modified in order to conform to conditions. In 1949 Article 48 of the new constitution stated: "The Hungarian People's Republic shall ensure the right to education to every worker . . . the Hungarian People's Republic shall implement the right by extending to all, educational facilities through a free and compulsory general school system, secondary and higher schools, educational facilities for adult workers, and financial aid to those receiving any kind of education." Although there was some degree of success in the achievement of this objective, there were also sufficient problems to warrant the gradual playing down of this theme. In 1954 the policy was modified slightly by conceding that, although the majority of students ought to be of working and peasant background, priority would be given to ability rather than to class origin. Finally, in 1963, the policy was virtually voided, and class background has been deemphasized in most policy statements since that time.

The fourth objective of communist education—and the only one that has not required modification—was to integrate education with everyday life. Law III of 1961 set forth two major goals to be achieved through education: closing the gap between school and daily life by means of relating practical activities to production; and unifying the individual and the state by molding "conscious, educated, patriotic, upright and law-abiding citizens who will be faithful to the people, will cooperate in building socialism with useful work, (and who) will build and protect the peoples' state."

COMMUNIST REFORMS IN EDUCATION

Broad Reforms

When the Communists took power in 1949, they began a series of broad reforms designed to eliminate certain features of precommunist education and to replace them with the means of meeting the new goals and objectives. Education for an eight-year period in coeducational schools was made compulsory in 1948. There was an overt attempt at this time to rid the school system of religious influences. Before World War II religion had been a compulsory subject in primary, secondary, and special schools. As early as 1947 religious instruction was no longer considered compulsory, and in 1949 it became, at least nominally, an elective subject. By 1948 denominational schools were nationalized, and church rights regarding school administration and textbook publication were curtailed. In the field of higher education, whereas there had been many religious-sponsored institutions in 1945, by 1954 there were none. On the primary and secondary levels, however, by the early 1950s certain agreements had been signed between the state and the Roman Catholic and Protestant churches that allowed some denominational schools to continue in existence.

In the first two years of reform there was a strong attempt to sovietize the entire educational system. Russian-language study became compulsory from the upper levels of the general school through the university. Many Soviet professors taught at Hungarian universities, much of the work of Soviet authors was utilized as course material, and Russian clubs were established. In the late 1940s the Gorki Institute of Budapest and the Russian Institute of Budapest University were founded. This sovietization policy was later modified in favor of a more Hungarian orientation

The communist leaders in order to elevate the educational level of students of worker and peasant origin—particularly at the higher levels of education where they previously had been barred—radically altered the admissions policy on the secondary level in favor of students from worker-peasant backgrounds. Similarly, in higher education, social background became the chief criterion for admission. Students from worker-peasant families who had not completed secondary school were allowed to enroll in an intensified one-year course that made them eligible for admission to universities.

By 1950 the entire school system had been nationalized. In the general schools, and other elementary schools remaining from the prewar era, a total of 639,335 pupils and some 18,000 teachers were under the aegis of the state. In higher education all universities and other institutions, which had been autonomous, were under state control. Marxism-Leninism had become the backbone of the curriculum by the early 1950s. A brief liberalization of this policy followed the death of Joseph Stalin but, seemingly as a response to the Revolution of 1956, a renewed effort to instill the spirit of Marxism in the schools had become evident by 1957. By 1961 all syllabi had been revised, new curricula had been implemented in elementary and secondary schools, and the teachings of Marx and Lenin had been incorporated into higher education.

Vocational training was one of the major objectives of the School Reform Act of 1961 and was made part of every kind of school at every level. A new course called practical skills was instituted to teach students basic techniques, and a new form of secondary education, based on a precommunist model but more specialized in scope, was established to deal exclusively with vocational education.

Before 1962 general or elementary school was free of charge, but secondary schools charged tuition fees. Pupils from worker-peasant families and exceptional students were generally eligible for scholarships. By 1963 all preschool, elementary, and secondary schools were tuition free. In addition, boarding schools, student homes, and study rooms were established to ease financial burdens, primarily those of children from rural communities. A decree by the minister of culture in 1963 stated that, in the field of higher education, students having high grades would be exempted from tuition fees. There were to be two forms of aid to students in higher education: benefits, such as room and board; and financial scholarships. Some 90 percent of higher education students received some form of assistance.

Specific Institutional Reforms

Whereas broad reforms were directed at eradicating past deficiencies as well as all noncommunist influences in the educational system, specific changes were instituted in the various branches of the school system in order to implement these reforms. In 1945 the general school was established as an eight-year elementary school for students from six to fourteen years of age, and all existing elementary schools became general schools.

Secondary schools were reorganized into four-year institutions; some were academically oriented along the lines of the precommunist gymnasium, whereas others were technical or vocational. The vocational secondary school, a branch of the school system greatly expanded by the Communists, was designed to train workers in agriculture, industry, and commerce. In 1948 there were three new kinds of secondary schools: the secondary modern; the technical or vocational; and the teacher training school. The teacher training school remained at the secondary level until 1958, when it was absorbed into higher education.

Reforms in higher education began in the early 1950s after all higher education had come under state control. By 1951 several polytechnical universities and colleges had been established. The trend toward specialization was accelerated by the founding of such new kinds of institutions as the Academy of Heavy Industry, the Academy of Transportation, and the Academy of Agricultural Engineering.

Workers' schools, which had existed as part of adult education before 1945, were established as separate institutions on three levels. The first level was the workers' general school, which was open to all workers who had finished the regular general school. The second level led to a so-called workers' diploma and enabled the worker to enroll in a form of higher education. The third kind was the correspondence school, which operated on both the secondary and university levels.

Reform Results

During the first five years of the communist regime, the number of children in nursery schools and kindergartens rose by 20 percent, and the number of pupils in primary schools increased by 50 percent. Between 1945 and 1965 the number of classes in the general school doubled, the number of teachers increased by 2½ times, and 98.8 percent of eligible children were attending elementary school. Of these students, 90 percent had completed their required courses within the usual period of time.

Between 1949 and 1954 secondary school graduates increased by 73 percent. Although the figures are disputed, the number of schools rose from somewhere between 173 and 397 in academic year 1937/38 to some 400 in 1954; some scholars placed the precise figure for 1937/38 at 250. Similarly, the number of pupils grew from between 44,000 and 53,000 to 162,000 by 1954. The worker-peasant percentage of the student body in secondary education rose from a mere 8 percent in 1948 to 42 percent in 1949. This percentage later declined as the policy was gradually deemphasized.

In higher education the number of institutions rose from sixteen in 1937 to forty-three in 1960. Students increased from 11,747 in 1937 to 44,585 in 1960. The worker peasant ratio in higher education reached a high of 66 percent in academic year 1949/50, but a number of these students failed to meet the curriculum requirements. This percentage, like the elementary-secondary percentage, later declined as there was a gradual return, dating from Stalin's death in 1953, to professional criteria rather than class origin as the main basis of admission.

ADMINISTRATION AND FINANCING

Administration

Before 1948 education had been under the administrative jurisdiction of the Ministry of Religion and Education, which was assisted in its functions by the National Council of Education. When the Communists took power, various aspects of education were placed under the tutelage of separate offices and ministries, and religious matters were placed under the authority of the State Office of Church Affairs. Formal education in 1949 was placed under the Ministry of Culture. By 1965 concern for education was so vast that the National Education Council was established as a consultative body to the Ministry of Culture and was very similar in function to the original National Council of Education, which had served the former Ministry of Religion and Education.

The administration of education in Hungary is highly centralized. Public education is set up in a strictly uniform pattern, and all public educational institutions are controlled and maintained by the state.

The single exception to this rule occurs in the case of church schools, although these too are assisted by the state and subject to its inspection. The final power of decision with regard to education rests with the main organs of the MSZMP. The Scientific and Public Education Section of the Central Committee of the party is the section most responsible for education.

The principal governmental body dealing with education is the Ministry of Culture. Within the ministry there are subsections dealing with education at the kindergarten level, elementary education, secondary education, vocational education, teacher training, and higher education. The ministry establishes an educational program based on political principles and the needs of the economy. Although the Ministry of Culture is responsible in an overall sense for all branches of formal education, other ministries actually oversee the administration of schools that fall into their field of specialization. The various ministries responsible for industrial, agricultural, and commercial affairs oversee both secondary vocational schools and higher technical school. All medical training comes under the Ministry of Health; agricultural training falls under the Ministry of Agriculture and Food; and colleges for physical training come under the Hungarian Physical Training and Sports Council.

Serving as an advisory body, the National Education Council establishes guidelines for both curricula and syllabi and evaluates the relative merits and deficiencies of the school system. Among the most important ancillary bodies dealing with primary and secondary education are the regional councils. Although their organizations are autonomous, they assist in planning in collaboration with central authorities. They also work at the local level with both teachers and parents and generally direct the work of the schools in their particular regions. The mass organizations are the last but not least important group dealing with the administration and functioning of the educational system. These are organizations, such as youth groups, trade unions, and parental work collectives, that strive to promote the development of the socialist school system.

Financing

Nearly all financial burdens for public education are borne by the state. Actually, the state allocates funds to cover 92.5 percent of the total cost of public education, parental contributions constitute 7.2 percent, and the remainder comes from individuals and industries who supply equipment or services to the schools. The cost of national education increased considerably from 1960 to 1970, although the percentage of the national income allocated to it remained relatively fixed. In 1960 education cost 5,872 million forints (for value of forint—see Glossary), which was 4 percent of the national income; in 1970 education cost 11,871 million forints, or 4.3 percent of the national income.

In 1970 general schools absorbed the greatest portion of the total revenue—36.5 percent; followed by higher education—18.8 percent; secondary education—15.9 percent; apprentice training—12 percent; kindergartens—10 percent; student homes or boarding facilities—5.2 percent; and extension courses—1.6 percent.

THE EDUCATIONAL SYSTEM

Hungarian education has been described as "socialist in content and national and European in character," a blend of the modern and the traditional. Although it is a highly pragmatic form of education—the teaching of practical skills is an indispensable requirement of the system—it also instills in its students a sense of respect for the culture of Hungary and of Europe as well. There is a great interest in adult education and, as a result, roughly the same number of adults attend class as do young people of school age. The formal school system is complemented by study circles, literary societies, debating teams, sports circles, and other extracurricular, party-dominated organizations.

Preschool Education

The first kindergarten was founded in Budapest in 1828. At this time there was strong opposition to the establishment of preschool institutions. By 1873 there were only three private kindergartens. The first state kindergarten was founded in 1876. The first legislation regarding kindergartens was enacted in 1891; it required the establishment of kindergartens in communities in which forty or more three- to six-year-olds were unsupervised. There was little real growth in the field until the end of World War II. Schools were frequently overcrowded and understaffed, and the emphasis was on discipline and religion.

When the schools were nationalized in 1948, there was a vast revision in the concept of kindergarten education. Children were to be educated in terms of the principles of socialist education, and preschool, especially in the kindergarten phase, was perceived to be built on three concepts of communist education—play, work, and learning.

There are two forms of preschool in Hungary—nurseries and kindergartens. Nurseries, or crèches, are for children from one month to three years of age. They function under the Ministry of Health and are maintained by such groups as people's councils, factories, enterprises, and cooperatives. The fee for this service is dependent on the income of the parents and the number of children in the family. Because of the ages of the children, nurseries are more in the nature of day-care centers than schools. Kindergartens are for children from three to six years of age and are the Hungarian child's first exposure to structured education. They operate under the Ministry of Culture and are maintained by local people's councils, state agencies, institutions, plants, cooperatives, social organizations, enterprises, and farms. There are six types of kindergartens: the half-day school, the full-day school, the seasonal day homes, the summer day homes, six-day kindergartens, and children's homes.

The total number of kindergartens and kindergarten pupils, as well as the overall percentage of children actually attending kindergarten, has improved greatly over the past decade, but problems remain. The number of kindergartens had increased from school year 1960/61 to 1970/71, as had the number of pupils. Nevertheless, even though the percentage of kindergarten-age children attending school had risen, it was still quite low (see table 6). There are not enough kindergartens in the country to satisfy demand, and many children have been refused admittance because of the shortage of schools. The government has taken some steps to alleviate this problem; trade unions, enterprises, cooperatives, and other organizations have been requested to create more kindergartens to fill the gap.

Table 6. Number of Hungarian Schools and Pupils Attending, School Years 1961 and 1971

Level	Number of Schools		Number of Pupils		Percentage of School-Age Children in School	
	1960/61	1970/71	1960/61	1970/71	1960/61	1970/71
Kindergarten	2,865	3,457	83,800	227,300	33.7	57.7
Elementary or general	6,307	5,480	1,392,300	1,116,000	98.5	98.4
Secondary	419	547	241,036	347,165	26.4	30.3

Source: Adapted from Hungary, Ministry of Cultural Affairs, International Conference on Education, 33d Session, "Report on Educational Progress in the 1970/71 Academic Year," Geneva, 1971; and *Statistical Pocket Book of Hungary, 1971*, Budapest, 1971, pp. 279–286.

Elementary Education

In 1777 the Ratio Educationis (Principles of Education) was passed under the rule of Queen Maria Theresa. This early decree attempted to regulate education and, like the communist system centuries later, articulated the concept that education was a state concern. After the Compromise of 1867, promulgated during the rule of King Francis Joseph I, the Fundamental Law of 1868 was passed, which regulated elementary education until World War II. Education was made compulsory for both boys and girls of six to twelve years of age. Later, compulsory education was extended to cover the three-year period of the so-called continuation schools. Under the Hungarian Council Republic of Bela Kun, who took power briefly in 1919, elementary education became an eight-year, rather than a six-year, process. Although this practice was not uniform throughout the country at that time, it became standardized in 1940 under Law XX. Until the Communists took power in 1948, however, compulsory education was not strictly enforced, especially in the rural areas. Similarly, coeducation, which was also part of prewar educational policy, existed only when separate classes for boys and girls were either too expensive or unsuitable.

Under the law of 1940, after the fourth grade, pupils could either proceed to the higher grades of the elementary school or choose one of three other courses: upper elementary school (a separate level of education); vocational school; or the eight-year secondary school. The upper elementary school was based on a German and Austrian pattern known as the *Bürgerschule* or citizen's school; these four-year institutions for boys or girls were established in large towns and cities in Hungary at the beginning of the twentieth century. In the 1937/38 school year, of 397 such schools, 160 were run by the state, 101 were communal, and the remainder were denominational.

After the communist takeover the compulsory eight-grade general school was established, which provided a standardized elementary education throughout the country. The aim of the general school, according to party officials, was to lay the foundation "for developing the communist man." The student was to be instilled with respect for the working man, appreciation of communist morality, and desire to protect the socialist fatherland.

There are two types of elementary education in Hungary: the general school, which is an eight-year school for children from six to fourteen years of age; and the continuation school, a two-year school for children between fourteen and sixteen (enrollment until sixteen years of age is compulsory) who are not planning to continue either academic or vocational secondary education.

Unlike preschool education, there was a decline in the number of schools and pupils, as well as a slight percentage decrease in the number of elementary-age school pupils attending elementary school; but the overall percentage of school-age children attending elementary school throughout the country is high. Moreover, 91 percent of the corresponding age groups graduated from the general school. The number of persons in the employed population enrolled in elementary school courses in 1970/71 was 21,275, as compared with 116,670 in 1963/64.

Problems still remain in the field of elementary education. There are still a number of so-called repeaters—pupils who lose one or more years of school—although the number had dropped radically in recent years. In 1952, 56.9 percent repeated; in the 1962/63 school year, 19 percent; and in 1970/71, 17.4 percent. This trend is especially prevalent in the first and fifth grades.

There is a shortage of qualified teachers, so that specific subjects are often taught by teachers not trained in that field. In some schools, owing to shortages of classrooms, pupils of different grades sit together in the same class. The state acknowledges the problems and works toward solutions, but progress is slow. At the Fifth Congress of the

Patriotic People's Front in 1972, the government declared that its goal was to have every school-age child complete all grades of the elementary school. Modernization of school equipment, introduction of new instructional methods, and establishment of more rural schools have been proposed as means to achieve desired goals.

Secondary Education

Like the elementary system, secondary education was based on the Ratio Educationis of 1777 and a later education law of 1806. A law of 1883 grouped secondary education into two formal categories: the gymnasium, which provided a classical education; and the *Real* school, which was more modern and scientific in orientation. By 1924 these two forms had evolved into three: the gymnasium; the *Real* gymnasium, in which modern languages were emphasized; and the *Real* school.

The first secondary school for girls was established in 1916. Legislation in 1926 provided that there be three types of schools for girls; the gymnasium; the lyceum, which emulated the *Real* gymnasium; and colleges, which were for girls terminating their education. Lyceums for both girls and boys were established in 1938. They were four-year institutions, which were to supply a practical rather than theoretical education.

Before the communist educational reforms, secondary education was essentially traditional, dominated by religious influence, and was accessible to only a small proportion—approximately 25 percent—of those students who completed the elementary school. The humanities were stressed, often at the expense of the sciences, and technical education was to a large extent minimized, despite the existence of technical and vocational schools. Secondary schools were roughly divided between state, community, and church schools.

Under the communist system, there are three major forms of secondary education: the gymnasium, which is further subdivided into academic and art sections; secondary *technikum* (a specialized technical school), which is being phased out; and vocational secondary schools. Each of these programs lasts four years. The gymnasiums operate under the Ministry of Culture, whereas the other two forms function under separate specialized ministries.

The gymnasiums are based on the educational laws of 1961. The objective of the gymnasium is to produce work-loving students, capable of absorbing further education in the institutions of higher learning, acquiring a skill, pursuing independent study, or filling a job commensurate with secondary school training. Furthermore, the purpose of the gymnasium is to develop the communist man, supply him with modern and general education, prepare him for life, and develop in him an interest in a particular field. In 1972 there were ten denominational gymnasiums still in existence. Of these, one was Jewish, one was Protestant, and eight were Roman Catholic. Gymnasium students made up approximately 50 percent of the total population of all three types of secondary education.

In the school year 1970/71 only one *technikum* remained. This was the Technical School for Miners. Previously, the *technikum* was of three types: industrial, agricultural, and commercial. They were to prepare the student for higher education in his particular field of specialization. These schools came under the broad jurisdiction of the Ministry of Culture but were under the specific tutelage of the appropriate ministries. The objectives of this type of education were to train patriotic and skilled citizens who would have a background both in the theoretical and in practical applications of their respective trades.

Vocational Secondary Education

As early as the so-called reform period in the first half of the nineteenth century, there was a demand for vocational schools. Before World War II there were a number of agricultural, industrial, and commercial vocational schools. By the 1937/38 school year there were 376 industrial schools and twenty-eight commercial schools in addition to a vastly greater number of agricultural schools in this largely agrarian country. Although the caliber of vocational secondary training was below that in the later communist system and the course was more general in nature, the precursor of the communist secondary vocational school was to be found in a new eight-year vocational high school, which was introduced on the secondary level in 1939. It provided a general education in the humanities as well as vocational training in a particular field.

Before the Communists took power in 1948, however, vocational education, although strong in terms of the number of schools, was weak in the quality of its training. Generally, vocational schools were far below the caliber of other kinds of secondary education. When the regime nationalized banking, transportation, and industry and collectivized farms, vocational education of necessity grew in importance.

Vocational secondary training is based on the 1961 educational laws, which require specialized training in a specific skill. Since 1965 training in skills has been stressed to an even greater degree. Vocational secondary schools function in collaboration with a shop or plant; they are designed to give a broader background than the *technikum*, which they are replacing. They, like the *technikum*, fall into three broad categories: industrial, agricultural, and commercial. The industrial schools were originally under the Ministry of Culture but are now under the aegis of the Ministry of Labor. The agricultural schools, similarly, are under the Ministry of Agriculture. The commercial schools have declined somewhat in importance in recent years but, overall, there has been a great increase in the popularity of vocational secondary schools; and many students favor them over the university-oriented gymnasiums.

In the mid-1960s many more students applied to these schools than could be admitted.

Secondary education in Hungary, unlike preschool and elementary education, is attended by less than a third of the entire corresponding age population, although the numbers of students and institutions are increasing. Almost twice as many attend day courses as evening and correspondence courses. The percentage of female students has increased slightly—from 54.4 percent in 1960 to 58.3 percent in 1970; women constitute a clear majority of the student population in secondary schools. A high percentage—70 percent in 1972—of school-age students graduate from secondary schools.

Many students tend to terminate their education with elementary school. Students of worker-peasant origin tend to enroll in continuation schools rather than proceed to secondary schools, although there are a few pilot projects designed to promote pupils of this background to secondary and higher education. The proportion of students of worker-peasant origin in secondary schools peaked at 64 percent in 1954; by the 1968/69 school year the percentage had dropped to 49.4 percent. There are severe shortages of schools—particularly of the boarding school variety—in secondary education, although the state in 1971 announced plans to create 14,000 additional places for secondary school students by 1976.

If the student has succeeded in completing his secondary education, he is then confronted by further difficulties. If he chooses to go on to higher education, which approximately one-half of secondary school pupils do, he finds that he is one of many applicants for very few admission spaces. A study completed in 1968 indicated that only one out of three students intending to go on to higher education could be accepted. On the other hand, of students wishing to find employment, 60 percent of this group wanted only white-collar jobs. The state's tentative solution to these problems is to offer intensified vocational guidance within the secondary school system.

Higher Education

The first institution of higher education, the University of Pecs, was founded by Louis the Great in 1367. In 1388 the second university was established at Obuda, followed by a third in Pozsony (Bratislava) in 1467. By 1547 all three of these universities had been destroyed during the Turkish invasions and ensuing occupation.

Five early universities, however, still survived by World War II. The first of these was the university in Nagyszombat, founded in 1635 by Peter Pazmany, leader of the Counter-Reformation; the university was later transferred to Budapest and called the Royal Peter Pazmany University. The second was the Royal Jozsef Nador University of Technology, predecessor of the Polytechnical University of Budapest, founded in 1872 as a school of engineering. The third was the university at Kolozsvar (later Cluj), founded in 1872, which later became the Royal Francis Joseph University in Szeged. The fourth and fifth were the reestablished University of Pozsony, which was later transferred to Pecs and called the Royal Elizabeth University, and the University of Debrecen, later called the Royal Istvan Tisza University, which were both founded in 1912.

Although the Communists greatly expanded the technical-school system, the first technical institution of higher education, the Mining College at Selmec, was actually established in 1763 and was one of the first technical schools in the world. By World War II there were polytechnical universities, economic institutions, institutions of fine and applied arts, specialized music institutes, and military academies. Religious seminaries continued to flourish; there were fifteen Roman Catholic seminaries, one Lutheran college, and three Calvinist schools. By 1937 there were sixteen secular institutions of higher education; during World War II, of course, many universities and institutes were suspended or operated on a reduced basis.

Higher education is organized in a more complex manner than the lower levels of Hungarian education, being under the jurisdiction of the Presidential Council, the Ministry of Culture and other relevant ministries, the National Planning Office, and the Hungarian Academy of Sciences. The Ministry of Culture has specific jurisdiction over the regular universities, the polytechnical universities, and the teacher training colleges and institutes; medical universities operate under the Ministry of Health. There are six major types of institutions of higher education: academic universities and colleges; medical universities; polytechnical universities; agronomic universities and colleges; vocational colleges, of which only one remained by 1972; and teacher training colleges and institutions.

There are five major academic universities. The term of study varies from faculty to faculty and university to university. Perhaps the most prestigious university is the Lorand Eotvos University, formerly the Royal Peter Pazmany University. Its particular strengths lie in the fields of foreign languages and education. Attila Jozsef University, formerly the Royal Francis Joseph University, has faculties in natural science, philosophy, and law and political science. The Karl Marx University of Economics was founded by the Communists in 1948 in order to train economists within the framework of Marxism-Leninism. Although it is a school of economics, it is also strong in foreign languages. The Lajos Kossuth University, formerly the Royal Istvan Tisza University, is the second smallest academic university. It offers courses only in natural science and philosophy; its school of law was discontinued, and schools of medicine and theology became separate institutions. The smallest academic university is the University of Pecs. Its only faculty is the School of Political Science and Law.

The medical universities are based on the educational reforms of

1950, which dictated that medical universities be separate from the academic universities. Generally the course lasts six years. The first three years are spent in general study; the next two are spent in practical clinical medicine; the sixth year is devoted to internship. Upon graduation, doctors must work in specified locations for a period of two years. Every three to five years, they must take five-month refresher courses at the Institute for Further Training of Physicians. The four major medical universities are located in Budapest, Debrecen, Pecs, and Szeged.

There are twenty-four polytechnical schools in Hungary. Although there were a small number of such schools in the 1937/38 school year, these schools grew primarily as a result of communist policy. Of the twenty-four higher technical schools, the four major ones are: the Polytechnical University of Budapest, which was established in 1782 and recently absorbed the Polytechnical University of Construction and Transportation in Budapest; the Polytechnical University of Heavy Industry at Miskolc, founded in 1949, which later absorbed the School of Mining and Metallurgy of the Polytechnical University of Budapest; the University of Chemical Industry at Veszprem, established in 1951; and the Polytechnical University of Gyor, which was set up by the Presidential Council in 1963.

The agronomic universities and colleges also form part of the higher technical school system. Before 1945 agronomic education at the higher levels came under the School of Agriculture and Veterinary Medicine at the Jozsef Nador University of Technology and Economics. The collectivization of farms by the Communists was the impetus for separate agronomic education. In 1945 the Agronomic University was established in Budapest and Godollo. By the late 1960s there were two universities and four colleges that specialized in agronomic education. Generally, the agronomic programs run from four to five years, leading to an engineering degree. The Agronomic University of Budapest and Godollo also includes the Institute for Further Training of Skilled Workers.

Many Hungarians in higher education study abroad. The explanation most probably lies in the fact that Hungarian universities lack sufficient places for their own nationals. Hungarians, however, have traditionally studied abroad. During the Middle Ages, Hungarian students studied in Italian, French, Polish, Dutch, Czech, and German universities. Since World War II, however, most Hungarian students have studied in the socialist-bloc countries, most frequently within the Soviet Union itself. In 1970 the number of Hungarian students studying in eighty-two universities in the Soviet Union alone was 1,300. Between 1952 and 1966 over 2,240 Hungarian students had studied in the Soviet Union. By 1972 a Hungarian student population of 1,700 had studied in other socialist-bloc countries. It was predicted that an additional 320 first-year Hungarian students would study abroad in

1972/73, predominantly in the Soviet Union, the German Democratic Republic (East Germany), Czechoslovakia, Poland, Bulgaria, and Romania.

Scholarships are provided by the National Scholarship Council, which since 1968 has selected students for study abroad. Scholarships to foreign universities are given if there are no places at a similar faculty in a Hungarian university or if the foreign faculty is considered to be superior. There are scholarships for undergraduates as well as for postgraduate students. In recent years there has been a great increase among Hungarian students in Western scholarships. In 1971 over 1,700 students applied for scholarships through the Institute of Cultural Relations; of these, British and Swedish scholarships were the most attractive to Hungarian students.

In 1972 there were 2,500 foreign students from seventy-eight countries studying in Hungary. Of these, the largest representations were from North Vietnam, Czechoslovakia, and East Germany—each having sent over 100 students. Syria and Sudan supply the greatest number of students from the noncommunist, developing countries. These students tend to concentrate their studies in the technical, medical, and agricultural fields. Western students, on the other hand, most frequently study art and the humanities. Five hundred first-year foreign students were expected to study in Hungary in the 1972/73 academic year.

Although women are still a minority in higher education, their proportion has risen steadily since before World War II. In 1937/38, of a total of 11,747 students in higher education, only 14.5 percent were women. By 1960/61 the number of women had risen dramatically; they then constituted 37.9 percent of the higher education population. In 1966/67, 43.3 percent of all day students were women. By 1970/71 women constituted 44.7 percent of the higher education population.

The highest percentage of women are in teacher training, where they constitute 94.4 percent of the total, and vocational colleges, where they represent 78 percent of the student body. During the 1960s there was a great increase in the number of women in medicine. In 1966/67, of the 8,353 medical students, 5,154 were women. The least popular fields for women are the technical ones; women constitute only 21.4 percent of the enrollment in the polytechnical schools. The number of university applications from women is rising. In certain schools applications from women are between 50 and 90 percent of the total number received. In the faculty of foreign correspondence of the Foreign Trade Academy, for example, women represented 93 percent of the total number of applicants.

The total number of institutions of higher education has risen from sixteen in 1937/38 to forty-three in 1960/61 and to seventy four in 1970/71. Thus, the number of institutions of higher education has more than quadrupled since World War II. Similarly, the number of students is approximately seven times the number of prewar students, growing from 11,747 in 1937/38 to 44,585 in 1960/61 and to 80,536 in 1970/71. Universities and colleges are the most popular form of higher education. The vocational colleges, most of which are no longer in existence, are the least popular. Engineering and architecture are the most well attended faculties within the university and college system, and pharmacy is the least well attended faculty.

Higher education in Hungary is the most problem-laden area of the entire educational system. A low proportion—7 percent—of persons from the corresponding age groups graduate from institutions of higher education. Students of worker-peasant origin have been poorly represented at this level ever since the policy of encouraging students from this background—initiated in the late 1940s and early 1950s—was moderated in 1963. This is considered a major problem by communist authorities. Although debates regarding the merits of this policy continue, the number of students having a worker-peasant background has dropped significantly. In 1949/50 this group constituted 66 percent of the higher education population. By 1963/64 it was down to 43.9 percent, and by 1969/70 it had declined to 39 percent of the total higher education population.

Another major problem is that there are many more applicants than there are places in most institutions of higher education in Hungary. The number of applicants is approximately two to three times the number of admissions. In 1972 a total of 34,000 applied for 14,000 places. Certain fields must turn large numbers of applicants away, whereas other fields fail to meet their quotas. For example, in 1972 in such fields as foreign languages, law, fine arts, history, and psychology—a very popular field—the demand for admission was overwhelming, whereas technical universities and faculties of mathematics in the universities have fewer applicants than places.

The state, which expresses concern over the fact that approximately two thirds of higher education applicants are rejected, has proposed tentative solutions to these problems. One is to offer more adequate counseling at the secondary school level. The other solution is to increase the number of openings at the higher educational level. In 1972 the number of places for 1973 was increased by 500, bringing the total to 14,500.

Other Types of Education

Although the Communists expanded and diversified education that did not fall within the strict limits of formal education, there was already an existing base for such activities under the precommunist system. Hungarians had long been aware of the need for special education for handicapped children. The first such institution was the Institute for the Deaf, which was founded in the small town of Vac in 1802. In 1825 a similar institute was established for the blind, and in 1875 one was established for the mentally defective. In 1922 the Training College for Teachers of Handicapped Children became a separate institution with the exclusive purpose of training teachers for special education.

The Communists have established special institutions and enacted specific legislation to care for handicapped children. In 1952 special institutes were set up for the vocational training of handicapped children, generally between the ages of twelve and eighteen. The educational law of 1961 dealt specifically with the problem of education for the handicapped. The law stipulated that mentally and physically deficient children should be educated in special institutions. By 1966 special institutes for the handicapped had been provided for 22,000 children; 6,000 of these were maintained at boarding schools. Health and educational authorities hope to keep approximately 50 percent of the handicapped population in boarding schools by 1980.

Each group of defective children is cared for in a separate institution dealing exclusively with a particular disorder. Mentally defective students have an entirely different curriculum from that of normal students: strong emphasis is placed on manual skills. Their training consists of one preparatory grade and eight formal grades. Deaf students have two years of preparatory grades followed by eight general grades. Blind students, similarly, have two years of preparatory school followed by eight general grades. Children defective in locomotor abilities are also taught in special institutions.

At the other extreme, there are special educational facilities for exceptionally intelligent children. At the primary level, students having special abilities, particularly in the areas of foreign languages and music, are provided with intensive classes. On the secondary level, there is intensified instruction in foreign languages, mathematics, and the natural sciences as well as in music. The concept of special education for exceptional children is continually being expanded in Hungary.

Minority elementary schools were set up on the basis of a 1923 law that stipulated that a community having a large number of children speaking a minority language was entitled to minority instruction. In the mid-1930s there were forty-seven German schools and seventeen Serbian schools, all courses being taught in the minority languages. There were 372 German, fifty-three Slovak, and sixty-four other diverse minority schools, in which classes were taught in both the minority language and in Hungarian.

There are also forms of vocational education, established in the early 1960s, which do not fall within the formal limits of education in Hungary. These schools, according to authorities, are "dedicated to training technicians who will be highly skilled and equipped with the most advanced theoretical and practical knowledge to serve the various branches of industry, construction, transportation, agriculture, trade, and public health." They function in collaboration with various factories, shops, and scientific organizations; they operate under the relevant ministries but within the broad domain of the Ministry of Culture. These schools are actually postsecondary vocational schools, although they do not fall into the field of higher education. They tend to admit students having eight years of general school and three years of vocational school, whereas institutions of higher education require twelve years of elementary and secondary education. Upon completion of the course, the student receives the skilled technician diploma.

There are also special programs for students in the fields of music, art, and sport. Under the communist regime the School of Dance Arts, later called the State Ballet Institute, was founded in 1949. In 1951 special secondary schools for music and both fine and industrial arts were established by order of the Presidential Council. In 1956 the Ministry of Culture assumed administrative responsibility for all music and art institutions. On the level of higher education, there is the Hungarian College of Fine Arts, which was founded in 1871 and which offers a seven-year course. The Hungarian College of Industrial Arts offers a four-year program. The College of Dramatic and Cinematographic Arts, which was founded in 1948, offers four-year courses for actors and five-year courses for directors. All of these colleges are under the tutelage of the Ministry of Culture. In the field of sports in higher education, the Hungarian College of Physical Education, which was established in 1959, offers a program of approximately four years. It is under the sponsorship of the Hungarian Physical Training and Sports Council and is regulated by the Scientific Research Institute of Hungary.

Party education in Hungary plays an important role in educating and indoctrinating the people (see ch. 11). The purpose of party education is threefold: to indoctrinate the population with the principles and objectives of the MSZMP; to increase the level of understanding of the people regarding political, economic, and social systems; and to train party activists who will further this work. Party education is both formal and informal and ranges from a form of university education down to conferences and lectures on the local level. At the highest level there is the so-called Party College, which falls under the jurisdiction of the Central Committee. The Academy of Marxism-Leninism, established in Budapest in 1951, operates in conjunction with the Faculty of Letters of the University of Budapest. Such subjects as Marxism-Leninism, political economy, dialectical materialism, and the history of the Hungarian labor movement are taught at this academy. Established later was the Political College of the MSZMP. On the intermediate level are the evening universities of Marxism-Leninism, which provide two to three years of party training, and the one-year evening secondary schools of Marxism-Leninism. The purpose of these schools is the indoctrination of people of worker-peasant origin. On the lowest level are the so-called theoretical conferences, which provide lectures on new economic reforms and current events.

In addition to formal party education, there are peasant academies, youth academies, parents academies and, the most popular form of education, the free universities. The free universities offer courses ranging from one to four years; the curriculum is comprehensive, offering such courses as electron physics, textile technology, history of art, logic, and languages. The Attila Jozsef Free University, for example, offers courses in sixteen languages—among them Chinese, Hindi, Arabic, and Turkish—to over 7,000 students.

Special attention has been paid to adult education since the Communists took power in 1949. As many adults had been deprived of formal education before World War II, many decided to avail themselves of the opportunity for education when it was attainable. In 1945 adult education was made available only in the evening; by 1951 adult education had been extended to include correspondence courses. By 1953 there were correspondence courses in all elementary and secondary school programs. These courses were geared primarily to the worker-peasant population. At this time there were preparatory courses for workers between the ages of seventeen and thirty-two to prepare them for higher education. This program was terminated in 1955.

In the Basic Education Law of 1961 adult education was incorporated into all levels of education: elementary, secondary, and higher. Adult education offers a very basic curriculum in composition, spelling, and Hungarian language and literature. Political forms of adult education, usually conducted in the so-called cultural homes, which are local centers of education and culture, are designed to raise the ideological awareness of the people. A specialized form of adult education is found in the factory workers' academies and the village cooperative academies, which offer lectures on subjects of practical interest to the population.

TEACHERS AND TEACHER TRAINING

The first formal institution for teacher training was established in 1828. In 1837 separate institutions began to train teachers who specialized in kindergarten work. In 1881 teacher training was expanded from a three-year to a four-year program. In 1923 it was again extended, this time to five years. By 1937/38 there were a total of fifty-five teacher training institutions—thirty-two Roman Catholic, eleven state, ten Protestant, and two Jewish. At that time there were four institutions for the training of kindergarten teachers—three under the control of the Roman Catholic Church and one under state control.

Teachers in Hungary generally enjoy a certain degree of prestige, primarily because of their educational background—teacher training was elevated from the secondary to the higher education level in 1958—but also because of their devotion to the field of education. Many university graduates enter the teaching field, although approximately 10 percent of the total teaching population leave the field every year to enter other professions. Hungarian law formerly guaranteed that there would be equal status among all workers, including teachers, but a policy of differentiated remuneration was instituted in order to reward the more qualified teachers. The policy appears to have been largely unsuccessful in terms of promoting a higher standard of education, however, as material gain assumed priority over educational concerns in some cases.

Apart from the university and postgraduate level, in Hungary there are six different forms of teacher training: kindergarten; elementary education; secondary education; art; music; and special education for the handicapped. In 1956 it was decided that kindergarten teacher training would be limited to secondary school graduates only; this plan was implemented in 1958. Kindergarten teacher training is a two-year course.

After World War II there was a great shortage of teachers in elementary schools. In 1947 the first pedagogical college was established in Budapest and was soon followed by pedagogical institutions at Eger, Pecs, and Szeged. At first the course was three years in duration; later it was reduced to two years because of the demand for teachers. In the early 1950s, when it was realized that the available institutions were not able to train elementary school teachers in sufficient numbers, teacher training institutes were introduced to train teachers for the lower elementary grades, and teachers colleges trained subject teachers for the upper elementary grades. Teacher training institutions operate under the Ministry of Culture and are attached to so-called practice elementary schools. The course runs for three years. Teachers' colleges, on the other hand, have four-year programs, during which the trainees are engaged in practice teaching as well as in practical work in government, factories, and shops.

With one exception, teachers of the handicapped are all trained in one institution, which was founded in Budapest in 1924. This college offers a four-year program in general education and a field of specialization. The general courses include developmental psychology, methodology, and the theory and practice of education. In 1963 a special institution, the Institute for Training Instructors of Motor-Disorder Victims, was established in Budapest on a four-year basis.

Training for teaching in the fields of art and music is acquired at various colleges of industrial and fine arts, music, theater, and cinematography. Training for teaching in the field of physical education, at both the secondary and higher education levels, is given at the Hungarian College of Physical Education. This is a four-year program. Like teacher training for the handicapped, this kind of training has risen in popularity.

The highest level of teacher training, apart from university professors and teachers engaged in postgraduate work, is for teachers in secondary schools. There were many problems in this field before World War II—such as weaknesses in courses in education and psychology and a lack of organized materials. These weaknesses still existed after the war. By 1948 certain reforms were instituted, which included compulsory attendance, certain required courses, and revised curricula and syllabi. In 1950 teacher training was reduced from five to four years. Students of worker-peasant origin were favored; by the mid-1950s this group formed approximately 50 percent of the student body. The program was again extended to five years in 1957. Almost all secondary school teachers are trained in the education departments of various universities, such as Attila Jozsef University, Lajos Kossuth University, and Lorand Eotvos University.

CHAPTER 7

ARTISTIC AND INTELLECTUAL EXPRESSION

Since the eleventh century Hungarian artistic and intellectual activity has developed within the framework of West European civilization, yet it has a distinct national character. Since the earliest periods, and especially as a result of the rise of the Hungarian vernacular in the sixteenth century, large segments of the population have shared in the creation and reception of one or another form of artistic and intellectual expression. Hungarian artists and writers have striven for a synthesis of specific national character and Western forms within the overall European cultural tradition.

The people take great pride in their cultural achievements. Artistic and intellectual creativity has been regarded not only as contributing to general human values but also as serving the Hungarian nation by nurturing its spirit. Artists and intellectuals have therefore always enjoyed a favored position in society as transmitters of the aspirations of the people. They are often looked to for leadership and guidance in times of national stress, more so than the politicians. For that reason, artists and intellectuals as a group continue to feel responsible for the spiritual well-being of the nation.

The communist government has promoted pride in the cultural heritage by devoting considerable funds and effort to the support and promotion of artistic and intellectual expression. It has been keenly aware, however, of the potential for protest and social criticism in art, literature, and music. Many times in Hungarian history cultural life has been more nearly the center of political activity than has the official political arena. Literature, in particular, has been a traditional vehicle for the expression of internal political ideas, for national reform, and for social criticism. For this reason, the communist leadership has tried to keep artistic and intellectual expression under control but has been comparatively liberal and has not imposed overbearing censorship. In recent years the nature of the cultural life has been a clear indicator of the political situation in the country.

Despite controls, artists and intellectuals have been active. Not all creative effort becomes public; some of it remains known only to a select circle until circumstances are propitious for making it public. Symbolism and allusion have been characteristic of Hungarian artistic expression through the ages. Artists are therefore able to communicate with their audiences even in times of relatively strict censorship as long as they do not provoke an audience into open protest.

THE ARTS AND SCIENCES UNDER COMMUNISM

Since 1949 artistic and intellectual activity has been subject to the cultural policy of the Hungarian Socialist Workers' Party (MSZMP— see Glossary). During the 1949-55 period the policy for the arts consisted of strict adherence to the concept of socialist realism as developed in the Soviet Union, whereby art, music, and literature were required to promote communist ideology and present an idealized picture of communist society. In order to impart the ideological message, artistic and intellectual expression had to be understood by the common man and, therefore, according to the Communists, could only take the form of straightforward representative statements. In the sciences, all scholarly work and research had to be based on the precepts of Marxism-Leninism and on the theories of accepted Soviet scholars, such as the later-discredited biologist Trofim Denisovich Lysenko. Basic research in any field was discouraged in favor of work directly related to the industrialization and socialization of the country.

Under the short-lived regime of Imre Nagy, cultural controls became less restrictive, and artistic and intellectual expression burgeoned with creativity and life. After the 1956 uprising, tight restrictions and controls were reimposed for a time, and cultural life was moribund until the early 1960s. Since that time considerable freedom of form and theme has existed, although the regime continues to determine what may or may not be made public. Provided that their work is not openly hostile to the regime or to the Soviet Union and does not pose a threat to the established order by promoting ideas that would undermine that order, artists and scholars have been free to express their ideas in whatever form or style they choose.

From time to time controls are tightened if the regime deems it necessary for domestic or foreign political purposes. The limits of freedom in artistic and intellectual expression, although not clearly defined, are well understood by both the intellectuals and the authorities. Intellectuals know that the government, in order to preserve itself, cannot allow complete freedom of expression. This was made especially clear by the Soviet invasion of Czechoslovakia in 1968. The government, on the other hand, knows that excessive controls and repression will lead to open revolt, as it did in 1956. Each side, therefore, tries to accomplish its aims without overstepping the limits. Self-censorship on the part of the artists and intellectuals, rather than government-imposed censorship, has been the controlling factor in cultural life.

A principal aim of cultural policy since 1949 has been to popularize the arts and sciences by making them accessible to all segments of the population and to utilize those mediums for the promotion of communist values. Science has been presented as the only logical and acceptable basis for a world view and for the customs and conventions that govern men's lives. The arts have been popularized by greatly expanding the facilities that present them to the public and by state subsidization. Many new orchestras, theater companies, publishers, and art galleries have come into existence since World War II. Touring exhibits and road companies take the arts into small towns and villages. Radio and television have been extensively utilized to promote the arts and learning. Through state support, the prices of books and admission tickets have been kept extremely low in order to bring them within the reach of everyone.

Efforts to mobilize artistic and intellectual expression for the indoctrination of the population with communist values and ideas proved unsuccessful during the regime of Matyas Rakosi. Artists and intellectuals refused to lend their efforts to the purpose and, for the most part, withdrew from public life. The public, for its part, showed little interest in art, music, literature, and scholarly work that was produced for propaganda purposes.

More recently the government and the party have adopted subtler methods for guiding the content of artistic and intellectual expression in the desired direction. An artist or scholar must communicate his ideas to an audience in order to achieve fulfillment. To reach that audience, his work must be accepted by a publisher, art gallery, theater company, radio, or other outlet, all of which are run by the state in conformity to the guidelines on cultural policy. Thus, only work that meets these guidelines can reach the public. Many artists and scholars, of course, are content to work for themselves or a limited audience of trusted friends. For the most part, however, they adapt their ideas and principles in order to reach a wider audience.

From a material standpoint, the life of a creative artist in contemporary Hungary is far more secure than that of his counterpart in a capitalist country. Creative expression is seen as a social function; therefore society owes the creative artist an assured livelihood. This livelihood is provided either through regular salaries from publishing houses, from academies of music or art, and from other agencies that employ artists or through stipends paid to creative artists who do not have a regular salary to depend on. Free or low-cost room and board are also available to creative artists and their families at special artists' colonies or retreats operated by professional unions in the creative arts and by government agencies for the promotion of the arts and sciences. Under this system, however, the artist is under constant pressure to produce in order to justify his salary or stipend. Many of the younger artists who do not yet have a reputation have complained that they must focus on quantity rather than quality in their artistic expression and thereby are inhibited from developing their true talents.

LITERATURE

The first literary productions in Hungary were hymns, historic chronicles, and liturgical compilations—all written in Latin. Ancient pre-Christian ballads and epic songs were passed on by word of mouth. Condemned by the Roman Catholic Church and the educated classes, they lived on among the common people and reached the lower nobility through renditions of troubadors. The Hungarian language was used in medieval times for conversation among all levels of the population and eventually replaced Latin in religious hymns, sermons, and prayers. The thirteenth-century *Funeral Oration* is probably the earliest written document in Hungarian.

The rise of the Hungarian vernacular began with the Protestant Reformation in the sixteenth century. In order to reach a wide audience, Protestant churchmen used Hungarian in spreading the religious tenets of the Reformation and in debates with the Roman Catholic Church. Because Protestantism was at that time regarded as the Hungarian religion as opposed to the Roman Catholicism of the Habsburgs, the vernacular also became a symbol of spiritual national resistance against efforts to germanize the population (see ch. 2). The first translation of the Bible was published in 1590.

Count Miklos Zrinyi was Hungary's first major epic poet. His *Siege of Sziget*, recounting his great-grandfather's heroic stand against the Turks, and his political essay *Medicine Against Turkish Opiate* became calls to resistance against oppression and to the rejuvenation of the national spirit.

Folk ballads and folk songs inspired the so-called *kurucz* ballads of Prince Ferenc Rakoczi's soldiers during the rebellion against Austria from 1703 to 1711. These ballads influenced Hungary's literature and music during the nineteenth and twentieth centuries and were popular with all segments of the population.

The Romantic Period, which reached its peak around the middle of the nineteenth century, is considered by Hungarians to be their golden age of literature. The period produced the nation's cherished triumvirate of poets—Sandor Petofi, Janos Arany, and Mihaly Vorosmarty—and its classic prose writers—Miklos Josika, Zsigmond Kemeny, and Mor Jokai. Politically, too, the poets and authors were the moving spirits of the era of national reform and of the struggle for independence.

Descended from a humble background, Petofi became the poet of the democratic intelligentsia and of the common people. His folksongs, his poetic themes of life, country, and freedom, and his rejoicing in battle made him the nation's hero. The defiant public reading of his *National Song* on March 15, 1848, sparked the War of Independence, in which he was killed in battle. His poems have remained popular over the years because of their exceptional lyricism and because they are the incarnation of Hungarian aspirations.

Arany is the contemplative genius of Hungarian epic poetry. His poems reveal a sound knowledge of history and familiarity with psychological problems. His principal epic work, the *Death of Buda,* is taken from the history and mythology of the Huns. His major work, the *Toldi* trilogy, is seen by Hungarians as the classic expression of the Magyar sense of destiny.

Vorosmarty wrote epics, lyrics, and drama. He is considered to be one of the masters of lyric poetry. Philosophy, worldly wisdom, and the patriot's grief dominate his poems.

Drawing extensively from the traditions of folksong and legend and from the imagery and typically descriptive qualities of Hungarian speech, these poets developed a colorful language of metaphor and symbolism. To this language the Hungarian reading public developed a special sensitivity, which has remained typical of their literary tastes.

The novel became a predominant literary form after the middle of the nineteenth century. During the second half of the century prose writers largely abandoned the romantic plot and elaborate style of earlier novels and, instead, portrayed the lives and environment of the various classes of society. Most of the novels, however, depicted the middle class, the gentry, and the peasantry—especially the last two—in an idealized manner and neglected their real problems and difficulties.

The first half of the twentieth century, especially the period between the two world wars, was an age of literary debates and cultural revaluation. The coffeehouse became an important arena of intellectual life. Artists, writers, and intellectuals in search of closer contact with the new artistic and intellectual trends of Western Europe associated themselves with a literary-political periodical called *Nyugat,* founded in 1908. In addition to embracing the new forms and thoughts and popularizing them in the form of translations, the authors of *Nyugat* synthesized these with Hungarian themes.

The greatest poet of the *Nyugat* generation was Endre Ady, who is considered to be the founder of modern Hungarian poetry and the most influential poet since Petofi. Like Petofi, Ady was a poet of sensuous love and strong expression of patriotism. His revaluation of the national destiny, however, was the antithesis of the romantic-patriotic concept of heroic past and promising future. According to Ady, the Magyar past was full of misfortune and oppression, and the fulfillment of the Magyar destiny at the crossroads of Europe was an impossible task. Despite this, Ady believed, the nation must fight with heroic compulsion. Ady stressed the Magyars' Eastern origins and their loneliness in Europe, but he also advocated a rapprochement between neighboring peoples. His concept of "tragic Hungarianhood" exerted a powerful influence on the generation of the interwar period. His sensitivity to the plight of the workers and to the horrors of war and his encounters with some of the eccentricities of capitalism promoted occasional outbursts of political radicalism that inspired a number of revolutionary poems.

The best scholar among the poets of the *Nyugat* generation was Mihaly Babits. An essayist of note, he was the leader of the elite of Hungarian literature during the interwar period.

An outstanding poet of the interwar period who was not affiliated with *Nyugat* was Attila Jozsef. In his poverty-stricken youth he formed a bond with the proletariat, and his poems tell of the life and sorrows of the poor. Jozsef joined the illegal communist party but was later expelled. Throughout his life he suffered mental illness, which drove him to suicide at the age of thirty-two. His poetry is considered by Hungarians to be the continuation of Ady's lyric tradition. His brief affiliation with the communist movement, his lower class background, and his fight against social injustice have elevated him to a position of exceptional honor under the communist regime.

A strong influence was exerted on the literature of the interwar period by the populist movement, which began before World War I. The populists considered folk culture the source of distinct Hungarian values and expressed the growing demand for social and political reform; they were especially concerned with the peasantry and demanded that they be given a major role in mapping the nation's future. The movement was supported by intellectuals in all fields, but its main impetus derived from artists and writers. Some elements of the movement, including authors Peter Veres and Pal Szabo, formed the National Peasant Party, which had a specific political program of economic and social reform.

One of the original populist writers was Zsigmond Moricz. He portrayed peasant poverty and the vacuity of rural middle class life in stark realism. A controversial writer before World War I and during the early years of the regime of Miklos Horthy, his popularity rapidly increased during the interwar period. Dezso Szabo, another populist author, was a fervent nationalist. He idealized the peasant's way of life and became its strong advocate.

The so-called second generation of populist writers includes, among others, Laszlo Nemeth and Gyula Illyes. Nemeth's long, analytical novels describe in careful detail the lives of middle class families and, through such descriptions, sketches all of Hungarian society. Although completely humorless and lacking a definite style, Nemeth convinces his reader by narrative power.

Gyula Illyes is regarded as the Hungarian poet laureate. He became famous after the publication of *The People of the Plains*, a sociological novel that deals with the lives of impoverished peasants on landed estates. He spent many years in Paris studying the modern French poets, and his lyric poetry was immediately acclaimed by Hungarian critics and readers. The force of Hungarian poetry, Illyes feels, is the uniqueness of the Hungarian language. Despite a strong commitment to examine the social issues of his time, including those of power and morality, Illyes' left-wing tradition and his stature at home and abroad have saved him from being silenced by communist censors.

During the first few years after World War II there was a burgeon-
ing of literature. Writers and poets who had spent the war in exile
returned and published their wartime writing. Others, who had remained at home in silence during the Nazi period, also brought forth
works that they had written but could not or would not publish earlier.
The themes of social injustice, tyranny, and human suffering permeated this postwar literature.

In keeping with established tradition, poetry was in the forefront of
the literary revival. Outstanding and most challenging among the postwar poets is Sandor Weores, who developed a highly personal style
through the assimilation of modern literary trends and aspects of
oriental philosophy. Together with Illyes, Weores is regarded as an
outstanding contemporary Hungarian poet.

A new generation of poets, most of them of peasant origin and communist oriented, came to the fore in the postwar years. From among
them, Agnes Nemes Nagy, Laszlo Benjamin, Laszlo Nagy, and Ferenc
Juhasz have emerged over the years as major talents. Their poetry is
strongly lyrical and full of modern imagery. All of them have experimented with new forms to express their feelings. Extremely popular
with the youth of the late 1960s was Ferenc Baranyi, whose free verse
appealed to their hopes and frustrations. Most critics, however, consider his poetry to have little lasting merit.

The period of the Rakosi dictatorship, 1949 to 1954, is often referred
to as the bleakest period in Hungarian literature. Most writers preferred to remain silent rather than submit to the dictates of communist
ideology. The literary production that succeeded in passing the censor
and being published was rejected by the public. When Imre Nagy's
New Course relaxed the controls on culture, writers sprang back to
life, and literature again became the outlet for expressing popular
dissatisfactions with the existing order. Writers and poets, following
Hungarian tradition, took on political roles as the spokesmen for the
demands of the people. This so-called writers' revolt was the prelude
to the Hungarian uprising of 1956.

The uprising was followed by a period of tight control and by reprisals against those writers who were held responsible for its instigation.
Many of them fled abroad; others were imprisoned. Since the early
1960s, however, literature has enjoyed the relative freedom characteristic of Hungarian life as a whole during the regime of Janos Kadar. An
extraordinary amount of poetry, prose, and other writing is published
regularly and eagerly consumed by the public. The literature represents
every conceivable style and deals with almost any subject that does not
undermine the authority of the regime. Well-established writers, such
as Illyes, Weores, Nemeth, and others of the older generation, continue
to be popular and exert their influence on younger authors. Younger
writers who began their careers under the restrictions of socialist

realism utilize their new freedom of expression by experimenting with form and style.

Literary criticism has also been lively. Writers, critics, and historians engage in lengthy polemics in the periodical press over the merits of a particular piece of literature, a particular author, or a specific style. Much discussion has also been devoted to examining the role of literature in socialist society.

THEATER

Hungarian theater is little known outside of the area that once comprised the Austro-Hungarian Empire because most of it deals with national problems and matters of local interest rather than with universal themes. A notable exception is Imre Madach's *The Tragedy of Man*, a monumental nineteenth-century drama examining man's destiny in the context of world history. Over the years, the play has been translated into many languages and played on many stages. Ferenc Molnar's plays are also internationally recognized, although many of his countrymen consider him an average playwright.

Hungarian theater, like that of other small nations in Eastern and Central Europe, developed primarily as a means for promoting national ideals and fostering the national language in the face of foreign domination. The opening of the National Theatre in Budapest in 1837 was an event of major significance not only to the cultural life of the city but also to the romantic movement of national revival of that time. Plays such as Joszef Kotona's *Bank Ban* and Vorosmarty's *Csongor and Tunde* aroused enthusiastic response from the public for their accent on national themes and, together with *The Tragedy of Man*, have become the great classics of the Hungarian stage.

To most Hungarians theatergoing is an important social and intellectual activity. Current plays are discussed in everyday conversation, and the Budapest theater audience has a reputation for being sophisticated and highly critical. Realism, naturalism, and symbolism were the representative trends in stage directing and acting until the mid-1950s. Since then, there has been a trend toward abstract, symbolistic expression and the use of modern stage techniques. Traditional forms of acting and staging are still popular, however. The same theater company is often three repertory companies in one: the company as a whole presenting large and elaborate productions in a large theater; a smaller group of some members of the company specializing in intimate theater; and an experimental group presenting new and different plays and techniques.

An extremely popular form of theater has been the presentation of satire in cabarets. Such satire flourished during the interwar period and was revived after the relaxation of political controls in the 1960s. The satire of cabaret shows is caustic and to the point. Politics and the trials and tribulations of daily life are favorite subjects. The communist leadership is said to tolerate satire as an escape valve mechanism for the people. The theory is that, if people can laugh at the things that make life difficult, they will not try to force a change.

All theater is subsidized by the government. The five leading companies are financed by the national government, and the others, by local governments. Ticket prices are extremely low, and free performances are often given for schoolchildren. The State Traveling Theater operates about a dozen road companies, which take theater into the more remote areas of the country. Many of the municipal theater companies also tour the smaller towns and villages in their areas. The repertory is chosen by the director of each company, subject to approval by government control organs. Companies often become known for a particular style of production that reflects the director's specialty or preference.

FILMS

After a promising start with silent pictures during World War I, the Hungarian film industry suffered a considerable setback in the economic crisis of the 1920s. It was during that time that the well-known directors Alexander Korda, Michael Curtis, and Joseph Pasternak left Hungary to gain fame in England and the United States.

After the mid-1930s the sophisticated tastes of the middle and upper classes brought about a regeneration of the film industry, which had been reduced to producing third-rate musicals and melodramas. Some of the leading novelists successfully wrote scripts and directed motion pictures; the novels of Mor Jokai were adapted to the screen; and Hungarian films became popular in other parts of Europe.

The communist regime considers motion pictures to be one of the major media for information and education and has devoted much energy and considerable resources to their production and distribution. The films produced in the Rakosi era, however, were blatant propaganda of no artistic merit.

The relaxing of restrictions in 1955 promised an artistic rebirth of the Hungarian cinema, which was stifled by the crushing of the uprising in 1956. Since the early 1960s several films of high artistic and technical quality have been produced by a group of young, talented directors. Such films as *Love*, directed by Karoly Makk, and *Falcons*, directed by Istvan Gal, have been called cinematic masterpieces by international critics.

MUSIC

Until about 1905 Hungarian-composed music and national folk music followed distinctly different paths. The former reflected mainly the influence of West European musical idioms, even though rhythmic and melodic characteristics of ancient folksongs and dances were discernible in some of the compositions. Folk music was alien to the

117

polyphonic development of European music and survived in pure form only among the peasantry. Its main characteristic was the Central Asian pentatonic scale and a descending melodic structure that conformed with the rhythmic pattern of the Hungarian language. Songs were learned by ear and passed from generation to generation. Hardly any of this music appeared in written form until around 1900.

Under the impetus of the romantic nationalism of the late eighteenth and early nineteenth centuries groups of characteristic songs and dances were composed that came to be regarded in Hungary and throughout Europe as the national music of Hungary. These compositions were not true folksongs, however, even though they were based on traditional folk rhythms and melodies. Their source was an old military recruiting dance, the *verbunkos*. Inspired by the ideal of Hungarian nationhood, the country's composers and music instructors transplanted the melody and rhythm of the *verbunkos* into the context of European musical idioms, notably four-four time and the major-minor keys. The outcome was a striking musical style with great instrumental flexibility, a broad but distinct melodic pattern, and a rich variety of rhythms. The so-called Hungarian compositions of great musicians like Haydn, Mozart, and Brahms reflect the distinct influence of the *verbunkos* style.

The stylistic successor of the *verbunkos* were songs composed in the style of peasant folksongs. They achieved spectacular success and popularity as a result of their rendition by Gypsy players, whose debut as popular musicians dates to the seventeenth century. In their highly ornamental and versatile interpretations, these compositions assumed striking forms and were regarded as genuine folk music both in Hungary and abroad.

Ferenc (Franz) Liszt was one of the most celebrated musicians of nineteenth-century Europe and a leading romantic composer. His symphonic poems, rhapsodies, and church music, resplendent with heroic pomp and glowing visions, are among the best musical expressions of romantic ideals. In his *Hungarian Rhapsodies*, *Saint Elizabeth's Legend*, and *Coronation Mass*, Liszt dramatically expressed that Hungarian musical substance that had emerged with the adaptations of the *verbunkos* and the peasant folksongs. He founded the Hungarian Academy of Music, where he was noted for his accomplishments in the pedagogy of the piano. He is still revered by his compatriots as a symbol of Hungarian musical creativity.

During the second half of the nineteenth century adaptations and commercialized versions of traditional folk music continued largely to represent Hungarian music abroad. The compositions of Jeno Hubay and Enro Dohnanyi, however, were also well known in the metropolitan cities of Europe. Audiences in Vienna, Budapest, and other parts of the Austro-Hungarian Empire thrilled to the operettas of Ferenc Lehar, Pongrac Kacsoh, and Imre Kalman; many of them are still popular.

An authentic national music came into being at the beginning of the twentieth century from the pens of Bela Bartok and Zoltan Kodaly. Their music celebrated the resolution of the basic problem of the Hungarian culture ethos—the expression of an Eastern cultural heritage in European form. The spectacular acclaim of Bartok and Kodaly also revitalized the Hungarians' sense of solidarity with Western culture.

Bartok and Kodaly devoted their early years to the intensive study of folksongs. They traveled from village to village in every region, recording dances, ballads, and songs, many of which pointed to the pagan past and revealed the Magyar musical heritage in its pure form. Bartok, who died in 1945, is considered one of the great modern musicians. In the context of its time, his music is novel in rhythm and harmony and singularly expressive in melody.

Kodaly renders the lyric depth and fiery pathos of folksong themes in the framework of classical compact forms. He initiated new concepts in choir techniques that revitalized choral singing and developed a system of musical education for children utilizing choral singing as a base. Under Kodaly's influence, new choirs and folksong ensembles gained national repute in the 1930s and have since become an outstanding feature of Hungarian musical life.

For the young composers of the post-World War II era, folklore influence in music is an exhausted style that they reject. Instead, they experiment with the various contemporary styles and techniques, revert back to classical forms and, often, attempt to merge the old with the new. Outstanding among the young composers is Sandor Szokolay, whose opera *Blood Wedding*, based on the play by Garcia Lorca, is performed all over the world.

Hungarian youth, like young people elsewhere, have embraced rock music as their own form of musical expression. One Western source estimated that some 4,000 rock ensembles performed regularly at various youth gathering places in 1971. Rock music is seen by the young as one of the few outlets of free self-expression open to them. The authorities have tolerated the rock boom despite occasional public condemnations of its bourgeois decadence.

Musical life in the early 1970s was active and varied. Its focus, however, was on performing rather than composing. Amateur orchestras and chamber music groups were found in all cities and larger towns. The five largest cities each have a professional orchestra, which presents concerts in their home city and in neighboring towns.

A large number of Hungarian performing artists have gained international reputations. Among the best known are conductors Antal Dorati, George Szell, and Georg Solti, pianist Geza Anda, and violinist Joszef Szigeti. Although they have all lived abroad for some time, they are a source of pride to Hungarians everywhere.

FOLK ARTS

The salient feature of the decorative folk arts, such as pottery, carving, and embroidery, is the rich but uncluttered patterns. Distinctive traits are present in the art of each region. The government has been promoting and subsidizing folk art in its various forms. The agency responsible for the promotion of folk arts, including folk dancing, is the Institute of Folk Art. There are a number of folk art cooperatives, notably in Mezokovesd, center of the famous Matyo embroidery, and in Kishunhalas, which is renowned for its lace. Most of the products of cooperatives and of individual artists are intended for export. Outstanding artists are awarded the title of master of folk arts. The use of motifs that symbolize socialist themes is encouraged, but most folk art continues to follow traditional lines.

Pottery has flourished on the Great Plain where suitable clay was available in large quantities. Before the nineteenth century, pottery was unglazed, varnished with pebbles, and smoked black in the kiln. Some of this black pottery is still manufactured in Nedudvar. The area of Hodmezovasarhely is famous for its green-glazed brandy flasks with patriotic inscriptions. Mezokut is known for its elaborately decorated jugs.

Carving is the specialty of herdsmen, who decorate their utensils, such as canes, whip handles, penknives, flutes, and pipes. The most frequently used motifs are scenes of everyday life, figures of national heroes, and patriotic symbols.

A characteristic branch of folk art is embroidery. Furriers and tailors decorate thick, woolen frieze coats, long sheepskin cloaks, and short sheepskin jackets worn by peasants and herders. The designs are lavish embroidery or colorful leather applique work that utilize floral patterns almost exclusively. The patterns are concentrated on the back and sleeves of the garment. Adaptations of these decorated coats and jackets have been popular with city dwellers in Hungary and in other parts of Europe.

The delicate lacework of Kiskunhalas is internationally appreciated. More than sixty varieties of crocheting stitches are used to execute the delicate lace patterns. Known as Halas lace, this was a consistently popular export item, which competed successfully with Brussels lace. The lacemaking cooperatives continue to receive active government support.

The traditional costumes, which used to be the main outlet for artistic creativity of the peasants, are no longer worn regularly. They have been replaced in daily use by standardized manufactured items, as have the embroidered linens, pottery, and carved wooden utensils formerly used in the peasant household. The costumes continue to be worn on festivals and special occasions and have become, in fact, costumes rather than the accepted attire that they once were.

The Hungarian people love to dance. Typical of the dances is the male solo. Even in the mixed dances of men and women, the man often becomes separated from his partner and performs a solo display of intricate steps and leaps. A proud military bearing is characteristic of the male dancing. The upper body remains erect and calm, and the rhythmic movement of the legs is often accentuated by the use of spurs.

The old military dance, the *verbunkos*, and the various herdsmen's dances are performed by men in groups, although they may also be danced alone. The emphasis is on display of individual virtuosity in performing variations of traditional steps, and there is little teamwork. The mixed dances of men and women combine graceful dignity with fiery rhythm. By popular usage, all dances performed by mixed groups of men and women are called *csardas*, even though each of the dances and their various figures have individual names.

The communist regime has supported folk dance research and encouraged folk dancing as a form of mass culture. Folk dance ensembles under special instructors are organized in many schools and factories. Professional folk dance troupes enjoy wide popularity at home and abroad.

FINE ARTS AND ARCHITECTURE

Hungary's achievements in the fine arts and architecture illustrate the nation's ready assimilation of West European art forms. Nevertheless, distinct national characteristics are discernible in painting, sculpture, and architectural forms. These are expressed mainly by a calmness and a simplicity that captures the essence without laborious detail. The monuments and remains of fine arts represent to Hungarians the nation's affinity with, and contribution to, Western civilization; they are a source of national pride known to most Hungarians.

During the Romanesque period, which lasted until the thirteenth century, the influence of northern Italian Romanesque art predominated. The church of Jak in western Hungary, with the fine ornamental details of its portals, is one of the outstanding Romanesque edifices of Central Europe.

The Renaissance period reached its apogee under King Matyas, whose Corvina Library exemplified the Hungarian Renaissance. Italian and Hungarian miniature painters and craftsmen decorated the pages and cut the exquisite, gold-embossed leather covers for this unique collection of books, the largest in Europe at the time. Several volumes from the Corvina are preserved in libraries abroad, including the Morgan Library in New York City.

During the period from the fourteenth century to the sixteenth century, goldsmiths and other metal craftsmen were noted for the design and workmanship in vessels, church ornaments, and jewelry. The wire-enamel technique they employed has been known in Europe as a Hungarian specialty. Working in gold and metal is one of the oldest forms of Hungarian artistic expression. The earliest examples have been found in graves dating to the conquest of the Carpathian Basin in 896.

During the national revival of the nineteenth century, fostering the arts became a national cause. The dominant themes of artists and sculptors were historical scenes, national heroes, and the peasants and their way of life, particularly those of the plains. The National Museum was built by public donations, and artists were sponsored by the middle classes as well as by the aristocracy.

Hungarian painters assimilated the dominant painting styles of Europe during that period. Historical painting was prominently represented. A tendency toward visionary expression led to a relatively early assimilation of symbolism, and impressionism was of lasting influence. The neoclassic style dominated architecture and sculpture. The characteristic architectural feature of Hungarian cities, however, is the baroque style of the late eighteenth century. Many excellent examples of baroque exteriors and interiors are found in the churches, castles, and other buildings in the larger towns.

The national revival painter Mihaly Munkacsi is commonly known as the greatest Hungarian painter. His best known paintings depict scenes from the lives of the less fortunate levels of the population. Munkacsi was one of the most celebrated painters in Europe during the second half of the nineteenth century.

Although Budapest was traditionally the center of artistic life, around the beginning of the twentieth century several art colonies were founded by outstanding painters who sought to express modern painting styles in the Hungarian ethnic and scenic milieu. The colonies attracted painters from other parts of Europe as well as from Hungary. The most important colony was that at Nagybanya in Transylvania, which exerted a strong influence on modern Hungarian painting of the twentieth century. Realism derived from a close observation of nature and combined with some of the techniques of the French expressionists was the characteristic style of Nagybanya painters.

Between the two world wars Hungarian painters continued to keep in touch with and absorb the various European styles, but cubism, fauvism, and surrealism had relatively few followers. The dominant painters of the period were the postimpressionists Istvan Csok and Jozsef Rippl-Ronai. Sculptor Ferenc Medgyessy won national acclaim with his simple, heroic forms. In architecture there were attempts to introduce elements of Hungarian folk art into the ornamental details of public buildings, whereas apartment houses reflected the influence of the German functional school.

The imposition of themes from socialist life and the policy of socialist realism limited artistic theme and quality after 1949. The requirement of universal clarity in artistic expression created a style that resembled photographs and propaganda posters. Nevertheless, outstanding artists, such as Istvan Szonyi, Aurel Bernath, Istvan Csok, and Gyula Rudnay, continued to paint in their customary styles and even received commissions from the government to decorate new public buildings. Landscapes and other neutral themes dominated the painting of the 1950s.

In the early 1960s the fine arts in Hungary again came under the influence of the main trends in Europe. Great variety has been evident in styles and in themes, especially among the young artists who experiment widely. The graphic arts have emerged as important mediums of expression, and Lajos Szalay is the most outstanding exponent. Bela Kondor is generally considered as the most original among the young painters.

Architecture since World War II has been dominated by the ornate, Soviet-monumental style in public buildings, on the one hand, and stark, functional concrete apartment complexes on the other. Many architectural monuments have been restored and renovated, but little originality has been evident.

SCHOLARSHIP AND SCIENCE

Hungarian scholars and scientists have been especially successful in the natural sciences and mathematics and have made notable contributions to contemporary philosophical thought. Many of their accomplishments are internationally recognized. Scientists and scholars have frequently played major roles in the country's political life and have enjoyed high social prestige.

The national revival during the nineteenth century invigorated literary and scientific activities. Its effect upon historical and ethnographic studies was to produce a romanticized and glorified interpretation of Magyar history and peasant culture.

A number of Hungarians made important contributions in the nineteenth century to the development of modern mathematics and technology. Janos Bolyai was an early contributor in the field of non-Euclidian geometry. Anyos Jedlik built the first electric motor in 1828 and an electric dynamo in 1861. Lorand Eotvos invented the gravity balance. Donat Banki invented the carburetor for fuel-burning motors. Titus Blathy developed the alternating current transformer.

The methods of disease prevention advocated by Ignac Semmelweiss were universally adopted after his death, although they had been discredited during his lifetime. His discoveries in pathology led to the conquest of childbed fever, which had caused the death of many women in childbirth.

Several ethnographers made important contributions to their field through their search for the ethnic origins of the Magyars in Asia. Among them were Sandor Korosi-Csoma and Aurel Stein.

Hungarian scientific and scholarly activities during the early twentieth century attained distinction both in scope and quality. Research in sociology, ethnography, and psychology was significant. Many of the followers of Sigmund Freud, who expanded on his theories, and many of the anti-Freudian psychologists were Hungarian. Much original research was performed in the natural sciences, medicine, and mathematics, which paved the way for major developments at later times.

After World War II much Hungarian scientific and intellectual talent was scattered beyond the country's borders. Albert Szent-Gyorgyi, the Nobel Prize-winning biochemist who isolated Vitamin C; Janos Neuman, the mathematician whose theories led to the development of computers; and Edward Teller, the noted nuclear physicist— all are of Hungarian origin.

Scholarship and science, which formerly had enjoyed a high degree of independence, came under complete state control after the Communists took power in 1949. The doctrinal demands of communism and the imposition of Soviet science as a model greatly hampered independent theoretical research, especially in the social sciences. Despite the restraints, however, most Hungarian scholars have found ways to remain faithful to scholarly integrity. Since the early 1960s the restrictions imposed by doctrinal demands and Soviet models have been greatly relaxed. Although they are urged to apply their work to Marxist ends, scholars and scientists may utilize non-Marxist theories in their research as long as this does not present a direct threat to the stability of the regime or to the relationship between the regime and the Soviet Union.

Recognizing the importance of the natural sciences in advancing economic production, the regime has extended considerable support to these branches of learning. The study of ethnography has also received strong backing.

The focus in ethnography has been the disappearing peasant subculture. Much research has been devoted to the collection of descriptive data about folklore and traditional peasant life in the various regions. Analytical research in the processes of social change has only recently caught the interest of Hungarian scholars.

A notable contribution in modern philosophy has been made by the Marxist philosopher George Lukacs. He first received recognition in 1923 with the publication of *History and Class Consciousness*, which has influenced both Marxist and non-Marxist thought since that time. Starting out as a classical Marxist, Lukacs later developed his ideas into what has been variously described as "democratic," "revisionist," or "humanist" Marxism. In the process, he repudiated many of his own earlier theories. In his later years, Lukacs became particularly concerned with developing an ontology and a system of ethics suitable to Marxist ideals. His final work, *Toward an Ontology of Social Being*, is scheduled for publication in 1973.

Since Lukacs' death in 1971, his student and follower, Agnes Heller, has pursued the same ideas and has developed them further. Her reputation and influence among both Marxist and non-Marxist philosophers are growing steadily.

Scientific research in both the social and natural sciences is carried out at all the universities, at special scientific institutes, and at research centers in industrial and agricultural enterprises. All research is supervised and coordinated by the Hungarian Academy of Sciences, which includes among its members the highest authorities in the various fields of learning. The academy is divided into nine branches of learning: language and literary sciences, sociological and historical sciences, mathematics and physics, agricultural sciences, medicine, technical sciences, chemistry, biology, and psychological sciences. Election to membership in the academy is one of the highest honors accorded to a scholar. In the mid-1960s the Academy of Sciences had thirty-nine research institutes devoted to basic research in both the social and physical sciences. Another ninety-two research institutes, guided by but not directly affiliated with the Academy of Sciences, were concerned almost entirely with applied research for industry and agriculture.

Research that is being done at the various institutes as well as other scholarly work is discussed and publicized in several dozen scholarly and scientific periodicals and books. The Academy of Sciences in the late 1960s published over two dozen such periodicals in Hungarian and an equal number in several foreign languages, including English.

SECTION II. POLITICAL

CHAPTER 8

GOVERNMENTAL SYSTEM

The government of the Hungarian People's Republic bases its legitimacy and organizational structure on the Revised Constitution promulgated by the National Assembly on April 17, 1972. Representing an extensive reworking of the Constitution of 1949, the revised document is purported to be an expression of the "fundamental changes that have transpired in the country's life, the historical achievements of the struggle waged for social progress, and of the work in the country's construction."

All power is held to derive from the working people and is to be exercised through elected representatives who are responsible to the people. Constitutionally, the highest organ of state power is the National Assembly, a unicameral parliament that theoretically controls all other government organs. In practice, however, much of the legislative authority of the assembly is exercised by the Presidential Council, and the day-to-day administration and supervision of the country's political, economic, social, and cultural activities are carried out by the Council of Ministers.

The most powerful organization in the country, however, is the communist party, known as the Hungarian Socialist Workers' Party (MSZMP—see Glossary). Its decisionmaking authority is superior to all of the constitutional organs of power and, owing to the placing of high-ranking party officials in key positions at all levels of the government, party control is absolute. For the most part, the organs of government on both the national and local levels serve as executors of programs and policies determined in the higher echelons of the MSZMP.

Below the central organs of state, government is organized on the county, district, and local levels through a hierarchical system of councils. The councils are designed to serve as both the local expression of national authorities and the expression of popular representation. Election lists are compiled by the Patriotic People's Front and, although all candidates must be approved by the party, a choice of candidates for a single office is sometimes presented to the voters.

THE CONSTITUTIONAL SYSTEM

Constitutional Development

Hungary's first post-World War II constitution was adopted on January 31, 1946. Oriented toward Western democratic traditions, it declared the country a republic, formally terminated the monarchy, and held that power derived from the people and was to be exercised through their elected representatives in the National Assembly. Provision was made for the country to be headed by a president, elected by the assembly, and for broad guarantees ensuring citizens' rights and freedoms (see ch. 2).

With strong Soviet support, however, the communist minority (the Hungarian Communist Party had received only 17 percent of the vote in the elections of November 1945) progressively gained power, placed stringent restrictions on civil liberties, and began a program to systematically eliminate all political opposition. After manipulating a merger with the Social Democratic Party to form the Hungarian Workers' Party in mid-1948, the Communists felt strong enough to conduct new elections and, through the façade of the Communist-Controlled People's Front of National Independence, called the elections for May 1949 and established a single voting list containing only the name of front-approved candidates (see ch. 2).

A month after the elections the new assembly was briefly convened to formally establish a special committee, completely dominated by ranking Communists, to draft a new constitution. Closely patterned on the Soviet Constitution of 1936, the draft constitution was ratified without modification by the National Assembly. It was entered into force on August 20, 1949, the date of a traditional Hungarian holiday known as Saint Stephen's Day in honor of the country's first king. The regime redesignated the day as Constitution Day.

The Constitution of 1949

Declaring the country to be a people's republic, the constitution described it as a state of workers and of working peasants. In the preamble, full credit for the liberation of Hungary from fascism was given to the Soviet Union, which was also credited with having "crushed the power of the great landowners and capitalists who were ever hostile to the people" of the country.

Consisting of eleven sections with a total of seventy-one articles, the 1949 Constitution was amended numerous times between 1950 and 1970 and extensively revised in 1972. In describing the country's social structure, primary emphasis was placed on the economic system. Although provision was made for the private ownership of property, the bulk of the means of production was designated as public property owned "by the state, by public bodies, or by cooperative organizations." Full direction of the country's economy was ascribed to "the state power of the people," the goal of which was described as the progressive elimination of "capitalist elements" and the building up of "a socialist system of economy." All economic activities and development programs were to be continually determined by a national economic plan.

All mineral resources, forests, waters, natural power sources, mines, larger industrial enterprises, means of communication and transportation, and all banking and postal services were declared to be the property of the state or of public bodies that function as trustees for the whole people. In the same manner, all foreign and wholesale trade were also ascribed to state enterprises, and all other forms of commerce were placed under state supervision. In agriculture, emphasis was placed on socialist development through the establishment of state farms and machine stations and the setting up of peasants' cooperatives.

In providing the constitutional basis for civil liberties, the guaranteed rights of the citizens were declared to include the rights to work, to rest, to recreation, to health care, and to education. In each instance the constitutional provision was supplemented with an implementation clause. The right to work and to remuneration in accordance with the quantity and quality of work, for example, was to be implemented "by means of the planned development of the forces of production and by a manpower policy based on economic planning."

All citizens were declared to be equal before the law, to have equal rights, and to be guaranteed "liberty of conscience" and freedom of religious worship. Constitutional guarantees were also extended to freedom of speech, of the press, and of assembly, to the inviolability of the person, and to the privacy of the home and correspondence. Discrimination on the basis of sex, religion, or nationality was made a punishable offense, and minority groups were assured the opportunity of education in their native language and the right to develop their national culture. At the same time, all citizens were held to be dutybound to strengthen the so-called people's democratic system, to seek to defend and increase social assets, and to work to further the country's economic strength.

The constitution established the National Assembly, the Presidential Council, and the Council of Ministers as the central organs of government. Although the Hungarian Workers' Party was not mentioned by name, the constitution declared that the leading force in the country's political and social life was "the working class, led by its vanguard and supported by the democratic unity of the whole people." Provision was made for the establishment of a variety of mass organizations, such as trade unions and associations of women and youth—all joined together in a single front organization that would function under the guidance of the leading force.

Later Amendments

The Constitution of 1949 provided for the possibility of constitutional amendments by a two-thirds majority of the National Assembly; and, although the fundamental content remained the same, at least ten modifications—some of major importance were made in the original document between 1954 and 1970. Changes in the judicial system were introduced in 1950 and 1954, and a significant modification (also passed in 1954) extended the authority of local government councils and made them responsible to the Presidential Council.

A detailed listing of the government ministries had been included in the 1949 Constitution; changing circumstances, however, necessitated the establishment of several new ministries and the merging or dissolution of others, and in 1957 the National Assembly deleted the list and substituted the provision that the number of ministries and the scope of their responsibilities would be determined by other laws. Important changes were made in the electoral system in 1966 and 1970.

The extent of the modifications in the constitution and the changes in the political, social, and economic environment prompted some of the country's legal experts to begin, in the early 1960s, to call for a new constitution. Similar sentiment was evinced at the Eighth Party Congress in 1962, at which time the party took the position that the laying of the foundations of socialism had been completed with the collectivization of agriculture and that, consequently, it had become necessary to synchronize the constitution with the realities of the existing situation.

For the next several years, party and government leaders debated the pros and cons of either revising the 1949 Constitution or replacing it entirely. The issue was finally resolved in favor of modifying the existing one when, in November 1970, the Tenth Party Congress decided that the time had not yet come to proclaim Hungary a socialist republic and, consequently, there was not yet a need for an entirely new constitution. Party leaders asserted that a revision of the existing document, in keeping with the changes that had taken place during "two decades of socialist development" would best reflect the continuity of the country's progress toward socialism.

Following the decision of the party congress, in January 1971 the National Assembly established a twenty-five-member committee to prepare the revision. By the first week of September the draft of the Revised Constitution was completed, and it was submitted to several of the leading mass organizations for discussion. These so-called social discussions took place over a period of six months, but none of the reported 600 suggestions for modification were ever published. The final draft of the Revised Constitution was made public on March 26 and was passed unaltered by the National Assembly on April 17, 1972.

The Revised Constitution

According to the revision committee, the Revised Constitution was designed to maintain in force all the features of the original document that had survived the test of time and, at the same time, reflect all the changes that had come about during the twenty-three years that had elapsed since the 1949 Constitution first became law. Observers of East European political affairs described the Revised Constitution as more of a catalog of cumulative change than a program for the future. On the occasion of the publication of the draft of the revision, the same perspective was affirmed by a party spokesman who asserted that the country's constitution "should first of all reflect what has already been achieved."

As compared with the 1949 Constitution, the revised version takes a longer view of Hungarian history and sees the struggle of the working people against the ruling classes as having endured for over a millennium rather than as originating with the communist movement or with the victory over fascism in 1945. According to First Secretary Janos Kadar, the Revised Constitution is a "bridge which leads from a thousand years of tribulation to a better future." At the same time, however, the importance of the events of 1945 is not overlooked, for the preamble declares that: "a new phase of our history began when the Soviet Union, in the course of the victories it scored in World War II, liberated our country from fascist oppression and opened the path of democratic development to the Hungarian people."

Some of the more significant differences from the 1949 Constitution are found in the chapter entitled "the Social Order of the Hungarian People's Republic." Although the country is still described as a people's republic, the Revised Constitution goes a step further than the earlier document and declares that the Hungarian People's Republic is a socialist state, a statement that some observers have described as a compromise between those who wanted to proclaim the country a full-fledged socialist republic and those who wanted to delay such a proclamation until after the development of a socialist society was fully completed. Party spokesmen explained that, although the country's socialist development had not yet been fully realized, the leading position of the working class and the social ownership of the means of production justified the description of Hungary as a socialist state.

Observers have also pointed out a significant change in the Revised Constitution's definition of what constitutes the social basis of political power. Extending the original constitution's declaration that all power is exercised by the working people, the revision broadens the description of the power base. Although it continues to assert that the working class is the leading class of the society, it declares that the power of the worker's class is exercised "in an alliance with the peasantry gathered in cooperatives and together with the intelligentsia and the rest of the working strata of society." Commenting on the greater inclusiveness of the revision, party leaders explained that the worker's class had been and would continue to be the leading force in the building of socialism but that the fundamental interests of all strata of the society coincide and that full socialist development required the cooperation of all citizens.

In the same chapter another addition is introduced in the Revised Constitution with the provision that "at their work places and homes as well, citizens participate directly in the administration of public affairs." This same point is reiterated in the chapter on citizen rights and duties, where it is stated that every citizen has the right to participate in the administration of public affairs and that each has, as well, the duty to fill public assignments conscientiously. Although party leaders have pointed to these provisions as evidence of the extension of democratic practices, some observers have commented that the type of participation desired by the regime is limited to administrative procedures rather than to involvement in policymaking.

Whereas the earlier constitution only alluded indirectly to the position of the party in the political system, the Revised Constitution is more specific, declaring that "the Marxist-Leninist party of the worker's class is the leading force of the society." As a supplement to this leading role of the party, the revision further asserts that the various forces of society are united in the Patriotic People's Front for the purpose of accomplishing their political, economic, and cultural tasks and for participation in the electoral process. Of the several important mass organizations combined under the front, the trade unions are singled out for mention in the revision and are ascribed the task of safeguarding and strengthening the interests and power of the working people.

Following the pattern of the Constitution of 1949, a considerable portion of the revised document is devoted to the underlying principles of the country's socialist economic policy. Under the Revised Constitution the social ownership of the means of production continues to constitute the basis of the economic system and, during the interval between the promulgation of the first constitution and the revision, the cause of socialist control was advanced to such a degree that the revision declares that "socialist conditions have become predominant in production in the Hungarian People's Republic."

Except for a few modifications, the Revised Constitution's catalogue of the "Fundamental Rights and Duties of Citizens" is identical to that contained in the original document. Among the more significant modifications is the addition of a paragraph of general principles at the beginning of the chapter. In brief, these principles assert that the republic respects human rights, that the civil rights of the individual must be "exercised in harmony with the interests of socialist society," and that rules governing citizen rights and duties are established by law.

STRUCTURE AND FUNCTIONING OF THE GOVERNMENT

The Central Government

The primary organs of the central government include the National

Assembly, the Presidential Council, the Council of Ministers, and the system of courts and public prosecutors. Local government, functioning on the county, district, and village levels, consists of a hierarchy of councils that are ultimately responsible to the central authorities. There is overlap and ambiguity in the roles assigned the central organs of the government, and the structure of authority differs from that depicted in the constitution. In actual practice, political power is concentrated in the highest bodies of the MSZMP: the Secretariat and the Political Bureau (Politburo) of the Central Committee. Overlapping of membership between these top party organs and the top government bodies results in a concentration of decisionmaking power in a small oligarchy of communist elites (see ch. 9).

The National Assembly

Constitutionally, the unicameral National Assembly is the supreme organ of both state power and popular representation. In theory, it is assigned all rights that derive from "the people's sovereignty," and it is to exercise these rights to ensure "the constitutional order of society." In addition to its legislative function, the assembly is assigned responsibility for the development of the national economic plan, the drawing up and implementation of the state budget, and the confirmation of the government's program. It also elects the Presidential Council from among its own members, appoints the Council of Ministers, and names the chairman of the Supreme Court and the chief prosecutor.

The assembly is also given basic responsibility for both the creation and implementation of the constitution as well as the supervision of all other organs of government to assure the constitutionality of their actions. In addition, the assembly is charged with the confirmation of international agreements and decisions regarding the proclamation of a state of war or the conclusion of peace.

Separate electoral laws that determine the number of assembly deputies and the division of electoral districts provided for a total of 352 deputies to be chosen in the general elections of April 1971. Constitutionally, the term of office for assembly deputies is fixed at four years, and a new assembly must be elected within three months after a term is completed. During its sessions, of which there must be at least two a year, the assembly is presided over by a president and two vice presidents, who are assisted in their duties by a group of six assembly clerks. In 1972 the president of the assembly was also a leading member of the MSZMP Politburo.

Authorized by the constitution to set up standing committees as necessary to deal with particular legislative questions, after the 1971 elections the assembly established or continued the following committees: administrative, legal and judicial; agricultural; commercial; cultural; foreign affairs; industrial; national defense; planning and budget; and social affairs and health. Also functioning as a permanent body under the National Assembly is the Interparliamentary Union.

At least half of the deputies must be present in order for the assembly to transact business and, except for amendments to the constitution (for which a two-thirds plurality is required), decisions of the assembly are reached by majority vote. Convening the National Assembly is the prerogative of the Presidential Council, although the constitution also requires that it must be convened on the written request of one-third of the deputies. Members of all other government organs are obliged to respond to requests of the deputies that are pertinent to assembly business.

The Presidential Council

Despite the provisions of the constitution that declare the National Assembly to be the supreme organ of the state power, much of the assembly's authority has been exercised by the Presidential Council. Elected from the ranks of the assembly, the twenty-one-member council has been described by observers as a body that combines the executive, legislative and, in some instances, judicial functions of the government.

Originally established by the 1949 Constitution, the council functions as a kind of collective head of state. Although it is nominally responsible to the National Assembly, it has broad executive powers and is authorized by the constitution to exercise the legislative function when the assembly is not in session. Inasmuch as the assembly is in session an average of only ten to fourteen weekdays annually, there is ample opportunity for the council to exercise its substantive function and to issue legislation in the form of decree-laws. The only legislative prerogative that the Presidential Council cannot exercise on behalf of the National Assembly is the amending of the constitution; however, in practice, the council has always left the adoption of annual budgets and long-term economic plans for assembly action.

In addition to its substitutive role for the National Assembly, the Presidential Council is assigned its own sphere of jurisdiction. Duties specifically assigned to the council by the constitution include: fixing the dates for elections; convening the assembly; initiating legislation; confirming international agreements; appointing and receiving diplomatic missions; and appointing career judges, undersecretaries of state, certain ranking civil servants, and senior military officers. The council is also empowered to create and bestow orders and titles, to exercise the right of clemency, and to call a plebiscite on issues of national importance. A decree-law of 1957 gives the council considerable influence in the filling of some of the leading ecclesiastical posts.

The Revised Constitution provides the Presidential Council with the authority to determine and proclaim a threat to state security and, in the event of such a threat, to create a national defense council vested with extraordinary jurisdiction. In the event of war or other national emergencies, the Presidential Council is also empowered to reconvene the National Assembly, even after the expiration of the assembly's term of office if new elections have not yet been held.

Constitutionally, the mandate of the Presidential Council continues until the first session of a newly elected National Assembly, at which time a new council is selected. Practice has shown, however, that there is little turnover of the council membership, the same persons generally being reelected each term. In theory, the council is responsible to the assembly, and the assembly has the authority to recall the entire council or any of its individual members. Nine members of the council, in addition to the chairman and secretary, are required for a quorum. The legally binding decisions of the council must be promulgated in *Magyar Kozlony*, the official gazette.

Another sphere where the areas of competence appear less than clear is in the matter of responsibility for the supervision of the councils on the lower levels of government. Constitutional supervision of the councils is assigned to the Presidential Council—supervision that includes the determination of election dates, the protection of the council's rights, and the power to dissolve councils "whose function is at variance with the constitution or seriously jeopardizes the people's interests." At the same time, the Council of Ministers is assigned the direction of the council and supervision "over the legality of their activities."

The degree to which the Presidential Council has exercised its substitutive role for the National Assembly is evident in the amount of legislation enacted by each; in 1966, for example, only three laws were passed by the assembly, and thirty-two decree-laws were passed by the council. Much the same pattern continued in 1967, when the count was seven assembly enactments as compared with forty-two for the council. Statistics from 1968 through 1970 reveal that the assembly passed a total of twenty laws during that period, whereas 119 acts were passed by the Presidential Council. Although the constitution formally requires that all decree-laws enacted by the council be approved by the assembly at its next session, the bills are generally voted on en masse, and observers report that there is never any opposition.

Some assembly deputies have called for a reduction in the Presidential Council's legislative activities and a corresponding increase in that of the National Assembly. Although several party congresses have endorsed the concept of expanding the role of the assembly, nothing has been done to restrict the council's substitutionary role, and the Revised Constitution drafting committee adopted the position that a fixed separation of the legislative functions of the two bodies would be too rigid and, consequently, not justified.

A striking example of the Presidential Council's assumption of the legislative function was the introduction of the New Economic Mechanism (known as NEM—see Glossary) in January 1968 (see ch. 12). As a program of economic reform providing greater autonomy to the socialist enterprises, the NEM was a matter of major importance to the entire social and economic life of the country. It was brought into being by a series of decree-laws with only minor involvement on the part of the National Assembly.

After examining the continued lack of involvement of the National Assembly in important issues, the Association of Hungarian Jurists, meeting in May 1969, stated that "it is disquieting to find that fundamental laws pass through parliament in half a day." Supporting an increased role for the assembly, the jurists suggested that "decree-laws should be used only as an exception." Although other groups, including some party organs, gave verbal support to these concepts, no basic changes were made and, in April 1972, the National Assembly passed the Revised Constitution unanimously, without alteration, in a brief morning session.

Observers have commented that in some areas the constitution does not make a clear distinction between the responsibilities assigned to the Presidential Council, the National Assembly, and the Council of Ministers. Both the assembly and the Presidential Council, for example, are assigned the task of overseeing the implementation of the constitution, and both are given the power to annul any actions of state administrative organs that are judged to be at variance with the constitution.

In a similar fashion, the Council of Ministers is assigned the responsibility of ensuring the implementation of laws and statutes and is empowered to annul or amend any action of a subordinate organ that infringes on the law. The same observers have further pointed out that a significant measure of discretion in this regard is reserved for the National Assembly and the Council of Ministers in the provisions that empower the assembly to annul any actions of government bodies that are considered "inimical to social interests" and enable the Council of Ministers to annul any measure that it deems harmful to public interests.

Council of Ministers

Whereas the 1949 Constitution described the Council of Ministers as the highest organ of state administration, the 1972 revision simply enumerates its duties and outlines its organization. Consequently, an understanding of the position of the Council of Ministers in relation to the other organs of the central government must be derived from the broad jurisdiction assigned by the Revised Constitution and from information provided by MSZMP and government spokesmen. During the years between the promulgation of the 1949 Constitution and its revision, observers reported a progressively increasing role for the council to the point that a prominent party leader, speaking in April 1972, could describe it as the highest collective body continuously and operationally running state affairs.

Appointed by the National Assembly on the recommendation of the Presidential Council, the Council of Ministers is described by official government sources as the direct executive organ of the National Assembly. Theoretically, the council is responsible to the assembly for its activities and is obligated by the constitution to make regular reports on its work to the assembly. As some observers have pointed out, however, the real status of the Council of Ministers derives from the fact that most of its members are also high-ranking party officials. At the beginning of 1972 all but five of the twenty-five members of the council were also members of the MSZMP Central Committee, and Premier Jeno Fock was a member of the party Politburo.

The council's constitutionally assigned responsibilities give it administrative control over all the country's political, economic, social, and cultural affairs. Headed by the premier and four deputy premiers, in mid-1972 the council included sixteen ministers and four chairmen of state offices assigned ministerial ranking. In addition to the members of the council, other officials and specialists may be invited to attend council sessions and, as the need warrants, special committees may be appointed to fulfill specific tasks.

The number of ministries and offices included in the council and the division of responsibilities among them have varied according to circumstances. The sixteen ministries listed in 1972 included: agriculture and food, construction and urban development, culture, defense, finance, foreign affairs, foreign trade, health, heavy industry, interior, internal trade, justice, labor, light industry, metallurgy and machine industry, and transportation and postal affairs (see fig. 5).

Functioning under the direction of a minister, each of the ministries is also provided with a consultative and advisory collegium consisting of appointed government officials and outside experts. Council regulations require that each of the collegia be convened on a monthly basis in order for the members to present their views to the minister. Each minister is personally responsible for the functioning of his ministry, however, and the collegium's views are not binding on his actions.

Several other administrative organs function under the direct authority of the council rather than through the individual ministries. The chairmen of four of these—the National Planning Office, the National Technical Development Committee, the State Office of Church Affairs, and the Central Bureau of Statistics—sit on the Council of Ministers with full ministerial rank.

Two of the other important organs functioning under the direct supervision of the council are the Central Arbitration Committee and the Central People's Control Committee. The Central Arbitration Committee, together with its subordinate network of arbitration committees, is authorized to mediate financial disputes between state and cooperative organizations or between enterprises. It was believed that the establishment of such a committee system would expedite the settlement of these disputes more rapidly than would be the case if they were under the jurisdiction of the regular courts. Local

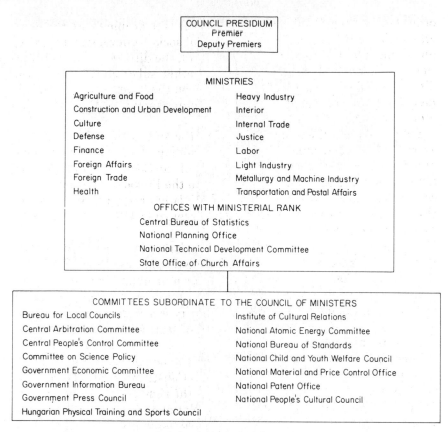

COUNCIL PRESIDIUM
Premier
Deputy Premiers

MINISTRIES

Agriculture and Food	Heavy Industry
Construction and Urban Development	Interior
Culture	Internal Trade
Defense	Justice
Finance	Labor
Foreign Affairs	Light Industry
Foreign Trade	Metallurgy and Machine Industry
Health	Transportation and Postal Affairs

OFFICES WITH MINISTERIAL RANK

Central Bureau of Statistics
National Planning Office
National Technical Development Committee
State Office of Church Affairs

COMMITTEES SUBORDINATE TO THE COUNCIL OF MINISTERS

Bureau for Local Councils	Institute of Cultural Relations
Central Arbitration Committee	National Atomic Energy Committee
Central People's Control Committee	National Bureau of Standards
Committee on Science Policy	National Child and Youth Welfare Council
Government Economic Committee	National Material and Price Control Office
Government Information Bureau	National Patent Office
Government Press Council	National People's Cultural Council
Hungarian Physical Training and Sports Council	

Figure 5. Hungary, Organization of the Council of Ministers, October 1972

arbitration committees are responsible to the county executive committees as well as to the Central Arbitration Committee.

Described by official government spokesmen as "the supreme body of general state supervision," the Central People's Control Committee also heads a hierarchy of committees that function on the county, district, and local levels. Except for the national committee, whose fifteen members are appointed by the Presidential Councils, most of the control committees consist of volunteers. The control organization functions in a watchdog capacity to oversee the operations of government organs, social organizations, and economic enterprises in order to ensure proper management and legality. In 1967, the latest year for which figures were published, the Central People's Control Committee reported a total of some 40,000 "volunteer controllers" working in its subordinate branches.

The first duty assigned to the Council of Ministers by the Revised Constitution is that of safeguarding and ensuring "state and social order and the rights of citizens." Some observers have commented that the priority shown in placing the protection of the state and social order before ensuring the rights of citizens is in keeping with the over-all policies of the regime in its program of socialist development. Other duties include the implementation of laws, the direction and coordina-tion of the work of the ministries and other subordinate offices, the direction and supervision of the councils on the lower levels of govern-ment, and the elaboration and implementation of the country's economic plans.

Policy defining the tendency of scientific and cultural development, as well as the determination and functioning of the system of social and medical care, is also the prerogative of the Council of Ministers. In almost the same words as that applied to the Presidential Council, the constitution also gives the Council of Ministers responsibility for con-cluding and confirming international agreements. Other duties may be assigned the council by law.

As long as there is no conflict with existing laws, the decrees and resolutions issued by the Council of Ministers are legally binding. The council is further empowered to annul or amend any measure passed by any subordinate organs that is considered to infringe on the law or to be harmful to public interests. Authority is also given the council to extend its direct control over any branch of state administration should such be deemed necessary.

There is no fixed term of office for the Council of Ministers, its man-date being given for an indefinite period. Constitutionally, the right to terminate a council's mandate as well as the right to recall any individ-ual council member are vested in the National Assembly. On begin-ning its term of office, each newly elected assembly either appoints a new council or simply confirms the existing one, which then continues in office.

Although the election of the Council of Ministers has always been the constitutional prerogative of the National Assembly, the governments headed by Gyula Kallai in 1956 and by Janos Kadar in 1961 were ap-pointed by the Presidential Council. Official statements indicate that this practice has been abandoned and that all future governments will be elected by proper constitutional procedure, but the Presidential Council is still able to make changes in the Council of Ministers via its substitutionary role for the assembly.

The Judicial System

According to the revised constitution, the role of the courts is to safeguard the state, the economic and social order, and the legal rights of citizens and to punish the perpetrators of criminal acts. In June 1972 the National Assembly passed a law, to take effect on January 1, 1973, substantially reforming the judicial system that had, until that time, operated under a 1954 law.

Among the changes called for by the new law was an expansion of the jurisdiction of the courts to deal with two categories of essentially economic disputes—those involving individual workers and employers and those between state enterprises. Labor disputes of the first type had been handled almost exclusively by enterprise arbitration committees in the first instance and by regional committees on appeal. It was expected that enterprise arbitration committees would continue to settle most disputes satisfactorily—as they had in the past—but that a new labor affairs court would provide full judicial protection of workers' rights on appeal.

Disputes between enterprises had been dealt with by economic arbitration committees, which represented the state administration, and were concerned chiefly with minimizing disruptions to the production process rather than dispensing justice. When the NEM was instituted in January 1968, it granted a good deal of autonomy to state enterprises, and judicial decision rather than administrative fiat came to be seen as a more adequate way of dealing with contractual and other civil disputes between them. The right of enterprises to go to the courts was not, however, established until January 1973, and it was not clear in early 1973 whether the courts would be able to deal with the considerable number of cases that may be brought to them.

The new law also permits citizens to appeal to the courts the decisions of state administrative organs. Specifically, it notes that "in matters affecting the fundamental rights and obligations of citizens . . . the parties can turn to the courts for reversal of decisions handed down by these organs in cases determined by the rule of law." The courts may also review decisions of state administrative organs with an eye to the legality of such decisions. These developments are considered of some importance by government and by others, although analysts suggest that uncertainties as to the precise nature of rights and responsibilities remain as to ambiguities of procedure. In any case the recency of these changes does not permit an assessment of functioning of the institutions and processes thus established.

At the base of the court hierarchy are the district courts and two kinds of specialized courts—the labor affairs courts and the military courts. The district courts function in the units into which the counties are divided, in the municipal districts of Budapest, and in the towns. Unless otherwise specified, district courts are the courts of first instance in all disputes. The labor courts operate in Budapest and in each of the counties. Although they may hear some cases as courts of first instance, the labor courts are to be concerned largely with judging appeals from the decisions of labor affairs arbitration committees and other extrajudicial dispute-settling entities concerned with labor matters. The military courts operate in some larger garrisons and in upper echelon military units. In addition to dealing with members of the armed forces, the military courts try civilian cases involving criminal acts which may directly harm the national defense.

The county courts (one in each county and the Capital Court in Budapest) act as courts of appeal from the decisions of the district courts and the labor affairs courts. Appeals from military courts go directly to the Supreme Court. The county courts act as courts of first instance in certain serious cases—for example, murder, willful homicide, and grave crimes against social property. These courts also function as courts of first instance in civil suits of a certain magnitude directed against the state, government officials, or socialist enterprises.

The Supreme Court acts as a court of appeal from the courts immediately below it and from the military courts. The Supreme Court— that is, one of its judges or a judge and lay assessors—may function as a court of first instance when important cases have been submitted to it. The decision of such a court may be appealed to a council of the Supreme Court. When the Supreme Court acts as a court of appeals, it is divided into councils, each of which is concerned with certain kinds of cases—criminal, civil, economic, labor affairs, and military. Appeals from these councils on points of law are heard by the Presidential Council of the Supreme Court.

Courts are manned by two kinds of persons: professional judges and lay assessors. All courts—district, county, and even the Supreme Court—when they act as courts of first instance consist of a professional judge and two assessors. Another new law is expected to permit some exceptions to this rule, particularly in the hearing of certain civil cases; lay assessors will be eliminated, and a single professional judge is to hear the case. According to the law reorganizing the judicial system, "lay assessors have the same rights and obligations as the professional judges." Courts hearing appeals usually consist of three professional judges. An exception is the Presidential Council of the Supreme Court, which is led by the president of that court.

Two entitles—the Supreme Court and the Ministry of Justice— share the supervision of the court system and its functions. Their tasks, however, are substantially different.

The new law gives the plenum of the Supreme Court—composed of all its professional judges—the power to issue "guiding principles or decisions in principle" when such guidance is necessary "in the interests of guaranteeing uniformity of judicial practice or on questions of legal interpretation." Three officials—the president of the Supreme Court, the minister of justice, and the supreme prosecutor—may propose that the Supreme Court consider specific matters for the purpose of issuing decisions in principle. The minister of justice and the supreme prosecutor attend the plenum of the Supreme Court with advisory powers. The minister of labor and the secretary general of the National Council of Trade Unions attend when labor matters are being considered. The issuance of guiding principles or decisions in principle is not to occur with respect to cases still being heard by the courts but is to be based upon problems raised by already adjudicated disputes and would apply to future ones.

The guiding principles and decisions in principle are binding upon the lower courts. By contrast, the decisions of the Supreme Court acting as an appeals court in specific cases are not binding as a matter of law, although they may in fact influence the decisions of lower courts.

In matters that do not require the issuance of a guiding principle but may require a statement of position by the Supreme Court in order to ensure uniformity in the application of the law, one of the collegia of the court may state such a position on issues within its field of competence. Each collegium consists of all of the professional judges who hear a certain range of cases. Just as there are five kinds of councils hearing appeals of specific kinds, so there are five collegia—criminal, civil, economic, labor affairs, and military. The new law does not specifically make positions of collegia binding, but these positions will presumably be influential.

The minister of justice is to supervise the general operation of the courts; in the case of the labor affairs courts, his authority is to be exercised in consultation with the minister of labor and the secretary general of the National Council of Trade Unions. The new law explicitly states that the minister of justice "must not violate the principle of the independence of judges in the course of carrying out his responsibilities." Nor are the minister and his officials to influence, directly or indirectly, decisions in cases under consideration by the courts.

Despite the limits placed on his powers by the new law, the minister of justice does have a number of important tasks assigned to him. He is to evaluate "the social effect of the judgment activity of the courts, analyze the social causes of the violation of the law, and take or initiate measures to end them." He is to observe closely the work of the courts and, on the basis of such research, he may bring to the Supreme Court issues on which the court may give guidance in principle.

Supervision over the observance of the law is vested in the supreme prosecutor of the Hungarian People's Republic, who heads a hierarchy of public prosecution offices organized on the national, county, and district levels. Two main categories of responsibility are included under the competence of the public prosecutor: criminal investigation and prosecution; and supervision over the legality of the actions of state, social, and cooperative organs. Only the highest organs of state—the National Assembly, the Presidential Council, and the Council of Ministers—are excluded from the authority of the public prosecutor.

Theoretically, the prosecutor's office is not subject to control by any other organ of government, although the supreme prosecutor is elected by the National Assembly to a four-year term and is constitutionally responsible and obliged to account to the National Assembly for his performance. The deputies of the supreme prosecutor are appointed by the Presidential Council; other officials of the central office and the heads of the county and district prosecution offices are appointed by the supreme prosecutor. The chief military prosecutor functions as a deputy of the supreme prosecution and is subordinate to him in his official duties.

In an advisory capacity, the supreme prosecutor is authorized to attend sessions of the National Assembly, the Presidential Council, the Council of Ministers, the Central People's Control Committee, and plenary sessions of the Supreme Court. The supreme prosecutor is the only government authority empowered to initiate action to suspend the immunity of National Assembly deputies or to institute criminal proceedings against a professional judge.

County and Local Government

Hungary is divided into nineteen counties and 120 districts. In addition, there are five cities of county rank, sixty-three towns classified as districts and, below the district level, 3,135 villages. On each of these levels the unit of government is the council, which purportedly fills a dual role, functioning on the one hand as the local arm of the central government and, on the other, as the organ of popular self-government (see ch. 3).

Originally established by an act of the National Assembly in 1950, the council system was reorganized by the assembly in 1954 and has undergone only slight modification since that time. According to the election law of 1970, council members on the lower levels (the village and the district) are elected on the basis of general, equal, and direct suffrage by voting citizens. County-level councils are elected by the district councils. The term of office for all council members is four years.

Each council elects, from its own ranks, a president and an executive committee, which must be approved by the council on the next higher level. The executive committee on the county level directs the activities of the lower executive committees within its territorial jurisdiction and, in turn, all county committees are responsible to the Council of Ministers. In almost every instance, the chairman of the county, district, and local councils are also members of the corresponding level of the MSZMP executive committees (see ch. 9).

In addition to the executive committees, councils on the county and district levels are also organized with a secretariat and with specialized departments having salaried staffs. Within their territorial jurisdictions, these council departments administer agriculture, industry, retail trade, housing, public utilities, education, health programs and facilities, child and youth welfare, and sports. The councils also have responsibilities in financial administration, in economic planning, and in labor management. Certain areas over which central organs of the national government exercise direct control are exempt from council authority, however; these areas include the military and police forces, customs, fire and postal services, railroads, waterways, telecommunications, land registry, vital statistics, and financial auditing.

Council organization on the lower levels is less complex and frequently consists of only the executive committee. In the smaller village units, where it would be impractical to have separate councils, two or three units may join together to establish joint councils. In 1972 there were an estimated 850 joint councils in existence.

Observers have pointed out that the vast network of councils on the lower levels serves as a means of involving large members of citizens in the affairs of local government and a means of mobilizing the population for the fulfillment of regime policies and programs. Projects and auxiliary committees set up by the local councils to deal with questions of economic, cultural, and educational affairs provide numerous opportunities for the involvement of voluntary workers.

THE ELECTORAL SYSTEM

The Electoral Law of 1970 states that all citizens have the right to vote provided that they have reached eighteen years of age and have not been deprived of this right by law. Those who are legally excluded from participation in the electoral process include persons under criminal sentence, persons who are considered mentally ill, and persons who are either under police surveillance or under preliminary arrest. Every eligible voter has one vote, every vote is equal, and everyone who has the right to vote may be a candidate for election.

Representatives to the National Assembly and members of the local and district councils are elected on the basis of general, equal, and direct suffrage by secret ballot. Members of the county-level councils are elected by and from the membership of the district councils. Assembly deputies and district council members are elected according to electoral districts.

For each of the electoral districts a voters' list is drawn up and maintained by a census commission appointed by the council executive committee. Law requires that these lists be posted in council offices for a period of eight days after their compilation and that every voter be notified in writing about his inclusion on a voting list.

Determination of the electoral districts is assigned to the Presidential Council. In general, each deputy to the National Assembly represents an electoral district of 30,000 residents. For the election of council members, the size of the electoral districts varies from one councillor for every fifty residents in the less densely populated areas to one councillor for every 700 residents in the heavily populated regions.

Election arrangements are under the overall direction of the Patriotic People's Front, the collective political front that brings the country's major mass and social organizations under the leadership and control of the MSZMP. The front organization's national council, acting at least thirty days before general elections, sets up the eleven-member National Election Presidium and election presidia in each of the counties and districts and their metropolitan equivalents.

These presidia are responsible for the legality of elections, the registration of candidates, the judgment of disputes arising out of election procedures, and the announcement of election results. Members of the National Election Presidium must be approved by the Presidential Council, and those for the lower level presidia must be approved by the appropriate council executive committee. In each of the election districts, the local organ of the Patriotic People's Front establishes election committees that function under the direction of the election presidia.

Nominees are selected at voters' meetings arranged by the presidia and the election district committees. At these meetings, nominations may be advanced by organs of the Patriotic People's Front, social organizations, enterprise worker organizations, and ordinary citizens. The law requires that one or more nominating meetings be held in each district and, although there is only a single-list ballot, more than one candidate may be nominated to fill a given position. Those who receive one-third of the total assembled vote at these meetings become candidates.

A decisive measure of control over the nominations is reserved to the election officials who "may refuse to register candidates for legal reasons." Appeals on such decisions, however, may be made by the local organ of the Patriotic People's Front and, in the event of such an appeal, the final decision is passed on to the next higher election presidium. Names of candidates must be published at least ten days before the election.

Dates for general elections are determined and published by the Presidential Council at least forty-five days before the election. On election day votes must be cast on an official ballot, and the voter marks his choice in the event that there is more than one candidate for a single office. Election results are tallied in each of the electoral districts by ballot committees and are supervised by the election presidia.

At the end of 1972 the most recent election had taken place in April 1971. In preparation for these elections, some 2.5 million persons reportedly took part in nomination meetings to decide on candidates for the local councils and the National Assembly. For the 352 assembly seats, only forty-nine constituencies nominated more than one candidate; for 68,946 local council seats, two or more nominations were made in only 3,016 constituencies.

The female proportion of the assembly candidates was 25 percent, an increase of 6 percent over the previous election. Twenty of the candidates were under thirty years of age, as compared to only one deputy in that age group in the preceding assembly. Official returns indicated that 7,334,918 voters, or 98.7 percent of those eligible to vote, participated in the elections and that the single list of candidates submitted by the Patriotic People's Front received 99 percent of the valid votes cast.

CHAPTER 9

POLITICAL DYNAMICS

All power for political decisionmaking rests in the Hungarian Socialist Workers' Party (MSZMP—see Glossary), which has assumed the leading role in determining the direction of all aspects of the country's political, economic, social, and cultural life. Within the MSZMP, primary political power is exercised by a ruling oligarchy of the top party elite who make up the Political Bureau (Politburo) and the Secretariat. Both of these organs function under the direction of MSZMP First Secretary Janos Kadar.

Effective party control of the government and the mass organizations is accomplished through its own personnel who occupy the leading positions in these bodies and, in some instances, through party organs that function in a supervisory capacity to ensure the implementation of party decisions. By means of the mass organizations, the party has sought to penetrate and mobilize all elements of the society to realize its programs and achieve its goals. Structured to incorporate all of the major interest and occupational groups, the mass organizations have served to preclude the development of any organized opposition to party rule.

After coming to power at the height of the 1956 uprising and after firmly reestablishing the party in an undisputed position of control, the Kadar regime has evolved a pragmatic approach to the country's economic and social problems. Although party membership continues to include only a small percentage of the population, its stability and its programs to improve living standards have served to enhance its image among the people.

In 1972 the country as a whole continued to benefit from the relatively relaxed political atmosphere. The regime remains sensitive, however, to any potential challenges to its rule and firmly maintains its leading position. Although the great majority of Hungarians have not adopted the ideology of communism, most, lacking other alternatives, are disposed to accept the continued rule of the MSZMP but feel that its leading role should result from merit rather than force and that its first priority must be responsiveness to the needs of the people rather than the perpetuation of its control.

MAJOR POLITICAL DEVELOPMENTS, 1968–73

When Hungarian military units joined with other Soviet-led forces of the Warsaw Treaty Organization (Warsaw Pact) in the August 1968 invasion of Czechoslovakia, the regime of Janos Kadar, first secretary of the MSZMP, had been in power for a period of almost twelve years. Ironically, Kadar's own rise to power had come about as the result of a similar situation—the crushing of the Hungarian rebellion by Soviet troops in November 1956—during which he emerged as the choice of the Communist Party of the Soviet Union to head the Hungarian party (see ch. 2).

Kadar first became party secretary on October 25, 1956, in the midst of the revolution as the Soviet-aligned communist leaders sought to regain control of the situation. As a part of this effort and in order to portray a break with the Stalinist past, on November 1 the old party was dissolved, and the MSZMP was instituted with Kadar as its chief. On November 4, the date of the main Soviet offensive that forcibly suppressed the revolution, he also became the head of the new pro-Soviet government.

After gaining power, Kadar successfully consolidated his control over the party and the state. Punitive measures were taken against the revolutionaries and those suspected of sympathizing with them. At the same time, the government carried out an intensive campaign to collectivize Hungarian agriculture. The stern tactics were continued throughout the period of consolidation, and it was not until 1962 that the regime felt secure enough to relax its stringent controls. Beginning in 1962, the regime gradually moved to what observers have described as a centrist position in domestic affairs and developed a pragmatic approach to the country's political and economic problems.

To political observers, the Eighth Party Congress, held in 1962, marked the beginning of the transition away from the rigid policies adopted after the revolution toward at least a limited degree of cautious relaxation; the tone was set by the congress' declaration of amnesty for the participants in the 1956 rebellion. Kadar declared his intention to make the party more responsive to popular demands and asserted that the efforts of the MSZMP would be directed toward the improvement of the political system and the modernization of the economy. At the same time, although Kadar's new course was strongly anti-Stalinist and antidogmatic, it remained staunchly pro-Soviet.

The drive for the much needed modernization of the country's economy resulted in the development of the New Economic Mechanism, which entered into operation on January 1, 1968. Involving a broad decentralization of economic planning, the New Economic Mechanism was designed to stimulate Hungary's economy by transferring greater responsibility to the managers of socialist enterprises and collectives and by giving some influence to the forces of the market. Observers reported that the party approved the new program without questioning its compatibility with orthodox Marxist principles (see ch. 12).

Although the economic reforms were not accompanied by political reforms of the same magnitude, the regime demonstrated some tolerance of criticism and differences on policy issues. Differences considered to be anti-Soviet or counterrevolutionary, however, were not permitted, and the regime continued to follow closely the lead of the Soviet Union in foreign affairs. It was this close dependence on the Soviets that resulted in Hungarian troop participation in the invasion of Czechoslovakia, involvement that proved difficult for the regime to reconcile with its own domestic policies. The only explanation offered came nearly two months after the event when Kadar asserted that "it is the fundamental principle of our foreign policy to cooperate with the Soviet Union." In accord with this principle, the regime also endorsed the doctrine of limited sovereignty for communist-controlled states put forth by Leonid Brezhnev, the Soviet party chief.

With Kadar firmly in control of the MSZMP and the party, in turn, fully in control of the apparatus of the government, Hungarian political developments have taken no startling turns during the period from the inauguration of the New Economic Mechanism in 1968 until early 1973. This is not to say that there has been complete unity within the MSZMP, however, as several factions are reported to exist among party regulars who are in positions of leadership just below the highest levels of authority.

On the one hand are the older conservatives who came into their positions during the Stalinist era of Hungarian communism and who advocate a more dogmatic form of socialism with a greater emphasis on Marxist-Leninist ideology and the maintenance of the strongest possible ties to the Communist Party of the Soviet Union. In general, however, the conservatives diminished in both power and numbers during the 1960s and have been progressively replaced by younger men loyal to Kadar. On the other hand are those who want to proceed with liberalization and democratization at a faster pace and to a greater degree than the regime is willing to allow.

Kadar and his supporters represent a middle ground between these two factions and pursue a generally pragmatic policy but, at the same time, are careful to maintain the supremacy of the party. Within the MSZMP, Kadar's strongest supporters consist of young and middle-aged party regulars, many of whom obtained their positions during his administration and are closely allied to him. Most of these might be classified as intellectuals or technocrats who were placed in their positions out of consideration for their professional competence as well as for their loyalty to the Kadar regime.

The liberalized internal atmosphere that the regime has allowed to gradually evolve does not mean a revival of the multiparty system or any reduction in the influence of the MSZMP. At the Tenth Party Congress, convened in November 1970, Kadar reiterated his position on communist party dominance, declaring that "the one-party system set up in our country facilitates the party's work and helps in the political cohesion of all creative forces of society."

One of the primary reasons that Kadar has been able to follow his own generally pragmatic policies in domestic affairs is that he has adhered closely to a principle of complete loyalty to the Soviet Union. This loyalty is itself partly pragmatic, for some 50,000 Soviet troops have been stationed in Hungary since the 1956 uprising. At the same time, however, Kadar is a confirmed communist and looks to the Soviet Union as the rightful leader of the communist world.

In November 1972 Brezhnev paid an official visit to Budapest, which was looked upon by observers as a sign of Soviet approval for the Hungarian regime's domestic policies. Brezhnev awarded Kadar the Order of Lenin and addressed him as a leader "filled with the majestic feeling of responsibility toward your people."

POLITICAL ORGANIZATIONS

The MSZMP

The first political movement in the history of the country to describe itself as communist was founded in 1918 and known as the Party of the Communists in Hungary. In March of that year, in the midst of the political turmoil resulting from World War I, the Communists seized control of the government and attempted to set up what they called a "dictatorship of the proletariat." Just five months later, however, the fledgling government collapsed, and the party was declared illegal and forced into a clandestine existence, which continued until World War II. Throughout this period the party's extensive underground activity was conducted under the pseudonym Hungarian Peace Party (see ch. 2).

During the final stages of World War II the party reconstituted itself as the Hungarian Communist Party and, with the advance of Soviet forces across the country, brought its activities out into the open. Although numerically weak, the Communists were well organized and well disciplined and, with Soviet support, were able to gain a significant measure of influence in the formation of the Provisional National Government, which was set up in December 1944, obtaining three of the twelve cabinet positions.

From this base of operations, the party worked to extend its influence over all elements of Hungarian political life. It received the active support of the Soviet occupation authorities, who aided the party's recruitment efforts by extending special food and employment benefits to party members, and it did not hesitate to use violence against its opponents. By mid-1948 the Communists were able to absorb the Social Democratic Party and gain full control of the government. After the merger with the Social Democrats, the party adopted the name Hungarian Workers' Party. Eight years later, after the 1956 revolution, the party renamed itself the Hungarian Socialist Workers' Party.

Although the Communists were in full control of the state apparatus by the end of 1948, the Constitution of 1949 contained no formal reference to the party, alluding to it only indirectly as the vanguard of the working people. A more specific recognition of the party's dominant position, however, is provided by the Revised Constitution, promulgated in April 1972, which asserts that the "Marxist-Leninist party of the workers' class is the leading force in society."

Organization

The general guidelines for MSZMP organization and functioning are laid down in the party statutes. Originally drawn up after the establishment of the Hungarian Workers' Party in 1948, the statutes have undergone a number of modifications as the result of leadership changes and political circumstances. Some of the more significant modifications were made after the death of Soviet Premier Joseph Stalin in 1953 and, again, after the party was reconstituted following the revolution of October 1956. Additional changes were made by the Tenth Party Congress, convened in November 1970.

The 1953 modifications were intended to strengthen the concept of collective leadership, improve party discipline, and increase the authority of the Politburo. In late 1956 the statutes were modified to redefine the leading political role of the MSZMP; 1970 changes included, among other things, a reduction of the age limit for party membership from twenty-one to eighteen years.

According to the party statutes, MSZMP organization is based on the Leninist principle of democratic centralism, which provides for the election of the leadership on the various levels of the party hierarchy but requires that each level be subject to the authority of the next higher unit. In accordance with this concept, although policy matters are to be freely and openly discussed, discipline requires that the resolutions of all higher party organs be unconditionally binding on all lower organs as well as on individual party members. In effect, the principle operates to limit debate; decisions of the party leadership are adopted with little or no discussion.

In theory, the highest policymaking authority in the party is the party congress. Consisting of delegates elected by the party organizations on the county level, the congress meets every four years to elect the MSZMP Central Committee and set the general guidelines for party policy. The Central Committee is assigned the overall direction of party affairs in the intervals between congresses. In reality, however, the Politburo of the Central Committee is the center of decisionmaking power, and the activities conducted at the congress sessions consist largely of hearing reports from ranking party officials and approving program proposals submitted from the higher echelons of the MSZMP.

Typical of the passive role filled by the party congress was the Tenth Congress, held in November 1970 and attended by 691 delegates, each representing approximately 1,000 party members. The congress agenda included receiving the report of the Central Committee and that of the Central Control Commission and the election of the members of the leading bodies. During the four-day session a total of fifty-six speeches were given by leading party functionaries and, in his closing remarks, First Secretary Kadar was able to note that "not one speech deviated on any essential issue from party policy."

In addition to the Central Committee, one other major party body, the Central Control Commission, is also elected by the party congress. As in the case of the Central Committee, the election is pro forma; the slate submitted by the central party authoriti. s is always approved by the congress without alteration. Duties assigned to the Central Control Commission focus on the maintenance of party discipline and the supervision of the Central Committee's financial affairs.

According to the party statutes, the Central Control Commission is to work to strengthen the MSZMP's ideological, political, and organizational unity and to promote the education of the membership. It is to keep watch over the member's political attitudes, loyalty, and "moral purity" and to fight against any antiparty or factional activities. The commission is empowered to call to account members who violate the principles of party discipline. In addition to the Central Control Committee of the party, a network of so-called popular control committees also exists within the organization of the various levels of the government.

Party statutes provide for the establishment of local cells—the basic party units—in all production enterprises, offices, and residential areas where there are at least three party members. On this level of the party structure the highest organ is the membership meeting, which must be convened at least once every two months. Officers for the basic organization are elected at the membership meetings and serve four-year terms. These officers direct the work of the cell and are responsible to the membership meetings for their activities. The number of officers in the basic organization depends on the size of the membership; units with less than ten members elect only a secretary and an assistant secretary. In November 1970 the party's first secretary reported a total of 21,000 basic organizations (see fig. 6).

The basic party units are responsible for the recruitment and indoctrination of new members, the dissemination of propaganda to nonmembers, and the interpretation of party programs and policies to the population as a whole. Party members are expected to function as representatives of the MSZMP in their places of work as well as in all of their social activities. Each local unit is required to uphold party discipline and take the lead in implementing policies established by the party leaders.

In all localities, factories, bureaus, and units of the armed forces where party membership exceeds 200 persons, the statutes require the election of party committees to coordinate and direct the activities of

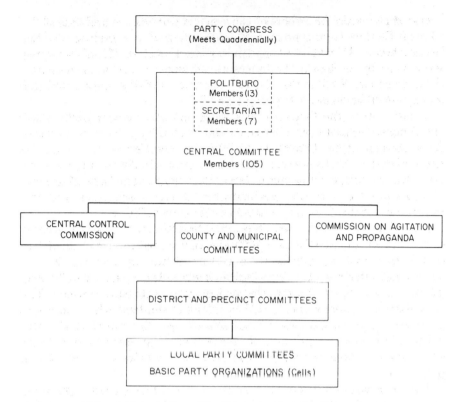

Figure 6. Organization of the Hungarian Socialist Workers' Party

the basic organizations. On this level, which is immediately superior to the local cell unit, the superior organ is the party conference. Convened at least every four years by action of the party committee, the party conference is the local equivalent of the national party congress. The conference elects the party committee, hears reports of the local party officials, and elects delegates to the party conference on the next higher level.

Almost all of the work of a party committee is conducted by a five- to seven-member executive committee, which the former elects from among its own ranks. The party committee as a whole is required to meet only once every three years, although it may be convened more frequently. The executive committee, which must meet at least every two months, is given the responsibility of directing the work of the party organization between sessions of the party committee and of implementing programs and policies set down by the central authorities of the MSZMP.

This system of party committees is repeated on each level of the party structure. Above the local committee level, district and Budapest precinct organizations function under the direction of executive committees and are responsible for the coordination and supervision of all party activities within their respective territories. The county and Budapest municipal organizations make up the next higher level of the party structure and are responsible directly to the MSZMP Central Committee. In almost all instances, the chairman of the corresponding level of the government council is a member of the party executive committee (see ch. 8).

In addition to the party statutes, some aspects of party organization and responsibility have been fixed by resolutions of the Secretariat. According to these resolutions, the tasks of the party organization on each level include the execution of party directives, the handling of assignments allocated by higher party authorities, and the preparation of suggestions for party activities within its territory. In addition, each party organization is assigned responsibility for the coordination of the activities of individual Communists in the government and mass organizations within its jurisdiction and for keeping them informed of party resolutions.

Defined by the statutes as the highest authoritative body of the MSZMP between sessions of the party congress, the Central Committee is assigned the overall direction of the party and is empowered to represent the party before all state organs and economic and social organizations and in international relations. It is also responsible for the direction of the party press and appoints the editors of the party newspapers and periodicals. Plenary sessions of the Central Committee must be held at least every three months. The Tenth Congress enlarged the membership of the Central Committee from ninety-nine to 105 members.

Within the Central Committee, the locus of political power lies in the Politburo and the Secretariat, and it is in these two bodies that the political elite of the country function. Although both of these leading party organs are theoretically elected by the Central Committee from among its own members, in practice the Politburo and the Secretariat are self-perpetuating bodies, and any membership changes are generated from within rather than from the Central Committee as a whole. In late 1972 five of the seven members of the Secretariat, including First Secretary Kadar, were also members of the thirteen-member Politburo. Before November 1970 the statutes provided for a period of candidate membership for the Politburo; on recommendation of the first secretary at the Tenth Party Congress, however, this statute was abolished.

The statutes assign the Politburo the overall direction of party affairs between Central Committee sessions and, by virtue of this assignment, the Politburo is the actual center of decisionmaking authority, its jurisdiction extending to all aspects of the country's political, economic, social, and cultural life. As the central executive organ of the party, the Secretariat is given the general task of supervising the administrative apparatus of the party and the execution of policy decisions. It is also empowered to appoint key personnel in the party, the government, and the mass organizations.

Throughout the era of the Kadar regime, there have been few changes in the makeup of the Politburo. What changes have taken place have been largely the result of the retirement or death of an incumbent and, in each case, the replacement has been a technically competent younger person owing loyalty to the first secretary. Observers have attributed this continuity of leadership at the highest levels of the party to Kadar's desire to ensure political stability and to the fact that he continues to enjoy the confidence of the party leadership.

Membership in the MSZMP Central Committee and the government overlaps at many points. In late 1972 at least fifty of the 105 members of the Central Committee also held important positions in the government. Of these, thirty-five were National Assembly deputies, and nine of the thirty-five were members of the Presidential Council. Nineteen Central Committee members, including some of those who were assembly deputies, also held ministerial positions in the Council of Ministers. This overlapping of membership serves to provide an interlocking of functions and authority at the highest levels of the party and government (see ch. 8).

Under the direction of the Secretariat there exists an extensive Central Committee bureaucracy that in many instances parallels the organization of the government. In addition to the Central Committee bureau, there are seven administrative departments, the Central Political Academy, the Institute of Party History, the Institute of Sociology, and the office of the Workers Militia. The departments are: administration; agitation and propaganda; international relations; national economy; party economy; party and mass organization; and science, public education, and culture.

Also attached to the Central Committee are five so-called working groups or collectives, which function as policy-formulating bodies. The role of these working groups is to assist the central party authorities in the development of long-term policy recommendations in their assigned areas of responsibility. Established during the two-year period following the reconstitution of the party in late 1956, the five policy groups are: Cooperative Policy Working Group, Cultural Policy Working Group, Economic Working Group, Party-Building Working Group, and the Youth Policy Committee. Each of these groups is chaired by a member of the Politburo or the Secretariat, and the membership of each includes a number of Central Committee members. The economic group is the largest, consisting of thirty-five members. Next in size is the cultural policy group with twenty-five members; each of the other three has approximately fifteen members.

In addition to the Economic Working Group there also exists a separate Committee on National Economic Policy. In late 1972 both of these bodies continued to function under the chairmanship of Rezso

Nyers, the party's economic expert who is considered by observers to be one of the most technically proficient members of the Secretariat. Although no precise information has been published on the relationship between these two economic planning organs, the Committee on National Economic Policy is heavily weighted with persons who hold leading positions in the party, the government, and the mass organizations and appears to be the more authoritative and powerful of the two.

One other body appointed by and responsible to the Central Committee is the Commission on Agitation and Propaganda, responsible for the expression and interpretation of the party's ideological line. Chaired by a member of the Central Committee, the commission sets the general propaganda guidelines, oversees the official press, and initiates policy concerning much of the training and indoctrination of party members. The commission has 400 full-time functionaries and 16,000 workers in local party organizations.

During the 1960s some MSZMP officials began to express concern that the duplication of governmental roles by parallel organs of the party was interfering with the activities of the government ministries. In response to these concerns, in 1970 the Politburo acted to reduce the number of party departments and limit their authority. In taking the action, the Politburo adopted the position that, since most of the members of the government are also members of the party, it is their duty to assert MSZMP policies in their places of work. One Politburo member explained, "We had to eliminate the approach, quite widespread before 1956, that every Communist working in the party apparatus is undoubtedly wiser than one working in the government apparatus."

Membership

At the beginning of 1945 the membership of the Hungarian Communist Party was estimated at only about 30,000. Strong support by the Soviet occupation authorities, however, resulted in the rapid growth of the party, and by May 1945 membership had increased to 150,000. Two years later the party claimed 650,000 members and, just before the merger with the Social Democratic Party in 1948, the membership was reported to total 884,000. After absorbing the Social Democrats and adopting the name Hungarian Workers' Party, the total membership reached 1.6 million.

There followed during the next two years an extensive purge, directed primarily at former Social Democrats, that reduced the membership by more than 600,000, leaving a total of about 860,000 members by the close of 1950. During the next decade new membership drives alternated with purges and changes in membership policy. Although the original statutes had set the minimum age requirement for entrance into the party at eighteen, the Central Committee decided in 1952 to assign all persons under age twenty-four to the youth wing of the party, which was known at that time as the League of Working Youth.

The events of October 1956 had a drastic effect on party membership statistics. So much were the Communists in disfavor during this period that in two months' time the party membership declined to only 96,000. After the crushing of the revolution and the installation of the Kadar regime, efforts were made to rebuild the party's numerical strength, and the membership increased to 500,000 by the end of 1962 and to 600,000 by 1970. In June 1971 the party reported a total of 686,000 members, a figure that represented about 6 percent of the total population.

Changes in entrance requirements contributed to the growth of the party. In 1966 the Ninth Congress abolished the status of candidate membership and brought some 35,000 persons on the candidate rolls directly into the MSZMP. With this change, between 1963 and 1970 the party maintained an annual average growth rate of 3.3 percent. This slow but steady rate of increase is in accord with what Kadar has described as his principle of party building: the qualitative improvement of the party's composition rather than a rapid increase in membership.

During the 1960s, however, there was increasing evidence that the number and proportion of party members under thirty years of age were decreasing while those of pensioners and persons over sixty were increasing. Statistics published in 1970 indicated that the average age of party membership had increased from forty-three to forty-four since the Ninth Congress. Inasmuch as the party had made a concerted effort during that period to invigorate its ranks by enrolling young members, the increase in the average age was a source of concern to the MSZMP leaders.

In June 1957 the minimum age for party membership was set at twenty-one. Concern over the decreasing ratio of younger party members, however, led to proposals that the minimum age again be fixed at eighteen. Advocates of this position pointed out that, since young people were constitutionally eligible to vote and young men were drafted for military service at the age of eighteen, it seemed unjust to exclude them from party membership. Against arguments that a reduction in the age requirement might bring opportunistic and unworthy persons into the party, the MSZMP leaders decided that the progressive aging of the party constituted a greater long-range peril than an influx of active young people.

After a decision by party leaders, in November 1970 the Tenth Congress lowered the age requirement to eighteen. Despite the lower membership age, however, the response among youth was less than anticipated. Party officials showed particular dissatisfaction with the number of young people in the eighteen-to-twenty-one age group seeking to join, and statistics for the first half of 1971 indicated that only 1.5 percent of the new party members belonged in this category. Less than 2 percent of the students in higher education were members of the party.

Although the MSZMP has always sought to portray itself as a party of the working class, the ratio of workers in the total membership has shown a steady decline. Industrial and farm workers made up almost 59 percent of the membership at the time of the Eighth Congress in 1962, but this ratio had dropped to 42.5 percent in 1966 and to 38 percent in 1970. In the face of this declining ratio and in order to maintain the image of a workers' party, Kadar, addressing the Tenth Congress, announced satisfaction with the MSZMP's social composition and declared that, according to their original occupations, some 70 percent of the members may be considered as workers.

Some party spokesmen have sought to emphasize that the MSZMP is the party of the working class not because its membership consists exclusively of workers but because it represents the interests of the workers. At the Tenth Congress one MSZMP functionary charged that many of the party organizations failed to actively recruit workers. He pointed out that 20 percent of the basic party organizations had failed to admit even one new member during a period of several years. In addition, statistics indicate that, of the 19,200 persons whose party membership was terminated during the 1966–70 period, 12,000, or 63.8 percent, were manual workers, a fact that was interpreted by observers as an indication of a significant degree of alienation between the party and the manual workers.

At the time of the Ninth Congress in 1966 women accounted for 22.9 percent of the total membership. By November 1970 the proportion had risen slightly to 24.4 percent. Figures for the period from June 30, 1970, through June 30, 1971, indicate that women made up 33 percent of the new members admitted during that period. The proportion of women in the party remains far below the ratio of women to the total population as statistics show that females make up well over half of the country's population.

As adopted by the Tenth Congress, the MSZMP statutes require that, in addition to the age requirement, a person seeking membership in the party must request admission in writing and include with the application the recommendations of two members who have been in the party at least three years and who know the applicant on the basis of "mutual activity." Members of the youth federation who apply are required to present only one such reference in addition to the recommendation of their local unit of the youth organization.

Persons who desire to become members must agree to adhere to the principles of Marxism-Leninism, to accept the party's guidelines and organizational rules, to regularly participate in the work of one of the basic organizations, and to pay the membership dues. Once having entered the MSZMP, the member is expected to continually improve his own ideological education and work for the growth and unity of the party. The statutes call upon all members to set an example in their places of work, to consistently maintain the rules of party discipline, and to follow the laws and regulations of the state. The member is further enjoined to seek to strengthen the party's relationship to the masses and actively participate in the country's political and social life as a representative of the party.

Although a member may express a contrary view at membership meetings or before a higher party body, the rules specify that, once a decision is reached on a particular issue, the member is obligated to support it and assist in its implementation even though he may not be in agreement with the decision. All members may participate in party elections and, after completing three years' membership, be a candidate for party office. The statutes provide for the waiving of this time requirement in exceptional circumstances.

The intent to withdraw from the party must also be submitted in writing and must state the reasons for the person's decision to leave. The withdrawal application must be presented to the membership meeting, and a member may not leave the party as long as he is under disciplinary proceedings. The statutes provide for disciplinary action in the event that a member does not perform as prescribed by the party rules or fails to participate for three months in the work of his basic organization. Party punishment may consist of reprimand, censure, strict censure, strict censure with final warning, or expulsion.

The training and ideological indoctrination of party members is one of the primary duties of the party organizations on the county and local levels. Under the overall supervision of the Commission on Agitation and Propaganda, subcommittees of the county and local party units cooperate in conducting the indoctrination courses and in determining which members shall be enrolled in particular courses of study. In general, classes provided include the fundamentals of Marxism-Leninism, party history, socialist economics, and the MSZMP's stand on current domestic and international problems.

Members in training for higher level party positions are enrolled in the Central Political Academy, which operates in Budapest under the direction of the Central Committee. Elevated to university status in 1968, the academy presented its first diplomas to forty-six graduating students in November 1970. Before entering the academy, members must have a full secondary education, have completed a three year course in Marxism-Leninism, and have five years' experience in party, state, or mass organization activity.

In addition to the formal training programs provided expressly for party members, political indoctrination courses are also directed at all segments of the population. In November 1970 Kadar announced that during the 1969/70 academic year over 2 million persons had received regular Marxist-Leninist training. This figure included 630,000 persons who were involved in courses under the sponsorship of the trade unions and 550,000 who received training in connection with the youth federation.

In late 1972 the regime expressed the desire that greater emphasis be placed on strengthening the party politically and qualitatively rather than numerically. Party leaders called upon all members to manifest exemplary communist behavior and seek to become better informed on party policy and international issues. As for the recruitment of new members, party spokesmen indicated that the emphasis is to be directed toward "deserving workers, cooperative peasants, technical intelligentsia, and youth."

Mass Organizations

Because the MSZMP, as the country's sole political party, incorporates only about 6 percent of the population, it has fostered the creation of numerous mass organizations to enlist the participation of the people in the fulfillment of party programs and policies. For the great majority of citizens these organizations represent the only type of political activity open to them.

Two types of associations are included under the rubric of mass organization: those that are based on common categories of persons, such as the youth and women's federations, and those that are based on interests or occupation, such as the trade unions and the scientific societies. The organizations fill a dual role, providing, on the one hand, channels for the transmission of policy and doctrine from the party to the general population and, on the other hand, at least a limited expression of group interests.

According to the MSZMP statutes, the ideological and political direction of the mass organizations is accomplished through party members who are active participants in those bodies. MSZMP members, on whom party resolutions are binding, are responsible for the realization of party policy in the mass organizations as well as in their places of work and in any of the councils of government on which they may serve. Communists in the mass organizations join together in work groups to promote the accomplishment of party goals.

In describing the relationship of the party to the mass organizations, Kadar reminded the Tenth Congress that the mobilization of society did not take place automatically but demanded the constant attention of the party. He stated that for the achievement of its established objectives, the party "relies partly on the masses, partly on mass organizations, and finally on the institutional organs of our people's democratic state and in local work on the councils." In late 1972 the Central Committee called upon the leaders and members of all mass organizations to work more actively to implement party resolutions and to involve broader segments of the population in their activities.

The Patriotic People's Front

All of the mass organizations are brought together under the guiding influence of the MSZMP through their association in the Patriotic People's Front, which coordinates and supervises their activities. Before its reorganization in 1954 the front was known as the Hungarian Independent People's Front and included the remnants of the former noncommunist political parties. After the establishment of the single-party system, the Patriotic People's Front was set up to provide the illusion of democratic practice and to give the party a means of controlling and utilizing the mass organizations.

Although the front has no separate membership of its own, it has committees on the village and precinct levels whose members are elected at public meetings. Other front committees are organized on the county and municipal levels. The highest authority of the front is the congress, which meets every four years, and the National Council of the Patriotic People's Front, which is responsible for front activities in the intervals between congresses. The 227-member council functions under the direction of its presidium; both the council and the presidium are elected by the congress. In 1972 the front reported a total of 3,847 committees having 110,000 members.

One of the more important tasks assigned to the front is the organization of elections. It arranges meetings for the nomination of candidates, prepares the single list ballot, and mobilizes the voting-age population to participate (see ch. 8). Front committees also take part in the elaboration of local development plans and sponsor community meetings for the purpose of introducing and explaining party programs.

The Trade Unions

The largest of the mass organizations is the trade union association. Consisting of some twenty member unions organized on industrial lines, the National Council of Trade Unions (Szakszerveztek Országos Tanácsa—SZOT) claims more than 3.4 million members, or approximately 92 percent of all wage earners and salaried employees.

Included in the SZOT are trade unions for workers in agriculture and forestry; the chemical industry; civil service; clothing industry; commerce, finance, and catering; construction, woodworking, and building materials; food industry; iron and metal industry; leather industry; mining industry; municipal and local economy; health services, including physicians; postal services; printing, paper industry, and press; railways; textiles; and transport and communications. Also included are the Trade Union of Teachers and the Association of Artistic Trade Unions, which itself consists of nine specialized unions.

As is the case in the organization of the MSZMP, in principle the highest authoritative body of the trade union association is the national congress, which convenes every four years and consists of delegates chosen by the member unions. Between congresses the council is empowered to conduct all of the association's affairs. The council itself functions under the direction of its thirty-five-member presidium, headed by a president and three vice presidents. The chief executive officer of the council is the secretary general, who in 1972 was also a vice president of the Presidential Council and a member of the MSZMP

Politburo. The secretary general is assisted by a corps of six executive secretaries, three of whom also held ranking party posts in 1972.

Seven council committees, headed either by one of the executive secretaries or a member of the presidium, function under the overall direction of the secretary general: agitation and propaganda; economic; organization and cadre; social-political; sports; women; and youth. In addition, the SZOT organization includes the following departments and institutions: Accounting Department; Cultural, Agitation, Propaganda, and Sports Department; International Relations Department; Labor Safety Department; Organization and Cadre Department; Production Department; Recreation and Sanatorium Board; Social Insurance Board; SZOT Central School; and the Wage and Labor Department.

Traditionally, the Hungarian communist regime has employed the trade union organizations as instruments of party policy for controlling and mobilizing the members of the working classes. In the immediate post-1956 era, the efforts of the Kadar regime to consolidate its control over the country led to the further concentration of trade union affairs in the hands of the party. During the early 1960s, however, the discussion regarding economic reform led to a reevaluation of the role of the union organizations, and the regime began to gradually shift its trade union policy from one of coercion to one of control through persuasion. With the development of the New Economic Mechanism, the party called upon the unions to organize greater worker involvement in the affairs of the economic enterprises. A new Labor Code, adopted coincidentally with the introduction of the New Economic Mechanism in 1968, contained new powers and activities for the labor unions, including veto powers over enterprise managers in some cases. Collective agreements that regulate working conditions, wages, and other matters are negotiated between the union and the individual enterprise management within specified guidelines.

Kadar regime spokesmen, attributing the origin of the party's coercive trade union policies to the pre-1956 era, described the revised policy as being one of "guidance based on ideological and political persuasion and wider cooperation with nonparty trade union activists." In September 1967 the National Assembly enacted a new labor code into law. Although much of the code deals with establishing the general framework of worker-management relations, a specific statement is given on the role of the trade unions, describing them as the organs representing and protecting the interests of the workers. Significantly, the code omits the previously defined function of the unions, which was to increase production, organize competitive work programs, and assure the leading role of the party.

Since the introduction of the New Economic Mechanism and the accompanying increase in the independence of the managers of the industrial enterprises, observers have noted that the union's role in

162

representing and safeguarding the worker's interest has become increasingly prominent. In 1970, SZOT Secretary General Sandor Gaspar declared that, although in Hungary the general interests of the state, the workers, and the trade unions were identical, "there could be, and are, differences of interests and opinions on concrete questions." He also asserted that in some cases, where there is disagreement between the trade unions and the state offices, the unions should be allowed to publish their contrary opinions. "This," Gaspar declared, "will be a new feature in the work of the trade unions."

Later in 1970 Kadar announced that the earlier practice of making party resolutions binding on the trade unions as a whole was to be ended in favor of making them binding only on the communist members of the unions. Inasmuch as almost all the leading figures of the SZOT are also members of the party, observers predicted little change in the general party-trade union relationship. There was other evidence during the 1970-72 period that, although there were increased efforts by the unions to protect jobs from being eliminated and to assert workers' rights, the party intended to maintain its control over the trade unions. The top leaders of the SZOT continued to be named by the MSZMP, and the party's ideological and political direction continued to determine the primary role of the unions. In late 1972 the status of the SZOT reflected the policy that the goals of national economic development take precedence over individual and group interests.

The Communist Youth League

As the official youth organization of the MSZMP, the Communist Youth League (Kommunista Ifjusagi Szovetseg—KISZ) has as its primary tasks the communist education of the country's youth and the organization of their political activities. Functioning under the direct guidance of the MSZMP, the KISZ is the only legal youth organization and is the most important source of new members for the party.

Known before the 1956 uprising as the League of Working Youth, the organization was reconstituted as the KISZ in 1957 during the Kadar regime's drive for full political control. Structured along lines that parallel the organization of the party, it has a congress, a central committee, a secretariat, county committees, and local units known as basic organizations. Membership is open to young persons between the ages of fourteen and twenty-six and, in 1970, the KISZ consisted of just over 800,000 members in nearly 26,000 basic organizations.

An organization for children six to fourteen years of age, the Association of Hungarian Pioneers, functions under KISZ direction. Organized with units based in the schools, the association serves as an instrument for the indoctrination of children along ideological lines established by the party. Although up-to-date membership statistics for the pioneer movement were not available in early 1973, observers estimated that approximately two-thirds of the country's 1,160,000 primary school children participated in the association.

Although leaders of both the MSZMP and the KISZ continued to emphasize the positive, there was, in late 1972, growing evidence of dissatisfaction with the youth organization. KISZ membership included only about one-third of the young people of eligible age, and the trend has been that the number of new admissions, 140,000 to 150,000 annually, only slightly exceeds the number of dropouts. The number of party members in the KISZ had dropped sharply and accounted for only 3.5 percent of the league's total membership.

KISZ leaders attribute the slow growth of the organization to a "failure of our educational efforts"; however, observers suggested that the primary reasons lay in a broad disaffection of youth with the propaganda orientation of the KISZ. During the 1960s the growing political apathy on the part of the nation's youth was countered with increased propaganda efforts that often resulted in even greater apathy. A 1964 survey published in *Magyar Nemzet*, the organ of the Patriotic People's Front, indicated that the organization is generally ineffective in influencing young people, and another newspaper survey published in early 1972 revealed that only 29 percent of the country's recent college and university graduates considered the KISZ units suitable places for open political discussions. Another survey indicated that only about 14 percent of the youth actively espoused Marxist values.

In 1968 the party reported that almost 35 percent of the KISZ membership was over twenty years of age. Statistics indicate that among school youth the organization is weakest in the secondary schools but has a higher membership ratio in the universities. KISZ numerical strength among university students reflects, at least in part, a realistic assessment by the students that there are more career and advancement opportunities available to KISZ members than to nonmembers.

No information has been published concerning the effect on the KISZ of the lowering of the age requirement for MSZMP membership voted by the Tenth Congress, but during 1971 the party leadership continued to manifest concern for improving the youth organization. One attempt to bolster the status of the organization was the new youth law passed in 1971 that provides for the KISZ to function as the official representative of youth in state organs. At the Eighth Congress of the KISZ, convened in December 1971, a party spokesman urged the association to take the initiative to establish new local units and to win over nonmembers to KISZ goals.

Other Organizations

In addition to the trade unions and the youth federation, two of the more important mass organizations are the network of women's associations, headed by the National Council of Hungarian Women, and the Hungarian National Defense Association. Another of the mass organizations with some measure of importance is the party-inspired network of local "peace committees" directed countrywide by the National Peace Council.

The women's council and its member associations have the assigned task of developing the "public and social activity of women," working for their equal rights, and mobilizing them in the accomplishment of party goals. On the national level the organization is structured with nine working commissions: economic affairs, family protection, legal affairs, education, homemaking, agriculture, foreign relations, cultural matters, and aesthetics. Local units are constituted on a territorial basis that conforms with the country's administrative divisions.

In October 1971 the women's council sponsored the first National Women's Conference attended by 600 women, some representing local units of the organization and others representing various professions. The task of the conference was to discuss the place of women in contemporary Hungarian society and ways to improve their economic and social position. Observers reported that the conference leaders were surprisingly frank in their criticism of some of the government ministries, particularly those of education, health, and labor.

The conference delegates were made aware of MSZMP statistics indicating that, whereas over 44 percent of the country's wage earners are female, very few women hold leading positions in their places of employment. In the primary schools, for example, 80 percent of the teachers are female, but they make up only 13 percent of the primary school directors. Similar situations were shown to exist in a number of the industrial enterprises and in the organs of local government. The president of the women's council called for the extension of professional training for women as a means of beginning to remedy this situation.

All sports activities are under the guidance of the Hungarian Union for Physical Education and Sports, an association consisting of a large number of sports clubs formed in schools, factories, offices, cooperative farms, and the armed forces. There were in 1972 an estimated 500,000 sports club members.

The National Peace Council heads a network of local peace committees that function largely as propaganda agencies of the party in regard to international issues. Affiliated with the communist-created World Peace Council, the peace council also provides a Hungarian presence at international peace demonstrations.

POLITICAL VALUES AND ATTITUDES

The Regime and the People

Sixteen years after the Hungarian uprising the impact of the events of the revolution remains a basic fact of the country's political life. At the height of the 1956 rebellion support for change was evident among all segments of the society, and the forcible repression of the revolution, accompanied by the return to harsh coercive tactics, resulted in an intense alienation of the people from the regime. Once again political power was in the hands of a Soviet-established oligarchy whose instrument of control was the communist party.

The leaders of the MSZMP, in order to reestablish the authority of the party, sought to extend their control to all aspects of the country's political, social, and economic life and to dictate the acceptable ideology. Fully aware that it had been instituted without popular support, the regime resorted to strict limitations on individual freedoms and relied on coercion to attain its goals. As had been the case under the preceding communist regimes, all expression of independent political thought was thoroughly circumscribed.

Powerless to change their circumstances, the people began to accommodate to the realities of their political situation; however, it was only after the regime began to moderate its policies in the early 1960s—a moderation that was initiated only after the party's control had been fully established—that it began to find a measure of popular acceptance. Symbolic of the regime's attempt to gain the allegiance of the people by less oppressive means was Kadar's declaration that "who is not against us is with us," a statement that reversed the previous attitude that those who were not actively in support of the party were its enemies.

After arriving at the policy that, as long as the leading position of the party is maintained, the preferable method of control would be persuasion rather than coercion, the party also became able to tolerate a limited amount of dissent. As in the attempt to restore the image of the MSZMP, the party's approach to the country's economic problems took on a tone of pragmatism. One observer described the regime's changes in the economic system, particularly the introduction of the New Economic Mechanism, as an abandonment of "ideological purity for the sake of economic expediency." Although the question of just how much dissent and individual initiative to allow poses a dilemma, in late 1972 a prominent characteristic of the Kadar regime was one of confidence, resulting from stability of leadership, continuity of policy, and the ability to chart a reasonably autonomous course in domestic affairs.

Popular Attitudes

Since the Ninth Party Congress in 1966, the Kadar regime has sought to emphasize that the construction of socialism is not a task of the party alone and has sought increasingly to involve the whole population. To this end, the primary propaganda efforts of the party and the mass organizations have been directed at implanting a "socialist consciousness" in the people. This, however, has been one of the party's major shortcomings. Despite the progress in improving the domestic political atmosphere, the regime has not accomplished its desired ideological conversion of the masses.

Although the regime's modified tactics and the country's substantial economic progress, including an increase in some consumer goods and a measure of improvement in the standard of living, have resulted in a significant degree of change in its public image, questions remain as to the depth of its popular support. Lacking any plausible alternatives, the prevailing popular attitude is to accept the Kadar regime as the best government that can be expected. In the eyes of the people, one of the main virtues of the regime is its stability. As long as there is hope for continued gradual economic and social improvement, any sudden changes in the top leadership and the accompanying uncertainty that would result are considered undesirable.

There is some evidence, however, of popular discontent with various aspects of official policy, and during the 1970–72 period there were indications that interest groups as well as individuals were becoming more assertive. One of the primary concerns most frequently voiced focuses on wages and prices; for example, people complained openly when the national economic plan for 1972 stipulated a 3-percent average price increase rather than the 1 to 2 percent of previous years. The seeds of discontent are also found in the growing disparity of incomes between workers in different sectors of the economy and between workers and management. In seeking to remedy the situation, in November 1972 the party acted to raise the lowest incomes by 8 percent and to increase others by 4 and 5 percent. To cover the raises, however, a number of price increases were put into effect, particularly prices on luxury items. Observers consider the price problem as the major challenge to the New Economic Mechanism.

Other criticism has been directed at administrative inefficiency in handling the everyday affairs of citizens. This lack of efficiency is said to result, at least in part, from the longstanding practice of awarding government positions on the basis of party loyalty rather than professional competence. Another source of inefficiency is the hesitancy of lower level officials to make decisions, preferring to take no action or to pass even routine matters on to higher officials rather than take the responsibility for decisionmaking themselves. One result of this lack of efficiency is a popular contempt for bureaucrats.

Discontent, however, does not necessarily indicate opposition to the socialist system. The majority appear resigned to the continued development of the country along socialist lines but prefer that it be in the context of increased freedoms and improvement in the living standards. Although most people are no longer hostile to the regime, only a minority are thoroughly committed to it; and in seeking to mobilize the population for the fulfillment of its socialist programs and policies, one of the greatest barriers that the party encounters is that of political apathy.

On the whole, the population tends to be skeptical of political programs and the propaganda that invariably accompanies them. In general, the values held by the population are essentially nonideological and individualistic, and the most evident commitments are to personal goals that focus on material demands. Party spokesmen have condemned such values as leading to so-called petit bourgeois tendencies (see ch. 4).

Another barrier the regime has encountered is nationalism, an attitude that one observer describes as "the strongest integrative and anticommunist force in Hungary." Confronted with this nationalistic sentiment, the regime has attempted to use it as a means of gaining popular support while, at the same time, being careful to avoid encouraging a nationalism that might be interpreted as anti-Soviet. In so doing, Kadar has attempted to identify his regime with patriotism but has sought to draw a distinction between national patriotic pride, which he considers desirable, and nationalism, which he considers dangerous to the socialist commonwealth.

CHAPTER 10

FOREIGN RELATIONS

According to official government and party statements, the foreign policy of Hungary is directed at the development of friendly and mutually advantageous relations with all states and is based on the concept of peaceful coexistence between countries of different economic systems. Throughout the period of communist control of the country, Hungarian foreign policy has mirrored that of the Soviet Union; Hungary has consistently supported the Soviet position on all important international issues.

The country's foreign policy is formulated in the Political Bureau (Politburo) of the Hungarian Socialist Workers' Party (MSZMP—see Glossary) and administered through the government ministries of foreign affairs and foreign trade. All policy decisions, however, take full account of the position of the Soviet Union. MSZMP spokesmen have repeatedly affirmed Hungary's commitment to the international communist movement and to the solidarity of all socialist states. Hungarian party leaders look upon the Communist Party of the Soviet Union as the center and guiding force of international communism.

Because of Hungary's strong political and economic ties to the Soviet Union, the direction and content of the country's foreign relations have been largely determined by outside political considerations. The growing détente among the superpowers, however, and its accompanying relaxation of political tensions in Europe have allowed Hungary a limited degree of initiative in seeking expanded relations with noncommunist states, although primary emphasis continued to be placed on dealings with other communist states.

In early 1973 Hungary maintained full diplomatic relations with more than eighty governments, sixty-five of which maintained embassies in Budapest. In addition, trade and cultural relations were conducted with a number of other states with which formal relations had not been established. Hungary is a member of the United Nations (UN) and several of the UN specialized agencies. It is also a member of the communist military alliance known as the Warsaw Treaty Organization (Warsaw Pact) and the communist economic alliance called the Council for Mutual Economic Assistance (COMECON).

During the 1970-72 period the regime made a concerted effort to cultivate relations with the developing states of Asia and Africa and with the nations of Latin America. During this same period relations also improved significantly with the states of Western Europe and with the United States.

HISTORICAL FACTORS

The terms of the armistice that ended Hungary's participation in World War II placed the country under the administration of the Allied Control Commission and made it a part of the Soviet area of military occupation. The Soviets effectively employed their chairmanship of the control commission to extend their control over the country and to strengthen the position of the Hungarian Communists.

The peace treaty, signed in Paris in February 1947, fixed Hungarian war reparations to the Soviet Union at US$200 million, and an additional US$50 million each was designated for Czechoslovakia and Yugoslavia. Hungary was also forced to return territories to Czechoslovakia and Romania—in effect, to reestablish the post-World War I borders (see ch. 3). As was the case with the other Axis powers, the treaty also prohibited Hungary from experimenting with or possessing atomic weapons, from manufacturing or possessing guided missiles, and from possessing long-range artillery pieces. In addition, strict limits were placed on the size of Hungarian military forces.

The economic reparations to the Soviet Union proved a severe strain on Hungary. Payments consisted of industrial and transportation equipment, grain, and livestock, the value of which was determined by the Soviets in a manner that significantly increased the prescribed amount of the reparations. In 1946 so-called Soviet-Hungarian joint stock companies were formed that effectively gave the Soviet Union control of Hungary's aviation, river transportation, and petroleum and bauxite industries.

By the end of 1948 Hungary had become a full-fledged Soviet satellite, and the country's foreign and domestic policies were fully subordinated to the policies of the Communist Party of the Soviet Union. The regime of Hungarian party chief Matyas Rakosi was closely patterned upon that of Soviet Premier Joseph Stalin, and Hungarian support of the international policies of the Soviet Union was automatic (see ch. 2).

In early 1948 the twenty-year Treaty of Friendship, Cooperation, and Mutual Assistance was concluded with the Soviet Union. This treaty was followed by similar accords with Poland, Bulgaria, Romania, and Czechoslovakia during 1948 and, in 1950, with the German Democratic Republic (East Germany). In 1949 Hungary became a member of COMECON, the Soviet-sponsored economic pact. Relations with Yugoslavia, however, differed from those with the other communist states of Eastern Europe. The Soviet-Yugoslav dispute in 1948 set the tone for Hungary's relations with that country and led the Rakosi regime to unilaterally terminate a 1947 trade agreement and to halt Hungary's reparations payments to Yugoslavia. The intensity of the Hungarian regime's anti-Yugoslav campaign, which included a series of contrived border incidents, made for openly hostile relations between the two states.

Hungary's relations with the United States also deteriorated during the 1948-53 period. The Rakosi regime lodged espionage charges against several members of the United States diplomatic corps, seized the property of United States citizens, and demanded ransom for the release of United States aviators who were brought down over Hungarian territory in 1951. In retaliation for these acts, the United States government closed the Hungarian consulates in the cities of New York and Cleveland.

After the death of Stalin in March 1953, Hungary followed the lead of the new Soviet leaders in instituting a measure of détente. The new Soviet policy included a reduction of tension in relations with the Western powers, the increased development of relations with the nonaligned states of Asia and Africa, and reconciliation with Yugoslavia.

Internal changes within Hungary, including a decline in the power of Rakosi, enabled improved relations with the Yugoslavs. In August 1953 the two governments signed an agreement to restore diplomatic relations on the legation level, and subsequent accords were reached on the matter of reparations payments. As evidence of the new level of relations, reciprocal visits were made by delegations of the communist parties of both states. Moderating influences in Hungary also led to friendly overtures toward noncommunist countries. Diplomatic relations were established with Indonesia, Sudan, and Burma; trade agreements were concluded with Turkey, Japan, Iran, India, and Egypt; and talks were opened with Austria concerning confiscated Austrian assets in Hungary.

Internal developments in Hungary led to civil unrest in October 1956, and this unrest rapidly evolved into a full-scale uprising that was anti-Soviet and anticommunist in content (see ch. 2). In the midst of the uprising, on learning that large numbers of Soviet troops were being moved into the country, Premier Imre Nagy announced Hungary's withdrawal from the Warsaw Pact, and the Council of Ministers declared Hungary a neutral nation. Two days later, however, Soviet military forces intervened to thoroughly crush the uprising and install a new government headed by Janos Kadar.

The Kadar regime quickly returned Hungary to a position of full compliance with the policies of the Soviet Union. In May 1957 the two governments signed an accord legalizing the continued stationing of Soviet troops in Hungary, and Hungary renewed its close ties to the other satellite states. Relations with Yugoslavia again followed the lead of the Soviet Union. Yugoslav condemnation of the Soviet intervention resulted in an accusation that the government of Josip Broz Tito was guilty of complicity in the uprising; relations remained bitter throughout 1957, and the execution of Imre Nagy in June 1958 brought

Hungarian-Yugoslav relations to a new low.

In general, throughout the remainder of the 1950s, Hungarian relations with noncommunist states depended upon the attitude of these countries toward the uprising and toward the legality of the Kadar regime. Beginning in the early 1960s, however, the regime increased its efforts to gain broader international acceptance and sought to improve relations with noncommunist states, but the Hungarian leaders showed no inclination to deviate from the international policies of the Soviet Union. By the beginning of the 1970s the Kadar regime could report a significant measure of success in reestablishing Hungary's position in international affairs and in developing a limited degree of foreign policy initiative.

PRINCIPLES OF FOREIGN POLICY

The Revised Constitution promulgated in April 1972 declares Hungary's willingness to cooperate with all people and countries of the world in the interests of peace and human progress. On the basis of this declaration, government and party spokesmen have described a basic principle of the country's international relations as that of peaceful coexistence between states of differing social and economic systems. In keeping with this principle, Hungarian leaders assert that the only qualifications placed on the development of relations with any foreign state is that recognition be given to the principles of noninterference in internal affairs and mutual observance of one another's national interests and that economic contacts be based on equality of rights and be beneficial to both sides.

Although such mutually beneficial and cooperative relations are desired with all nations, Hungarian policy places primary emphasis on relations with socialist states, and government leaders have declared that being a member of the socialist world is the most important single element of Hungarian foreign policy. Policy statements coming out of the Tenth Party Congress, held in December 1970, indicate that the MSZMP leaders continue to view the world as divided into two camps—one socialist, the other imperialist. In propaganda statements the world socialist system is held to be the decisive factor in international politics, and the principle of peaceful coexistence is said to be based upon the premise that war is not necessary to the ultimate triumph of socialism.

Party historians have described Hungary's post-World War II foreign policy as focusing on three sets of problems: redefining relations with the great powers; reestablishing harmonious relations with neighboring countries; and restoring the country's reputation as an advocate of peace and democracy. The communist takeover settled the foremost of these problems—the country's relationship to the major world powers—in favor of the Soviet Union. Throughout the period since 1948, the successive Hungarian regimes have considered full loyalty to the Soviet Union as a basic tenet of foreign policy.

To a large extent the second issue was also settled by the communization of Eastern Europe. Under the preponderant influence of the Soviet Union, the communist parties of these states achieved at least an outward display of unity and joined together in active forms of cooperation. The two primary multilateral instruments of cooperation with other socialist states are the economic alliance of COMECON and the military alliance of the Warsaw Pact. Relations with neighboring Austria developed more slowly and followed the pattern of Soviet policy toward that state. After the Soviets agreed to the conclusion of an Austrian peace treaty in 1955 and after Austria declared itself a neutral state later that same year, Hungarian-Austrian relations improved significantly.

In regard to the third set of problems—the reestablishing of the country's reputation and the increase of Hungarian influence in world affairs—the task has been more difficult. Much of the effort that had been expended toward these ends during the 1948-56 period was destroyed by the crushing of the 1956 uprising and the installation of the Kadar regime. The result of these events was widespread criticism of the action and charges that the Kadar government with both illegitimate and a betrayal of the aspirations of the Hungarian people. Two resolutions of the United Nations General Assembly condemned the Soviet Union's intervention and both the Soviet and Kadar regimes for consistently defying the attempts of the assembly to send a team of observers into the country to investigate the situation.

One direction the Kadar regime has followed in its efforts to gain acceptance has been the cultivation of political and economic relations with the developing countries. During the 1965-72 period numerous agreements were concluded with African, Asian, and Latin American nations, and the Tenth Party Congress declared continued Hungarian support for movements of national liberation and for states that have emerged from colonial status. Support was specifically declared for the so-called Provisional Government of the Republic of South Vietnam (Viet Cong), for the Arab states in their conflict with Israel, and for the independence movements in Portuguese colonial territories.

INTERNATIONAL TREATIES

Another important set of foreign policy determinants consists of international treaties. The Paris Peace Treaty that terminated the state of war existing between Hungary and the Allied powers was concluded in February 1947 and entered into force in September of that year. Because a number of the states included in the treaty had concluded bilateral agreements with Hungary before the war, these states were given a period of six months after the peace treaty became effective to decide which of the bilateral agreements would remain in force.

Few of the existing treaties were terminated, and some of those that

173

were maintained included extradition treaties with the United States and Great Britain and the copyright convention with the United States. Hungary's multilateral treaties also continued in force, including the Brussels agreement of 1890 on the suppression of slavery and the conventions adopted by the Hague peace conferences of 1899 and 1907 on the regulation of warfare.

Accords with communist states include both bilateral and multilateral treaties. Bilateral treaties of friendship, cooperation, and mutual assistance have been concluded with the Soviet Union, Poland, Bulgaria, Romania, Czechoslovakia, East Germany, and the People's Republic of China (PRC). In general, these treaties run for a period of twenty years and have automatic five-year extensions unless one party terminates the agreement in writing.

The multilateral Warsaw Pact was formed in May 1955 and included Albania, Bulgaria, Czechoslovakia, East Germany, Hungary, Poland, Romania, and the Soviet Union. Contracting states were bound to provide mutual military assistance for purposes of individual or collective self-defense, and units of the armed forces of each state were organized under a joint command. In theory the Warsaw Pact is open to other states irrespective of their political or social systems. Albania ceased its participation in the pact in 1961 and formally withdrew in 1968 as a gesture of protest against the invasion of Czechoslovakia by military forces of all the other pact states except Romania.

The other important multilateral accord binding Hungary to the Soviet Union and its allied communist states in Eastern Europe is that which forms the basis for COMECON (see ch. 12). Among the foremost objectives of the COMECON organization is the coordination of economic planning and the integration of production among the member states. Advocates of such COMECON cooperation assert that the member countries accept the forms of integration not out of compulsion but because it is in their interest to develop a socialist division of labor. According to Hungarian economists, one of the primary COMECON difficulties is the lack of a common socialist currency, a deficiency that results in excessive bilateral negotiations to settle accounts between members.

COMECON cooperation is designed to extend not only to economic planning, production specialization, and trade but also to the development of technology and scientific research. As one of the stronger advocates of COMECON integration, Hungary has been critical of nationalistic tendencies and protectionist policies among some of the member states. On this issue a Hungarian spokesman declared that national sovereignty must not become a basis for constant rivalry among the Danubian peoples but that each government must seek to promote understanding and cooperation.

A multilateral treaty important for Hungary's access to sea transportation is the 1948 convention on navigation of the Danube River, which superseded the post-World War I convention. Under the terms of the new convention, the riparian states undertake the obligation to maintain the river in a navigable state and to secure all the conditions necessary to expedite navigation. The convention established a permanent agency, the Danube Commission, which is headquartered in Budapest, to exercise supervision over river transport and draw up work plans for the maintenance of river channels and port development.

Another form of Hungary's interstate relations is that manifested in a broad series of bilateral cultural agreements. In addition to numerous such agreements with socialist states, during the 1960s a number of conventions were concluded with countries in Asia, Africa, Latin America, and Western Europe. In general, these agreements are valid for a period of five years and provide for the reciprocal establishment of cultural institutions in the territory of the signatories; the exchange of printed materials and films; and exchange visits of university personnel, students, and representatives of science, the arts, journalism, and broadcasting.

CONDUCT OF FOREIGN AFFAIRS

Policy Formulation

Exclusive jurisdiction over foreign policy is reserved to the central government and, constitutionally, this responsibility is lodged primarily in the Presidential Council and the Council of Ministers. The Revised Constitution, in authorizing both of these bodies to conclude and confirm international agreements, is not specific on the division of responsibilities between them. Other information, however, indicates that the Council of Ministers ordinarily initiates international agreements and that the Presidential Council, acting in its role as the collective head of state, provides the formal confirmation.

The Revised Constitution also assigns the National Assembly the powers of ratification of international agreements; however, the assembly never challenges or questions the recommendations of the Council of Ministers or the Presidential Council, and neither of these bodies acts without the prior consent of the senior organs of the MSZMP (see ch. 8). As is the case with important decisions of domestic policy, the major lines of foreign policy are formulated in the higher echelons of the party, where primary decisionmaking powers are concentrated in the Politburo. Although this body is the principal Hungarian authority for both domestic and foreign policy, its members give careful attention to the international policies of the Communist Party of the Soviet Union. Speaking to the Tenth Party Congress, Kadar affirmed the dependence on the Soviets and declared that the Hungarian "relationship to the Soviet Union is clear and unshakable, based on firm principles and internationalist foundations, and completely accords with our national interests."

Administration

Within the structure of the Council of Ministers, foreign relations are conducted primarily through the Ministry of Foreign Affairs and the Ministry of Foreign Trade. For the most part, these agencies function as the administrative agents for policy decisions emanating from the MSZMP. The party's Department of International Relations serves as an advisory body to the Politburo and functions in a watchdog capacity over the organs of the government in their conduct of foreign affairs.

A number of the government ministries also have departments responsible for international contacts within their areas of jurisdiction. International relations departments exist in the ministries of agriculture and food, culture, health, and light industry. The Ministry of Metallurgy and Machine Industry has a department of international cooperation, and the Ministry of Finance includes a department of international financial relations. Also functioning in the area of international affairs under the Council of Ministers is the Institute of Cultural Relations. This body, which is the central organ for the cooperation of Hungary's cultural relations with foreign countries, is organized in three principal geographic departments that are in turn subdivided into desk offices, each having responsibilities for specific states.

Responsibilities of the Ministry of Foreign Affairs include the overall direction, coordination, and implementation of the country's foreign policies and the protection of the nation's interests in international relations. In addition to Hungary's diplomatic relations with foreign states, the ministry also has general responsibility for cultural and scientific relations with other states and international organizations. Foreign economic relations are conducted through the Ministry of Foreign Trade (see ch. 12).

In early 1973 the Ministry of Foreign Affairs consisted of an extensive bureaucratic organization that functioned under the direction of the minister and five deputy ministers. The deputies directly supervise the work of the three ministry divisions responsible for state relations, as well as the Department for Consular Affairs, the Department of International Organizations, and the Diplomatic Service Bureau. The first deputy minister also directs the ministry's press department.

In September 1972 the Council of Ministers created the Hungarian Foreign Affairs Institute. Under the supervision of the minister of foreign affairs, the institute pursues research on general aspects of international relations, compiles and analyzes data important to Hungary for policy, and supplies the government with information to aid in decisionmaking. In the research program of the institute, emphasis is placed on relations between socialist states and "advanced capitalist countries." Rather than a historical study of past relations between states, the goal of the institute is to draw up a prognosis on the possible trends of international developments and evaluate Hungary's role in the future of Europe.

Foreign Policy Issues

A primary concern of the Kadar regime has been to gain international recognition of its legitimacy. After the 1956 Hungarian uprising, many states looked upon Kadar and his government as puppets and a mere facade for Soviet control. In the years after 1956, and particularly during the 1960s, the Kadar regime made extensive efforts to establish its credibility as the legitimate government of the Hungarian nation and to regain the country's lost stature in international affairs.

Closely related to this drive to improve the country's international position has been the status of the large numbers of Hungarians living abroad. In addition to the Hungarian minorities living in countries bordering on Hungary, the total number of Hungarians resident abroad in 1970 was estimated at 1.5 million. Of these, some 700,000 were in the United States; an estimated 140,000, in Canada; and the rest, primarily in Austria, Sweden, and the Federal Republic of Germany (West Germany).

To bring about a rapprochement with these Hungarians living abroad, the regime encouraged the formation of the World Association of Hungarians. As a result of the work of this body, which set up its own travel bureau and information office, nearly 100,000 of the expatriates visited Hungary in 1970. Emphasis was placed on 1970 as the millennium of the birth of Saint Stephen and as the twenty-fifth anniversary of the liberation of the country from Nazi occupation. In addition to the festivities held in Hungary, the world association also organized celebrations in other countries.

The official position of the communist regime is that those who left Hungary for either political or economic reasons were mistaken and that they will come to recognize their errors as they become aware of the faults of capitalist societies. In encouraging the policy of rapprochement, major emphasis is given to the Hungarian language as the most important tie binding the Hungarians living abroad to Hungary and its culture. Observers consider the rapprochement program to be a carefully calculated policy aimed at creating permanent ties with Hungarians living abroad.

Other policy issues focus on economic relations between the member states of COMECON and on relations with the two German states. Hungary has followed the Soviet lead in seeking a rapprochement with West Germany; a primary reason for the development of relations with the Bonn government is the desire for expanded trade and other economic ties.

Issues growing out of COMECON relations focus primarily on Hungary's desire for increased economic integration among the member states. In 1970 Hungary made a series of proposals for the reorganization of COMECON in order to facilitate direct relations between enterprises of the member states and to expedite the integration of COMECON markets (see ch. 12).

The development of stronger relations with several Western nations, including the United States, was hindered throughout much of the post-World War II period because of the failure to reach agreement on matters of indemnities for confiscated properties. During the 1970–72 period, however, negotiators reached a number of indemnities agreements that paved the way for improved relations.

INTERNATIONAL RELATIONS

As of early 1973 Hungary maintained diplomatic relations with eighty-four countries and the Viet Cong. Of this total, sixty-five governments and the Viet Cong maintained embassies or legations in Budapest; seven others conducted relations through their embassies in Moscow; six, through their embassies in Prague; five, through their embassies in Belgrade; and one, through its embassy in Rome. Trade relations were conducted with a number of other states even though no formal diplomatic ties existed.

Relations with Communist States

The Soviet Union

Except for the brief period of the 1956 uprising, the successive Hungarian communist regimes have been closely allied with the Soviet Union. The Kadar regime has proved to be no exception, particularly as it owes its rise to power to Soviet armed force. For geographic, economic, political, and military reasons, Kadar actively supports the Soviets in all matters of international relations.

In the Sino-Soviet dispute, from the beginning Hungary clearly sided with the official Soviet attitude. At the same time, however, Kadar sought to encourage a compromise between the two communist powers and requested both sides not to air the dispute openly in the press where it might be "read and seen by all our enemies." Whereas the Romanian Communists sought to exploit the dispute to gain a greater measure of autonomy for their country, Kadar faithfully followed the Soviet line.

In response to the Hungarian support, the Soviets took the initiative in signing a new twenty-year treaty of friendship, cooperation, and mutual assistance with Hungary in September 1967, fully five months before the existing treaty was to expire. On the occasion of the signing, Leonid Brezhnev, the Soviet Union's Communist Party chief, hailed Kadar as "a true patriot of his country, consistent internationalist, and prominent leader of the world communist movement." In turn, Kadar proclaimed the complete identity of views between the two countries on every basic international issue. High-level party delegations exchanged visits and affirmed the "complete unanimity" of views. In 1968 Hungarian troops participated in the Soviet-led invasion of

Czechoslovakia by forces of the Warsaw Pact.

In its efforts to reestablish its leadership of the international communist movement, in 1966 the Communist Party of the Soviet Union proposed a communist summit meeting. The Kadar regime moved quickly to support the proposal and took an active part in the conference when it was held in Moscow in June 1969. The major ruling communist parties of five countries, however—the PRC, the Democratic People's Republic of Korea (North Korea), the Democratic Republic of Vietnam (North Vietnam), Yugoslavia, and Albania—representing over 21 million of the world's 46 million communist party members, boycotted the conference.

The MSZMP signed the main conference document, a 15,000-word statement entitled, "Tasks at the Present Stage of the Struggle Against Imperialism and United Action of the Communist and Worker's Parties and All Anti-imperialist Forces." The document called for support of the communist forces in Vietnam, aid to movements of national liberation, the prevention of the spread of nuclear weapons, and the enforcement of the Non-Proliferation Treaty. In addition, the statement called for a European security conference designed to secure the inviolability of Europe's existing frontiers. Support was also declared for East Germany in negotiations with West Germany and for the Arab states in their conflict with Israel.

After the conclusion of the conference, the Kadar regime continued to support the leading position of the Soviet Union in the communist world and to identify Hungary with the Soviet stance on major world problems. In early 1972, however, some observers believed that they had detected indications of disagreements between Moscow and Budapest. At the center of these disagreements was thought to be Soviet concern over Hungary's domestic reforms.

Observers noted an unusual increase in the number of high-level visits between the two capitals and interpreted these visits as manifestations of Hungarian-Soviet differences. Later evidence served to substantiate that there were well-defined differences over economic relations between the two states, stemming primarily from Soviet reluctance to satisfy certain Hungarian import needs. A report by Hungarian Premier Jeno Fock indicated that one of the problems lay in the failure of the Soviets to agree to raw material deliveries necessary to improve the structure of Hungarian industry (see ch. 14).

In late 1972, however, Brezhnev visited Hungary, and the official communique released at the conclusion of his visit gave strong support to Hungary's economic reforms and asserted that the Hungarian economy "provides a firm basis for meeting the material and mental demands of the working people." In speaking to a group of factory workers, Brezhnev declared that within the larger framework of unity and common goals there was room for diversity in the approach to problem-solving by socialist states. Before concluding his visit,

Brezhnev awarded Kadar the Order of Lenin.

Other Communist States

Relations with the other communist states of Eastern Europe derive in general from the country's relations with the Soviet Union and are governed by the Warsaw Pact, COMECON, and a series of bilateral agreements. Relations with Yugoslavia and Romania have been less consistent than has been the case with East Germany, Poland, Bulgaria, and Czechoslovakia. Hungarian-Yugoslav relations have followed the pattern of relations of the Soviet Union with the Tito regime, and policies toward Romania have also matched policies of the Soviet Union. Relations with Albania have fluctuated from cool to openly hostile, paralleling developments in the Sino-Soviet dispute in which the Albanian regime sided strongly with the PRC.

To a significant degree, Hungarian relations with the other communist states of Eastern Europe were determined by developments that followed the 1968 invasion of Czechoslovakia. According to observers, the Hungarians had been reluctant to take part in the invasion but did so under pressure. An estimated 15,000 Hungarian troops participated in the Warsaw Pact action.

After the invasion the Kadar regime avoided comment on the Czechoslovak situation as much as possible, but it gradually came to echo Soviet criticism directed at Czechoslovakia's leadership. After Gustav Husak replaced Alexander Dubcek as head of the Czechoslovak communist party, relations between the two states showed a marked improvement; the new Czechoslovak leaders, seeking to benefit from the experience of the MSZMP in dealing with problems that followed the 1956 Hungarian uprising, initiated a number of contacts with the Kadar regime.

In the aftermath of the Czechoslovak crisis, Romania, the only Warsaw Pact state that did not take part in the invasion, was highly critical of the action, and Hungarian-Romanian relations since that time have been cool. At the same time, however, the two governments have indicated a continuing willingness to carry on business as usual in spheres unrelated to the points of contention. The two states differ on the proper role of the Soviet Union in the socialist community, and when Romania initiated closer ties with the PRC, Hungarian party leaders criticized the action.

By the end of November 1971 relations had improved to the extent that both governments agreed to renew their treaty of friendship, cooperation, and mutual assistance. Although the original treaty had expired in 1968 the treaty continued in force under its automatic five-year extension clause. Observers of East European politics point out that the Hungarian-Romanian treaty differs in several ways from other such agreements between Warsaw Pact states. One of the most notable differences is the omission of the statement affirming that the contracting parties "will act according to a common standpoint established in accordance with their mutual interests." In lieu of this statement, the Romanian-Hungarian treaty simply asserts that the two states will "inform and consult each other" about the development of cooperation between them and about international topics of mutual concern.

Another significant departure from the usual pattern of friendship treaties between communist states is that the Hungarian-Romanian treaty was signed only by the premiers of the two governments and not by the party leaders as well. Some observers concluded that the failure of Kadar and Romanian party chief Ceausescu to add their signatures was indicative of continuing interparty differences.

Despite these differences, however, spokesmen for both states emphasized the cooperation and good relations between the two countries. Ceausescu stated that different points of view should not be an obstacle to improved relations. Similar statements by Kadar indicate the evolution of a Hungarian policy of restraint in dealing with disagreements within the international communist movement.

Relations with Yugoslavia have also reflected Soviet-Yugoslav relations. After Yugoslav President Tito strongly condemned the invasion of Czechoslovakia, Warsaw Pact military maneuvers were held along the Romanian border; and several Soviet divisions were sent into Bulgaria, an action that raised concern in both Romania and Yugoslavia that they might be the targets for further military action. After the crisis passed, relations remained strained and only began to improve significantly in 1970.

Both Hungary and Yugoslavia indicated a willingness to improve relations during the 1970–72 period and trade contacts increased significantly. Given the Hungarian regime's dependence on the Soviet Union and the Yugoslav regime's determination to develop its own course in international affairs, the political debate is most likely to continue while economic relations are developed outside the context of the polemics.

Relations with East Germany have generally focused on Hungarian support for East Germany's drive to gain international acceptance as a second German state and on economic relations. In May 1967 the two states concluded their first twenty-year treaty of friendship, cooperation, and mutual assistance. After signing the treaty, the two governments began a program under which Hungarian workers took jobs in East German industries.

In 1970 the Ministry of Labor reported that some 15,000 Hungarian workers were employed in 180 East German industrial enterprises. Although officials of both states praised the program, a number of problems were reported by nongovernmental sources—among them the workers' lack of necessary skills, the language barrier, and the workers' dissatisfaction with their living conditions in East Germany.

Relations with Noncommunist States

Throughout the post-World War II period, relations with the states of Western Europe have been determined by the Soviet position on the major issues of East-West relations. The growing détente between the superpowers, however, and the 1970 accord between the Soviet Union and West Germany allowed a measure of improvement in Hungary's political relations with Western Europe, and the Kadar regime made a concerted effort to expand and cultivate these relations.

A primary concern of the Hungarian leaders was the problem of European security, and Hungary has actively supported the proposal for a conference of European states to deal with this issue. In January 1967 Hungary was a cosponsor of a proposal to put this question on the agenda of the United Nations General Assembly. In the view of the Hungarian party and government leaders, a settlement of the German question was the central problem of international security in Europe, and Kadar declared that, without an acceptable settlement of this matter, "European security is inconceivable."

Despite problems in the development of political relations, during the late 1960s trade relations with Western Europe increased significantly, and West Germany became Hungary's largest Western trading partner. In October 1970 the two states concluded their first long-term trade agreement. After the signing MSZMP spokesmen outlined the framework of Hungarian policy, stating that, whereas before 1970 political circumstances in West Germany had made relations difficult, there was new hope for continuing improvement and, despite a number of unresolved differences between the two states, the outlook for better relations was highly favorable. At the same time, however, party leaders declared continued support for the recognition of East Germany.

In early 1971 a major problem between West Germany and Hungary was settled when representatives of the two states completed negotiations on an agreement for indemnities to Hungarian victims of Nazism. Under terms of the agreement, Hungarians who were the objects of Nazi medical experiments were to receive direct individual settlements, and a lump sum was to be paid to settle all other claims.

High-level contacts continued throughout 1971, and in mid-1972 the MSZMP spokesman for international affairs declared that "at the appropriate moment" diplomatic relations could be resumed. A precondition of this resumption, however, was the normalization of relations between West Germany and East Germany. Discussions on the establishment of relations reportedly were intensified later in the year after direct talks were initiated between the two German governments.

Relations with other states of Western Europe also improved during the 1970-72 period. In late 1971 it was announced that a consortium of seventeen banking institutions for six countries, some from outside Europe, had concluded a US$50 million loan to Hungary. Economics experts explained that the willingness of the banks to make the loan was based on Hungary's good record in repaying past loans on schedule, its willingness to redeem a part of its prewar debts, and the success of its domestic economic reforms.

Although bilateral relations with West European states continued to show improvement, in mid-1972 a number of prominent Hungarian officials expressed disappointment over the trade policies of the European Economic Community (EEC, known as the Common Market). These officials declared that the EEC had established a broad system of preferential agreements among its members that were damaging to the interests of other countries. Inasmuch as the EEC serves as the main market for a number of Hungarian agricultural products, the officials declared that Hungary considered these agreements as discriminatory and expressed concern that the development of political relations might be adversely affected.

The United States

Hungarian leaders have manifested interest in strengthening relations with the United States. After the 1956 crisis and the installation of the Kadar governments, Hungarian-United States relations were reduced to the chargé d'affaires level. Legations were again raised to embassy status in 1966. Throughout the 1964-68 period, there was an increasing number of high-level contacts, and in August 1969 negotiations led to a settlement of several outstanding issues. Another major impediment to the development of closer relations—the question of war damages and indemnity for nationalized American property was settled in early 1973.

In July 1972 United States Secretary of State William P. Rogers paid an official visit to Hungary, marking the first time a United States cabinet member had been received by the Kadar regime. On the occasion of this visit, a consular convention was signed, and an agreement for scientific and technical cooperation was concluded between the Hungarian Institute for Cultural Relations and the United States National Science Foundation. Secretary of State Rogers assured the Hungarian leaders of United States interest in participating in the proposed Conference on Security and Cooperation in Europe, and the two governments also agreed to explore the possibility of drafting an agreement on cultural and scientific exchanges.

After the Rogers visit, negotiations were renewed concerning the claims of United States citizens for property seized after the Communists took power in 1948. The United States had conditioned the approval of Hungary's request for most-favored-nation trade status on an acceptable settlement of these claims. The negotiations led to a preliminary agreement on the issue in October 1972; formal ratification of the agreement was anticipated early in 1973.

Official Hungarian attitudes toward the problems of Vietnam and the Middle East fully accord with the policies adopted by the Soviet Union. The United States action in Vietnam was officially labeled as aggression, and Hungary pledged to provide continuing aid to North Vietnam and the Viet Cong. Under the terms of an agreement concluded in 1967, Hungary provides North Vietnam aid in the form of industrial machines, agricultural equipment, and some consumer goods. The communist Viet Cong government is officially recognized by Hungary as the legitimate government of South Vietnam and maintains an embassy in Budapest. When a cease-fire was signed in January 1973, Hungary was one of four states that pledged troops for the purpose of truce supervision.

In regard to the Middle East conflict, the Kadar regime quickly responded to the Soviet lead and condemned Israel as the aggressor after the outbreak of the Arab-Israeli war in 1967. Along with the Soviet Union and several other Warsaw Pact states, Hungary broke diplomatic relations with Israel and joined in a pledge of political and economic support to the Arab states.

Relations with the developing countries of Asia, Africa, and Latin America have focused primarily on the development of economic ties. Regular trade relations are maintained with about thirty of these states and account for about 7 percent of Hungary's total foreign trade. Of these thirty states, twelve can be considered the most important, accounting for about 75 percent of the country's trade with the developing countries. These are: Argentina and Brazil; Egypt, Libya, and Nigeria; Iran, Iraq, Kuwait, Lebanon, and Syria; and India and Pakistan.

Hungary has also actively sought to increase trade relations with Algeria, Morocco, Sudan, and Tunisia; and with Bolivia, Colombia, Ecuador, Peru, and Venezuela. According to observers, Hungary has experienced problems with currency convertibility in its trade relations with some of the developing states; however, despite difficulties, a number of agreements were concluded during the 1969–72 period. Examples of these agreements are a joint pharmaceutical enterprise with Nigeria; a cooperation agreement for the manufacture of electric bulbs in Ceylon; a joint cheese factory in Lebanon; and a series of ten cooperative agreements with India, the most important of which are joint enterprises in the aluminum and vehicle manufacturing industries.

In addition to Cuba, in Latin America Hungary maintains full diplomatic relations with Argentina, Bolivia, Brazil, Chile, Ecuador, Peru, Uruguay, and Venezuela. Special attention has been given to the cultivation of relations with Brazil because of the large number of people of Hungarian descent—an estimated 150,000—residing in that country. On the whole, Hungary experiences an unfavorable balance of trade with all of these countries, purchasing goods worth seven times more than it sells. Since the administration of Salvador Allende came to power in Chile, economic relations with that state have expanded considerably.

PARTICIPATION IN INTERNATIONAL ORGANIZATIONS

Although Hungary began participating as an observer in the work of several of the UN specialized agencies during the early 1950s, it did not obtain membership in the UN until 1955. At the beginning of 1973 Hungary also held membership in the following UN specialized agencies: The United Nations Educational, Scientific and Cultural Organization (UNESCO); the World Health Organization (WHO); the International Labor Organization (ILO); the International Atomic Energy Agency (IAEA); and the United Nations Industrial Development Organization (UNIDO). It also participates in the work of the United Nations Conference on Trade and Development (UNCTAD) and has applied for membership in the General Agreement on Tariffs and Trade (GATT).

The two major communist organizations to which the country belongs are COMECON and the Warsaw Pact. COMECON was organized by the Soviet Union in 1949 as the communist counterpart to the Marshall Plan, and its original intent was to be a division of labor among the member countries under the guidance of Soviet economic planners. Hungary, although having no raw materials resources, was assigned an industrial role, as was Czechoslovakia, whereas Romania and Bulgaria were to concentrate on agricultural development. Poland was to have a combination of industry and agriculture. In view of COMECON's benefits for industrial development, Hungary has been one of the most ardent supporters of the economic integration of the member states.

In 1955 the Soviet Union sponsored the creation of the Warsaw Pact as a twenty-year mutual defense organization. The pact has served as an instrument of Soviet foreign policy and has been employed by the Soviets to maintain hegemony in Eastern Europe and to provide the legal basis for the presence of Soviet troops in the territory of some of the participating states.

In addition to its membership in COMECON and the Warsaw Pact, Hungary also participates in a large number of international communist-front organizations. Among the more important of these are the World Federation of Trade Unions and the World Federation of Democratic Youth. The MSZMP also actively maintains party-to-party relations with many nonruling communist and workers' parties that participate in the international communist movement.

CHAPTER 11

MASS COMMUNICATIONS

Mass communications are almost exclusively in the hands of the government. The press is still the principal medium—as it was before the communist takeover—although radio and a rapidly developing television network are gaining importance as sources of information as well as entertainment. Publishing, libraries, and films are also seen by the government as instruments of the mass communications network and are under overall state supervision. Informal means of communicating with the masses have been developed to a large degree under the regime and, despite their more limited audiences, are viewed by the government as a vital link in the communications chain.

The Revolution of 1956 had a great impact on the government and, in turn, on the mass media. A member of the Political Bureau (Politburo) wrote in 1970 that the party would "never forget the lessons of 1956." Party leader Janos Kadar himself refers to the revolution as "those dark days." The overall effect on the regime's attitude toward the masses and the mass media, however, was paradoxical. On the one hand the government recognized that its continuation in power depended on public support to a greater extent than previously calculated. This in turn signified that more freedom of expression was required as an outlet for the public. On the other hand the revolution inspired in Kadar and his regime a greater awareness of the desires of the people. If these desires were not fulfilled, the leadership feared that the people would seek to destroy the party and even the Hungarian People's Republic itself. This feeling, combined with an implicit faith in the party and the leadership of the Soviet Union, led Kadar and his regime to seek greater control over, and identity with, the people; the use of mass communications was one means toward that end.

Given this paradox, the government has manifested in recent years an ambivalent attitude toward mass communications. Generally, however, a certain moderation and relative freedom in overall policy has prevailed. The attitude of the regime and Kadar in particular since 1956 has been characterized by three predominant traits. The first trait is a degree of tolerance, manifested in the 1962 decision by the Eighth Congress of the Hungarian Socialist Workers' Party (MSZMP—see Glossary) to allow the free expression of criticism at local party meetings. The second trait is a general hesitation to run against the strong nationalistic sentiment of the country, despite the regime's deeply rooted belief that national patriotism should be expressed only within the framework of communist internationalism. Kadar has attempted to fill the Soviet-oriented government with Hungarian substance or content or, as one writer expressed it, "to fill the imported hive with Hungarian honey." The third trait is the avoidance of cant and dogmatic ideology unless provoked by particular circumstances. Kadar appears to believe that polemics do not successfully convert people to the socialist credo and that a certain amount of free exchange of opinions is healthy.

A more liberal policy toward the people and the media does not signify the absence of governmental supervision and control. The mass media, particularly the press, are still viewed as effective means of articulating governmental views and decisions to the people. Propaganda is still a vital concern to the party and the government, which oversee all mass communications. Propaganda tends to be all-pervasive in the sense that, once the government has adopted a particular position, the decision is generally reflected universally—principally in the press, radio, and television—so that the public is subjected to the party line on many fronts. The greatest latitude in terms of governmental control is granted to the media that are perceived to have less widespread and less direct political impact—publishing houses, libraries, and the film industry—whereas more stringent control is maintained over the media that have both tremendous and direct impact—the press, radio, and television.

The press is the most highly controlled medium. Governmental decisions and policies are most often expressed through it; but the press, particularly periodicals and specialized newspapers, represents other interests as well. Both radio and television are also tightly controlled, as they are perceived as having educational significance. Listener and viewer preferences, however, often prevail. Book publishing, with the exception of textbooks, is relatively free from censorship. Western and even anti-Soviet literature is read by many Hungarians. Libraries, although they are an integral part of the socialist educational system, generally serve a wide variety of interests and tastes. Films are perhaps the most nearly free from governmental control, despite their early origins as propaganda vehicles. Many films are imported, and a high percentage come from the West.

CONTROL OF THE MEDIA

The ambivalence of the regime, as a result of the 1956 Revolution, regarding the decision to increase or decrease governmental control over the media is reflected in the Revised Constitution of 1972, which differs considerably from that of 1949. In the Constitution of 1949 there was no distinction made between the various branches of the media, all of which were to be the property of the state. In the 1972 revision only radio and television are specifically mentioned as being state property, although in fact all the media are under the overall control of the state.

In the 1949 Constitution all freedoms of speech and the press were guaranteed without qualification in word if not necessarily in fact. In the 1972 version a vital clause was attached to the section dealing with freedom of speech and the press. These freedoms are now guaranteed only if they are "in accordance with the interests of socialism." This ambivalent strain runs through all governmental policy toward the media and is expressed in the content of the media.

On the one hand there seems to be relatively great tolerance under Kadar. In addressing the Union of Hungarian Writers in 1968, Kadar stated that, although the goal of the party was the construction of a strictly socialist society, writers should concern themselves with all subjects and must have "enough freedom for creative work."

Many Western writers have observed greater liberalization in the Hungarian media, which some attribute to the general relaxation of the environment surrounding the New Economic Mechanism (known as NEM—see Glossary) (see ch. 12). These observers state that the relaxation in the economic sphere has spread outward to include the political, cultural, and ideological areas as well.

The press has printed questions and letters to the editor in newspapers that have dealt with sensitive issues. Although Western journals are not easily accessible in Hungary, some Hungarians do read such American publications as *Time* and *Newsweek*. The radio has ceased its jamming of Radio Free Europe and the Voice of America. Television has since 1968 featured forum shows that allow viewers to call in questions on political subjects. Slightly dissident literature has appeared under the auspices of the state in recent years, although in limited editions. Films are made that deal with deeply philosophical questions regarding socialism. In all aspects of the media there is a great deal of exchange and importation of Western films, books, and plays.

There are several specific examples of this liberalization policy. In 1969 the party purges of the early communist years were reopened for public discussion. Although Laszlo Rajk, a leading party member, had been executed by the Communists as a traitor in 1949, articles were written twenty years later that questioned his entire trial and execution. In a 1971 article in a Hungarian journal an author openly discussed the so-called neurotic nature of Hungarian socialism and criticized the mass media for their failure to promote more humanistic education. In 1972 Hungarian students demonstrated against the government on the anniversary of the 1848 Revolution for independence. Although the leading Hungarian newspaper objected to Western coverage of the event, it commented that the views of such demonstrators were considered tolerable under socialism.

On the other hand liberalization of the media has not, by any means, been total. Most Western writers agree that, despite Hungary's relatively free media, neither anti-Kadar nor anti-Soviet views would be tolerated. Similarly, although suggestions for improving conditions within the political framework can be made, suggestions for actually changing the system itself would be unthinkable.

The world outside the socialist bloc is still often perceived by the regime and portrayed by the media as a dangerous enemy. The Hungarians stood staunchly by the Soviet Union in the United Nations General Assembly in 1972 in its opposition to the use of satellite television. Satellite transmission was viewed as threatening to the regime, as it would allow the Hungarian viewer to select programs from any part of the world. The Hungarian arguments were presented in terms of foreign threats and interference in internal matters, arguments reminiscent of polemics of an earlier era.

Similarly, major newspapers have addressed themselves to the issue of the foreign threat. One article by the chief of the party's Agitation and Propaganda Department (Agitprop) declared that the nonsocialist countries still intended to destroy the socialist bloc but were cloaking their evil intentions under the guise of a new policy of relaxation. Another major newspaper, *Magyar Hirlap*, warned the people of the "intellectual contraband" contained in foreign, anti-Marxist literature.

Still another journal listed a wide variety of threats coming from both foreign and domestic fronts, warning against foreign tourists, missionaries, economic and cultural exchanges with foreign countries, Western radio and television, and letters and messages from Hungarian refugees. The domestic dangers cited were nationalism, which was perceived as divisive, and religion, which was viewed as anti-Kadar.

ADMINISTRATION OF THE MEDIA

Policy on propaganda and public information is broadly formulated by the MSZMP, which places its members in leading positions in the various agencies of the media as well as in mass organizations. Agitprop, which is under the Central Committee of the party, supervises the mass media (see fig. 7). Under the Council of Ministers is the Information Office, established shortly after the revolution in 1956. This office has nationwide authority. Its functions are: the organization of all public information; the dissemination of information to the press, radio, and television; the issuance of newspaper licenses; the distribution of newsprint; and the control of foreign publications.

The press—like the other media—is controlled by the MSZMP. It is the most strictly supervised of the media, in part because Hungary's high literacy rate leads the government to consider the press the principal means of conveying information to the people. Individual newspapers operate under the auspices of various groups, such as the trade unions and mass organizations, but party control is no less rigid for these than for official newspapers.

The Information Office is in charge of the national news agency, the

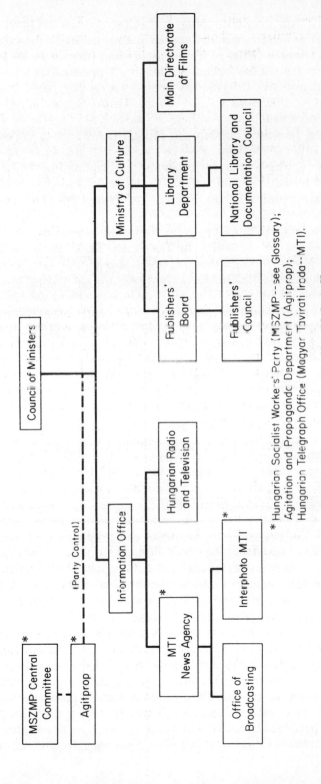

* Hungarian Socialist Workers' Party (MSZMP--see Glossary);
Agitation and Propaganda Department (Agitprop);
Hungarian Telegraph Office (Magyar Tavirati Iroda--MTI).

Figure 7. Administration of the Mass Media in Hungary

191

Hungarian Telegraph Office (Magyar Tavirati Iroda—MTI), which has a central office in Budapest and approximately twenty regional offices. Within MTI are the Office of Broadcasting and Interphoto MTI, which prepare information for foreign audiences. A press office within each government ministry informs the press on a regular basis. The press department of the Ministry of Foreign Affairs keeps foreign correspondents informed.

Radio and television, under the Hungarian Radio and Television (Magyar Radio es Televizio) are state owned and also under the Information Office, which prepares program material and provides broadcasting and telecasting equipment. The technical aspects of radio and television are handled by the Ministry of Transportation and Postal Affairs.

Publishing is structured on the Soviet model, and both publishers and booksellers are controlled by the state. The Publishers' Board, within the Ministry of Culture, is the administrative organ dealing with these matters. All publishers must have the sanction of the board, which controls all matters of finance. The Publishers' Council, a branch of the Publishers' Board, is essentially an advisory board composed of representatives of the state as well as publishing experts.

Libraries have also been controlled by the state since 1949. The Presidential Council has regulated all library activities since 1956. Overall practical responsibility for libraries is the task of the Library Department of the Ministry of Culture, which is assisted by the National Library and Documentation Council. Libraries are divided broadly into five categories: the National Szechenyi Library, which encompasses all historical libraries; the Hungarian Academy of Sciences, which includes all scientific and specialized libraries; the public libraries, which are principally those of the local councils and the trade unions; the school libraries, which fall under the Central Library of Education; and various miscellaneous libraries.

Films also are nationalized and under the control of the state. The Ministry of Culture generally controls the production, distribution, exhibition, and import and export of films through the Main Directorate of Films. The Ministry of Interior is in charge of film censorship, although the film medium is the least controlled of all mass communications in Hungary. The Institute for Film Teaching (Iskolai Filmintezet) produces educational films for school use.

There are various other miscellaneous administrative organs that deal with the mass media. One is the Mass Communications Research Center of Hungarian Radio and Television, which—despite its name—deals with all branches of the media. This organization, in existence since 1968, examines the impact of programs and explores the tastes of the public. It conducts a vast amount of public opinion research.

Another peripheral organization of the media is the Institute for Cultural Relations, established in 1949. It is essentially the counterpart of the All-Union Society of Foreign Cultural Relations in the Soviet Union and functions under the Council of Ministers. Its principal tasks are to propagate Hungarian culture abroad and to disseminate information regarding foreign cultures in the country.

Media for the young and for mass organizations fall under the aegis of the party. Agitprop, under the Central Committee of the party, decides policy regarding indoctrination of both party and nonparty members.

THEMES OF THE MEDIA

A major theme of the mass media, particularly the press, is expression of Soviet-Hungarian friendship. In 1967, on the anniversary of the signing of the Hungarian-Soviet friendship treaty, all three leading newspapers praised the leadership of the Soviet Union. An article in *Nepszabadsag* stated that "in the Soviet Union we esteem our liberators, our ally and our true friend and helper. On the basis of the experience in the last twenty-five years, we can say that the long-term and unalterable policy based on Hungarian-Soviet friendship is in perfect harmony with our national interests and with the internationalist standpoint which ensues from our common ideas and aims."

During the period of the Czechoslovak uprising, the Hungarian press abstained from the condemnation of Czechoslovakia voiced by the other socialist countries. When this abstinence was no longer tenable, Kadar stated in the press that the danger of so-called counterrevolution (by the liberals) in Czechoslovakia had become a menace. Shortly thereafter the press began once again to stress the importance of Soviet-Hungarian friendship.

A second major theme of the media deals with socialism and the conflict between socialism and nationalism. Kadar, in an article in *Kritika*—a literary magazine—discussed the building of socialism. He extolled the virtues of the socialist system and praised workers and collective farm workers for their role in its development. In a 1971 interview Kadar adopted an orthodox socialist stance on the issue of nationalism. He explained that there was no unique Hungarian road to socialism, but that all forms of socialism were contained in the principles of Marxism-Leninism.

A third theme of the media—exploitation of the masses in other lands—has a dual purpose: to further alienate the public from the capitalist West while simultaneously attempting to identify Hungary and the entire socialist bloc with the struggles of the developing countries. For example, an article in the journal *Beke es Szocializmus* claimed that the so-called third world could only achieve progress through class struggles and that only through anti-imperialist unity could true national liberation be achieved.

The fourth major theme of the media is economic policy. After the advent of the NEM in 1968, the media have discussed both its problems and its progress in the press. The propaganda agency has attempted to strengthen public confidence in the new economics by portraying the previous economic system as delaying progress in the economic field, but serious criticism of problems has also been expressed.

THE PRESS

The Hungarian press began as early as the sixteenth century in the form of handwritten papers or broadsheets. The first newspaper, *Mercurius Hungaricus*, was published in Latin in 1705. This newspaper was designed to evoke awareness of the war of independence against the Habsburgs. Other newspapers appeared in the eighteenth century but were printed in either Latin or German, languages that only the aristocracy could read. The first Hungarian newspaper, printed in 1780, was *Magyar Hirmondo*.

Publications were printed in Hungarian, as well as Latin and German, beginning in the early eighteenth century. When Hungarian newspapers were censored and repressed in the eighteenth century after a brief flowering stimulated by the Enlightenment, Hungarian liberals began to view such journals as the principal means of propagating their progressive ideas. The first periodical of this genre, published in 1788, was called *Magyar Museum*.

The Reform Era of the nineteenth century was a prosperous period for Hungarian journalism. There was a great demand for political newspapers from the early 1800s until 1849. Lajos Kossuth, a leader in the Hungarian nationalist movement, was one of the leading figures in the political press and began his own newspaper called *Pesti Hirlap* in 1841 (see ch. 2).

During and after the Revolution of 1848, there was a tremendous proliferation of daily and weekly newspapers. The failure of the war of independence, however, marked the opening of a dark era for the press. The laws passed in March 1848 pertaining to freedom of the press and the abolition of censorship were rescinded, and most newspapers were suppressed.

After the Compromise of 1867 conditions improved to some extent. The labor movement, which was beginning in Hungary, launched major newspapers, most notable of which was *Nepszava* which started in 1877. It became the official newspaper of the Social Democratic Party in 1890 and is today the daily newspaper of the National Council of Trade Unions.

In the early twentieth century the typical daily newspapers emerged. They represented the interests of particular parties as well as of private enterprise. Advertising became a source of income for newspapers, but government subsidies also assisted the publishers. In the early 1900s there were approximately twenty daily newspapers in Budapest. The largest one in terms of circulation was *Az Ujsag*. So-called sensational newspapers, known as the yellow press, began to appear.

In the interwar years, between 1919 and 1940, the press was largely in the hands of the government. During the brief communist regime of Bela Kun, the communist newspaper *Varos Ujsag* became the official newspaper of the short-lived Hungarian Council Republic. When the communist government was overturned, newspapers began to serve the interests of the new government of Miklos Horthy, although a communist press continued underground through World War II. A number of government newspapers began to represent the ideas of fascism, and there were a number of other rightwing newspapers, some representing political parties.

During World War II the communist party continued to operate illegally, and in 1941 the communist newspapers *Szabad Nep*, *Nepszava*, and *Magyar Nemzet* became active. Despite the general caution and fear that prevailed among publishers, the press was still vigorous at that time. By 1942 there were 101 daily newspapers and 1,278 periodicals. There was worldwide news coverage, and throughout Europe the Hungarian press maintained a good reputation for the diversity of its coverage.

Although the press was nominally independent during World War II, the official government party exerted a great deal of influence over it. The Ministry of Interior had the right to suspend publications that criticized the government. A censorship board was established to screen all material before publication. A decree in 1942 required the press to publish cabinet ministers' speeches according to a prescribed form. A so-called press fund subsidized all newspapers. The MTI—on which the press was dependent for news—became an official government agency. The government controlled the supply of newsprint.

When the coalition government took power in 1945, the decision was made to reorganize the press. The only newspapers published were those of the legal political parties; these were the communist *Szabad Nep*, the Social Democratic Party *Nepszava*, the Smallholders' Party *Kis Ujsag*, the National Peasant Party *Szabad Szo*, and the Social Democratic Party *Vilag*.

By 1948 the press was reorganized once again. Four morning newspapers were published: *Szabad Nep*, which was the official organ of the Hungarian Workers' Party; *Nepszava*, the organ of the trade unions; *Magyar Nemzet*, an intellectual, so-called nonparty organ; and *Szabad Ifjusag*. During the early 1950s, when the so-called cult of personality surrounding Matyas Rakosi prevailed, both newspapers and other periodicals suffered (see ch. 2). The total number of newspapers was reduced, and those that survived were dull and uninformative. After the Revolution of 1956 the government reduced the dogmatism in the newspapers in an attempt to increase their popularity.

Since the communist takeover, the Hungarian press has attempted to speed up and broaden its coverage of events. In addition to Hungarian, newspapers are printed in German, Serbo-Croatian, Slovak, and

Romanian. The press attempts to cover both domestic and foreign news, governmental policies, economic and cultural events, literature, and the arts. Another fairly recent feature of the Hungarian press is the incorporation of suggestions and criticisms by the reader. Editorials and commentaries discuss issues that have been mentioned by the public in letters to the editor. In addition, sources state that members of newspaper staffs meet with readers in factories, offices, and farms in order to listen to the comments and criticisms of their readership.

News Agency

The Hungarian national news agency, MTI, although established in 1880, is patterned on the Soviet Union news agency. MTI is composed of four major departments: cultural and internal policy, economics, agriculture, and sports.

The news agency is an arm of the government, as is the case in most communist countries. It transmits official and semiofficial news information to the domestic and foreign press as well as to the radio bureau. MTI also transmits news dealing with production to agencies that are directly concerned with the "construction of socialism." It provides foreign news to the press and the radio bureau and develops provincial news services.

MTI deals actively with other countries in the exchange of news. Since the mid-1960s there have been over 2,000 foreign correspondents in Hungary. Similarly, MTI had correspondents all over the world. It received press material from twenty news agencies and had exclusive distribution rights for Reuters, Agence France Presse, and the Associated Press. It relied almost exclusively, however, on the Soviet agency for foreign news policy.

Newspapers

In 1972 there were approximately 400 dailies, weeklies, and monthlies. The principal means of newspaper distribution was through subscription; 80 percent of the morning dailies were distributed in this manner. The Post Office had an extensive system by which dailies, weeklies, and monthlies were delivered to towns and villages. Almost all of the 3,270 inhabited localities in the country received either daily or weekly newspapers.

Dailies

The number of daily newspapers increased from twenty-four in 1960 to twenty-nine in 1972. The average daily circulation of newspapers was 2.2 million according to the latest available figures. This averaged approximately sixteen daily newspapers to every 100 persons. Four of the five Budapest dailies sold a total of about 1.5 million copies, which circulated nationally. In the order of their popularity, they were *Nepszabadsag* (810,000), *Nepszava* (290,000), *Esti Hirlap* (250,000), and *Magyar Nemzet* (110,000).

Nepszabadsag is the main organ of the MSZMP and is the principal newspaper of Hungary. It was called *Szabad Nep* before 1956 but was refounded in 1956 under its current name. This newspaper sets the tone for the other Hungarian newspapers. It is, in content and format, patterned on the Soviet Union's *Pravda* and, in like fashion, is required reading for all party members. It is also read aloud in farms and factories and over the radio.

The other daily newspapers are generally devoted to international issues as well as domestic affairs. They are actively concerned with the international labor movement and problems of developing countries. They also carry short stories, poems, and other literary works. The Sunday issues of daily newspapers, which have a greater circulation than the weekday editions, have cultural supplements that review plays, films, and books and discuss social and cultural problems. There are special sections that deal exclusively with sports, women, and children.

Weeklies

Weekly newspapers still enjoy considerable popularity despite their overall decline from sixty in 1960 to fifty-four in 1971. Ten of these weeklies appeared to have the largest circulation. *Nok Lapja*, an illustrated newspaper produced by the National Council of Hungarian Women, had a readership of approximately 510,000. *Orszag-Vilag*, an illustrated newspaper of the Hungarian Soviet Friendship Society, had a circulation of approximately 235,000. *Ludas Matyi*, a satirical newspaper, had approximately 608,000 readers, and *Kepes Ujsag*, the illustrated newspaper of the Patriotic People's Front, which was geared to the rural population, had a readership of 265,000. *Film-Szinhaz-Muzsika* had 174,000 readers, and *Elet es Tudomany* had 151,000. *Tukor*, an illustrated political and scientific weekly, had 79,000 readers, and *Magyarorszag*, a foreign affairs weekly, had 74,000 readers. The two sports weeklies, *Lobogo* and *Kepes Sport*, had 60,000 and 81,000 readers, respectively.

In addition to the daily and weekly newspapers, many other, more specialized newspapers were available. In 1971 there were nine literary reviews, five of which were published in Budapest. *Kortars* was the official publication of the Union of Hungarian Writers. Trade union newspapers were published once or twice a week; there were twenty-one trade union newspapers with a combined circulation of 465,000. Each individual factory also published its own newspaper in which particular problems of production were discussed.

Despite the overall policies of most socialist countries, in 1971 religious newspapers continued to be published and often had high prestige. There were twelve published with a combined circulation of approximately 147,000. *A Kereszt* and *Uj Ember* were Roman Catholic newspapers; *Evangelikus Elet* was Lutheran, and *Uj Elet* was Jewish.

Periodicals

Journals in Hungary increased from 175 in 1960 to 318 in 1971. The major journal of MSZMP was *Beke es Szocializmus*. It was, in essence, a version of the *World Marxist Review*, which was founded in 1958 and appeared in twenty-four different languages in thirty-two independent national editions; it was distributed in 125 different countries. The intent of the journal was to both reflect and analyze the conditions of the international communist movement.

In 1971 a wide variety of periodicals in Hungary served special interest groups. Sixty-six technical journals, with a combined circulation of 274,000, ranged widely in subject matter, including such diverse fields as architecture, electronics, transportation, communications, and textiles. There were twenty-eight medical journals with a total circulation of 77,000 copies. *Orvosi Hetilap*, a medical journal, was established over 100 years ago. Twenty-one different publications for teachers of primary, secondary, and university levels had a combined circulation of 273,000. Seventeen agricultural journals, with a circulation of 148,000, discussed such topics as plant cultivation, livestock breeding, and fruit farming. There were other journals for photographers, librarians, musicians, and painters. Particular societies—such as the Hungarian Red Cross or the Hungarian Philatelists—had their own specialized journals.

The total circulation of exported journals was over 286,000 in 1971. The major ones were: *Magyar Hirek*, an illustrated weekly published by the World Federation of Hungarians, and *Latohatar*, a literary magazine for Hungarians abroad. Hungarian magazines published in English and circulated abroad were *Hungarian Review*, dealing with politics, economics, and culture, and the *New Hungarian Quarterly*, dealing with social, political, and cultural issues. Other Hungarian magazines circulated abroad, which deal exclusively with foreign trade, were: *Foreign Trade, Hungarian Heavy Industries*, and *Hungarian Exporter*. Many scientific journals also appeared in foreign languages. These were generally published by the Hungarian Academy of Sciences or the various Hungarian universities.

Youth Press

Young people have a unique impact on the media, particularly the press, in two senses: they form a large audience for the regular media—special radio and television programs as well as extensive press coverage are devoted to them—and a mass press network publishes for them.

Research has shown that 50 percent of the youth-age (university level and below) population reads daily newspapers, and 80 percent of those read them several times a week. Officials complain, however, that many young people read only the sports news. Such leading newspapers as *Nepszabadsag* and *Nepszava* publish a weekly youth page.

198

Other newspapers deal with youth issues continually in domestic political columns, social issue spaces, and youth pages. Specialized newspapers, such as factory newspapers, are also read by a large youth population.

In 1971 a press for youth, almost all of which was party dominated, was also maintained. The Communist Youth League (Kommunista Ifjusagi Szovetseg—KISZ, see Glossary) and the Pioneers press accounted for 1.4 percent of the country's press products and 4 percent of all copies. *Magyar Ifjusag* was the central newspaper for all youth. Other youth newspapers were *Pajtas* and *Ifju Kommunista.* The Youth Publications Enterprises published 51 million copies of youth newspapers and journals annually. Sixteen percent of the young readers were reached by subscription, a much lower percentage than for the general public newspapers. The rest were distributed through the movement: 90 percent in the case of *Pajtas* and 20 percent in the case of *Magyar Ifjusag.*

There are also secondary school and university newspapers. Although the party pressure is less direct on these than on the communist youth newspapers, its influence is strong here as well. Nearly 200 secondary school newspapers are designed to play a role in the promotion of communism within the school, in the strengthening of relations between pupil and teacher, and in the increased activity of political life among the students. At the university level nineteen institutions of higher education have a total of nine newspapers. Although this news paper work is supervised by university committees, the editorial boards are appointed by KISZ.

The aims, functions, and aspirations of the youth press are all in line with party concepts. They have a dual purpose: to assist KISZ leaders in their practical work as propagandists and to stimulate the political interests of the young population. In order to achieve these ends, the youth newspapers provide information on domestic and international events, on decisions of the party, the government, KISZ, and other social and mass organizations, and on contemporary issues of youth policy.

RADIO

Hungarians claim that a Hungarian engineer, Tivador Puskas, a collaborator of Thomas Edison, first invented the concept of radio broadcasting. As early as 1893 he began what was called telediffusion, broadcasting through telephone lines and entertaining his audience with news, music, and lectures.

Standard radio broadcasting was first started in Hungary on December 1, 1925. Radio developed rapidly, and by 1928 the first transmitter, with a power of twenty kilowatts, was in operation. A second, 120-kilowatt, transmitter was constructed in 1933. Overseas shortwave broadcasting began in 1934.

Early radio programs tended to be dull and repetitive, consisting largely of band music and opera. Later plays, lectures, commentaries, and live concerts were added. Radio also became more internationally oriented during the 1930s; Hungarian programs were transmitted to Western Europe, and concerts from the United States and Western Europe were received in Hungary. As radio programs grew in scope, the number of radio owners or subscribers increased. In 1928 there were 168,000, and by 1938 there were 419,000, or 46 per 1,000 of the population.

During World War II the Hungarian Broadcasting Company, although nominally independent, was under the control of the Ministry of Propaganda. The principal radio station, a 120-kilowatt station, was still in Budapest; there were six relay stations as well. The number of listeners continued to rise during the early years of the war, nearly half of them tuning to foreign broadcasts.

When the war ended, Hungarian radio was virtually destroyed. The antenna tower, which had been one of the tallest in Europe, was completely demolished. The Broadcasting House, completed in 1928, was destroyed in the siege of Budapest in 1944–45.

The revival of radio began in 1945. During that year Radio Budapest was once again on the air. By 1948 a 135-kilowatt broadcasting station had been constructed. Although there was a ban on radio receivers that was maintained for a time after the war—because of stipulations in the armistice agreement—when it was lifted, the number of radio subscribers rose from 178,000 in 1945 to 539,000 in 1949, or 58 per 1,000 of the population, surpassing the number of prewar subscribers.

By 1955 there were thirty radio studios, each having a separate amplifier, and twelve mobile transmitters. Hungarian radio broadcast internationally on a daily basis in German, English, Italian, Spanish, Turkish, Arabic, and Greek. There were separate programs for Hungarians living abroad in Western Europe and the United States. The number of subscribers continued to rise from 1.3 million in 1955 to 2.2 million, or 222 per 1,000 of the population, in 1960.

Hungarian Radio, a division of Hungarian Radio and Television, is state owned. The state owns all central transmitters and controls the use of individual receivers through their registration with the Post Office. The Post Office, under the Ministry of Transportation and Postal Affairs, provides services to prevent receiver interference and polices the installation and use of receivers.

In 1971, despite the advent of television, there were over 2.5 million radio subscribers, or 245 per 1,000 of the population. Between 85 and 90 percent of the families owned radios. The number of radio subscribers began to level off in the late 1960s, a fact attributable to the rise and popularity of television.

The two principal radio stations are both in Budapest. Radio Kossuth, which transmits Program I, is broadcast on mediumwave twenty-four hours a day. Radio Petofi, which transmits Program II, broadcasts on mediumwave during the morning hours and on ultra-shortwave in the evening. These two radio stations complement each other. There is, in addition, one very high frequency transmitter, which broadcasts musical and literary programs.

Programs

The four principal programming sections of Hungarian Radio are: the Department of Actual News, the Literary and Dramatic Department, the Music Department, and the Children's and Youth Department. Hungarian Radio attempts, through such departmental programming, to serve a dual purpose, which is to satisfy the interests and tastes of the general public and to inform the listeners in conformity with the tenets of the party.

An official publication presents the policy of the state toward radio programming: "the Hungarian Radio is an institution charged with social responsibility in the field of art, education, information and entertainment and in filling this role, the Hungarian Radio is guided by a socialist programme policy." An example of this policy can be seen in the fact that, although there is a great popular demand for so-called sentimental music, Hungarian Radio restricts the amount of such music in order to improve the taste of the public.

Music, however, still predominates over all other types of radio programs. Another kind of program that, despite some mild governmental disapproval, enjoys wide popularity is the so-called light entertainment program. The most popular of these, according to the Mass Communications Research Center of Hungarian Radio and Television, is the thirteen-year-old series known as "The Szabo Family." Its audience is composed primarily of housewives, elderly people, and agricultural workers. Another popular light program is entitled "Saturday Night Vaudeville."

A second kind of radio program is the show that gives either practical or moral advice to specific groups. There are such shows as "The Code to Good Taste," "Girls and Women," "Answers to Our Listeners," and "Medical Advice." Some of these advice shows are geared specifically to rural areas and the agricultural population. An early morning show entitled "Villager's Radio" includes technical information and advice.

A third kind of radio program deals with news, current events, and reviews of cultural affairs. News bulletins are presented hourly. Among the most listened-to news programs are "The Evening Chronicle," "Economic Press Reviews," "Events Seen and Heard," and "Guide to Foreign Politics." Cultural reviews are dealt with principally by "Thought," a literary weekly program, and "Globus," a cultural review.

A fourth kind of radio program and one that the government actively promotes is the informational or educational program. In addition to broadcasts for schools and adult education institutions—which are transmitted daily—there are radio courses in Russian and French, including "The Radio Free University," "Literary Encyclopedia," and programs that offer the listener "visits" to specific institutions. Two major radio programs allow the listening audience the opportunity to ask questions of specialists on the air. They are "Press Conference" and "Editorial Room."

Foreign Broadcasting

Hungarian Radio broadcasts to foreign countries on mediumwave and shortwave for approximately twenty-two hours a day. The principal languages used in these broadcasts are Arabic, English, German, Italian, Spanish, Greek, and Turkish in addition to Hungarian, which is principally for the benefit of emigrants overseas. The foreign-language broadcasts are aimed chiefly at Western Europe, the Middle East, and North and South America, although broadcasting to Asia is increasing. Many of the programs broadcast from Hungary are cultural. There are music exchange programs with over 120 foreign radio stations. Hungarian Radio features chiefly cultural events from overseas, such as the Salzburg Festival and the Zagreb Musical Biennial.

TELEVISION

In 1949 television was first considered for use in Hungary. By the 1950s the country began its first technical experiment with the medium, but it was the end of 1952 before the government had definitely decided to promote television in the country.

In December 1953 experimental telecasting was begun from a 100-kilowatt station. The production of television sets for home use was initiated in 1955. In 1956 the first transmitter was operational, and the building of studios was begun. Although there was some delay during the period of the 1956 Revolution, a mobile transmitter was made operational by February 1957. In 1958 a high-power transmitter was established in Budapest, consisting of a thirty-kilowatt video transmitter and a ten-kilowatt audio transmitter. Two television studios were opened that year.

Regular telecasting was begun in 1958. There were only 16,000 subscribers at that time. By 1960 the number of subscribers had grown to 104,000, and by 1967 there were nearly 1.2 million subscribers.

The state-owned and -operated central television station is located in Budapest. A second channel, featuring experimental transmission in color, was put into operation in 1971. Programs occupy 4½ hours each day from Monday through Friday and 20½ hours on the weekend.

Hungarian Television, a division of Hungarian Radio and Television, is affiliated with Intervision, the International Organization for Radio and Television of the socialist bloc. Eurovision, the television network of the European Broadcast Union, is the Western European counterpart of this organization. A limited number of Hungarian television shows are received in such diverse areas as Monte Carlo and Alexandria. A much larger number of television programs are received by Hungary from other countries. Although the great part of these are from Intervision countries, a substantial percentage come from Western Europe.

Television, like radio and the press, has a definite propaganda purpose in addition to its value as entertainment. An editorial in *Tarsadalmi Szemle* stated: "Television, radio and the press are the best tools for agitation and propaganda. They must always strive to inform . . . with the needed political decisiveness and purpose and a perseveringly Marxist spirit. . . . Television program editors should realize that they . . . work for . . . the broad public. . . . They must always figure with the political effect on the masses."

The political aims have been achieved to some extent by Hungarian Television through such shows as "Forum"—in which experts answer questions from the viewers—a foreign affairs series, a political lecture series, documentaries, party decree discussions, language courses, scientific lectures, educational programs, and seminars on collective farm and factory problems. Generally, however, there is a minimum of dogmatic material on television.

According to a poll taken in the late 1960s, Hungarian viewers prefer news films, theater performances, sports events, and movies, in that order. To meet the demands for news Hungarian television offers the viewer a feature entitled "TV Newsreel," which features international news, as well as many news programs—particularly in the evenings— that cover general news and industrial and cultural events. The demand for theatrical performances is met by an average of six to eight live plays each weekend. Sports news is featured daily, with special coverage of particular sports events. The demand for films is generally met, frequently with foreign productions. Swedish, Japanese, and other nonsocialist films are frequently purchased to fill the gaps in Hungarian film production. On an average, of the films shown on television, only one out of four is from a socialist country. Other miscellaneous features of television are operas, detective stories, music, children's features, and quiz programs.

Hungary's plans regarding the future of television are extensive. In 1970 the government prepared a fifteen-year development plan that had detailed decisions covering 1970 through 1975. Major emphasis will be placed on color telecasting, which is expected to begin in 1973. Seventy small relay transmitters were under construction in the early 1970s. Plans are being formulated to improve reception, particularly in the rural areas. Although the number of radio subscribers is expected to increase very slightly, the growth in the number of television owners is anticipated to be very great in the next few years (see table 7).

Table 7. Hungary, Number of Television Sets and Ratio per 1,000 Population, Selected Years, 1958-71

Year	Number of Television Sets (in thousands)	Ratio of Subscribers per 1,000 Population
1958	16	2
1960	104	10
1967	1,169	114
1971	1,943	187

Source: Adapted from *Statistical Pocket Book of Hungary, 1972*, Budapest, 1972, pp. 41-42, 298-304; and *The Europa Yearbook, 1972*, London, 1972, p. 23.

PUBLISHING

Book publishing began very early in Hungary, paralleling developments in western Europe. In the eleventh century Latin codices first appeared. By the fourteenth century some libraries contained as many as 200 to 300 manuscript volumes. The first Hungarian printing press was established in Buda in 1472 by Andras Hess. The first book printed in Hungary, the *Chronica Hungarorum* (History of Hungary), was in Latin and appeared in 1473. The first Hungarian text printed in Hungarian was printed in Poland.

During the sixteenth century, despite the Turkish wars, publishers continued to be active. Printing presses were supported mostly by the various churches of the Reformation, which were concerned with spreading the concepts of the Reformation through the printed word. By the end of the sixteenth century and the beginning of the seventeenth century, permanent printing presses were set up, and educational books appeared, ending the religious monopoly on book publication. In the last half of the seventeenth century nearly 600 books were published; this was almost double the number produced in the first half of the century.

In the eighteenth century books, like newspapers and other periodicals, began to discuss openly the war of independence against the Habsburgs. At the end of this war the Nagyszombat printing house, controlled by the Roman Catholic Church, was the largest in Hungary. Debrecen was the location of the chief printer of the Calvinist Church, although it too was dominated by the Habsburgs. New printing houses began to appear at that time. The first private press appeared in 1724. By the end of the century Buda and Pest were active publishing centers.

Censorship, which was prevalent in the eighteenth century, relaxed somewhat under the rule of King Joseph II in the nineteenth century, and books dealing with politics, education, philosophy, and fictional subjects appeared. There was a new emphasis on national culture, and the Hungarian language was actively promoted. During the reform era, particularly at the height of the Revolution of 1848, the demands of the revolutionaries were printed. Hungarian translations of works of foreign authors—such as Charles Dickens, Molière, Victory Hugo, and Johann Wolfgang von Goethe—began to appear.

By 1848 there were fifty printing houses. Editions began to appear in thousands, rather than hundreds, of copies. After the Compromise of 1867 private enterprise in publishing expanded greatly. By the end of the nineteenth century there were 680 printing houses.

In the late nineteenth century a socialist press began to take root, and the works of Karl Marx were published in Hungarian. Trade unions established libraries, and peasants started reading circles. Shortly after World War I, under the brief rule of Bela Kun, book publication was nationalized. The writings of Vladimir Ilyich Lenin were translated into Hungarian, and classics, particularly Russian ones, were printed in cheap editions.

Between the two world wars, socialist printing was suppressed by the Horthy regime, and there was a general return to clerical, scientific, technical, and fictional publications. Despite limitations in the scope of publications, however, the field grew tremendously in volume. In 1938 there were 731 printing houses, and the number of booksellers had expanded to 528. In Budapest alone there were 192 bookshops.

Private publishers continued to function for a number of years after 1945, although fascist publications were prohibited by the government. Communist publishing houses emerged quickly, however. The party publishing house, Szikra, and the publishing house of the Hungarian-Soviet Cultural Society, later renamed the New Hungarian Publishers, quickly began the publication of Marxist works. Works that were considered anti-Marxist were suppressed by the Communists.

Reorganization of book publishing was begun in 1948. All large publishing companies were nationalized, and the National Book Office, under the direction of the Ministry of Culture, was founded. In 1949 book publishing, printing, and bookselling were developed as separate entities. The publishing houses were placed under the Ministry of Culture; printing was under the Ministry of Light Industry; and bookselling was under the Ministry of Home Trade. By 1950 the publishing house of the Hungarian Academy of Sciences was reorganized. Smaller publishing houses were placed under specialized ministries, all of which were under the broad direction of the Committee of Ministerial Publishers. In 1953 the Council of Ministers established the Publishers' Council; in 1954 the Publishers' Board was founded under the control of the Ministry of Culture.

The overall administration of publishing and the formulation of publishing policy were performed by the Publishing Board in the early 1920s. Other administrative bodies under this organization were the Copyright Office, founded in 1952, and the Hungarian Publishers and Booksellers Association.

The Kultura Hungarian Company for Books and Newspapers exports books. This organization, which maintains relations with eighty foreign countries, exports approximately 3 million books a year, printed both in Hungarian and in foreign languages. The Kultura company also directs the importation of books. Approximately 5 million books are imported yearly, primarily from socialist countries, although books from the United States, the United Kingdom, France, and the Federal Republic of Germany (West Germany) are also imported.

Book Week

A special week—Hungarian Book Week—is designed to focus the attention of the public on book publishing. In 1972 it was held in connection with the International Book Year of the United Nations Educational, Scientific and Cultural Organization (UNESCO). Such organizations as the National Trade Union Council, the Patriotic People's Front, KISZ, and the local councils were hosts, although book week is generally sponsored by cultural affairs specialists. In honor of the event meetings between readers and writers, exhibitions, recitals, and conferences were held. Special book tents were established for foreign—generally socialist—publishers, national minority groups, and local printing houses.

Types of Publications

Although Hungarian publishing houses cater to a wide variety of specialized interests, they publish six predominant types of books. They are professional, text, educational, literary, scientific, and juvenile, listed in the order of the number of individual works published in the field (see table 8).

Table 8. Types of Books Published in Hungary, 1971

Type of Book	Number of Titles	Number of Copies (in millions)
Professional	1,986	5.0
Text	1,180	15.8
Educational	801	10.8
Literary	721	14.9
Scientific	620	1.4
Juvenile	182	5.1

Source: Adapted from *Statistical Pocket Book of Hungary, 1972*, Budapest, 1972, pp. 41–42, 298–304; and *The Europa Yearbook, 1972*, London, 1972, p. 23.

The principal publishing houses for professional publications are: Kossuth Konyvkiado Vallalat, publishing on politics, history, economics, and philosophy; Medicino Konyvkiado, publishing on medical topics; and Kozgazdasagi es Jogi Konyvkiado, publishing on economic, social, and juridical matters.

The principal publisher of textbooks is Tankonyvkiado Vallalat, which specializes in school and university texts, pedagogical literature, and language texts. Generally, the greatest number of texts is for secondary schools, followed by general schools, universities, and special and professional classes. All textbooks are designed to conform to the principles of socialism.

Educational publications differ from textbooks in that they are less uniform and deal with a wider variety of subjects. The Corvina Publishing House publishes tourist guides, cookbooks, and books on foreign languages, art, and musicology. The Gondolat Konyvkiado deals in popular science and educational publications. Publishers in this field attempt to make broad areas of knowledge available to all strata of society.

The principal publishing houses for literary works are Europa, which translates world literature into Hungarian; Megveto Konyvkiado, a literary house; and Szepirodalmi Konyvkiado, which publishes modern and classical Hungarian literature. Classical works hold a prominent place. In addition to Hungarian classics, Dickens, Rudyard Kipling, Mark Twain, Alexandre Dumas, and Jules Verne are widely read.

The principal publishing house for scientific publications is Akademiai Kiado, which publishes for the Hungarian Academy of Sciences. It publishes dictionaries, encyclopedias, and works on pure and applied science.

The principal youth publishing house is Mora Ferenc Ifjusagi Konyvkiado, which publishes children's books exclusively. Although there are several educational series for children—such as research books and children's encyclopedias—there is an attempt to expose children to all aspects of life through the publication of novels, science fiction, adventure stories, and biographical fiction.

Book publishing in Hungary is not expected to serve propaganda and other political functions in quite the same way as the publication of newspapers and periodicals. An official source states: "The principal objective of socialist publishing and bookselling is to make books available to everybody, to arouse and satisfy the demand for education and worthwhile recreation, to acquaint the masses through books with the achievement of science, literature, and the arts, and to promote creative work in every field."

There is some socialist content in the publication of Hungarian books. A new series entitled "Discovering Hungary" was initiated in 1970 on the twenty-fifth anniversary of the liberation of the country. The series, based on the precommunist series that opposed the Horthy regime, is designed to present socialist writing in terms of documenting results already achieved and discussing problems still unresolved.

Generally, however, Hungarians are free to enjoy nonsocialist publications, in which they have expressed a strong interest. Only socialist literature—primarily Soviet—was accessible in the early years of the communist regime, but there have been several million copies of foreign works sold in Hungary. Since that time foreign publications have been translated in ever-increasing volume. Since 1945 approximately 12.7 million copies of American and English works have been sold in Hungary. Budapest bookshops regularly sell American Penguin books. French, German, Swiss, and Italian literature is also widely distributed. Anti-Stalinist literature is not uncommon in present-day Hungary.

LIBRARIES

The remains of early libraries and their documents are more fragmentary in Hungary than in the rest of Europe, primarily because of the Turkish invasions of the sixteenth century. One of the most famous early libraries was the Bibliotheca Corvina, established by King Matyas, who reigned from 1458 to 1490. Through this library the king introduced Italian humanism into Hungary during the Renaissance. This library, no longer in existence, had 7,000 volumes; only the Vatican Library in Rome exceeded it.

School libraries grew up during the sixteenth century. Printed books began to replace the handwritten codices, and the demand for books increased greatly because of the impact of the Reformation, the extension of the educational system, and the consolidation of towns and cities. The counter-Reformation and the controversy surrounding it also gave impetus to the development of libraries.

The eighteenth century witnessed tremendous development in Hungarian libraries as new universities were established. Contributing to the great demand for books by scholars and historians was the development of the nationalist movement, which was concerned with collecting documents dealing with the history of the nation. By the end of the century Hungarian literature was found on the shelves of many of the country's libraries.

In the nineteenth century individuals and the government began to share in the establishment and maintenance of libraries. In 1802 Ferenc Szechenyi donated 15,000 books, 2,000 manuscripts, and 10,000 foreign-language books to Hungarian libraries, thus founding the National Museum and Library, later called the National Szechenyi Library. Jozsef Teleki donated 30,000 books as the foundation for the Library of the Hungarian Academy of Sciences. By 1885 there were 2,270 libraries in Hungary, with a total of 7.3 million works.

The establishment of village libraries began in the nineteenth century. In 1873 the Central Committee for the Development of Rural Libraries was created. At the end of the century the National Council for Museums and Libraries was developed; 748 libraries were created by the early twentieth century. The Ministry of Agriculture organized 3,000 village libraries during the period.

The early twentieth century libraries were solvent financially and employed modern library methods. During the brief reign of Bela Kun in 1919, there was an attempt to reorganize libraries under the National Institute for Librarianship and Bibliography.

Between the two world wars libraries were in disrepair because of the stagnating economic situation, and they virtually ceased to exist in towns and rural areas; toward the beginning of World War II, however, there was some growth in the library system.

After the war the government began to restore and rebuild the libraries that had been devastated. By 1949 several libraries were reopened under the new socialist cultural policy. The state assumed control of all libraries, increasing the number of both libraries and works and attempting to make literature more readily available to the masses. Mobile libraries began to reach into the rural areas. Networks were established for the rural areas; the county library was the center, stretching outward to all districts, towns, and villages. By 1953 almost every village had its own library. Trade union libraries also increased rapidly. By the mid-1960s there were 9,514 of these libraries, having over 19 million volumes.

In 1956 laws were enacted that regulated the library system. Most libraries from that time on were classified under one of several organizational headings, among them the networks of the Library of the Hungarian Academy of Sciences, the university libraries, technical libraries, agricultural libraries, medical libraries, public libraries, and school libraries.

Among the achievements of the communist library system were: the introduction of the international decimal system, the standardization of library administration, the introduction of a central catalog for the entire country, regular publication of an up-to-date national bibliography, preparation of subject indexes for periodicals, and the introduction of microfilms.

Public education libraries—in Hungarian library terminology—are those libraries that belong to the trade unions and local councils (administrative organs of the government that operate on the local level), whereas national libraries are enjoyed by the general public. The number of local council libraries increased from 4,688 in 1960 to 5,293 by 1970. On the other hand, the number of trade union libraries decreased from 5,105 in 1960 to 3,958 in 1970. Similarly, the readership in the local council libraries rose from 919,000 in 1960 to 1.6 million in 1970, but the number of readers in the trade union libraries declined from 708,000 in 1960 to 642,000 in 1970. Available information does not provide a reason for the decline.

There were nine major national libraries in Hungary. The largest was the National Szechenyi Library, which had 5.2 million volumes of various kinds in 1971. This library had a special collection of books from the sixteenth century, medieval codices, and early documentations of the Hungarian language. The National Szechenyi Library maintained the central catalog of foreign books and periodicals for the entire country.

The Library of the Hungarian Academy of Sciences had 1.2 million volumes in 1971, principally scientific publications. It also had works dealing with histories of antiquities, linguistics, and literary sciences, and it had an extensive Oriental collection. This library exchanged periodicals with most of the major libraries in the world. It was also the center for seventy-two academic institutes in Hungary.

In 1971 the Library of the Lorand Eotvos University, known as the University Library, had approximately 1.2 million volumes, most of which dealt with general scientific subjects. It held a large collection of works on medieval and contemporary history and one on modern philology; 176 handwritten codices were preserved in this library.

The National Technical Library and Documentation Center was merged with the Technological Documentation Center in 1952. In 1971 it had approximately 803,000 books and 60,000 periodicals. Its main collections were in the fields of mathematics, physics, and chemistry. It was the center for 106 faculty libraries of technical universities in Budapest.

The Parliament Library, established originally for members of parliament, has been a public library since 1952. It had over 465,000 volumes, dealing principally with modern history, political science, law, and administration. It had a separate United Nations collection of about 350,000 books and 40,000 periodicals.

The Library of Lajos Kossuth University had over 900,000 books and 100,000 periodicals in 1971. Most of these deal with scientific topics. The Municipal Ervin Szabo Library is a general library, which has more than 1.3 million volumes. Two of the more specialized libraries in Hungary are the Library of the Central International Statistical Office and the National Agricultural Library and Documentation Center. The statistical library has approximately 340,000 volumes, 70,000 of which deal with official statistics. The agricultural library has over 85,000 volumes and more than 1,100 foreign reviews and journals.

Both the Roman Catholic Church and the Reformed Church in Hungary have library collections. One of the main libraries of the Roman Catholic Church is the Central Main Library of the Benedictine Order of Pannohalma. Another major Roman Catholic library is the Chief Catholic Library in Esztergom. Both have codices and manuscripts as well as standard volumes. The libraries of the Reformed Church are the Raday Library in Budapest, the Library of the Reformed College of Debrecen, and the Library of the Reformed College of Sarospatak.

FILMS

The first public performance of films in Hungary was presented in 1896. The first original Hungarian film, entitled *A Dance*, was made in 1901. Its documentary style was later to become the principal form of Hungarian films.

Between 1910 and 1915 the documentary style grew in popularity.

Events of World War I were recorded in films. The Pedagogic Film Studio, which concentrated exclusively on documentaries, was founded in 1913. Many films produced by this studio were used to assist with teaching in the public school system.

Nondocumentary film making developed in approximately the same time period. The government prohibited the importation of English, American, French, Italian, and other foreign films during the war years, and Hungarian film making flourished. By the end of World War I there were thirty film producers in the country, and they were producing either documentary or dramatic films.

During the brief regime of the Hungarian Council Republic the film industry was nationalized. In the interwar years, 1918–40, avant-garde films began to be produced. Because of the critical economic situation in the country, however, few films were made. During the Horthy regime there was a high degree of censorship, and a vast number of propaganda films were made. The government began to subsidize film production and eventually founded the Hunnia Film Studio Company, which was partially owned by the state.

By the end of World War II over 400 sound films had been produced. Although some sound films were concerned with social commentary, generally they were operettas and light comedies.

Educational films developed rapidly in the 1930s. By 1942 films were used as a vehicle for instruction in nearly 700 schools, particularly at the secondary level.

Hungarian film making continued to expand during the war years. In 1940 there were thirty-four feature films produced, as opposed to ten or fifteen per year before the war. In 1943 fifty feature films were made. During World War II American and British films were prohibited, causing the Hungarian film industry to boom. The government continued to subsidize propaganda films, some of which were characterized by anti-Semitic and anti-Soviet attitudes.

Towards the end of World War II film studios were devastated, and equipment was ransacked. The coalition government reorganized the film production industry, and foreign, primarily Soviet, films were again imported.

In 1948 the film industry was nationalized under the Communists. An official source states the view of the government toward the industry: "The film came to be regarded as an integral part of culture and education." A central studio for news films and documentaries was established. The personality cult that surrounded Matyas Rakosi and prevailed until the death of Joseph Stalin created both bureaucratic and aesthetic problems in the film industry. Newsreels at that time consisted mostly of dull propaganda, dealing exclusively with events in Hungary and the Soviet Union. Documentaries played almost exclusively on the theme of the downtrodden peasant but were often over-dramatized and unrealistic.

After 1953 films began to be both more original and more accurate.

In newsreels and documentaries lessons were learned, not only from Soviet film experience, but from English and French as well. The scope of documentaries was expanded and made more realistic. Feature films again began to be produced.

After the Revolution of 1956 the government decided to decentralize film studios in order to create a freer atmosphere for film artists. In 1959 a film was produced that dealt directly with the causes of the revolution. In 1963 a film was produced that actually treated the subject of the inner conflicts of the socialist man.

The film industry is nationalized, although considerable latitude is given to individual film producers and studios. The production, distribution, exhibition, importation, and exportation of films are broadly controlled by the Ministry of Culture. There has been considerable decentralization in recent years, however, and managers of film enterprises have more freedom to exercise judgment than was previously allowed.

The Institute for Film Teaching produces educational films and distributes projectors, films, and slides to both elementary and secondary schools. It also maintains film archives and exchanges films with educational film organizations abroad. The College of Dramatic and Cinematographic Arts trains people for careers in films; the Hungarian Institute of Cinematographic Research and Film Archives performs research in film history and contemporary theory.

The number of films in all major categories—feature films, newsreels and documentaries, and dubbed films—increased substantially between 1960 and 1971. The number of motion picture houses, however, dwindled. Similarly, attendance over the same time period decreased (see table 9).

Table 9. Number of Motion Picture Houses, Performances, and Admissions in Hungary, 1960 and 1971.

	1960	1971
Motion picture houses	4,558	3,813
Performances	846,000	738,000
Admissions	140,000,000	75,000,000

Source: Adapted from *Statistical Pocket Book of Hungary, 1972*, Budapest, 1972, pp. 41–42, 298–304; and *The Europa Yearbook, 1972*, London, 1972, p. 841.

Although film importation before 1958 was almost exclusively from the socialist bloc, in recent years there has been a rash of imports from the Western countries. In 1971, however, Soviet films still led the field with thirty-eight, followed by the United States with eighteen, the United Kingdom with fifteen, and France with fourteen. Hungarian films were exported almost exclusively to the socialist bloc countries.

Hungarian films are perhaps the most nearly free from propaganda or socialist content of all the mass media. Even they, however, often deal with socialist themes laden with ideological overtones. The theme of the struggles of the peasantry persists, but more contemporary socialist problems and issues have also been introduced. Peasants were the heroes of such famous Hungarian films of the early 1960s as *Calvary*, *Summer Rain*, and *Autumn Star*. In the late 1960s films such as *The Father* discussed the problems of the personality cult of the early 1950s. In 1972 a color film called *The People Are Asking For More* dealt with the plight of agricultural workers around 1900.

On the other hand, Hungarian film producers are eager to experiment with nonsocialist techniques and content, and they appear to be at relative liberty to do so. Although the weight of Soviet influence has been incalculable in Hungarian film making, Hungarian film producers are also indebted to Italian producers, particularly in the area of neorealism. Foreign films are tremendously popular in Hungary, particularly Italian films, such as Michelangelo Antonioni's *Blow-up* and *Zabriski Point*. Hungarian producers have also made relatively controversial political films, such as the anti-Stalinist *Love* and *Gal*.

SECTION III. ECONOMIC

CHAPTER 12

CHARACTER AND STRUCTURE

OF THE ECONOMY

At the beginning of 1973 the Hungarian leadership was drawing up a balance of the successes and failures of the five-year-old liberalized system of economic management that was meant to cure the ills associated with the former traditional communist method of centralized administrative controls. The general, publicly expressed conclusion was that the reform principles had proved to be sound but that technical changes of regulations were needed to make the reform effective. In an address to the Central Committee Plenum of the Hungarian Socialist Workers' Party (MSZMP—see Glossary), Janos Kadar, the party leader, emphasized his conviction that all the major and minor problems, difficulties, and errors arose not as a consequence of the reform principles but as a result of their inadequate translation into practice.

Difficult economic problems faced the country. Strong inflationary pressures over the preceding three years were slowed but not arrested. This situation had been engendered by excessive investment and an unplanned rise in consumption. Politically sensitive problems were posed by the leadership's policy of restraining the rise in wages and incomes and by the need to raise consumer prices in order to reduce the drain on the state budget through price subsidies. Official measures introduced in the 1971-73 period in efforts to cope with the difficulties constituted, in effect, a partial though unacknowledged retreat from the reform policies. In an address to the National Assembly at the end of 1972 a party secretary stressed the groundlessness of prevailing rumors about impending grave problems and a reversal of economic policy.

The basic purpose of the economic reform was to make the country's productive mechanism more efficient in order to speed up economic growth, raise the population's standard of living, and make Hungarian products competitive in world markets. The reform was successfully introduced, but its first five years demonstrated that some of the country's endemic economic problems would require more time for solution than originally was thought necessary.

NEW ECONOMIC MECHANISM

Slow economic growth under the traditional communist system of economic management led Hungarian political leaders to seek a new method of running the economy without surrendering political control. The failure of partial measures introduced in 1957 led to a concerted effort by leading economists and public officials to develop a viable new economic management system. After prolonged deliberation and debates a set of economic reform principles was officially announced in the fall of 1965 and approved by the party's Central Committee in May 1966.

The reform principles constituted a compromise between liberal and conservative elements in the MSZMP. After the introduction of a few minor preliminary measures to prepare the way, the new economic management system, the New Economic Mechanism (known as NEM—see Glossary), was formally put into effect on January 1, 1968. A transitional period of three years was envisaged during which the new system would be perfected; thereafter NEM was expected to enter into full force as a smoothly functioning economic guidance system.

The basic aspect of the reform was the decentralization of economic management to allow enterprise managers greater scope of decisionmaking in the operation and development of individual enterprises but to retain the function of overall economic planning and direction at the level of central government authorities. The traditional system of assigning a mass of detailed targets for each enterprise was replaced by an interrelated system of mostly indirect economic regulators governing all economic activities, which was meant to provide the framework for decisionmaking by enterprise managers in accord with the broad, centrally established policies.

The wide variety of economic regulators is generally subdivided into six groups. The first group reflects the government's price policy. The policy calls for a high degree of stability in the majority of retail prices but seeks to develop competitive conditions in the formation of producer prices for goods other than most essential raw materials through freely negotiated contracts between buyers and sellers. For the longer run the policy aims to achieve a closer relation between prices and costs and between domestic and world market prices.

The second group of regulators supports the official policy regarding the growth of personal incomes. Through budgetary controls and rules concerning the use of enterprise incomes, the state regulates aggregate incomes in producing enterprises and public institutions. Within these general regulations, enterprises retain a certain measure of freedom in determining the wages and salaries of individual employees. Goals for the annual and long-term growth rates of personal incomes are stipulated in the national economic plans.

The third group of economic regulators is designed to help implement the government's investment policy. Under this policy a substantial part of total investment is undertaken on the initiative of individual enterprises. The state's influence in this area is supposed to assert itself mainly through its policy on investment credits. In addition, however, the state can influence the investment trend through central government decisions on major investment projects, by allocating funds for designated investment purposes and by making direct investments out of the state budget. The remaining three sets of economic regulators establish the framework for credit operations, foreign trade, and fiscal and budgetary management.

The position and role of individual enterprises were significantly modified by the reform. In contrast to the prereform era, when enterprise operations and investments were generally financed through the state budget, enterprises under NEM have been expected to be financially independent after an initial grant of state funds and some subsidies to ease the transition. Prices established in 1968 were to ensure profitable operation for most enterprises and adequate returns to provide for needed investment and profit sharing among enterprise personnel.

An elaborate system of income and wage regulations was instituted to promote better utilization of labor resources, greater productivity, modernization of production processes and products, and elimination of obsolete and uneconomic output. The basic purpose of these regulations was to create a framework within which the enterprises' interest in maximizing profits would lead to improved economic performance and more equitable distribution of economic rewards—thus harmonizing personal interests with the interests of society.

Enterprise profits are separated into three distinct funds in accordance with complicated regulations that take into account the gross value of assets and the total amount of the annual wage bill. The development fund is destined for investment in improvements and expansion. The profit-sharing fund—also known as the participation fund—provides cash payments and benefits in kind to all enterprise personnel in officially prescribed proportions. A portion of this fund must be set aside as a reserve for the next year. A reserve fund provides a cushion against unforeseen contingencies, including primarily unfavorable price changes.

A complex and frequently revised system of taxation diverts a large portion of the profits to the state budget. Aside from providing budgetary revenue, profit taxes—especially those levied on the development and participation funds—are also intended to influence enterprise policies in the fields of labor utilization, wages, productivity, and investment.

ORGANIZATION AND STRUCTURE

Socialized ownership of the means of production is virtually complete, including agriculture, where almost all of the land area is in the socialized sector (state or collective farms). A certain amount of private property, other than personal, is nevertheless allowed, including the ownership of land, small farms, and housing. In 1970 the socialized sector was reported to have produced 98.1 percent of the national income, including 70.8 percent by state and 22.8 percent by collective enterprise; an officially designated "other socialist sector" produced the balance of 4.5 percent. This reference may be to cooperatives of small-scale individual producers, often located in urban areas, who raise poultry and other small livestock for the market. The private sector, with almost 5 percent of the economically active persons, accounted for only 1.9 percent of the national income. Its contribution had declined from 9 percent in 1960 and 3 percent in 1965.

Under NEM the country's economic activity is guided by broad MSZMP policy directives that are quantified as specific targets for major areas of the economy in a five-year national economic plan. The targets relate to such aspects of the economy as national and personal income, investment and consumption, industrial and agricultural production, employment and wages, technology and productivity, and foreign and domestic trade. Plan targets are supposed to be attained by production and trade programs independently developed by individual enterprises under central agency guidance in conformity with the plan. Conformity is to be secured through so-called indirect regulators—a set of complex, state-imposed formulas and regulations that link every phase of enterprise activity and financing to the enterprise's profit-sharing fund.

This fund consists of a specified proportion of the enterprise's total profit, and its size determines the magnitude of profit distributions to the manager and workers at the end of the year. Enterprises have therefore been primarily interested in maximizing their profits, as they were expected to do under the provisions of the reform. Many of them, however, have pursued this aim without regard to adverse economic and social consequences of their actions—a development that went counter to the MSZMP axiom that under socialism personal and social interests necessarily coincide. This unforeseen result grew out of the discrepancy between the theoretical and the practical working out of the indirect regulators.

Organization

Individual enterprises constitute the basic units of the economic management pyramid. Grouped into economic and industrial branches according to the nature of their activities, they are subject to supervision and ultimate administrative control by branch ministries, such as the Ministry of Agriculture and Food or the Ministry of Heavy Industry, and by functional ministries and other central government agencies having economy-wide jurisdiction, such as the Ministry of Finance, the Hungarian National Bank, and the National Material and

Price Control Office. These government bodies, in turn, are responsible to the Council of Ministers and, ultimately, the MSZMP leadership (see ch. 8). Although the outward appearance of the economic management structure, with minor variations, has remained substantially unchanged, the degree of authority exercised by the supervisory bodies over enterprises was significantly reduced by the economic reform.

In contrast to the prereform era, when government directives spelled out all details of enterprise operations, enterprises under NEM have gained a significant degree of independence and have been able to make major decisions concerning internal organization, production, investment, purchasing, marketing, and, in many instances, pricing. Sole responsibility for the enterprise is vested in the government-appointed manager. The leadership has explicitly rejected enterprise self-management through workers' councils and has also denied authority of a self-management nature to the trade union organization within the enterprise. MSZMP opposition to self-management has been officially defended on the grounds that this form of management would break up state property and would undermine the foundation of effective central planning and state control.

Supervision of enterprises by superior government agencies has been officially justified on the grounds of government ownership. Ministries are supposed to assist enterprises in planning, in improving performance, and in achieving planned targets. They are also responsible for ensuring enterprises' adherence to applicable laws and regulations. The ministries' ability to influence enterprise decisions rests mainly on their power to appoint, reward, and discipline managers.

Supervision and control of enterprises is executed by means of comprehensive evaluation studies by the appropriate ministry's staff. In the case of large enterprises, performance may be evaluated at ministerial conferences, at which ministry officials are joined by representatives of the National Material and Price Control Office, the Hungarian National Bank, and the Hungarian Investment Bank and by representatives of district party and factory trade union organizations. In theory the enterprise is not obliged to accept the findings and recommendations of the conference, but the legal power of the ministry over the enterprise manager may suffice to elicit compliance. The work of enterprise supervision is also carried out by a number of enterprise supervisory committees, information on the composition of which is not available. In 1971 these committees were active in about 6 percent of the state enterprises.

The extent of ministerial involvement in enterprise affairs has varied between branches of the economy and industry and over time. Ministerial supervision has often been criticized for being lax and, in a number of instances, ministries have been accused of advancing the interests of their branches and enterprises to the detriment of the economy. Growing economic difficulties led to a tightening of governmental controls in 1971 and 1972. Special attention was to be given to about forty to fifty of the largest state enterprises that account for a substantial portion of the country's industrial output.

The internal organization and management of enterprises, many of which consist of several component units, have been frequently criticized in the Hungarian technical press. Cited shortcomings included: overcentralization of decisionmaking that excluded middle level managers from participation in the solution of problems; excessively long chains of command that impeded optimum efficiency; and inadequate operative autonomy for the constituent plants, production divisions, and shops. The quality of middle level management was also said to be in need of upgrading.

In December 1971 the MSZMP Central Committee adopted a resolution on raising the standards of enterprise organization and management in the shortest possible time. The most important aims to be achieved by this measure are greater efficiency in production, larger contributions to the state budget from enterprise profits, better coordination of production and trade, improved working conditions and wages, and a streamlining of the excessively bureaucratic administration. The president of the National Planning Office and branch ministers were made responsible for the implementation of the resolution.

Detailed recommendations for solving the organizational and management problems were to be prepared by May 15, 1972. The Central Statistical Office and the branch ministers were required to devise methods for evaluating the success of the adopted measures and to report regularly on actions taken and progress achieved beginning in 1973. Responsibility for evaluating improvements made by individual enterprises was assigned to the ministers concerned, the ministers of finance and labor, and the president of the Hungarian National Bank. Their findings are to be taken into account in the evaluation of overall enterprise performance and in determining the remuneration of enterprise managers.

Structure

According to official data, the national income (net material product) in 1970 amounted to 277.3 billion forints (for value of forint—see Glossary). In terms of official prices, which do not adequately reflect the relative scarcity of resources or production costs, the contributions of major economic sectors to the national income, in round figures, were: industry, 42 percent; construction, 12 percent; agriculture, 17 percent; and trade, 15 percent.

During the 1961–70 period national income rose by 81 percent at an average annual rate of 6.1 percent. Whereas the contribution of industry to national income doubled and the contributions of construction and trade increased by almost 80 percent, the value added by agriculture remained virtually unchanged. This disparity in development was a consequence of the leadership's economic policy, which gave preference to industry over other sectors but was constrained by political considerations to allow an increase in the supply of consumer goods on the domestic market.

There is no evidence of any intent to modify the trend of the intersectoral structural development. The leadership, however, has been seeking to bring about structural changes within industry and agriculture. In industry the major aim is to shift production from obsolete and low-quality products to technologically more advanced models capable of competing in world markets. In agriculture the drive has been centered on raising the volume and improving the quality of livestock production in order to eliminate sporadic domestic food shortages and to increase the volume of traditional exports.

PLANNING

National economic planning serves as the basic instrument for guiding the development of the economy. The long-term plan for a period of fifteen or twenty years outlines the long-range objectives of national economic development and foreign economic relations. The five-year plan is used as a tool for the management and control of the economy by central authorities. This plan is oriented toward the long-range objectives and establishes quantitative interim goals for all sectors of the economy. The annual plan defines current targets that are based on the five-year goals, taking into consideration existing economic conditions and short-range prospects. In 1973 the country entered the third year of the Fourth Five-Year Plan (1971-75).

In contrast to the prereform system, the national economic plan is no longer compulsory in the sense that the fulfillment of each individual plan target is compulsory. Under NEM the plan is considered to be compulsory only in its entirety—in that it prescribes the direction in which individual economic units should proceed.

The attainment of the planned goals is to be ensured through the system of indirect economic regulators that are intended to guide enterprises in the direction prescribed by the plan. The government, nevertheless, is legally empowered to issue direct instructions to enterprises whenever it judges such intervention to be in the best interest of the economy. Unforeseen changes in circumstances or initial miscalculations by planners necessitate modifications of original plans from time to time.

The planning apparatus, which consists of the National Planning Office and planning units of ministries, local governments, and enterprises, has not been able to develop effective methods of integrated planning under the more decentralized system introduced by the reform. Neither has it been possible for the government to develop the system of accounting and statistical reporting to a point where it could provide planners in adequate time the needed range of reliable data.

Based on the objectives of the five-year plan and within the framework of the economic regulators, enterprises draw up their own five-year and annual plans under the guidance of central government authorities. The formulation and execution of the plans is supposed to help disclose unused resources, accelerate technological development, and increase the efficiency of production. Several variations of the plan must be prepared, and the traditional tendency of setting targets below the potential of the enterprise must be avoided. In the capital goods sector, however, central government organs still make between 35 and 40 percent of the decisions concerning development.

In practice enterprises are severely handicapped in formulating realistic plans by frequent changes in the regulators. One of the most basic regulators, for instance, was modified three times in the first four years of NEM. A committee of economists and government officials that reviewed the experience gained under NEM during that period concluded that a long-range system of regulators could not be established in advance and that annual changes of many basic regulators, including prices and controls over the supply of materials, must be integrated each year in the annual plan. This procedure is to be followed at least until 1980.

Another difficulty in planning by enterprises is the difficulty of anticipating market trends and the failure of the trading organizations to provide this information. With the exception of agriculture, most enterprises in 1971 planned higher growth rates than the overall rates in the national plan. Many enterprises continued to emphasize the expansion of plant and output above a more intensive use of available resources and greater efficiency. This led to the planning of a much higher growth in investments than the growth planned by central authorities. Few enterprises made any plans for marketing their products, and most preferred to sell the bulk of their output in the domestic market. In accordance with NEM policies major emphasis in enterprise planning is placed on maximizing profits.

Only a minority of enterprises have succeeded in organizing their planning work efficiently. Most enterprises lack the necessary managerial capabilities and long-range outlook. In 1972 the National Planning Office made several recommendations to improve the quality of enterprise planning. These recommendations called for unity of viewpoint and action among state and social organs (for example, the Patriotic People's Front) in relation to the objectives of enterprise planning and for a clearer definition by central party and government organs of short- and medium-term enterprise planning policy and of the role of central agencies in enterprise planning. They also drew attention to the need for a realistic appraisal of capabilities and trends and for an improvement in the supply of information to enterprises. Useful experience for both enterprises and central agencies was reported to have been gained in the planning of the Fourth Five-Year Plan and of the annual plans to 1972.

The National Planning Office functions as a commission with ministerial rank; it has no responsibility for enforcing the implementation of plans. Control over implementation is diffused among branch and functional ministries (for example, the Ministry of Heavy Industry and the Ministry of Finance) and other central government agencies, such as the National Material and Price Control Office and the national, investment, and foreign trade banks. During the prereform era control over plan implementation was centered in the planning office, which exercised its authority through the branch ministries and banks.

During the first five years of NEM the decentralized system of economic planning and control failed to ensure the attainment of several essential goals and intensified certain inimical conditions that it was supposed to eliminate. In November 1972, therefore, Kadar drew attention to the need for more precise planning, better integration of the planning work, and stricter supervision over plan fulfillment. In his view this required greater centralization of efforts and authority. He proposed to enhance the authority of the National Planning Office and called for the establishment of a state planning commission as an organ of the Council of Ministers, in order to coordinate the planning work of ministries and other central government agencies, to regulate the economy, and to supervise the implementation of the national plan. Kadar also called for enhancing the authority of branch ministries with reference to planning and technological development.

PRICE SYSTEM

The price system established under NEM was intended to promote the rational use of resources, adaptation of production to effective demand, product innovation, equilibrium between demand and supply, and price stability. Prices were to reflect the combined effects of production costs, domestic market valuation, foreign competition, and state-determined priorities. These goals were only partially attained during the first five years of NEM. Economic difficulties developed that necessitated a substantial rise in state subsidies, with a consequent increase in inflationary pressures.

In the price reform of January 1, 1968, prices paid to producers were raised substantially with the intention of eliminating production subsidies and enabling enterprises to create investment funds out of profits. Retail prices, however, were left virtually unchanged. The leadership has attached great importance to the maintenance of a stable retail price level in order to avoid the emergence of public discontent, particularly in view of the decision to allow only a minimal rise in wages, at least until 1975. The increased disparity between producers' and retail prices was absorbed by the budget through a rise in price subsidies to the trade network and to producers selling directly to the public.

Prices for domestic products that are also imported in significant quantities, mainly raw materials, were set in relation to purchase prices from communist and Western suppliers. Prices for a wide range of manufactured products, however, were formed in the traditional manner. These prices reflected total domestic input costs and also included an element of predetermined profit calculated as a percentage of cost. Because of pressure from industry and in order to maintain the supply of scarce goods, a high rate of profit was also granted to high-cost producers using obsolete technology, especially in light industry. Subsequent price increases in excess of planners' expectations contributed to the maintenance of a high profit level in this industry despite strict government control measures.

The price system includes four different types of prices: fixed, maximum, variable between fixed limits, and free. The more basic or scarce the product, the more rigid is the price. The level of fixed prices and the limits of maximum and variable prices are set by the government, generally in some relation to the average calculated costs of the products. Free prices, as the name implies, may be set by individual enterprises, subject to review by higher authorities.

According to one Hungarian source, in the beginning of 1972 fixed prices applied to 10 percent of industrial products; maximum prices covered 29 percent of the products; and free or flexible prices prevailed for 61 percent of the products. The price structure in the consumer field was reported to have been significantly different. Eighteen percent of the prices were fixed; 21 percent were in the variable price category; and only 33 percent were free. The remaining 28 percent of prices were, presumably, in the maximum price category.

Another source reported that between January 1968 and mid-1970 the proportion of industrial production governed by fixed prices declined from 10 to 5 percent, and the share of output subject to maximum prices declined to 27 percent. In agriculture 80 percent of the product volume marketed in 1970 was subject to various forms of price limitation, including 60 percent of the volume governed by fixed prices.

Adequate information on the mechanism of price formation and on price control since 1968 is not available. The National Material and Price Control Office is authorized to deal with all price questions except for those the Council of Ministers has reserved for itself and for questions that were delegated to appropriate ministers and local authorities by the president of the price office. The state (presumably the Council of Ministers) establishes general guidelines for price policy and price regulation and determines the official prices for important products and services. In some cases—whenever required measures exceed the competence of the various price agencies—the state can exert a direct influence on the price level. The upward revision of certain consumer prices in January 1973 is an example of such state intervention.

Effective supervision of prices by the authorities has been hampered by the complexity of the price system and the multiplicity of applicable regulations. It has also been handicapped by the failure of legal provisions to authorize decisive action by price authorities in cases involving unjustified increases in free prices. The relevant law merely admonishes enterprise managers to proceed with proper care in the formation of prices.

Nevertheless, it was reported in 1972 that ministries were beginning to pay closer attention to pricing by enterprises under their jurisdiction. There is no evidence whether, or to what extent, the ministries have applied sanctions, in the form of reducing or withholding premium payments, to managers pursuing irresponsible price policies.

Supervision is relatively simple in the case of fixed prices, where the task is limited to checking whether the legal prices are in fact being maintained or whether enterprises find loopholes in the regulations to circumvent the prescribed maximums. In the area of maximum and variable prices the common practice among enterprises has been to raise prices to the maximum level. The most difficult problem is presented by free prices.

At the time for the introduction of the new price system it was expected that free prices would be determined by competitive market conditions. These conditions materialized in only a few cases. Many manufacturing enterprises have continued to enjoy a monopoly position and to set prices accordingly; trade enterprises have passed on the price increases to consumers. The anticipated moderation of domestic monopoly prices through competition from imports did not take place, in part because the limited availability of foreign exchange precluded an adequate volume of imports and in part because of price equalization through the import-pricing system.

Beginning in 1973 trade enterprises were placed under stricter obligation not to pass on production cost increases to consumers, and measures were introduced to enable them to absorb increased costs. A decision was also announced to impose controls over many previously free prices in the building construction industry. In his report to the National Assembly on the budget for 1973, the minister of finance noted that the first signs of more effective price control were already discernible. He warned, however, that action by state and social organizations was also indispensable to end illicit price increases.

One of the aims of NEM is to bring prices gradually more closely in line with production costs. Nevertheless, retail prices for most consumer goods, especially foods, have continued to be divorced from costs of production and prices paid to producers. With the exception of high prices for clothing and for products in the free price category under monopolistic enterprise control, consumer prices are generally lower than producer prices and are heavily subsidized by the state.

This has been particularly true in the field of staple foods, where consumer prices remained relatively stable despite significant increases in farm prices. For political reasons, maintenance of the artificial consumer prices has been considered essential by the leadership, despite its awareness that this policy militates against desirable changes in the consumption pattern and retards the evolution of a more rational production structure.

An increase in retail prices for milk, dairy and tobacco products, and alchoholic beverages other than beer and wines could not be avoided in January 1973, after a substantial rise in farm prices introduced earlier to stimulate farm production. As an offset to the price increase—an average of 28 percent for milk and dairy products, from 3 to 11 percent for baked goods containing significant quantities of milk or cheese, 25 percent for tobacco products, and 15 percent for alcoholic beverages—provision was made for greater social assistance to annuitants and large, low-income families.

To allay public discontent the government also drew attention to the special wage increase for workers in state industry and building construction scheduled for March 1, 1973, and to the further rise in real wages and collective social benefits provided for in the economic plan for that year. For political reasons an economically needed and justified rise in the retail price of meat was postponed. In reporting on this subject to the MSZMP Central Committee, the party leader recommended that an increase in the price of meat be considered sometime at the beginning of the next five-year plan (1976–80), when it could be balanced with wage and social policy measures and with price reductions for textiles, clothing, and other manufactured articles.

Prices up to 1973 reflected a distorted valuation of resources, especially in relation to costs of capital and labor. Because investment costs have been high and rising under the impact of NEM regulators, enterprises in capital-intensive industries have tended to raise prices for their products. As a result Hungarian economists believed capital-intensive products to be overpriced and labor-intensive products to be underpriced with reference to the optimum use of resources. They also believed that relative undervaluation of labor costs inhibited a rise in productivity through more intensive use of capital assets. Economists have therefore suggested the need to modify the proportion between labor and capital costs that enter into price calculations by raising the cost of labor through appropriate taxation.

Economists also consider that a disparity exists between the levels of industrial and agricultural prices, in that the former is too high and the latter too low in relation to economically justifiable levels. This disparity is reflected in high returns on capital and excessive profits in industry at the same time that prices in agriculture, even though supplemented by government subsidies, are insufficiently remunerative to stimulate a significant rise in production. This gap continues to exist despite repeated increases in farm prices. Economists estimated that a rise of 25 percent in farm prices was needed to attain parity with industry at the price levels that prevailed in 1970.

There is disagreement among economists about the economic effects of the industrial-agricultural price disparity. Some believe it to constitute an impediment to economic development. Others justify it on grounds of differences in the taxation of the two sectors, by virtue of which a much larger proportion of income is withdrawn from industry. They argue that taxation tends to narrow the gap between agricultural and industrial incomes and that it may be better policy to strive for income parity rather than price parity. In any case, they maintain, parity should be attained by reducing industrial prices and not by raising farm prices.

Severe problems have arisen under the new price system for enterprises that must buy a portion or all of their materials at free prices and sell their output, or a significant proportion of it, at maximum or fixed prices. The rise in free prices since 1968 has depressed the income of these enterprises to the point where they must appeal to the state for additional budgetary support. These enterprises have been unable to provide to their workers the yearend distributions out of profits, which constitute virtually the only means for raising wages. The resultant wage disparity among workers in different enterprises has contributed to the creation of social tensions.

The NEM price system has also perpetuated and, in some instances, intensified difficulties in foreign trade. The unplanned rise in prices and profits of many enterprises and the consequent failure of these enterprises to make any efforts to raise the efficiency of production have further complicated the foreign trade problems (see Foreign Trade, this ch.).

WAGES AND INCOMES

The regulation of wages has proved to be one of the most intractable and controversial problems in economic management. In a statement to the National Assembly at the end of 1972, the minister of finance remarked that neither past nor current wage regulation methods succeeded in producing the desired economic effects. He noted that the development of a comprehensive and enduring wage system would require a considerable length of time and that amendments to the current regulation would be relied upon in the meantime. He also observed that wage regulation was still widely regarded as experimental and that experimentation with a new approach to the problem had been undertaken on a limited scale earlier in the year. A short time before the minister's statement, the chairman of the National Material and Price Control Office reported the existence of a wide divergence of opinion on the subject of wages and profits.

The wage system introduced in 1968 was intended primarily to contain the total rise in purchasing power within planned limits. It was also meant to interest both managers and workers in the profitable operation of the enterprise and to bring about a more efficient use of the labor force. To accomplish these aims wages were linked to the enterprise participation (profit-sharing) fund, and a limit was set on the average annual wage that may be paid by the enterprise without incurring financial penalties.

Wages and salaries consist of a fixed-base pay in accordance with a wage schedule determined by central authorities and of a share in any enterprise profits. The wage schedule is based on seven levels of skill and four categories of working conditions. In 1971 the average worker's share in profits was equivalent to between twenty-two and twenty-three days' wages, but there was a wide divergence in the amounts actually received by individual workers.

Initially, any excess in total wage payments above the sum based on the prescribed average wage had to be paid out of the participation fund, thereby reducing the amount available for distribution to managers and workers. This method was subsequently replaced by a progressive tax on the profit-sharing fund. Limits were imposed on the total amount of profits that may be distributed to each personnel category in relation to its position and aggregate annual base pay. For the management group, which constitutes about 0.5 to 1 percent of the personnel, the total profit distribution could not exceed 80 percent of the aggregate salaries. The comparable limit for technicians, who account for about 4.5 to 12 percent of the enterprise complement, was 50 percent; for workers, who constitute from 87 to 95 percent of the work force, the maximum was a mere 15 percent. Within each category, however, no limits were set on individual profit shares; distribution was at the discretion of the enterprise director, presumably based on his judgment of relative individual merit. The profit share of the director was determined by the relevant ministry. This system was greatly modified after one year because of worker discontent over its apparent favoring of managers. Strict percentages were abolished and greater flexibility in profit sharing was introduced.

The low limit on profit distribution to workers was intended to minimize the disparity between earnings of workers in similar positions employed in enterprises with widely differing profit levels. Relatively large differences in managers' incomes under the same circumstances were generally thought to be acceptable because managers are primarily responsible for the success or failure of the enterprise. Workers' incomes are better protected than incomes of other personnel in enterprises suffering losses that cannot be compensated by reserve funds. In this event management personnel may receive only 75 percent of their salaries; technicians may be granted 85 percent of their pay; but workers must be paid their full wages.

Far from accomplishing its intended purpose, the wage regulation had several inimical consequences. In order to avoid the penalty for exceeding the average wage limit, enterprises that needed to hire highly qualified, and therefore relatively highly paid, technicians resorted to the expedient of simultaneously hiring larger numbers of unneeded unskilled workers at below average wages. This practice served to perpetuate low productivity and intensified the labor shortage, but it ensured to managers and to the workers already on the job a higher income than would the economically desirable alternative of reducing the work force and upgrading the qualifications of workers.

The wide disparity in profit levels among enterprises brought about an inequality of workers' and managers' earnings through profit distributions from participation funds. The linkage of wages and profits penalized not only inefficient enterprises but also worked to the detriment of personnel in efficiently managed enterprises that must operate very largely under conditions of fixed and maximum prices. Many of these enterprises are in essential industries. In order to keep workers' discontent within tolerable limits, the government found it necessary to subsidize wages in unprofitable enterprises, without regard to the efficiency of management. The wage regulation thus failed to promote greater efficiency because it failed to establish any relation between productivity and financial rewards.

The disparity in workers' earnings, coupled with the tight labor market, encouraged excessive labor turnover. Large numbers of workers quit their jobs in favor of better paying jobs elsewhere. Along with other factors this situation tended to obstruct the achievement of the government's plans for improvements in the economic and industrial structure (see ch. 14).

Technical changes in the wage regulation were made each year after its introduction without, however, altering its fundamental character. In 1970 a small reduction was made in the financial penalty for raising the average wage, and some financial penalties were introduced for increasing the size of the work force. In 1971 a complicated formula was introduced that linked permissible increases in the average wage level to productivity expressed in terms of per capita wages plus profits. A steeply progressive tax on the participation fund was instituted as a penalty for raising the average wage level beyond the limit sanctioned by the new productivity formula. The tax was also supposed to arrest the growth in the inequality of workers' wages. In the event of a decline in the productivity index, the tax on the participation fund was levied even in the absence of an increase in the average wage. The revised regulation was expected to be more effective than the earlier version in promoting a rise in productivity and a more economic management of labor resources.

The productivity formula was criticized by economists and officials for its failure to take into account the use of capital and for its disregard of the wide differences in the structure of enterprises and in the possibilities open to them for increasing productivity. Under the new formula, low-profit enterprises had to attain a higher rate of increase in profits than did high-profit enterprises in order to afford an equivalent increase in the average wage.

At the end of 1971 a high party and government official declared that the wage regulations had become so complicated that even enterprise experts found it difficult to carry them out. Yet the new measures did little to improve the wage situation or to promote the economic aims of the reform. Under the prevailing wage structure it still remained worthwhile for many enterprises to pad their work forces in order to avoid the penalty for exceeding the average wage limit. Furthermore, because profits could generally be raised most easily by increasing the volume of traditional output, many enterprises found it expedient to hire additional workers to operate their machines and to work longer hours at overtime rates of pay.

The same official also pointed out that the trend of income and wage policy, though not unequivocal and not undebated, pointed in the direction of loosening or eliminating entirely the existing relationship between profit sharing and the wage level. He suggested that it may even prove necessary to go further eventually and, in the spirit of the reform, allow enterprises independently to work out wage policies best suited to their particular conditions, provided that certain general regulations are observed.

The development of an effective wage system has been hampered by contradictory policy aims and by the egalitarian attitude of some officials and of a large segment of the population, notably blue-collar workers. Adequate wage differentiation is generally admitted to be essential as an incentive to better work and for the acquisition of improved skills by workers. Yet a substantial disparity of incomes is shunned because it is widely believed to be incompatible with a socialist society. Wage differentiation had been virtually eliminated as a matter of policy in the 1952–65 period when public dissent had less influence on official decisions. A resumption of a trend toward wage differentiation under NEM has produced social tensions that constitute a political problem.

Dissatisfaction with the wage structure is particularly strong because differences in earnings are not always related to the workers' qualifications or performance but are often based on fortuitous circumstances beyond the workers' control. Resentment was also aroused by the much more rapid growth of managers' incomes compared to workers' wages. A large majority of workers expressed themselves in favor of substantially egalitarian wages and of wages unaffected by the profit position of the enterprises. At a national trade union convention held in 1971 a demand was voiced for the formulation of appropriate concepts and methods to ensure a desirable level of income to workers employed in unprofitable manufacturing enterprises.

Economists and officials who recognize the need for wage differentiation disagree as to the limits of income differentiation that would be acceptable and yet suffice to attain the efficiency aims. A study by the Hungarian Academy of Sciences found this subject to be highly controversial and hazarded a tentative conclusion that a difference of 10 to 15 percent would probably be acceptable. The study warned, however, that an unambiguous relationship between productivity and wages could not be maintained even at the level of the economy as a whole, let along at the enterprise level. A basic problem was posed by the lack of a generally accepted concept and measure of labor productivity.

The first step in an apparent retreat from the profit-linked wage system was taken with the abolition of that system in coal mining and in the electric power industry effective January 1, 1973. It was replaced by the discredited former method of regulating the wage fund—the total amount of wages paid out by an enterprise. A further revision of the wage system was indicated by the simultaneous official announcement of two projected measures. A new national wage schedule is to be worked out that will establish uniform rates of pay, according to trade, for similar kinds of work in all industrial enterprises and for equal levels of qualification and achievement. At the same time, the new schedule is to ensure above average pay for work requiring higher qualification or greater effort and for work performed under difficult conditions. The government is also developing a modified set of economic regulators, of which the wage system is an important component, to be introduced in 1975 in the context of the next five-year plan.

In the meantime, a special differentiated wage increase, averaging 8 percent in industry and 6 percent in building construction for workers and foremen in state enterprises, was announced effective March 1, 1973. This increase is in addition to the rise of 4 to 5 percent in workers' earnings scheduled for 1973 in the five-year plan. There will be wide variations from the average in the rates of increase awarded to individual workers, based on their training, achievement, and other unannounced considerations.

INVESTMENT

In the 1968-71 period the share of national income devoted to net capital formation increased from 24 to 28 percent. Investment in the economy in 1971 rose to an all-time high of 110 billion forints, 9.5 percent of which was accounted for by private enterprise. The sum was 74 percent larger in current prices and 34 percent larger in comparable prices than the amount invested in 1968—the first year of NEM. The difference in the rates of increase reflected a rise of 25 percent in the cost of investment over the three-year period. The increase in investment far exceeded the level projected by the Fourth Five-Year Plan. The situation was brought about by the loosening of central controls over investment activities of individual state and collective enterprises and by the initial underestimation of the financial resources that would become available to enterprises as a result of the price and tax reforms of 1968.

Whereas investment by central authorities was 55 percent higher in 1971 than in 1968, investment by state and collective (mostly farm) enterprises rose by 122 and 69 percent, respectively. Investment by private enterprise, however, increased by only one-third. In the first six months of 1972 investment rose by 12 percent, although investment outlays in that year were to be strictly controlled and restricted to the level of 1971 through regulation of enterprise incomes and through budgetary and fiscal policies.

The unplanned overinvestment exacerbated economic difficulties that the reform was intended to alleviate. The excessive demand for investment goods and labor aggravated existing shortages and intensified inflationary pressures. The official policy of maintaining a stable price level forced the government to absorb the rising costs through a substantial increase in subsidies, with resultant budgetary deficits. In an effort to curb the rapid development, the government reduced its own investment program in 1972 and, contrary to the philosophy of the reform, adopted direct administrative measures to restrain investment by enterprises. At the end of that year the leadership believed it had gained firmer control over runaway investment but realized that the restoration of a proper balance would require several more years.

In the 1968-71 period, after the initial reallocation of investment authority under NEM, decisionmaking power concerning investments in the socialized sector of the economy shifted further from central government authorities to individual enterprises. In 1971 the proportions on total investment decided upon at the two levels were: central authorities, 44 percent; state enterprises, 43 percent; and collective enterprises, 13 percent. The reform also brought about a major shift in the sources of investment funds. In 1971 the state budget provided 48 percent of the investment funds; enterprises supplied 42 percent out of their own resources; and bank credits covered the balance. In 1966 the respective proportions of investment financing from state and enterprise funds were 82 and 16 percent.

The traditional shortcomings of investment realization—overextension, inadequate economic justification, poor project planning and execution, long construction delays, growth in the volume of unfinished projects, and massive cost overruns—have not been eliminated by the reform. According to a report by the Hungarian Academy of Sciences, it took an average of 6.3 years to complete individual state investment projects—virtually twice the length of time usually required in the West. The volume of uncompleted investment projects almost doubled in the 1968-71 period and approached the volume of a full year's investment. A Hungarian economist placed the responsibility for overinvestment and its associated evils mainly on the shortcomings of the investment planning and decisionmaking process.

In the area of direct state investments the National Planning Office's control or influence over large projects has been inadequate. Individual ministries are primarily interested in the construction of physical facilities in the shortest possible time. The ministries generally possess more complete information than the planning office and are in a position to use their knowledge to elicit favorable decisions from the higher authority.

In the case of decentralized investments, enterprises have often undertaken projects in excess of their financial resources in the confident expectation that the state would come to their assistance in the event of financial difficulties. At least until mid-1972 central government agencies actually provided this assistance in the overwhelming majority of instances. Banks have been accused of contributing to the problem by their superficial analyses of requests for investment credits. Banks often feel obligated to make questionable loans in order to avoid what they consider possibly greater losses to the economy.

For a period of years the leadership has been concerned over the disproportionate share of investment consumed in building construction as against the funds used to acquire new machinery. Investment in buildings rose from 41.9 percent of the total in the 1961-65 period to 48.6 percent in 1971, whereas investment in machinery declined from 44.3 to 41.8 percent. Imported machinery gained in importance compared to machines of domestic production; in 1971 imports accounted for more than half the investment in machinery. Although imports from other Eastern European communist countries predominated throughout the period, their proportion declined from 73 to 55 percent, while the share of imports from Western states almost doubled.

In the 1961-71 period there was a minor shift in the distribution of total investment in favor of agriculture, housing and public buildings, the construction industry, and trade at the expense of industry, transport, and communications. In 1971 the relative investment shares of the major economic branches were: industry, including construction, 41.6 percent; agriculture and forestry, 21.1 percent; and transport and communications, 11.9 percent. Four percent of the investment in that year was devoted to trade, and 9.3 percent was spent on housing. The balance of the investment was absorbed by various communal service facilities.

BUDGET

Official information on the country's finances has not been published. Only fragmentary data may be gleaned from press reports, the annual budget presentations to the National Assembly by the Ministry of Finance and the Council of Ministers, and reports on fulfillment of the budget as published in the *Official Gazette*.

Budgetary revenues in the 1968-72 period increased by more than 10 percent annually, and a rise of 7.7 percent was planned for 1973. The budget for 1973 provided for revenues of 229 billion forints and expenditures of 231.7 billion forints, leaving a deficit of 2.7 billion forints. Annual deficits in 1970, 1971, and 1972 amounted to about 3.8 billion, 3.3 billion, and 3.2 billion forints, respectively. In his address to the National Assembly in December 1972, the deputy chairman of the Council of Ministers pointed out that the minor improvement planned for 1973 did not signal a quick return to balanced budgets.

Budgetary imbalance after 1968 was brought about mainly by excessive investment and an upsurge in consumption at state-subsidized prices. A rapid improvement in the budgetary situation is precluded by the continuing need for large-scale subsidies to inefficient producers and for price subsidies to maintain relative price stability. The leadership considers a rapid elimination of the budgetary deficits to be undesirable because such a retrenchment would slow down the growth of the economy and unfavorably affect the standard of living.

More than 80 percent of the budgetary revenue is derived from state and collective enterprises. Levies on enterprises include a tax on profits; a 5-percent charge for the use of capital (interest); and taxes on wages and salaries and social insurance contributions, amounting to an average of 25 percent of the total wage bill. Turnover taxes, levied mainly on consumer goods at the manufacturing or wholesale level, have declined in importance but still accounted for 18 percent of the budgetary revenue collected from enterprises in 1968. Other levies on enterprises include a production tax that is akin to a rental charge, the withholding of 40 percent of depreciation allowances, and customs charges. About 40 percent of the revenue derived from enterprises is absorbed by subsidy payments. Subsidies made up 60 percent of enterprise profits in 1970 and 58 percent in 1971.

Less than 20 percent of budgetary revenue has been collected from sources other than economic enterprises, including direct taxes on the population. In 1970 and 1971 direct taxes constituted only about 5.5 percent of budgetary receipts. In 1971 and 1972 official measures were being prepared to increase taxes on high incomes. These measures were directed mainly at the remaining small private sector of artisans, retail merchants, and intellectuals but were also aimed at stopping real estate speculation and the common practice of moonlighting. Taxes were also to be raised on rental incomes and real estate transactions. The revised taxation system was to introduce a differentiation based on the social usefulness of the particular income-producing activity. Indirect evidence suggests that at least some of the tax measures were in effect in early 1973. At that time the introduction of a new tax on real and movable property was under consideration by the MSZMP and the government.

Information on the distribution of budgetary expenditures for various purposes is more scarce than data on receipts. In the 1973 budget more than 20 percent, or 46 billion forints, was earmarked for investment, and about 97 billion forints, or 42 percent, was allotted to collective social consumption, including almost 30 billion forints for health, education, and culture. Subsidies to economic enterprises were to increase by 7 billion forints to a level of 58 billion forints, or 25 percent of total expenditures. All reported categories of expenditures reflected increases over the preceding year.

BANKING

Until 1971 the country's major banking institutions included the Hungarian National Bank, which functioned as a bank of issue; the Hungarian Investment Bank; the Hungarian Foreign Trade Bank; and the National Savings Bank. During the second half of the year a reorganization of the banking system was carried out for the purpose of rationalizing central government control over credit extension and particularly over credits for investment purposes. In the reorganization the Hungarian Investment Bank was abolished, and its functions were distributed among the Hungarian National Bank, the National Savings Bank, and the newly created State Development Bank. Functions related to the financing of local economic enterprises were transferred from the Hungarian National Bank to the National Savings Bank.

Under the prereform economic system detailed bank supervision over enterprise activities was an integral part of the central government's control mechanism. At the inception of the economic reform, bank supervision became the subject of intensive debate. Many participants in the debate considered control by the banks to be incompatible with the spirit of the reform and questioned the need for bank control on the grounds that the new economic regulators created adequate incentives for enterprises to use borrowed funds wisely and to complete investment projects expeditiously and efficiently.

In addition to serving as the bank of issue and regulating the activities of all other banking institutions, the Hungarian National Bank, within the revised banking system, handles all applications for loans to cover fixed and current capital requirements that arise from project decisions made by enterprise management. The bank also finances the working capital requirements of the construction industry and of all investment planning enterprises. The Hungarian National Bank and all other financial institutions are subject to the direction and supervision of the minister of finance.

The National Savings Bank may use its funds to extend loans to individuals, collective enterprises, savings unions, and certain noneconomic institutions. The bank handles the accounts of all local governments and local government institutions and provides development loans for these agencies. It also extends loans for private housing construction in conformity with municipal and regional government development plans; engages in real estate transactions and acts as real estate agent; organizes and operates lotteries; and manages the proceeds from state bond issues.

A decree on the functions of the National Savings Bank issued by the minister of finance in October 1972 appointed the bank to be the agency for the conduct of selected foreign exchange transactions, such as estate transactions. The bank is empowered to handle foreign exchange accounts of persons residing within and outside the country. The Hungarian National Bank continues to exercise a monopoly over foreign exchange. It handles Hungary's international financial transactions and provides finance for imports and exports. The Hungarian Foreign Trade Bank is responsibile for financing special foreign trade operations.

The newly created State Development Bank, the legal successor to the Hungarian Investment Bank, is supposed to finance large enterprise investment projects that are supported by government loans. Its jurisdiction does not extend over state investment projects financed by local government funds. In performing its financing function the bank must keep under close scrutiny all aspects of the investment work. The bank is directed to participate in the formulation of decisions concerning state subsidies for enterprise investments and to monitor in detail the use of subsidy funds. The bank may organize new enterprises and sponsor the creation of economic associations for the purpose of promoting the attainment of social goals.

There is no clear demarcation between the kinds of projects to be handled by the Hungarian National Bank and those to be financed by the State Development Bank. By mutual agreement of the banks' managers the State Development Bank will finance only the largest state-supported investment projects. A definition in value terms of what constitutes the largest projects is not available. A jurisdictional question between the two banks arose in connection with the financing of large highway construction projects and afforestation. It has been suggested that the Hungarian National Bank is better suited for this task because of its large network of rural branches. The problem of division of authority between the State Development Bank and other government agencies, such as the National Planning Office and the economic ministries, and the limits of the bank's authority over enterprises remained unresolved in the spring of 1973.

CURRENCY

The country's currency is the forint, divided into 100 fillers. The currency is not convertible and is usable only in domestic transactions. The forint is defined as containing 75.758 milligrams of fine gold, which implies a theoretical parity of 10.81 forints per US$1. This official rate is not used in practice. Several rates of exchange have been created, each applying to a different set of international financial transactions. A rate of 27.63 forints per US$1 is used for most noncommercial transactions.

In foreign trade so-called price multipliers that are used for accounting purposes were introduced on January 1, 1968. They serve as the base for determining the amount of state subsidies or other financial adjustments provided by the government for exports and imports. The multiplier in dollar and other hard currency trade was set at 60 forints per US$1. In trade with the Soviet Union and other ruble area trading partners, the multiplier was set at 40 forints per 1 ruble; this is equivalent to a rate of 33.3 forints per US$1.

Bilateral ruble clearing accounts are used in trade with partners in the Council for Mutual Economic Assistance (COMECON). Trade with less developed states is also based on bilateral clearing accounts. Obligations arising from this trade are sold outside Hungary at discounts of 2 to 22 percent.

Strict government controls are in effect over all foreign exchange transactions. Trading in gold is illegal, and the import or export of diamonds and jewelry is prohibited. Residents who have permission to travel to the West may obtain an allocation of about US$140 or the equivalent amount in other hard currencies for each trip abroad.

FOREIGN TRADE

A dearth of natural resources makes Hungary heavily dependent on foreign trade. In emphasizing the importance of trade for the country's economy, statements have often been made that 40 percent of the national income is realized through foreign trade. What is implied by these statements is that the annual volume of foreign trade is equivalent to 40 percent of the national income. According to official statistics, however, the ratio of foreign trade to national income rose from about 18 percent in 1968 to 21 percent in 1971. The figure of 40 percent is actually the five-year plan target for 1975.

One of the main problems faced by the leadership in expanding foreign trade is the slow progress in developing the production of export goods that could compete in world markets with regard to quality and price. The lag is owing mainly to the insufficiency of investment allotted for this purpose. Despite the provision of liberal subsidies and other benefits to exporters, most enterprises prefer to produce for the domestic market because of the lower risk and investment needs and the generally higher earnings in domestic trade.

The country's foreign trade suffers from a lack of flexibility because the nature of two-thirds of its trade volume is determined by long-term bilateral trade agreements with members of COMECON that, in effect, constitute barter trade. The limitation on the freedom of trade serves to perpetuate the existing structure of industry.

The reform of foreign trade was intended to bring the pressure of foreign competition to bear on the domestic economy with a view to stimulating greater efficiency through cost reduction and improvements in the structure and quality of output. The overriding policy of maintaining domestic price stability and protecting domestic industry, however, necessitated the introduction of measures to attenuate substantially the effects of world price fluctuations on the domestic price level.

Liberalization of trade in order to stimulate more efficient production will be a slow process, according to the deputy minister of finance. A more rapid exposure of domestic producers to foreign competition, he stressed, would entail a substantial loss of production, widespread unemployment, increased balance-of-payments deficits, and other economic ills. Enterprises must be enabled to recoup their production costs and to obtain a profit either from sales or from state subsidies.

State monopoly of foreign trade was maintained in the reform of 1968. A system of economic regulators was introduced, however, that was intended to guide the foreign trade activities of large industrial and specialized foreign trade enterprises along policy lines and in accord with generalized export and import plans formulated by the government. Innumerable exceptions from the general provisions, however, have had to be made for individual enterprises for diverse reasons, so that the government has continued to be involved in detailed direction of trade, although by somewhat different means than before the reform.

The economic regulators of foreign trade consist of what are known in the country and generally referred to as foreign exchange multipliers (in effect, foreign exchange rates used for domestic accounting purposes) and various so-called financial bridges that help span the gap between foreign and domestic prices. The financial bridges include various state subsidies, import and export taxes, government rebates and tax remissions, price fluctuation reserve funds, and a customs tariff applicable to noncommunist countries. Administrative controls include export and import quotas, foreign trade licensing, and discretionary credit administration.

Different exchange multipliers and sets of financial bridges are applied to the ruble and the dollar trading areas because trade with communist countries is conducted on the basis of bilateral clearing accounts for predetermined lists of commodities at specified prices. Administrative responsibility and supervision over foreign trade is shared by the Ministry of Foreign Trade, the Ministry of Finance, the Hungarian National Bank, and several economic ministries. Trade promotion is carried on by the Hungarian Chamber of Commerce.

The level at which foreign exchange multipliers were to be set was a subject of prolonged debate before 1968. As a compromise, rates of forty forints to the ruble and sixty forints to the dollar were finally adopted. At these exchange rates about half the exports entailed losses in the first year of the reform, although a number of enterprises were able to earn above average profits. Subsequent fluctuations in world market prices produced wide-ranging changes in the profitability of individual imports and exports based on the fixed exchange multipliers. Under these circumstances a complex and constantly changing mix of state supports and taxes has been used to maintain the domestic price level, ensure profitable operation for all enterprises engaged in foreign trade, divert a portion of the profits to the budget, and protect domestic supplies. Because of conceptual imperfections and faulty administration of the financial bridges, their effectiveness proved to be far below the original expectations.

The unfavorable trend of the foreign trade balance was arrested in 1972 through administrative measures and adjustments in financial supports, although at the cost of a continuing drain on budgetary resources. A substantial improvement in the trade balance was officially reported at the end of the year, but an excess of imports over exports was, nevertheless, anticipated for 1973.

In the 1961-71 period the volume of foreign trade almost tripled to a level of 64.5 billion foreign exchange forints (roughly equivalent to US$1.6 billion); imports grew somewhat faster than exports. The expansion of trade, however, was erratic. Annual rates of growth fluctuated between 3 and 20 percent. The most rapid growth of trade took place from 1969 through 1971, after the relaxation of government controls under NEM. In these three years the volume of trade increased by 53 percent, including a rise of 66 percent in imports but only 40 percent in exports. Regulations that had been framed by the government to facilitate the importation of essential raw materials were used by enterprises to augment their profits through imports of a wide range of products, including consumer goods.

Trade with communist countries in the 1960-71 period fluctuated between 65 and 73 percent of the annual volume and averaged 68.5 percent for the entire period. The lowest level was reached in 1970, a year in which imports from the West rose by an unprecedented 43 percent— an increase far in excess of the level projected by the economic plan. Virtually all trade with communist states was oriented toward COMECON partners; nonmembers in this organization accounted for less than 3 percent of the trade. The Soviet Union has been by far the most important trading partner; it has accounted for roughly one-third of total trade and a little more than half the trade with other communist states.

In the trade with the West advanced industrial states predominate, particularly the Federal Republic of Germany (West Germany), Italy, Austria, the United Kingdom, and France. These six countries accounted for more than 60 percent of the trade with the industrial group in 1970. Trade volume with developing countries has been of minor significance and has been declining as a proportion of the total trade. Countries in Asia and Africa have not been able to export a sufficient volume of goods to pay for imports from Hungary, whereas Hungary has been unable to repay in exports for goods imported from Latin America because it cannot compete with other exporters to that area. Foreign exchange difficulties of all these countries have largely precluded a monetary settlement of outstanding balances.

In the 1960-71 period the overall trade balance was positive in only three of the twelve years, and the balance with Western states was favorable only once—in 1969. The cumulative trade deficit for the entire period amounted to 11.5 billion foreign exchange forints, or one-third the value of imports in 1971; half the deficit was incurred in 1970. Under the usual trade agreements among COMECON members the deficit of 2.3 billion foreign exchange forints with communist countries must be repaid in goods and services. The debt of 9.3 billion foreign exchange forints to Western trading partners requires settlement in convertible currency. Information on the balance of payments and the manner of international debt settlement is not available. In December 1972 the minister of finance assured the National Assembly that the country's ability to meet its foreign obligations remained stable. A reputable Western source estimated Hungary's indebtedness to the West at the beginning of 1971 to have been at least US$152 million, including a debt of US$78 million to the United States. This sum did not include a 25 million Euro-dollar (see Glossary) bond issue that was floated in Europe that year.

In the 1965-71 period a significant shift took place in the composition of imports from industrial and agricultural raw materials, semifinished products, and foods to finished capital goods and manufactured consumer goods. The share of the first product group was almost three-fourths of the total at the beginning of the period but only two-thirds in its last year. The proportion of machinery, transport equipment, and other capital goods rose from 20.6 to 25.5 percent; the share of consumer goods increased from 5.6 to 8.8 percent after having reached 9.9 percent in 1970. Most of the increase in machinery imports occurred in 1971 after the removal of a high protective tariff against these imports from the West. The tariff was removed on the urging of economists and enterprise directors who saw it as an obstacle to the modernization of industry—one of the leadership's high priority goals.

The composition of exports remained somewhat more stable than that of imports in the 1965-71 period. A small reduction in the share of semifinished products was balanced by an increase in the share of raw materials and spare parts. Similarly, a minor decline in the proportion of finished capital goods was offset by a rise in the share of manufactured consumer goods. In 1971 manufactured capital and consumer goods accounted for almost half the exports. Of the remainder somewhat more than half consisted of raw materials and semifinished products, and somewhat less than half consisted of agricultural and food products.

The commodity pattern of exports to communist and Western countries reflects the state of Hungary's industrial development and its qualitative limitations. Although a high proportion of exports consists of manufactures, only a small part of these exports, particularly machinery, is sold in the West. In 1971 manufactures, including semifinished products, constituted 77 percent of the export volume to communist states but only 48 percent of a much smaller volume to Western countries. In the case of machinery, transport equipment, and other capital goods, the relative proportions were 33.4 percent to communist countries and 7.6 percent to the West. In terms of value machinery sales in the West were less than 10 percent of exports to the communist area. By contrast agricultural and industrial raw materials and foods constituted less than one-fourth of exports to communist states but more than half the exports to the West. Unfinished products purchased with convertible currencies in the West were incorporated in finished products that were not competitive in world markets and that had to be traded under COMECON agreements, exchanged for food products from developing countries, or sold on credit.

CHAPTER 13

AGRICULTURE

The agricultural organization consists of state, collective, and private tiny farms. Since 1968 farm enterprises have had relative freedom to plan production and investment—but not marketing—within a framework of government regulations and financial incentives. This framework, however, has not been conducive to rapid progress, particularly in the field of livestock production. The main reasons for the unsatisfactory advance have been the shortage of resources for agricultural development owing to the leadership's industrialization policy and inadequate production incentives because of low prices and profitability. Government measures to stimulate production through price adjustments and new subsidies after 1969 showed initial signs of limited success in the following three years.

In 1970 agriculture employed 24 percent of the workers active in the economy, received 16 percent of the investments, and contributed 17 percent of the national income (net material product) according to official Hungarian statistics. The farm output covered almost all domestic food consumption and provided about one-fourth of the country's exports. Agricultural imports to the extent of about half the volume of exports, however, were necessary to balance domestic needs, including substantial quantities of livestock feed and plant protective chemicals.

CLIMATE AND SOILS

Natural conditions are generally favorable for agriculture. The country is well endowed with fertile soils, and the climate is warm enough for the cultivation of such crops as wheat, corn, rice, and grapes. Wide annual variations in the seasonal pattern and rainfall, however, accompanied by periodic droughts and floods, cause significant fluctuations in the volume of farm output.

The basically continental climate is moderated by Atlantic air currents and is further influenced by the Mediterranean Sea. The Mediterranean influence assures even to the northern portion of the country warm and sunny weather through early fall. Annual precipitation averages more than twenty-five inches in portions of Transdanubia but less than twenty inches in some sections of the Great Plain. Heaviest rainfall occurs in the months of May through July and again in October. Marked regional differences in climate exist despite the relatively small size of the country. Weather conditions are subject to extreme variations from year to year depending upon the relative strength of the individual climatic factors (see ch. 3).

The country's varied soils are scattered in a mosaic pattern. Of greatest value to agriculture are: the rich chernozem (black earth), most of which lies in the Great Plain east of the Tisza River and in the eastern portion of Transdanubia; the fertile alluvial meadow soils along the rivers; and the relatively fertile brown forest soils that compose most of Transdanubia and the Northern Range. Poorer soils, however, may also be useful. Some of the finest fruits and vegetables are grown in light sandy soils in the region of Kecskemet, between the Danube and the Tisza rivers. Swamp soils are fertile when drained, and alkaline soils can be reclaimed for rice cultivation, afforestation, and fishponds.

Two million acres of acid, alkaline, and sandy soils were improved in the 1961-70 period, but in 1971 about half the available farmland—8.6 million acres—still required some form of improvement to become fully productive. During the same period irrigation extended over an average of 500,000 acres annually, or less than 3 percent of the agricultural land. Only 340,000 acres were irrigated in 1971. The maximum area that could be irrigated in 1972, if all unserviceable irrigation equipment were repaired or replaced, amounted to 914,000 acres. Farmers, however, lacked the necessary funds to undertake the task of rehabilitation. They were offered some assistance at reasonable fees by the national water authority.

LAND USE

In 1970 agricultural land comprised 17 million acres, or 74 percent of the country's land area. More than 73 percent of the agricultural land was arable; meadows and pastures constituted less than 19 percent; vineyards, orchards, and gardens accounted for the remaining 8 percent. The proportion of arable land in the total land area—54 percent—was one of the highest in Europe.

In the 1960-70 period the agricultural area declined by 657,000 acres, and the acreage of arable land was reduced by an almost equal amount, mainly through diversion to industrial and urban uses. At the same time the area of vineyards, orchards, and gardens increased by 383,000 acres at the expense of meadows and pastures. The increase was largest in the case of orchards, the area of which more than doubled.

The area sown to crops declined from an annual average of 12.4 million acres in the 1961-65 period to 11.9 million acres in the years 1966 through 1970. Grains occupied about 64 percent of the sown area during the decade, including about 25 percent of the area under corn. The wheat acreage increased from an annual average of 21.6 percent of the sown area in the first half of the 1960s to 25.6 percent in the second half, under the stimulus of relatively favorable prices. During the same period the areas under rye, barley, and oats declined from a total of 17 to 14 percent of the sown area. Expansion of the corn acreage by reducing the area under wheat, which economists consider essential for the development of livestock production and desirable for purposes of export, has been inhibited on most farms by a shortage of labor, a low level of mechanization, and an unfavorable cost-price ratio relative to wheat. Corn production is more profitable than the cultivation of wheat only on highly mechanized farms.

Owing to declining supply of farm labor, the acreages of such labor-intensive crops as potatoes, vegetables, sugar beets, tobacco, and sunflowers were reduced to a point where production failed to keep pace with growing requirements. Beginning in 1971 the government introduced incentive measures for tobacco, sugar beet, and vegetable growers in an effort to counteract this undesirable trend. The average annual acreage under major fodder crops remained virtually unchanged from the first to the second half of the 1960s.

ORGANIZATION

Collective farms constitute the dominant form of agricultural organization. In 1970 they comprised 78 percent of the agricultural land and 80 percent of the arable acreage. State farms and farms under the jurisdiction of local governments contained about 15 percent of the farmland and 14 percent of the arable area. The remaining small acreage portion of 6 to 7 percent consisted of unfavorably located, private tiny farms and plots cultivated by nonagricultural workers and annuitants mainly for personal consumption but also for the market. State farms have enjoyed strong support from the government in the form of investment funds, technical personnel staffing, and priorities in the distribution of fertilizers and other farm supplies.

State Farms

In 1970 there were 180 state farms with an average of 12,000 acres of agricultural land, about three-fourths of which was arable. In terms of their total landholdings they ranged in size from less than 5,000 acres to more than 25,000 acres. During the preceding ten years the number of farms was reduced by almost half, and their size nearly doubled through consolidation. State farms employed 157,000 persons, or 13 percent of total employment in agriculture. They had at their disposal a disproportionate share of farm buildings and machinery—more than double in value the amount per hectare (1 hectare equals 2.47 acres) available to collective farms; they were also much better supplied with professionally qualified managers and technical experts. State farm personnel are state employees working for salaries or wages and entitled to share in the profits of the farm on which they work.

The management of state farms is entrusted to directors appointed by the state. Under the economic reform of 1968 managers acquired the power to determine the structure of production and investments, in contrast to the earlier period when all decisions were handed down by higher authorities. Under the influence of the incentive system based on profit sharing, state farm managers were quick to take advantage of the new freedom to concentrate production on profitable lines and to reduce the share of less profitable, labor-consuming activities, disregarding to some extent national needs and government policies. The government, however, exercising its right to interfere administratively in urgent situations, directed the farms to expand the production of vegetables and sugar beets.

The main function of state farms until the late 1960s was to expand production maximally along lines determined by the government, particularly the production of essential items in short supply. The change in production policies after 1967 contributed to the exacerbation of supply problems that they were intended to alleviate. State farms have been called upon in the 1970s to intensify production, improve their management and marketing methods, and generally raise the level of efficiency. They have also been given the task of disseminating modern production methods and experimenting in so-called vertical integration by developing cooperative ventures with collective farms and with the food industry for production, processing, and marketing.

Crop and livestock yields have generally been somewhat higher on state farms than on collective farms. The difference, however, has not been significant considering the far superior technical endowment of state farms.

Collective Farms

Types and Size

Collective or cooperative farming exists in several forms. By far the most important organizations numerically and in terms of land and output are so-called agricultural producer cooperatives, which are large-scale farms engaged in mixed farming. Other forms include specialized agricultural cooperatives (no information is available on the nature of the specialization); grape-growing and garden cooperatives; and associations within the consumer cooperative structure that specialize in raising small animals for food, such as rabbits, pigeons, and poultry. Published information deals mainly with agricultural producer cooperatives, or collective farms, which were officially reported to have numbered 2,441 in 1970.

In that year collective farms held about 12.5 million acres of agricultural land, 76 percent of which was arable. Thirteen percent of the acreage consisted of small plots allotted to farm members for their personal use. The farms had a complement of almost 1.1 million persons, including 773,000 members, 128,000 members' dependents, and 176,000 hired employees. About 143,000 of the members were retired, but some continued in light work after retirement. The 500 smallest farms had an average area of less than 2,500 acres and 146 members; the largest thirty-seven farms averaged more than 12,500 acres and almost 1,200 members.

Collective farms own all their productive resources, but barely one-third of the land they cultivated was held in common in 1971. The state owned 13.5 percent of the land, and more than half was in the possession of private individuals, including collective farm members. Transfer of land to collective ownership was accelerated by a legal provision enacted sometime in 1970 or 1971 that required nonmembers inheriting collective farmland to decide within three months whether to join the collective or sell the land to it. Individuals who have neither land nor other productive resources to contribute find it difficult, if not impossible, to acquire membership in a collective farm. Those that are accepted are generally required to pay an entrance fee.

Legal Status and Organization

The legal status, organizational form, operating methods, and income distribution of collective farms are governed by the farmers' cooperative law of 1967, the standard cooperative law adopted in the fall of 1971, and supplementary government decrees. The law of 1971 granted to collective farms equality with state enterprises and protection against interference by state administrative organs except by mutual consent in unavoidable cases. In accordance with the reform principle of enterprise independence, collective farms are allowed freedom of decision within the framework of national economic plans in such matters as the structure of production, the pursuit of ancillary nonagricultural activities within prescribed limits, and cooperation with other collective and state farms in production, processing, and marketing.

State authorities may legally intervene in the affairs of a collective farm only if decisions of its general assembly violate any law or regulation. There is evidence, however, that local government and party organs have in fact injected themselves into the work of the farms' control committees, the election of new farm leadership, and economic policy discussions. The extent of such interference on a national scale could not be determined in early 1972.

Authority for governing a collective farm is vested in the general assembly of all members. The assembly elects a management body, including a president, and several specialized committees, three of which are mandatory under the law—the supervisory (control) committee, the arbitration committee, and the women's committee. The management body and the committees receive their direction from and are accountable to the general assembly. In order to make internal supervision by the supervisory committee more effective, farms may employ qualified accountants and are obliged to engage—at least once every two years—outside expert accountants for a general audit of their operations.

The arbitration committee is charged with settling disputes concerning labor and compensation. Except for minor matters, the committee's decision may be taken to court by the aggrieved party. Earlier arbitration methods were ineffective and biased against members and workers because they relied upon grievance committees subordinated to managers.

Collective farms are organized into regional associations which, in turn, are federated in the National Council of Producer Cooperatives. The National Council of Producers Cooperatives is represented in the National Cooperative Council—a consultative body and national forum for the entire cooperative movement that also includes consumer and artisan cooperatives. The National Cooperative Council also serves as an advisory body to the government on general questions of cooperative policy.

In contrast to the prereform era, the associations and federations are not supposed to be hierarchical superior authorities but rather democratically elected representative organs of the collective farms, operating within a framework of legal stipulations. According to a high party and government official, well formulated recommendations by the associations and the national federation carry great prestige. Collective farms discuss the recommendations in their general assemblies, adopt them as binding directives, and act accordingly. The requirement for mandatory outside audits, for instance, was adopted on the initiative of the National Cooperative Council.

Remuneration

The remuneration of collective farm members consists of a rental payment for the land they contributed to the collective and a share in the distribution of the farm's net income after taxes, based on the amount of work performed during the year. Payments are made in cash and in kind. Many farms have introduced a system of fixed monthly payments combined with profit sharing. A substantial portion of the members' personal income is derived from crops and livestock raised on their personal plots.

In mid-1972 a move was initiated in response to a resolution by the second national congress of collective farms to reward members for good and loyal work in the interest of better membership relations. The first collective to adopt this scheme decided to provide a wage supplement of 450 forints (for value of forint—see Glossary) per month to members who had served the collective for at least ten years and who had completed the statutory number of workdays in the last five years. The reward is payable to men over sixty years of age and women over fifty-five years, regardless of their place of work or annual income. The new reward scheme parallels a practice of long standing in industry.

A substantial proportion of the collective farms have been operating at a loss, particularly in years of poor harvests. At the end of 1970, for instance, more than 500 collectives had deficits totaling in excess of 1.5 billion forints, mainly because of bad weather and destructive spring floods. About 400 of these farms had no prospects of rehabilitation without financial aid. The government covered 0.5 billion forints of the farms' debts by a grant from the budget and provided a medium-term credit at an annual interest rate of 9 percent. The conditions attached to the state's financial assistance imposed a limit on payments to members, which a number of collectives found to be too low to ensure the members' continued active participation in the collective work. In the interest of keeping the members' personal income at an acceptable level, they reduced the amount of expenditures for the modernization of production. Individual incomes from the collective enterprise remained below 15,000 forints per year through 1972 for more than 35 percent of the active collective farm members, compared to an average income of 28,416 forints for blue- and white-collar workers on state farms in 1970.

Household Plots

The collective farm members' personal plots make a substantial contribution to the food supply. Although they constitute only 13 percent of the collective farm acreage, they have accounted for more than one-third of the farms' output and about one-fourth of the country's total agricultural production. Work on the household plots has been performed mainly by the older and retired farm members; younger members have tended to avoid the hard manual labor involved in cultivation by traditional methods.

In contrast to some of the other communist states and to the leadership's earlier policy, the party and government have come out in support of the personal farm plots to forestall difficulties in the food supply and in meeting export obligations. Various measures have been proposed to facilitate work on these plots. Plots are to be allocated closer to members' homes. Collective farms are to encourage their more intensive cultivation by providing technical assistance in production, marketing, and the purchase of supplies. Tools, garden-type equipment (such as small tractors with attachments), and milking machines are to be made available. The interest rate on loans for the purchase of equipment and the improvement of the farms is to be lowered from the prevailing rate of 8 percent per year.

A shortage of funds and continued opposition or indifference on the part of local authorities and some collective farm leaders have militated against a rapid improvement in production on the personal farm plots. In 1971 many collective farm members expressed a preference for cash compensation by the collective in lieu of continuing to farm their plots in the traditional manner.

Auxiliary Activities

Before the introduction of the economic reform, collective farms were not allowed to engage in any activity other than strictly agricultural production. Under the circumstances farms were unable to provide year-round employment for their members, and collectives that were farming poor land were able to provide income for members only with the aid of substantial state subsidies. The elimination of this restriction by the reform encouraged many farms to engage in a wide variety of ancillary activities, including not only food processing and marketing, as proposed by the government, but also more profitable industrial, transport, and service undertakings unrelated to agricultural production. This step enabled many collectives to provide full employment for their members and to realize substantial profits in place of former losses. Three-fourths of the profits from industrial operations were used for the development of agriculture and for investments that otherwise would have had to be financed with funds from the state budget.

Thirteen percent of collective farm income in 1970 was derived from sources other than farming, food processing, and lumbering. Particularly in the Budapest region, but also in poor agricultural areas near other industrial centers, farms engaged in lucrative industrial production, partly as suppliers for state industrial enterprises and partly for direct sale to consumers. Objections to the farms' industrial operations were raised on the grounds that these operations offered serious competition to state industrial enterprises and caused qualified workers to leave industry because they were able to realize higher earnings in the farm workshops. Most of the skilled workers who moved from industry to the farms were former farmers and rural residents who had been commuting to their jobs in the city.

The 1971 law that regulates the operation of collective farms does not explicitly limit the range of permitted industrial activities but allows the government to forbid or otherwise restrict some of these activities. Accordingly, new regulations issued in 1971 prohibited a number of the farms' industrial operations entirely and made advance ministerial approval necessary for others. Prohibited activities were to be phased out by mid-1972 unless permission to continue them was obtained from the appropriate ministry. Specific tax measures were also introduced to discourage activities unrelated to agriculture. At the local level, authorities fearing competition for their own enterprises have been reluctant to grant requisite licenses for auxiliary activities by the farms and have raised rents on premises leased to the collectives in instances where auxiliary ventures had been approved.

At the same time the leadership wanted to encourage the expansion of food processing and direct marketing by farms, as well as machinery repairs, construction, and small-scale local industrial production and services in competition with private artisans. The merits of the new regulations were questioned in the country's press because many collective farm industrial activities were considered beneficial for the national economy. Spokesmen for the farms urged in early 1972 that only those activities be liquidated that were demonstrably harmful.

FARM LABOR

In 1970 there were 1.2 million persons actively employed in agriculture—only two-thirds the number employed in 1960. Of these, 78.5 percent were employed on collective farms (including some of the overage annuitants), 14 percent worked on state farms, and 7.5 percent were small private farmers.

On collective farms the labor situation has been deteriorating steadily, and concern has been expressed for their future because the rate of mechanization has not kept pace with the loss of able-bodied workers. At the end of 1970 more than 44 percent of the collective farm members were over sixty years old, including 39 percent over the retirement age of sixty years for women and sixty-five years for men. The great majority of the overage members had ceased to do heavy farmwork. Only 9 percent of the members were under the age of twenty-six. Of the nonmember workers, 25 percent were more than fifty-five years of age, compared to less than 9 percent in industry.

There has been a continuous flow of workers in both directions between collective farms and industry, but the outflow from the farms has been much greater—60 percent in 1970. Only 20 percent of new members admitted in 1970 and 1971 were below the age of twenty. A loss of 340,000 collective farm members through aging and out-migration has been projected for the 1971–75 period.

The main reasons for the reluctance of young people to remain on collective farms or to join them are the more arduous working and living conditions and inferior social benefits compared with those enjoyed by industrial workers. The working day on collective farms is ten hours long, excluding work on the household plots, compared to an eight-hour day in industry. The retirement age for farmers is five years higher, yet such benefits as pensions, paid vacations, and day-nursery care for children are lower. The rural areas also lack the housing and sanitary amenities and the cultural and recreational facilities demanded by the increasingly educated youth. Neither the farms nor the economy possess the resources needed to meet the demands of the young people.

On state farms the labor situation is more stable. Because of the much greater capitalization of state farms, state farm workers enjoy relatively better working and living conditions than collective farmers. They are also accorded the same social benefits as industrial workers.

INVESTMENT, CREDIT, AND SUBSIDIES

Investment

Published statistics on agricultural investment do not allow a precise evaluation of trends because of changes in definition, methodology, and prices. Official data in current prices show a rapid rise of investment beginning in 1967 to almost 16 billion forints in 1970 and an increase of 65 percent in the 1966-70 period over the investment during the preceding five years. Yet a comparison of investments during the two periods in physical terms, including farm buildings, machinery, irrigation, soil melioration, livestock, and poultry, shows a substantial decline in volume. Apart from any statistical discrepancies, the difference between the indicated trends of the monetary and physical investment volumes was due to rising costs. Investment costs in agriculture during the 1968-70 period alone were officially reported to have risen by 15 percent.

Collective farms absorbed about three-fourths of the agricultural investment in the 1966-70 period, and state farms received one-fourth. On the basis of agricultural land acreage, however, investment in state farms was about 75 percent higher. Investment funds were provided from three sources—the budget, farm income, and bank credits. The sums invested directly by the state or by the farms out of income cannot be determined because published statistics lump these data with investments in forestry and water management. In 1970 investment subsidies from the budget amounted to about 1.4 billion forints for state farms and 4.2 billion forints for collective farms. In the same year state and collective farms received investment credits of 1.4 billion forints and 7.4 billion forints, respectively. Much larger investment funds, however, are needed to construct modern facilities on collective farms and to modernize and expand the inadequate farm machinery inventory. Many farms do not have the requisite resources.

Information on the distribution of agricultural investment by type of investment project was not available in late 1972. According to an unofficial source, 70 percent of the investment by collective farms in the 1960s was used for building construction, primarily for livestock; the proportion of investment devoted to this purpose is scheduled to rise in the 1971-75 period. Priority during this period is also to be given to a rapid expansion of mechanization, including equipment that will lighten the physical burden of livestock raising and help reduce manpower requirements. The sum earmarked for the supply of farm machinery in the 1971-75 period has been variously reported as 16 billion forints and 18 billion forints.

Credit

Investment and production credits are made available to farms through rural branches of the Hungarian National Bank in accordance with guidelines issued by the government in December 1971. Conditions for granting loans were modified with the introduction of the economic reform in 1968, including an upward adjustment of interest rates. In each of the succeeding three years interest rates were further raised by a total of from 50 to 100 percent in efforts to curb excessive credit demands in the economy. The added cost of credit has placed a heavy burden on agriculture; unlike industry, farms cannot pass the cost to consumers because prices for the bulk of the farm output are fixed by the government. The problem has been aggravated for farms that must resort to increased borrowing to cover crop failures caused by conditions beyond their control.

Credits to agriculture are provided for investment and operating purposes. Investment credits with a maximum maturity of fifteen years generally carry an interest charge of 8 percent per year. Credits at an annual rate of 6 percent, however, may be granted for the construction of barns and hogpens and for the expansion of milk- and meat-processing facilities. Short-term production credits with maturities of up to twelve months are provided at an annual interest rate of 8 percent. Intermediate-term loans for investment and operating purposes with maximum maturities of five and three years, respectively, carry a charge of 9 percent per year.

For the first six months of 1972 the Hungarian National Bank authorized new investment credits to be allocated for the acquisition of essential farm machinery, for soil melioration, and for food-processing installations. Credits for investment projects connected with cattle and hog raising, truck farming, and irrigation were made subject to the provision by recipients of matching funds from their own resources and of proof that subsidies from the state budget for these projects had been approved.

In the 1966–70 period collective farms received investment credits averaging 7.8 billion forints per year. The actual amount of the credits was somewhat higher than the average during the first two years of the period and lower during the last three years. Operating loans were first granted to collective farms in 1967. From that year and through 1971 the annual credits averaged 1.8 billion forints.

State farms were financed entirely through the state budget until the end of 1967. After the reform of 1968, they were placed on a self-financing basis and were made eligible for bank loans. In the 1968–71 period investment credits to state farms rose from 0.2 billion forints to 1.4 billion forints, and operating credits increased from 1.3 billion forints to 2.1 billion forints. Information on the repayment record of state and collective farms is not available.

Available bank credit resources have not been adequate for the needs of agriculture, particularly in years of poor harvests. A movement therefore arose among collective farms to establish a mutual aid fund through which resources of well-to-do farms could be used to assist farms in financial distress. Although originally reluctant to dilute its monopoly control over credit, the government eventually provided a legal framework for mutual aid in the cooperative law of 1971. Under the statute a portion of collective farm reserves set aside from profits after taxes may be used for mutual support. Farms are free to decide on the extent of their participation and on the division of their contribution between the regional and the national association assistance funds.

Subsidies

Over the years farm income has been too low to provide adequate funds for the modernization and expansion of agricultural production and, in many instances, even for current farm operation. A system of state subsidies for investment and operating purposes has therefore been used to fill the gap.

Provisions governing the granting of investment subsidies were changed in 1967. Before that date a subsidy was granted only after the investment project had been completed, and the credit was used to cancel an equal amount of outstanding indebtedness. The amount of the subsidy was determined by the priority rating of the agricultural branch in which the investment was made and by the physical characteristics of the specific investment project. In the construction of buildings for livestock, for instance, a fixed amount was allowed per cow or per hog to be housed.

Since 1967 subsidies for approved projects have been disbursed before the start of construction as supplements to the farms' own resources and bank loans. The amount of the subsidy is based on a percentage of the estimated cost and is differentiated in accordance with the projects' priority ratings. No information is available on provisions that govern subsidies for operational needs.

In the 1966–70 period the volume of subsidies to state and collective farms rose from 3.8 billion forints to 9 billion forints, including an elevenfold increase in investment subsidies from 0.5 billion forints to 5.6 billion forints. The subsidy of 9 billion forints was equivalent to 17.5 percent of the farms' net output in that year. Each of the budgets for 1971 and 1972 earmarked a sum of 7.5 billion forints for farm subsidies. The reduction from the peak level of 1970 reflected the restrictions imposed by the government on new construction as part of its program to control inflation (see ch. 12).

MEANS OF PRODUCTION

Farm Machinery

Mechanization of agriculture is urgently needed to increase productivity and to offset the continuing loss of manpower on collective farms. The farm machinery problem has been accentuated by the obsolescence of the existing inventory and an acute shortage of spare parts. For the country as a whole, about 40 percent of the main types of machines were beyond working age in 1971 and ready to be scrapped. The shortage of essential machines has been particularly pronounced with regard to labor-saving machinery for planting and harvesting corn, potatoes, and sugar beets on collective farms.

The country's machine-building industry has been unable to meet the requirements of agriculture, and more than half of all machinery, including 80 percent of the tractors, must be imported. Most of the imports have come from the Soviet Union and Czechoslovakia but also to some extent from the German Democratic Republic (East Germany) and Western countries. As a result the machinery inventory has been highly heterogeneous, which has complicated the problem of spare parts and repairs. Maintenance of the available machines was reported to require 42,000 different spare parts in 1971. Shortages of parts have immobilized much of the available equipment during the critical planting and harvesting seasons.

Although about 50,000 new tractors are to be provided for agriculture in the 1971-75 period, the number will not be sufficient to replace all obsolete units; at the end of the period there will still be about 12,000 overage tractors. The situation is similar in the case of grain combines and other crop-harvesting equipment. To improve the supply of spare parts, domestic and foreign suppliers of new farm machinery have been required to provide spares for their products. A new domestic farm machinery manufacturing trust has been made responsible for the production of spares for discontinued models and of parts that cannot be imported. The trust undertook to produce about 2,000 parts in 1971.

An important consideration in the mechanization of agriculture is the financial ability of farms to buy machinery. To facilitate its acquisition, the government has provided subsidies, based on manufacturers' or import prices, of 10 percent on tractors, 47 percent on other types of machinery and equipment, and 23 percent on spare parts; the subsidy on sugar beet planting and harvesting machinery was set as high as 70 percent. Many collective farms, nevertheless, have been too poor to buy the machinery they need even at the reduced prices. In 1971 the farms were unable to take advantage of 300 million forints in subsidies for machinery because they lacked the funds needed for purchase. A proposal made that year for raising the subsidy on tractors was rejected by the government.

The problem for the farms has been complicated by rising machinery prices. Many of the price increases have been hidden; they were introduced through minor model changes that did not significantly improve performance. Other price increases were based on rising costs of imported materials, particularly nonferrous metals. Hidden price increases in the 1968-71 period were reported to have ranged from 10 to 40 percent on individual machinery and parts items and to have been more than fourfold on one essential part. In addition, subsidies on parts for machines considered obsolete were discontinued during that period. On March 1, 1972, the government raised machinery prices by an average of 8 percent, but for some items the increases were as high as 30 to 40 percent. As a consequence, many farms had to curtail their planned purchases.

An anomalous situation existed in 1971 and 1972 with regard to bank credits for the procurement of farm machinery. Banks refused to grant credits for the acquisition of new machinery but were willing to advance credits for the purchase of parts to repair obsolete equipment at a cost almost equal to the price of new machines. Information on the rationale for this bank policy has not been available.

Fertilizers

Fertilizer consumption increased fivefold during the 1960-70 period to a volume of 837,000 tons of plant nutrients, or an average of 134 pounds per acre of arable land and perennial crops. Domestic production has been unable to meet requirements, so that one-third of the tonnage used in the years 1965 through 1970 had to be imported mostly from the Soviet Union and East Germany but also from Western nations. The proportion of imports in total consumption rose from about 23 percent in 1966 to 38 percent in 1970.

Maintenance of steady production and orderly distribution of fertilizers has not been possible because of inadequate storage capacity and the financial weakness of many collective farms. In the fall of 1971, for instance, collective farms canceled about 20 percent of the orders for fertilizers they had placed earlier because of a shortage of funds. Since the distributing agency's warehouses were full and large stocks were accumulated in the yards of producers, the industry curtailed its output.

Later in the year the government decided to grant a special fertilizer credit to the farms, which was to be repaid out of the proceeds of the 1972 crop; a longer maturity period was provided for financially weak farms. When farms began to buy fertilizer during the first quarter of 1972, a shortage of about 130,000 tons developed, largely because of the cutback in production. The shortage could not be alleviated through imports because the traditional suppliers did not have sufficient stocks at the time. The construction of adequate storage capacity is therefore considered to be an urgent task for the coming years.

In terms of fertilizer use per acre, Hungary occupies a middle position among the countries of Eastern Europe. Its fertilizer application was just half that of East Germany but six times larger than the amount used in the Soviet Union. Many farmers have not yet learned the correct use of fertilizers, particularly the proper proportion between the different types.

Plant Protective Agents

The use of plant protective agents, including herbicides, pesticides, and fungicides, is reported to have grown rapidly from a low level in the early 1960s. Their application has been made mandatory by law, the effective date of which is not known. In terms of value, the amount of these agents used on farms was reported by one source to have increased from about 1.5 billion forints in 1969 to 1.8 billion forints in 1970 and 2.3 billion forints in 1971. Another source, however, cited a figure of only 1 billion forints for 1970. The application of herbicides was reported to have been extended from 4 percent of the arable acreage in 1960 to 28 percent in 1970.

Domestic production of plant protective agents has been far below requirements. Imports from Western countries increased from the equivalent of about US$10 million in 1968 to US$18.8 million in 1971 and were expected to reach US$30 million in 1972. The high cost of the imported materials and the drain that they constituted on foreign exchange reserves led an official of the Ministry of Agriculture and Food to advocate the development of domestic manufacture on the basis of technologies known to the chemical industry. The proposal suggested as a possibility cooperation with other East European countries or, as an extreme measure, with Western firms.

MARKETING

State farms deliver their produce to state procurement agencies. Collective farms and private agricultural producers may sign delivery contracts with state purchasing and food-processing enterprises; sell directly to retail stores, restaurants, and public institutions; or bring their produce to free markets for direct sale to the population.

For several years the government has urged collective farm leaders to establish their own retail food outlets in order to shorten the distributive chain and to increase farm income. Progress in this direction has been slow, mainly because of a shortage of capital and credit but also because of opposition by local governments and a lack of marketing experience. In 1972 collective farms still sold 90 percent of their output to state enterprises. The main products sold on the free market included fruits and vegetables, poultry, eggs, and wine.

The predominance of state trade and the absence of local farm markets result in excessive crosshauling of produce with a resultant loss in quality. Products often move from villages to state purchasing centers and back again to the points of origin for sale through state retail outlets. Such roundabout trade is also encouraged by the government's policy of subsidizing retail food prices. In the case of pork, for instance, the retail price in 1972 was 25 percent below the cost of production and also lower than the government's procurement price. Hog raisers were therefore unwilling to slaughter hogs for their own consumption and preferred to buy meat at the local state stores. A similar situation prevailed with regard to bread and milk. Supplies of these products at the state stores were often short of needs.

The official milk procurement price in 1970 was 20 percent higher than the retail price of milk at state stores. Even with a state subsidy it did not pay producers to undertake the processing of milk. In 1969 milk producers sold 69 percent of their output to the state processing industry, compared to 39 percent in 1960. This shift necessitated a large increase in shipping capacity and resulted in doubling the volume of milk sales without any significant increase in milk production.

With few exceptions, prices for farm products are regulated by the government. The economic reform of 1968 was intended to reduce the influence of government and increase the importance of the market in the determination of farm prices. Three price categories were expected to emerge: fixed prices for stable commodities and foods set by the central government; variable prices set within centrally established guidelines for important foods, such as fruits and vegetables, poultry, eggs, and wine, that are subject to seasonal fluctuations and that were expected to be traded extensively on the free market; and free prices for less essential items. Adequate information on the actual situation in 1972 was not available—either on the items included in each category or on the relative importance of the categories in terms of the volume of output.

Contrary to the reported original plan, prices for vegetables have been in the free category at least since 1969 and rose at retail much higher than prices for other foods. In 1970 retail prices for vegetables in state stores were 26 percent higher than in 1968 and 65 percent above the price level of 1965. The price inflation was caused by a shortage of supplies, particularly after 1969, owing to inadequate production incentives. Under long-term agreements with other communist countries of Eastern Europe, notably the Soviet Union, 40 percent of current vegetable production must be exported, and the remaining quantity is not enough to satisfy the domestic demand.

The government's policy of using prices instead of administrative directives to regulate production and market supplies has not been entirely successful, and numerous price adjustments have had to be made in the 1968–72 period. All but a few of the price changes were upward. Nevertheless, farm prices have been generally kept below the cost of production on less efficient farms and on farms cultivating poorer lands. These marginal farms have been kept financially afloat through state subsidies. Government procurement agencies have at times taken advantage of their monopoly positions to depress prices on products falling within the free or variable price categories.

PRODUCTION

Total Output

Gross agricultural production is officially reported to have amounted to 97.6 billion forints in 1970. This volume represented an increase of 22 percent over the output in 1960 but a decline of 10 percent from the peak production attained in 1969. Net output in 1970—that is, gross output less farm produce used for further production—amounted to 70 billion forints, and value added (net output less the cost of nonagricultural inputs), which constitutes the contribution of agriculture to national income, was 43 billion forints.

The value added was of the same magnitude in 1970 as it had been ten years earlier. Its failure to advance was due to the disproportionate rise of industrial input prices relative to prices for farm products. Whereas the cost of agricultural materials used in production was somewhat lower than it had been in 1960—reflecting in part fairly stable prices for basic grain crops—the cost of nonagricultural materials rose more than fourfold. This phenomenon, generally known as the scissors effect in agriculture, led collective farm leaders in the spring of 1972 to urge the establishment of a government intervention fund to compensate farms for income losses suffered through advances in industrial prices.

The relative importance of crop and livestock production fluctuated during the 1960s. In 1969 the respective shares of the two groups of products in gross output were 60 and 40 percent. Preliminary data for 1970 indicate a decline in the proportion of crop production to less than 55 percent and a corresponding rise in the proportion of livestock products. This shift was caused by a poor harvest due to inclement weather and floods and by a spurt of hog and poultry production in response to financial incentives offered by the government.

Crops

Production of major crops was generally higher in the 1966-70 period than it had been in the preceding five years. To a large extent the rise in output resulted from higher yields achieved through better cultivation practices and greater use of fertilizers. The largest increases were achieved in the output of wheat (49 percent), corn (20 percent), hay (24 percent), and vegetables (18 percent). The output of potatoes and sugar beets, however, advanced by less than 3 percent (see table 10).

Although production of sugar beets was somewhat higher for the five-year period as a whole, it declined steadily from a high of 3.6 million tons in 1966 to 2.2 million tons in 1970. To counter this unfavorable trend, which entailed a large increase in imports of sugar, alcohol, and livestock feed, the government launched a program for self-sufficiency in sugar from domestic beet production by 1975. As expanded in December 1971, the program provides for an increase in the procurement price of sugar beets and also a special bonus for collective farms that conclude production agreements with refineries for a total of at least four years and that agree to increase their sugar beet area by 10 percent over the acreage in 1971. The overall procurement price advance amounts to 30 percent, and legislation has been

(in thousand metric tons)

Product	1961–65 (Average)	1966	1967	1968	1969	1970
Wheat	2,020	2,350	3,022	3,361	3,585	2,723
Corn	3,350	3,958	3,580	3,841	4,820	4,072
Legumes	125	136	152	80	136	126
Potatoes	1,997	2,907	1,855	1,632	2,013	1,813
Vegetables	1,470	1,750	1,833	1,708	1,843	1,517
Sugar beets	3,093	3,570	3,356	3,471	3,303	2,175
Oil seeds	129	125	105	121	155	157
Hay	3,415	4,407	3,971	3,639	4,629	4,458
Corn for silage and green feed	4,528	5,726	4,821	5,274	5,848	4,442
Fruit	955	1,000	1,258	1,008	1,516	1,430

Source: Adapted from *Statistical Pocket Book of Hungary, 1971*, Budapest, 1971, pp. 241-242.

enacted to ensure that the additional income from this source does not increase tax liability.

At the same time the government acquired in the West a substantial number of modern beet harvesting machines and a large quantity of weed killers and pesticides for sale to collective farms at heavily subsidized prices. Domestic production of advanced harvesting machinery has been undertaken under foreign license, and new facilities have been constructed to produce single-grain seeds, which reduce the labor of sugar beet thinning.

A subsidy of 70 percent is granted to collective farms for the purchase of machinery, weed killers, and pesticides for use in the production of sugar beets. To enable financially weak collectives to take advantage of this opportunity, the Hungarian National Bank raised its credit limit for collective farms. The response to the government's program in early 1972 was reported to have been favorable, and by the end of March 96.5 percent of the planned acreage for that year was covered by contracts with refineries.

A situation similar to that in the case of sugar beets has also prevailed in the production of vegetables. Output was fairly stable from 1966 to 1969 but declined substantially thereafter. On collective farms production stagnated because of the growing scarcity of labor and the lack of machinery for modern mechanical operation. Small producers were unable to expand output because they lacked the necessary gardening equipment and tools, fertilizers, and other essential supplies.

Expansion of the vegetable output was considered imperative in order to meet export obligations and domestic requirements. In the winter of 1971/72, therefore, the government was reported to have worked out short-range and long-term plans to encourage vegetable growing. As a first step, the procurement price for vegetables was raised about 5 to 6 percent, which meant an increase in income of about 200 million forints for vegetable growers in 1972. Some tax relief was also granted to these growers, but the regulations needed further clarification to be fully effective.

The government also undertook to persuade small growers to increase production and backed up its appeal with larger supplies of seeds, fertilizers, and other supplies and with a 47-percent price reduction on a wide range of garden equipment. Modern Western machinery was to be provided to collective farms that agree to conclude contracts with state canning enterprises and other state trading agencies for a minimum period of five years. Provision has also been made for research in modern production methods in cooperation with foreign experts. These measures were beginning to show results in the summer of 1972, when the Canning Industry Trust reported its vegetable purchases up to that date to have exceeded procurements in 1971 by 20 percent.

Livestock

Expansion of livestock production has been an important facet of agricultural policy, not only because of the political importance to meet domestic requirements for meat and dairy products but also in order to secure substantial hard-currency export earnings. Progress in this field, however, has been uneven. Over the years livestock production has faced major obstacles: shortages of fodder; obsolete physical facilities and an insufficiency of investment funds for modernization; inadequate slaughterhouse and meat-processing capacities; rising costs; and low, officially set selling prices. Although hog and poultry production responded favorably to financial inducements offered by the government in 1970, the number of cattle continued to decline (see table 11).

To reverse the unfavorable cattle trend, which jeopardized a large

Table 11. Livestock and Poultry in Hungary, Selected Years, 1960–71*

(in thousands)

	1960	1965	1968	1970	1971
Cattle	1,971	1,964	2,096	1,933	1,917
Cows	(879)	(798)	(779)	(738)	(735)
Hogs	5,356	6,963	6,609	5,970	7,510
Sheep	2,381	3,400	3,311	3,024	2,657
Horses	628	321	274	231	219
Poultry	n.a.	48,594	56,902	62,972	72,018

n.a.—not available.
* As of March 31.

Source: Adapted from Statistical Pocket Book of Hungary, 1971, Budapest, 1971, pp. 250–251.

foreign exchange income from beef exports and necessitated recourse to imports of butter and powdered milk, the government limited the slaughter of cows beginning January 1, 1972. This measure was judged by cattle raisers to have been ill conceived since it required the retention of cows that produced neither milk nor calves. Ninety percent of the cattle herd consists of the Hungarian piebald breed; cows of this breed produce an average of about 2,500 quarts of milk per year, or only half the average quantity produced by cows in Western countries. A breeding program to upgrade the native cattle is therefore a prime requirement for more efficient and profitable cattle production.

Further measures to promote cattle raising are to go into effect on January 1, 1973, as part of a long-range plan through 1985. The plan established a profitability target for cattle raising of 9 percent, compared to a return of only about 1 percent for a number of years. To this end, procurement prices for beef and milk are to be raised. In addition, state and collective farms will be granted a subsidy for every calf and for every quart of milk sold to the dairy industry. Large farms that increase the size of their herds over the level of March 31, 1972, will also receive a sizable grant for every additional cow and will be allowed more favorable repayment terms on loans for the development of feed production. The range of 50-percent subsidies already payable to state and collective farms for specific aspects of cattle production development will be extended to include the construction and modernization of barns, silos, granaries, and feed-processing installations.

Cattle raising on private and subsidiary farm plots is also to benefit from government support. Beginning in January 1973 the state will pay an annual subsidy for every cow upon a guarantee that the cow will be kept the entire year. The National Savings Bank is to grant credits to the operators of these plots for the purchase of cows. Eighty percent of the financial requirements for the cattle-raising plan is to be provided by the food-processing industry, and about 0.5 billion forints annually will come from the state budget. The meat industry was reported to have made a profit of 1 billion forints in 1971.

The projected government support measures are expected to increase the income of collective farmers and others who raise cattle above the level envisaged for these groups by the five-year plan for 1975. To compensate for this increase the government raised the price of mixed protein feeds by 7 percent as of October 1972 and, beginning in 1973, will raise the land tax of collective farms by 15 percent and their gross income tax by 27 percent. The land tax imposed on small plot owners will also be increased by 27 percent.

The announced cattle program was received with mixed feelings by the agricultural community. Only those engaged in cattle raising may benefit from the program, provided that the countermeasures that it contains do not wipe out the entire gain in income. Collective farms and individuals who do not raise cattle, however, will definitely suffer a reduction in income through higher taxes.

CHAPTER 14

INDUSTRY

Toward the end of 1972 industry continued to expand, although at a somewhat lower rate than the annual average for the preceding decade. Faced with a declining and unbalanced supply of new manpower and with an urgent need to make industrial products competitive in world markets, the country's leadership was seeking ways to stimulate greater productivity and technological advance. The leadership was also concerned about the longrun threat of raw material shortages and the related need to develop new sources of imports outside the circle of traditional communist-state suppliers.

The economic reform of 1968 was intended to create conditions for rapid industrial and economic growth through more intensive use of available resources. The reform measures have only partially attained this objective. Problems in the fields of investment and labor continued to hamper industry.

ORGANIZATION

Virtually all industry is state owned. In 1971 state enterprises possessed 99 percent of the productive fixed assets and motive power in industry; they employed 83 percent of the industrial work force and produced 93 percent of the industrial output. Collective industrial enterprises accounted for 6 percent of the output, and independent private artisans, engaged mainly in construction, servicing, and repair work, contributed the balance of 1 percent.

At the beginning of 1971 the state industrial establishment consisted of 812 enterprises operating 5,681 industrial plants and employing more than 1.5 million workers. Enterprises, generally, were of large size; one-third of the total number, excluding those in the food industry, employed from 1,001 to 5,000 workers, and 6 percent employed from 5,001 to more than 10,000 workers. By contrast, only 9 percent of the enterprises employed up to 100 persons, and 20 percent of the total number employed from 101 to 300 persons. Concentration in the food industry was less marked. In this branch 36 percent of the enterprises employed from 101 to 300 persons, and 17 percent employed not more than 100 persons. The large size of many enterprises is reputed to have placed them in a monopoly position.

Available information on the regional distribution of industry is confused, contradictory and, in part, outdated. It is nevertheless evident that industry has been highly concentrated in Budapest and its environs within a radius of twenty miles. Roughly half the industrial workers have been employed in this area, where manufacturing predominates. Two other areas, with a total of 30 percent of the workers at the time, were cited as industrially important in 1964—one with its center at Gyor and the second centered on Miskolc. Szeged and Debrecen were the least developed of the industrial areas.

In the 1960s the government embarked on a program to encourage the geographical dispersion of new industrial investments away from Budapest through the selective use of credits, building permits, and incentives. The Hungarian Academy of Sciences estimated in the late 1960s that another fifteen to twenty years would be needed to achieve a more balanced distribution of industry.

Despite continuing official emphasis on the need to modernize the industrial structure, the relative importance of major industry groups in 1971 was virtually identical with the structure in 1960. Within the different industry groups only minor changes took place during the intervening period. In terms of employment, the proportions of industrial branches in 1971 were: heavy industry, 58.3 percent; light industry, 27.1 percent; food industry, 10.5 percent; and other (unspecified) industries, 4.1 percent. In the heavy industry group the importance of mining, metallurgy, building materials, and vehicle production had declined slightly, and the importance of machine building and of chemicals increased correspondingly. A very small decline also occurred in the relative position of the textile industry.

Under the economic reform introduced in 1968, state ownership of industry has been coupled with a significant measure of autonomy for the enterprises and trusts (see ch. 12). The state, nevertheless, retains the right to create new enterprises and to abolish obsolete or inefficient ones. The state can order internal reorganizations to be made within economic units, can effect mergers, and can change the affiliation of enterprises with trusts and ministries. The state also appoints enterprise directors and their deputies and broadly regulates the range of enterprise activities. Authority to engage in foreign trade transactions, for instance, requires specific government permission.

The state's authority over industrial enterprises is exercised through several economic ministries and other central government agencies, including four ministries specifically responsible for industrial affairs. These ministries include the Ministry of Heavy Industry, the Ministry of Metallurgy and Machine Industry, the Ministry of Construction and Urban Development, and the Ministry of Light Industry.

The Ministry of Heavy Industry has jurisdiction over mining, oil and gas extraction, and the aluminum and chemical industries. The Ministry of Metallurgy and Machine Industry is responsible for the production of iron and steel and for the several branches of machine and instrument production. Both ministries are concerned with the electric power industry, but information on the division of authority between them has not been available. The cement industry is within the jurisdiction of the Ministry of Construction and Urban Development. The main industries supervised by the Ministry of Light Industry are those producing textiles, clothing, leather, and shoes.

The main function of industrial ministries is to further the development of the industry branches under their jurisdiction and to ensure compliance by enterprises with the government's economic policies and regulations. Although enterprises were given relative freedom to plan and organize their operations, they have had to function within a framework of specific and increasingly stringent rules that have progressively narrowed their range of choice. The ministries can also bring their influence to bear on the formulation of enterprise policies through their power to appoint, reward, punish, and dismiss enterprise managers. In late 1972 many of the largest industrial enterprises were placed under more direct control of the ministries because the managers had not adequately executed the reform measures introduced in 1968 (see ch. 12).

RAW MATERIALS AND ENERGY

The country is poor in raw materials and sources of energy, with the exception of bauxite, and is heavily dependent upon imports. Imported raw materials account for about 20 percent of the industrial output value. About 80 to 85 percent of these imports have come from the communist countries of Eastern Europe—primarily from the Soviet Union. Uncertainty about future supplies has posed a major problem in long-range industrial planning. Because a large proportion of Hungarian industrial output is exported to the Soviet Union, cooperation agreements between the two countries are crucial to Hungarian economic planning. The terms of these agreements pertaining to long-range Soviet deliveries of raw materials have not been made firm enough to allay the fears of Hungarian economic planners. In 1972 economic planners estimated that from 65 to 70 percent of raw material import requirements could be obtained over the long run from the communist trading partners. Importation of raw materials from the West is limited by the shortage of foreign exchange.

Fuels

Domestic sources of mineral fuels are inadequate to supply the current needs of industry. A substantial expansion of crude oil and natural gas imports will be needed to support the planned industrial development.

Coal and Lignite

Reserves of hard coal are almost exhausted. Deposits in the only hard coal basin in the Mecsek Mountains lie at relatively great depths, and the seams are thin and folded. The prevalence of firedamp and underground water makes mining conditions hazardous. Mechanization of the mines is difficult, and the cost of coal extraction is consequently high.

Reserves of brown coal and lignite are larger, but the caloric content of these fuels is low. The best brown coal is found in deposits along the northern margin of the Bakony Hills, which are located in the western part of the country, northwest of Lake Balaton. The major brown-coal mining centers are located at Dorog and Tatabayana.

The annual output of coal declined from 31.4 million tons in 1965 to 27.4 million tons in 1971. During that period 70 percent of the coal output consisted of brown coal, and the balance was evenly divided between hard coal and lignite. About half the brown coal and lignite output has been used to fire electric power stations located near the mines. Two million tons of coal have been imported annually to supplement the inadequate domestic supply, mainly in the form of coking coal for use in the metallurgical industry.

Oil and Natural Gas

Crude-oil production is centered in the region of Szeged. Output has been maintained at close to 2 million tons per year. At this rate of production, known reserves will be exhausted by 1981. Despite prospective discoveries of new oil deposits, domestic needs will have to be met increasingly through imports. Shipments of crude oil from the Soviet Union amounted to more than 17 million tons in the 1966–70 period; they are expected to rise from 4.3 million tons annually in 1970 to 6.5 million tons by 1975. Small quantities of crude oil have also been imported from Egypt.

With a view to future needs the oil industry has carried out oil prospecting and drilling in Iraq on a commission basis, and negotiations have started between the two countries for joint undertakings in research, production, and pipeline construction. Similar negotiations were reported to be underway with Egypt, Libya, and Nigeria.

Reserves of natural gas were estimated to exceed 3.5 trillion cubic feet in 1972; they are expected to last about thirty years. The most important deposits are located at Hajdszoboszlo, southwest of Debrecen, and in the area of Szeged. Natural gas output increased elevenfold after 1960 to a level of 131 billion cubic feet in 1971. Seven billion cubic feet have been imported annually under a long-term agreement with Romania. Estimated requirements of about 230 billion cubic feet in 1975 are to be covered by domestic production of more than 187 billion cubic feet, the usual imports from Romania, and imports of more than 35 billion cubic feet that are scheduled to begin in that year under an agreement with the Soviet Union.

Energy Balance

Because of the inadequate supply, poor quality, and high cost of domestic coal and in order to keep pace with technological developments abroad, a program has been adopted for increasing the proportion of oil and natural gas in the balance of energy sources—a process that has taken place in all industrially developed countries. In the 1960-70 period the proportion of coal in the total amount of energy consumed declined, in terms of calories, from 74 to 51 percent, whereas the proportion of oil increased from 20 to 31 percent, and that of natural gas rose almost fivefold, to 16 percent. Firewood still accounted for 2 percent of the energy supply in 1970.

By 1975 the combined proportion of oil and gas in the energy balance is scheduled to reach 55 percent. Increased use of gas and oil poses serious difficulties because of the high cost of pipeline construction, a declining fuel export potential of communist trading partners, and the consequent need for eventual large imports from hard currency sources or from developing countries.

Metallic Ores and Metals

Reserves of metallic ores are very small, with the exception of bauxite, the resources of which are among the largest in the world. Information on other nonferrous ores, including copper, lead, zinc, and tin, is not available.

Bauxite, Alumina, and Aluminum

Bauxite deposits are located along the northwestern edge of the Bakony and Vertes hills. Two-thirds of the bauxite is contained within a triangle formed by the towns of Kislod, Sumeg, and Tapolca at the southwestern tip of the Bakony Hills. The ore, consisting of aluminum hydroxide, occurs in thick beds close enough to the surface to allow open-pit mining. Major production centers are located in the Gant field in the Vertes Hills and at Iszkaoszentgyorgy, Halimba, and Nyirad in the Bakony Hills.

Production of bauxite increased from 1.2 million tons in 1960 to 2.1 million tons in 1971 and is scheduled to rise to 3 million or 3.5 million tons by 1985. About one-third of the output has been exported to Czechoslovakia, Poland, the German Democratic Republic (East Germany), and the Federal Republic of Germany (West Germany). The remaining bauxite has been converted to alumina, the bulk of which has also been exported for smelting in the Soviet Union and other Council for Mutual Economic Assistance (COMECON) countries because the available electric power supply is inadequate to convert more than a fraction of the alumina output to metal. Forty percent of the alumina exported in the 1960-71 period was shipped to the Soviet Union for smelting on a toll basis under a long-term agreement and reimported in the form of aluminum ingots for further processing or export.

Production of alumina more than doubled in the 1960-71 period to a volume of 467,000 tons, but the output of crude aluminum rose by only one-third of 67,000 tons. Net exports of crude aluminum in 1971 reached 57,000 tons, compared to only 9,000 tons in 1960.

Iron Ore, Iron, and Steel

The only source of domestic iron ore is a deposit in the vicinity of Rudabanya in the northern mountains. The ore seam is thin, and the quality of the ore is low—the iron content is less than 25 percent. The production of ore declined from 762,000 tons in 1965 to 629,000 tons in 1970 but rose to 687,000 tons in 1971. The domestic output covers less than 12 percent of industry's needs, so that almost 90 percent of the requirements in terms of iron content must be imported. The Soviet Union has supplied 95 percent of the imports, and India, most of the remainder.

Production of pig iron increased from about 1.6 million tons in 1965 to almost 2 million tons in 1971. During that period the output of crude steel rose from 2.5 million tons to 3.1 million tons. Although most of the raw materials for iron and steel production have had to be imported, Hungary has been a net exporter of rolled steel products.

Manganese

Small amounts of manganese ore—ranging from 213,000 tons in 1965 to 156,000 tons in 1968 and again in 1969—have been mined for use by the steel industry. Increasingly large amounts of ferro-alloys have had to be imported to supplement the inadequate domestic supply.

Uranium

With assistance from the Soviet Union, uranium ore has been mined under difficult conditions in the Mecsek Mountains and enriched in unknown quantities. Production of uranium ore began in 1956; the output increased by 90 percent in the 1961-65 period but rose by only 7.5 percent in the years 1966 through 1969. In 1970 the Mecsek reserves were reported to be of sufficient magnitude to allow production for fifteen to twenty more years. Absolute figures on uranium reserves and output have been treated as a state secret. The entire output of uranium ore has been shipped to the Soviet Union under an arrangement on which information is not available.

Other Raw Materials

Available resources of nonmetallic minerals are sufficient for the needs of the building materials industry, but production has lagged behind requirements. The agricultural sector supplies all the raw materials needed by the food industry. Although domestic resources provide a portion of the basic material needs of the petrochemical industry—coal, oil, and natural gas—available supplies must be supplemented by imports. All or most of the materials needed for the production of sulfuric acid, phosphate and potassic fertilizers, chlorine, and lye have to be imported. Imports must also be relied upon to supply the full requirements for natural and synthetic rubber, cotton, and jute. Other basic material requirements that must be covered to a very large extent through imports include: cellulose and paper, raw wool, flax and hemp, synthetic fibers, hides and skins, and leather substitutes.

Electricity

The country's hydroelectric power potential is insignificant. One small hydroelectric station on the Tisza River produces a fraction of 1 percent of the electric energy output. Thermal stations fueled by coal, oil, and natural gas must be relied upon to meet the growing electrical energy needs.

Information on the installed generating capacity is not available. Efficiency of the powerplants has been improving, in part as a result of the construction of new, more modern installations and in part through the gradual shift in fuel consumption from coal to oil and natural gas. In the 1960–71 period the proportion of coal in the fuel consumption, in terms of calories, declined from 94 to 65 percent, while the proportion of oil and gas increased from 6 to 35 percent. During the same period the heat consumption per one kilowatt-hour of generated electric energy declined from 4,079 to 3,092 calories. The efficiency level, however, remained below the level of up-to-date powerplants. The high cost of coal mining has kept the cost of electricity above the average for European countries.

Production of electricity in 1971 amounted to 15 billion kilowatt-hours—almost double the output in 1960. The increase in output, however, has not been able to keep pace with growing requirements, thus necessitating steadily rising imports of electricity from neighboring countries. Net imports of electrical energy increased from 536 million kilowatt-hours in 1960 to 4.3 billion kilowatt-hours in 1971—that is, from 7 to 29 percent of domestic production.

Two-thirds of the electrical energy supply in 1971 was consumed by industry, 13 percent was used for residential purposes, and 5 percent was used in transportation. The remainder of the power supply was devoted to various unspecified uses. Large industrial users of electricity must adjust their consumption according to a centrally determined daily and monthly schedule. The schedule is drawn up to harmonize industrial requirements with the available capacity of the national power system. Private individuals are not subject to any restrictions in the use of electricity.

In an effort to overcome the country's power deficiency through the use of domestically mined uranium, the government signed an agreement with the Soviet Union in 1966 for the construction of a nuclear power station at Paks on the Danube. Construction of the main building was to begin in 1971, and the first unit was to start operation in 1975. In December 1970 an announcement was made that the construction project had been postponed for five years. Subsequently released information disclosed that the nuclear power station would have a capacity of 1.9 million to 2 million kilowatts, ultimately to be expanded to 4 million kilowatts. Under a new agreement signed with the Soviet Union in mid-1972 the first unit of 440,000 kilowatts is scheduled to begin operation in 1980.

INVESTMENT

In the 1966-70 period investment in industry amounted to 131 billion forints (for value of forint—see Glossary), a sum that was 46 percent larger than the amount of investment in the preceding five years. The volume of investment accelerated markedly after 1968; it rose by 70 percent in three years, reaching the sum of 38.4 billion forints in 1971. The upsurge was a direct result of the change in investment policy under the economic reform that granted to individual enterprises greater latitude than previously in making investment decisions (see ch. 12).

According to an unofficial source, about 32 percent of the industrial investment in 1971 was consumed in building construction, and 58 percent was devoted to the acquisition of machinery; the remainder was used for installation work and other related activities. Another source reported somewhat lower figures for investment in machinery. More than half the new machinery was imported, and 55 percent of the imports originated in Western countries. Imported machines have generally been technologically more advanced and of better quality than machines of domestic manufacture.

The distribution of industrial investment among industry branches reflects the government's continuing policy of assigning priority to the development of heavy industry, particularly machine building, in the belief that this policy ensures the most rapid economic growth. Four-fifths of the industrial investment in the 1966-70 period was allocated to heavy industry, and only one-fifth was devoted to light industry and the food industry, even though the food industry makes a large contribution to exports.

Although the primacy of heavy industry has been maintained, greater recognition was nevertheless given after 1965 to the needs of previously neglected branches of industry. Whereas investment in the 1966-70 period was higher than the investment level in the preceding five years by 74 percent for the food industry, 54 percent for light industry, and 59 percent for the building materials industry, it rose by only 39 percent for heavy industry (excluding building materials). The adjustment in investment emphasis was an outgrowth of the government's concern to achieve a better balance in industry and the economy, to improve the supply of consumer goods in order to ensure political stability, and to increase the potential for food exports.

The largest consumer of investment funds has been the machine-building industry; it received 18.5 percent of the industrial investment in the 1966-70 period at an average of 4.9 billion forints per year. In 1971 investment in machine building reached 6.7 billion forints—an increase of 60 percent over the investment level in 1968. The growth in physical investment was somewhat slower because of rising investment costs.

Other major recipients of industrial investment funds were the chemical industry and mining, followed by electric power production and metallurgy. The building materials industry received by far the smallest share of investment despite the chronically short supply of essential building materials.

In line with the economic reform policy of transferring authority from central authorities to enterprises, industrial investment financed through the budget was scheduled to decline from a prereform level of about 75 percent to only 31 percent of total outlays by 1975. A correspondingly rising share of investment was to be undertaken by enterprises with their own funds and bank credits. The proportion of these so-called decentralized investments rose from about 51 percent in 1968—the first year of the reform—to 64 percent in 1971. The absolute volume of decentralized investments more than doubled during this period, but state investment was only 22 percent higher, after a slight retrenchment from the level of 1970. Enterprise investments rose by more than 5 billion forints from 1970 to 1971 to a level of about 24 billion forints.

Enterprise investment policy has generally favored new building construction and expansion of capacity at the expense of modernizing production technology. This tendency—a carryover from an earlier stage of industrial development—has been encouraged by continuing demand pressures under conditions of rising incomes and shortages of goods. It has also been perpetuated by outdated regulations concerning investment financing, the use of credits, and the treatment of enterprise investment funds. These regulations place enterprises that renovate their plants in a disadvantageous position with regard to profits.

One of the consequences of the prevailing investment policy has been the coexistence in many industrial plants of modern, high-quality machines, imported from the West at a substantial cost in foreign exchange, with obsolete equipment of low productivity. There are many plants where imported high-capacity installations cannot be fully utilized because of bottlenecks created in the production line by the old equipment. The resultant loss to the economy is reported to be high, but avoidance of modernization safeguards the profit position of enterprises.

Official measures for dealing with the problem of modernization were being drafted in late 1972. Earlier in the year, in the context of measures adopted to curb excessive investment, a decision was made to give preference to investment for the acquisition of new machinery over investment for construction of buildings. The relative economic advantages of reconstruction over new construction, however, had not been established.

LABOR

The number of persons earning incomes in industry in 1970 was 1.8 million, or 38 percent of active earners in the economy. State industry employed 1.5 million persons; the remainder were either members and employees of industrial collectives or independent private artisans. Women constituted 40 percent of the state work force and accounted for 55 percent of the collective and private artisans. The work force in construction consisted of 361,500 persons, 75 percent of whom were in state enterprises. Women made up only 17 percent of workers employed in state construction enterprises and 40 percent in collective and private enterprises.

In the 1960-70 period industrial employment increased by 31 percent. The growth in the three different sectors, however, was uneven. In state industry employment grew by 33 percent, and in collective industry it rose by 48 percent. In private enterprise, however, employment declined by 25 percent. In construction the number of employed increased by about 50 percent.

Almost two-thirds of all employees in socialized industry were engaged in heavy industry, and more than half were in the machine-building branch, including the manufacture of transportation equipment. Light industry employed 37 percent of the industrial work force, and other (unspecified) industry employed the remaining 4 percent. The growth of employment in the 1960-70 period was largest—71 percent—in the "other industry" branch. In heavy industry, employment increased by 34 percent, including a rise of 53 percent in the machine-building branch. During the same period employment increased by 30 percent in light industry and 35 percent in the food industry.

Little discussion has appeared in the Hungarian technical press about the qualification of industrial labor beyond occasional references to the discrepancy between the vocational structure of the labor force and the needs of the economy or to the shortage of personnel in specific professional categories. The absence of discussion suggests that worker qualification may pose no major problem. In fact, government officials anticipate that the number of young skilled and semiskilled workers entering the labor market will be greater than the capacity of the economy to absorb them.

In the 1965-70 period about 42 percent of the industrial labor force consisted of skilled workers. The proportion of so-called trained workers (the difference between skilled and trained workers is not known) rose from 37 percent in 1965 to 39 percent in 1970, while the number of unskilled workers and juvenile assistants declined correspondingly from 21 to 19 percent.

The industrial labor supply has a paradoxical aspect—a labor shortage exists along with underemployment. Wage regulations introduced by the economic reform have led many enterprises to hire and hoard excessive numbers of low-paid unskilled workers (see ch. 12). Because the free manpower pool is limited essentially to the declining number of youths entering the labor force, other enterprises have been unable to fill vacant positions. The shortage has been aggravated since 1967 by the transition from a workweek of forty-eight hours to a forty-four-hour workweek.

A shortage of 58,000 workers was reported in Budapest alone during the last quarter of 1971—a number equivalent to 5.7 percent of the workers needed to operate enterprises without interruption. In construction the labor shortage reached 7.8 percent—the equivalent of 10,000 workers. The number of surplus workers employed by state industry was estimated by the Hungarian Academy of Sciences to have been 12 percent of total employment in 1969, or 200,000 persons. A large number of workers could also be freed through mechanization of auxiliary work processes where the current level of mechanization is extremely low, such as materials handling, warehousing, and shipping. It is generally recognized by the leadership and the country's economists that the labor shortage is, in large measure, an outgrowth of low productivity and that an improvement in the organization and management of labor within enterprises is therefore urgently needed.

The labor shortage has stimulated an excessive turnover that was brought about by competitive bidding for workers among labor-hungry enterprises after the elimination of administrative controls over labor mobility at the end of 1967. According to a statement by the minister of labor, enterprises engaged in labor enticement that often included extralegal and socially offensive wage practices. In search of better pay or working conditions some workers developed the habit of job-hopping and changed jobs several times a year.

Labor turnover in industry amounted to 37 percent of employment in 1968; it rose somewhat in 1969 and declined to about 30 to 31 percent in 1970. A further slight improvement was anticipated in 1971. Much of the labor turnover represented legitimate movement of workers for personal and professional reasons. From one-half to one-third of the job changes, however, were deemed by officials and economists to be unjustified and economically harmful. Labor turnover in construction was almost twice as high as in industry. In an effort to deal with the problem several restrictive administrative measures were introduced in Budapest and other industrial cities in 1971 (see ch. 12).

PRODUCTIVITY

Both the absolute level and the rate of growth of productivity in industry have been low in comparison with Western industrial nations and also in relation to other East European communist countries. The growth of productivity was also uneven. In the 1961-65 period the output per person employed in socialized industry rose at an average annual rate of 5.1 percent. In the years 1966 through 1969 the average rate of increase was only 2.8 percent because productivity had stagnated altogether in 1968 and 1969. An improvement took place in 1970 and 1971, when productivity increased by 7 and 5 percent, respectively.

The productivity record in terms of output per unit of fixed assets was also poor. After having risen by 5 percent in 1967, the output declined by the same percentage in the first two years of the reform and remained at that level in 1970. Economists and public officials have attributed the unsatisfactory advance in productivity after 1967 primarily to unexpected adverse effects of the regulations introduced by the economic reform (see ch. 12).

Many industrial plants are technologically obsolete, and the proportion of outdated machines is steadily increasing. Available machinery is only partially utilized, and the level of mechanization of work processes is very low. Less than 2 percent of the machinery inventory used in industry is scrapped each year. In the machine-building industry, machine tools operate on the average little more than one shift per day; they are used less than three-fourths of the time during the first shift and about one-third of the time during the second shift. Technologically advanced special-purpose machine tools constitute only 4.5 percent of the machine tool inventory, and the proportion of presses is less than 20 percent.

Of all industrial workers, only 25 percent of those in factories are involved in fully mechanized work, and little more than one-third work with machines and mechanical equipment. More than half the industrial workers use no power-driven machinery or equipment whatever on the job; they use only their bare hands in mostly hard physical labor.

Productivity has suffered from low worker morale, expressed in loafing on the job and in a general lack of work discipline. The morale problem has been caused by the disaffection of workers over the blocking of wage increases under provisions of the economic reform and over inequities in the operation of the profit-sharing system. Although the wage system was intended to stimulate and reward improvement in productivity, a negative correlation actually developed between productivity and the wage level. Branches within heavy industry that have attained the greatest advance in productivity rank among the lowest with reference to wage scales (see ch. 12).

Industrial managers have had little experience in effective labor management. For years industry has operated under conditions in which labor has been cheap and mechanization has been expensive. Only toward the end of the 1960s did demographic reality force enterprise managers to face the necessity of more efficient labor utilization. The prevailing wage, profit, and tax regulations, however, have inhibited managers from undertaking reorganization programs that would necessitate the discharge of superfluous workers. Dismissal of any significant number of employees for reasons of efficiency has also

274

been shunned because of the government's full employment policy and the associated widespread assumption that enterprises have an obligation to ensure the employment of their workers.

As in the case of labor management, modernization of the industrial plant has been hampered by regulations concerning enterprise finances and investment and by restrictive rules for foreign trade and exchange governing the importation of machinery from the West. In the absence of effective competition and with the continued existence of a seller's market, there has been no incentive for enterprises to modernize production in order to increase efficiency. The modernization process entails a temporary lowering of profits that reduces managers' incomes, whereas losses from ordinary enterprise operations are generally covered by subsidies from the budget. Eighty percent of all industrial enterprises received government subsidies of one kind or another in 1972.

The urgent need to raise industrial productivity has been one of the leadership's main concerns. In December 1971 government agencies and enterprises were instructed to outline measures that would serve to make production more efficient. The ministries and the Government Economic Committee were to make plans for the most important enterprises. The majority of enterprises, however, were called upon to develop their own plans for action but were unable to proceed promptly because ministries were slow to issue relevant directives. The work had not been completed by September 1972. Articles published in economic journals at the time indicated that far-reaching new measures would soon be adopted. They also reported that proposed measures would expand the responsibilities of ministries and enhance their influence over enterprises in matters related to the efficiency of production.

PRODUCTION

The gross output of industry in 1971 was about 391 billion forints; in the first nine months of 1972 it increased at a rate of 5.7 percent. Average annual growth rates of the industrial output were officially reported to have been 7.8 percent in the 1961–65 period and 6.2 percent in the years 1966 through 1970. In the 1966–71 period industry contributed 42 percent of the national income (net material product). Changes in prices and statistical methods introduced in 1968, however, destroyed direct comparability with earlier data so that the validity of the reported figures cannot be assessed.

In line with the leadership's traditional policy, heavy industry advanced at a substantially higher rate in the 1960–71 period than either light industry or the food industry. Within heavy industry the most rapid growth was attained in the output of chemicals, followed by machine building and electric power production. The outputs of the building materials industry and of mining increased at less than half the rate attained by the chemical industry. In light industry the growth in production of textiles, clothing, leather, and shoes lagged behind the advances made by the wood-processing, paper, and printing industries.

Official statistics on the production of major goods cover hundreds of items that range from coal, oil, and steel, to bathtubs, locomotives, and bicycles, to kitchen cabinets, baby clothes, and brooms. Progress in the output of basic commodities and essential capital and consumer goods in the 1960–70 period was uneven (see table 12).

A major problem in production has been posed by the continued manufacture of obsolete products and the slow pace of product innovation. In the machine-building industry, for instance, more than one-third of the output in 1972 consisted of models that had been in production longer than ten years, whereas new products made up only from 6 to 7 percent of the output.

The industry has relied almost entirely upon domestic research and development for its technological progress. Little more than 3 percent of its output in 1970 was based on foreign licenses that were purchased in order to acquire advanced technology. Production under foreign license, however, usually begins from one year to as long as six years after the need for the particular machines has been determined. Under the circumstances a large proportion of new machines is no longer up to date by the time they are produced. In the mid-1960s 14 percent of the machine-building industry's products measured up to world standards, 39 percent were partly obsolete, and 47 percent were completely out of date.

The chemical industry, in the judgment of the minister of heavy industry, has lagged behind developed Western nations by from eight to ten years in several important areas. Much of light industry's output has also been below world standards. For these reasons manufactured industrial products have accounted for only about 30 to 40 percent of exports to the West. Resistance to accepting mediocre-quality goods has also developed among communist trading partners and among domestic consumers.

Product innovation has been retarded by some of the same factors that have adversely affected the pace of plant modernization. An important role has also been played by the small size of the domestic market, which discourages the introduction of products that can be economically manufactured only in large volume. Another drawback has been the failure of the trade network to inform manufacturers adequately of changes in consumer preferences. Although much discussion has been devoted to the problem of innovation, no solution has been found.

(See Table 12, pages 278–279.)

Table 12. Output of Selected Industrial Products in Hungary, Selected Years, 1960-71

Product	Unit of Measure	1960	1965	1970	1971
Electric power	million kilowatt-hours	7,617	11,177	14,542	14,990
Coal and lignite	thousand metric tons	26,524	31,437	27,830	27,400
Crude oil	do	1,217	1,803	1,937	1,955
Natural gas	billion cubic feet	12	39	123	131
Iron ore	thousand metric tons	516	762	629	687
Manganese ore	do	123	213	169	n.a.
Bauxite	do	1,190	1,477	2,022	2,090
Pig iron	do	1,244	1,577	1,822	1,970
Crude steel	do	1,887	2,520	3,108	3,110
Alumina	do	218	267	441	467
Crude aluminum	do	50	58	66	67
Cement	do	1,571	2,383	2,771	2,712
Nitrogenous fertilizers*	do	57	148	350	377
Phosphatic fertilizers*	do	45	117	167	170
Tractors	units	2,649	2,961	1,930	1,611
Diesel motors	do	891	670	967	1,180
Diesel trucks and buses	do	4,447	6,305	9,798	10,335
Bicycles	thousand units	256	257	275	255
Roller bearings	do	6,568	12,574	16,462	n.a.
Center lathes	units	2,577	2,492	2,996	2,987

Milling machines	do	1,176	1,083	985	791
Drills	do	3,054	5,128	4,843	5,660
Telephone sets	thousand units	37	126	60	97
Pine lumber	thousand cubic feet	7,557	8,581	9,959	n.a.
Plywood	million square feet	98	172	140	n.a.
Cellulose	thousand metric tons	24	60	53	49
Paper and cardboard	do	138	174	259	269
Cotton textiles	million square yards	295	386	364	366
Woolen textiles	do	38	43	47	49
Silk textiles	do	34	43	68	67
Knitwear	thousand metric tons	8	11	13	14
Household electric sewing machines	thousands	144	182	165	162
Household electric refrigerators	do	9	103	242	278
Radio sets	do	212	228	206	215
Television sets	do	139	267	338	371
Sugar	thousand metric tons	380	428	280	241
Beer	million quarts	376	469	529	532
Tobacco (cured)	thousand metric tons	18	25	21	n.a.
Cigarettes	billion units	16	19	22	24

n.a.–not available.

*In terms of plant nutrients.

Source: Adapted from *Statistical Pocket Book of Hungary, 1972*, Budapest, 1972; and *Statistical Yearbook, 1970*, Budapest, 1972.

SECTION IV. NATIONAL SECURITY

CHAPTER 15

PUBLIC ORDER AND SECURITY

In 1973 the party-controlled government—through its ministries of interior and justice—controlled all of the various police and security forces, the courts, and the penal institutions. The party also sponsored and directed the programs of several large organizations designed to attract and to elicit the cooperation of masses of people from a wide variety of age and special interest groups. Although these organizations had a social character, their role in national security was considered by the country's leaders of importance equal to that of the security and law enforcement agencies.

The Ministry of Interior's agencies included regular military and paramilitary units and local and national security police. The ministry's civil police performed the usual criminal and regulatory police functions in villages and cities, and its frontier guards monitored and regulated all transits of the country's borders. The ministry's internal security troops, organized and equipped as mobile military units, were able to move to any major trouble spot in the country. Its security police operated in uniform or in plain clothes against activities—political or economic in nature—threatening the state or society. The ministry's Workers Militia—the only part-time paramilitary organization of the group—functioned as a national guard. The courts and penal institutions of the Ministry of Justice complement the security forces and are directed to use their facilities to enforce conformity with the society's standards and to rehabilitate persons who have deviated from those standards.

Crimes against the state, socialist property, or society in general are considered more serious in Hungary than in Western countries, and crimes against private property are considered less serious. During the late 1960s and early 1970s juvenile crime and crimes against the person, particularly those involving violence, increased. Petty crime, such as small thefts of government property and disturbing the peace, were rampant. Crimes against private property and serious economic offenses decreased, and political crimes became a rarity.

Hungary's communist regime has had a tumultuous history since seizing power in 1948. Its first adherents represented a small minority, and during the early years much of the opposition was bitterly hostile.

The oppressive measures it employed to solidify its controls were highly unpopular, and the system for all practical purposes disintegrated in 1956. Despite this background and the fact that the regime of Janos Kadar was imposed upon the country by the armed force of the Soviet Union, in 1973 the regime had effective control of the country and appeared to have a considerable amount of popular support. By far the greatest portion of the people who could not actively support the regime found it tolerable enough to cooperate with it (see ch. 9).

INTERNAL SECURITY

A relaxation of internal security controls has been experienced throughout Eastern Europe and the Soviet Union since Joseph Stalin's death in 1953. The liberalizing process was most pronounced through the mid-1950s and, in general, a slower liberal movement has been tolerated, if not encouraged, by controlling groups in the various countries over the longer span of time. At times, however, the people have demanded freedoms at a pace faster than their regimes felt that they could be granted. Popular discontent developed into protest, and protest into violence—in the German Democratic Republic (East Germany) in 1953 and in Poland and Hungary in 1956. Hungary's was by far the most violent of the revolts—including the later one in Czechoslovakia—and by far the greatest amount of blood was shed when it was crushed.

Stalinist-type police activity endured in Hungary until 1953, but oppressive controls were relaxed in the mid 1950s. Terror as a means of control was characteristic of the period from 1948 until 1953, under the inspiration of party chief Matyas Rakosi. Although muted after that date, the same secret police and internal security forces continued to exist, and the people continued to despise them. The secret police force was virtually eliminated in October 1956 after they had fired into unarmed crowds of demonstrators. The security forces were the first target of the revolutionaries, and within a week the hated organization was officially abolished.

When the security forces were rebuilt after 1957, strict measures were again resorted to, both within the police units for disciplinary reasons and also to impress their authority on the population. As the situation stabilized, police practices were again moderated. The public no longer fears the police to the extent that it did before 1956.

Civil Police

The civil police are the local law enforcement officers who perform the day-to-day regulatory functions in direct dealings with the people. They deal with criminal activity that is confined to their areas, and they handle traffic, local licensing, and a major portion of the official contacts with the individual citizens.

Although the civil police function in local jurisdictions, they are centrally organized under the Ministry of Interior. As police work has become more complex, even at the lowest levels, the ministry has raised the level of police training. Until the early 1970s, if prior military experience had not been considered sufficient, police officers were trained at various defense or interior department schools, but in the autumn of 1971 a police officers' academy was opened. At that time the academy was the latest and most important of a series of moves designed to improve the professional capabilities and political reliability of higher level police officers.

Various types of special units also exist within the civil police organization. Air police control civil airfields, regulating such things as sports flying and crop dusting. They may provide overhead assistance to police on the ground and to water police. They are helpful during searches for criminals, for locating the causes of vehicular traffic problems, or in any way in which their mobility and extra visibility can be used advantageously. Their helicopters also perform rescue work during floods or at scenes of major accidents.

Water police patrol the major rivers. Most of their work is in cooperation with the border guards, assisting in the prevention of illegal border crossings and smuggling. Water police in the Budapest area patrol warehouses and other river-oriented enterprises.

The police issue identification cards and maintain records on all adults. To keep them current the cards are reissued every two years. The cards provide a check on a citizen's work and place of residence. An increasing amount of police work deals with the control and regulation of motor vehicles. It includes giving vehicle operator driving tests and issuing and revoking operator permits. Tests may be taken by those eighteen years of age and older. Drivers' licenses are revoked if a person becomes physically or mentally disabled or if an individual is apprehended operating an unsafe vehicle, disobeying regulations, or causing an accident. A license may be revoked temporarily or, if the circumstances are sufficiently serious, permanently.

Workers Militia

The Workers Militia, or Workers Guard (Munkas Orseg), was formed in late 1956 or early 1957 to participate in the fight against the 1956 revolutionaries. In addition to assisting in regaining control of the country under Kadar, the militia was conceived as an armed organization to provide a more localized base of support for the regime, as it was more closely related to the daily life of the people than were the Internal Security Troops. Like a national guard, it was, therefore, drawn from the workers, who did their training after working hours and in their home areas. By 1972 over 80 percent of the guard were party members. Average age of guard members was thirty-eight years, and over 65 percent of them were agricultural or industrial workers. Women may also join, and their numbers are increasing. They constituted only 2 percent of the total membership in 1972, but about 8.5 percent of the new members recruited during 1971 were women. Estimates of the militia's membership vary widely, some observers believing it close to 250,000. Interest in militia work fluctuates, and the effectiveness of units in different parts of the country varies, depending upon the quality of local leadership, tasks they may be required to perform, and other local factors.

There are few restrictions on membership in the militia. New members may be active reservists in the armed forces or may have had no previous military experience. They may have university degrees, or may not have completed elementary schooling. Whether they are fifteen or over fifty years of age, however, they must be able to indicate that they have some enthusiasm for paramilitary organizations and activities.

Unit commanders attend twelve weeks of training at the militia's central school in Budapest. About 35 percent of the curriculum consists of theoretical subjects; the other 65 percent of the time is spent on practical exercises. Age and background of the commanders vary in about the same degree as does the organization's membership. Students at a typical commander school class in 1972 were from twenty-two to fifty-five years of age and represented a wide spectrum of the labor force from manual laborers to managing engineers.

National leaders acclaim the militia as a "well trained and well disciplined armed body, a worthy companion-in-arms to the other armed forces." Maintaining public order and security remains its primary mission, but the militia joins other agencies in civil defense work and preinduction military training, and units are activated at times of natural disasters and other emergencies. An engineer company of the militia, for example, was decorated for its work during the heavy floods of June 1970.

Internal Security Troops

The Internal Security Troops (Belso Karhatalom) have existed since the earliest days of the communist regime. Their mission has always been to put down internal disorders and to protect the regime but, in 1956, many of the men proved to be sympathetic with the rebelling population, and the organization had to be completely re-formed in the years following the revolt. Its personnel are most frequently referred to as interior troops and occasionally as the constabulary.

Because they are designed to combat local disturbances, rather than heavily equipped foreign armies, they are lightly armed. They are required to be able to respond quickly to a disturbance in any part of the country, however, and for this purpose they have a considerable amount of mobile equipment, including armored personnel carriers. Career men serve on a voluntary basis; basic personnel are acquired from the annual draft of eighteen-year-old youths. Those conscripted serve from two to three years.

The force numbers roughly 15,000, much smaller than it was during the years between 1949 and the mid-1950s. It is a uniformed force that operates in typically organized military units. Uniforms are the same as those worn by the army, but they can be distinguished by the blue backgrounds on rank shoulderboards and collar insignia.

Industrial Guards and Government Guard Command

Industrial guard units were also formed shortly after the 1956 revolt, in the same period that the Workers Militia was organized. At that time the authorities feared that industrial plants might be special targets of rebellious groups. The newly created force was charged not only with preventing sabotage but also with containing theft, which was rampant during that period. The units that remained in 1972 were small, but the men served as full-time guards on a regular work and salary basis.

A newer guard unit, the Government Guard Command (Kormanyarseg Parancsnoksag) was formed in 1972. In its initial announcement the Ministry of Interior solicited soldiers and noncommissioned officers to join the new group. Among the requirements, applicants for the government guard must be in good health and physical condition, be five feet six inches or more in height, have completed eight years of schooling and their mandatory military service, and have no criminal records. Applicants are advised that they will serve in the capital and that they will receive generous pay, travel, leave, clothing, and quarters allowances. The Government Guard Command is presumably to become the elite unit for ceremonial functions and for contacts with important officials and visiting dignitaries.

Security Police

Security, or secret, police symbolized Stalinist terror in the post-World War II period and for a time after the 1956 revolt. In 1973 these police were still in existence but markedly less influential. Although the State Security Authority (Allamvedelmi Hatosag—AVH), from which the initials are derived, existed under that name for only a few years, the secret police are still generally referred to as the AVH.

Detested, hated, and feared, the AVH and the earlier security police forces permeated all areas of the regime, all major institutions, and all levels of the society. In the days when they were earning their reputations, they operated stealthily, making arrests at night and holding their victims incommunicado. Persons who ran afoul of the AVH would, after brutal interrogation, often confess to treason, sabotage, or some other crime against the state. Some were executed; most were sentenced to long terms in prison or detention camps. Frequently it was years before their fate became known to relatives or friends.

During their years of greatest terror, these forces had at least seventeen administrative divisions to monitor the internal political and economic life of the country. Their interests included religious organizations, youth groups, and mass organizations and all other groups having a social, political, educational, scientific, or entertainment character. They controlled passports, monitoring all movement of people into or out of the country. They conducted surveillance of the governmental organization, the military and other security agencies, aristocrats of the precommunist society, and any high-ranking individual brought to their attention as potentially subversive. Two divisions conducted the prosecutions and trials of individuals apprehended by the agency. Another maintained personal files on all persons who had membership in any political group other than the communist party and who were therefore considered potentially dangerous to the regime. The so-called invisible group provided high-ranking party and government officials with guards and security.

The AVH was dissolved during the 1956 revolt and, although it was re-formed under a new name, the worst of the old extralegal secret police practices have not again been resorted to. The people transfer their distaste to the renamed organization, but they do not fear or hate its personnel as individuals. Political trials, prepared and conducted as they were in the Stalin era, have been very rare, although the law states that certain cases may be tried in private.

Frontier Guard

The Frontier Guard is similar to the Internal Security Troops in personnel strength, organization, training, and equipment. The troops also wear army uniforms, distinguished by green backgrounds on shoulder and collar insignia. Most of the force is deployed along the land boundaries, but small river guard units operate in the Danube and Drava rivers along the Czechoslovak and Yugoslav borders.

Border defenses are minimal on the Soviet, Romanian, and Czechoslovak borders. Along those with Austria and Yugoslavia, where more illegal trading and border crossings are attempted, barriers may include double barbed-wire fencing, strips of plowed and carefully raked earth, watchtowers, searchlights, landmines, and twenty-four-hour patrols using trained dogs.

CIVIL DEFENSE

Civil defense has been a concern of Hungarian leaders since the end of World War II. In the early period responsibility for civil defense work was given to air defense organizations. They modernized shelters built during the war, built new ones of the same type, arranged for emergency stockpiles of medical supplies, dug ponds for use as fire-fighting basins in public parks, and arranged educational programs.

When it became necessary to think in terms of nuclear and biological warfare, unventilated shallow shelters were seen to have little or no value. Emphasis changed to stockpiling food and to such measures as evacuation of urban populations. Deeper shelters were constructed, usually under large buildings. Underground facilities in new construction—such as sports clubs' dressing rooms, restaurants, garages, bowling alleys, and firing ranges—were equipped to double as shelters.

Civil defense exercises have become larger and include more activities. Before 1965 they rarely involved more than one factory or enterprise. Since 1967 several have been countrywide and have involved up to 100,000 persons. Simulated radiation dosages are measured, water and food are tested for contamination, and plans for relocation of industrial plants and evacuation of population are examined.

Despite continuing efforts, enthusiasm for such projects fluctuates. It flagged during the early 1970s and, to restimulate interest and rejuvenate the effort, a mandatory program has been instituted for the 1972-75 period. Authorities are determined to give people few opportunities to evade the program. All citizens are required to participate except active duty military and police personnel, women more than four months pregnant, mothers with a child under six years of age or three children under fourteen, disabled persons, and workers having regular jobs plus a full schedule of high priority after-duty work. Annual training is increased from fifteen hours—which had been voluntary— to a mandatory ten to thirty hours. Some material is presented by television, radio, or in the press. Groups assemble for the greater portion of the required hours, however, and for testing on that which is disseminated by the media.

The new program also provides for construction of additional warehouses to store food and medical supplies. Increased food stockpiling is aimed at storing fifty-five to sixty days of supplies, instead of the twenty that satisfied earlier requirements. Wherever practicable, factories are required to install auxiliary power units, emergency water pumps, and filtered ventilation equipment.

Other than activities centered on the organization's main reason for existing, the study of Marxism-Leninism and classes on a variety of economic, political, foreign policy, and other theoretical subjects are encouraged. During the 1971-72 period about 37,000 study course leaders conducted classes attended by 700,000 party members and nonparty activists. Trade unions were the most active in getting the participation of their members in these classes. Union leaders claimed that nearly 20 percent of their members attended 22,000 such courses.

PUBLIC ORDER

Social Organizations

In the Hungarian system, like those of the other countries that operate on the Soviet model, the less subtle controls exercised by the police and other armed forces are balanced by the pressures exerted by a large number of social organizations engaged in all kinds of activities. The mass organizations and other large social associations are designed to attract people from as many interest groups as possible and to influence them to support the establishment.

The trade union and youth groups are the largest of the mass organizations and, in 1972, claimed memberships of about 3.4 million and 780,000, respectively. All of the mass organizations are approved by the party and receive their more basic guidance from it. In turn, all of them support the party, giving it advice on procedural and local matters when their contacts prove helpful (see ch. 9).

The Patriotic People's Front—dating from 1944, when it was named the National Independence Front—was created to develop a coalition of parties to assist in an eventual communist takeover. Since that time it has existed as a coordinating agency. The party, all of the approved mass organizations, and various social, economic, and cultural associations work under its aegis. The front, however, is subordinate to the party (see ch. 9). During its twenty-fifth anniversary celebrations in 1972, spokesmen for the front stated that it had over 3,800 committees, more than 110,000 members, and "several hundred thousands of activists."

The Hungarian National Defense Association, with the support of the army and the mass organizations, directs programs designed to strengthen love of country throughout the population, to assist in defense education and, more specifically, to coordinate preinduction training of the youths approaching military age and the training of reservists who have completed their active duty tours. Its programs are carried out in schools, places of work, and in programs of the party and the Communist Youth League (Kommunista Ifjusagi Szovetseg—KISZ).

The association was founded in 1968, superseding the Defense Sports Association, and grew rapidly in its first few years. By 1972 it had 140,000 members in 5,000 clubs throughout the country. Its sports competition for young people drew 800,000 participants from pioneer organizations. The association has also developed quality competitive sports, arranging training in meets for 23,000 of the country's best athletes. These programs determine the country's representatives at, among others, the Olympic games. Also, by 1972 its premilitary training programs were available to 80 percent of the young men of draft age.

Hungarians have long had a tradition of joining clubs or associations, and such groups have been formed in large numbers. Approximately one-half of the 9,000 clubs that existed in 1972 were sports associations. These were divided again into departments for individual sports, including—in the order of their popularity—soccer, table tennis, and handball. Volunteer fire departments are also considered associations, and there are about 2,700 of them. Hunting, fishing, animal breeding, scientific, and artistic and cultural associations account for most of the remainder. As a group, the associations are much smaller than the mass organizations but, because there are so many of them, their total membership is large (see ch. 9).

Youth Programs

Hungarian youth appears to be an enigma to the authorities. On the one hand, party dogmatists have been convinced for years that—although the new society might be accepted with less enthusiasm by older people who are set in their ways and beliefs—young people were its great hope. The youth, they believed, would accept the new concepts and work enthusiastically for them. Although those expectations have been borne out to a degree, it is also true that youthful elements much too large to be ignored do not cooperate with the regime. Most of the uncooperative youth is politically apathetic; a few of the more rebellious ones question the basic tenets of the communist ideology.

Only a small percentage of the young people adhere to the groups whose conduct is deplored by the regime. Particularly disturbing is the fact that one-half of juvenile crimes are committed by those between the ages of fourteen and seventeen and that many of the offenses involve senseless violence and destruction. Authorities associate youthful crime with unsatisfactory family life, poor environmental factors, the increased use of alcohol, and the indifference of society. Other factors contributing to their uncooperative behavior that are frequently cited are anticommunist ideologies, shown by imitation of various Western customs and life-styles, and tendencies toward credulous attitudes and provocative dress and behavior. Police officials feel that social organs and their pressures are the best avenues to a reduction in juvenile crime but that quick and effective disposition of juvenile crimes is also essential.

Attempting to gauge the degree of youth apathy, the leadership experimented for a time with opinion-sampling polls. In two such polls, the results of which were published in 1972, about 20 percent of the youths questioned had positive political convictions or an active interest in politics. About 70 percent, however, professed indifference to, or no interest in, politics. The remaining 10 percent were cynical or hostile to the subject of politics.

Questioned as to whether or not they would discuss politics freely under certain situations, 90 percent of university students said they would express themselves openly in friendly student groups. Almost 50 percent of the KISZ members, on the other hand, said that KISZ meetings would be unsuitable for uninhibited political discussions.

Possibly as a result of such polls, the party has withdrawn its approval of public opinion surveys. According to a party spokesman, such surveys divide and isolate the people—rather than guide them to uniform and correct solutions to society's problems.

Although authorities have probed many new means of dealing with youth problems, the oldest measures—albeit with improved programs and new emphasis in certain directions—had as of early 1973 proved most effective. Among them was the mass organization for youth fifteen years of age and older. The KISZ had a membership of nearly 800,000 in 1972, representing about 40 percent of the population in this age bracket. About 60 percent of the members are working youth. Of those still considered to be students, 16 percent are in college, 47 percent are in secondary school, and 37 percent are skilled-worker apprentices.

The KISZ gives its youth organized sports and recreation, introduces them to hobbies and skills, and gives them some influence in the party, the government, and the community. For their efforts, the party and the regime have the opportunity to indoctrinate the young people along the lines they consider correct. Specifically, the KISZ is charged with keeping youth in, and interested in, schools; contributing to their more complete education; and teaching them the theories and practices of good citizenship.

About thirty thousand of KISZ's members are also members of its Youth Guard. The guards are organized along typical military lines, with battalions, independent companies, and platoons. Guards receive three years of training that entails much more work and is considerably more comprehensive than the more widely attended in-school premilitary training programs. Youth Guard members have an age spread—up to twenty-six years—permitting their use alongside other paramilitary forces in national emergencies. Those who serve in the guard before their induction into the army are said to show early superiority over their colleagues.

The KISZ's Agricultural Youth Council is the organization of youths working in agriculture. The council's tasks include the political education of the youths working in agriculture, experimentation in new methods of agricultural production, and the improvement of vocational training of rural youths. This group represents the interests of its members and all other young people in the villages. It is attempting to make rural life more attractive and to show its merits to the younger generation.

A few of the KISZ's programs have been less than total successes. Its summer youth construction camps or youth labor camps, in their fifteenth season during the summer of 1972, are one such example. Some 40,000 secondary and university students served at eighty-four camps, usually for a two-week stay, and the quality of their experience varied widely. The camps are situated at vineyards, orchards, road construction sites, and the like. Young people do a day's work, for which they are paid, and they are provided with sports and cultural programs, amusements, recreation, and entertainment.

The camps are designed to provide a two-week camping vacation, usually with a group of friends from the same school, with worthwhile and interesting programs for afternoons and evenings. To keep its experience variable from year to year, no school sends it students to the same camp two consecutive years. With these advantages, plus wages, the six hours of work per day are, in theory, amply compensated. Some students having special interests work individually rather than at camp, although their work may be a part of the KISZ camp program. Medical students replace vacationing nurses, for example, and university students help archaeologists at their digs.

The KISZ, however, has not been provided with sufficient funds to operate the camps well. It has run a deficit each year and has been forced to skimp on services. Food and entertainment provided for youth have suffered and often have been of marginal quality. Youths complain that those who work on construction jobs are paid at lower than the adult rate. Those paid hourly rates at state farms are actually paid for work norms. Persons new at a task are rarely able to achieve the norm and as a result do not get the pay they were led to expect. Users also have complaints. State farms complain that the camps cost them more than they profit from them. Other enterprises allege that the young people do not like the camps, are pressured into volunteering for them, and do as little as they can at them.

Leaders believe, however, that over the years the youth camps have achieved positive results far more frequently than they have fallen short of their goals. In their fourteen years the camps have reclaimed many square miles of land, have built new roads and improved old ones, and have dug over 200 miles of irrigation canals, and the work that their people have done on agricultural land has been statistically impressive.

The Pioneers, a pre-KISZ organization having retained its name and organization since 1946, is among the oldest of the organizations within the country that has not undergone nearly complete reorganization. Its young members are taught patriotism and ideology but in general terms. Members are drawn from the six- to fourteen-year age group and include a majority of the children in elementary and primary school. In 1970 approximately 75 percent of those eligible were members. The Pioneers have been looked to since about 1970 as one of the best vehicles for reducing juvenile delinquency. A test program that year was believed responsible for reducing the number of crimes committed by fourteen-year-old juveniles in the test group by 22 percent.

Authorities remain convinced that young people must and can be persuaded to support the country's system. Several steps have been taken in order to elicit more interest and cooperation from them. More youths are being appointed as representatives to the national parliament, and provincial leaders are being urged to select more of them for positions on local councils and on their subcommittees. Trade unions are being urged to use young men in positions where their views can be heard and where they can make decisions. The party has reduced the minimum age for its members from twenty-one to eighteen and has done strenuous recruiting among those who are potential members.

CRIME AND THE PENAL SYSTEM

Crime

Total crime and the number of criminals are increasing, and the upswing in crime has reached serious proportions. Statistics for the three or four years after 1965 showed decreases from earlier figures, but largely because crimes against property had been redefined and were not included unless they entailed the loss of 500 forints (for value of the forint—see Glossary), as opposed to 200 forints theretofore. Also, a general amnesty in 1970 erased statistics for a great number of cases that had been on criminal records during the late 1960s.

During 1970 and 1971 the number of crimes against public order and against persons, of crimes of violence, and of juvenile crimes again increased. The number of crimes against private property decreased. Crimes against socialist property decreased in 1970 and increased again in 1971. In relation to the total number of criminals apprehended, the percentages of recidivists and juveniles rose slightly. Although by far the greater number of crimes committed by juveniles were those classed as hooliganism or crimes against public order, serious and violent crimes were up sufficiently to be of official concern. Gang crimes were considered to have reached dangerous proportions. The percentage of crimes committed by women rose steadily until 1966; between then and 1972 it declined. Peripheral crimes such as begging and prostitution, nagging to the regime because it can see no place for them in the socialist society, have also shown increases, particularly in the Budapest area.

There are fewer complaints than during the early days of the regime that capitalist countries are attempting to overthrow the regime, but authorities in Zala County on the Austrian border blame some of their troubles on bourgeois propaganda. Citizens in that area are exposed to Austrian television and radio and to many tourists.

Alcohol is a factor in about one-fourth of all crimes and in one-half or more of attempted murders, crimes against juveniles, and crimes against public order. It was also involved in a large portion of traffic accidents and drownings. Of the 4,000 drivers' licenses revoked in 1970, by far more were for drunken driving than for any other cause. Hungary's suicide rate is the highest in the world, and at least one-half of all suicides have been committed during or after heavy drinking. Economic losses attributed to alcohol include production shortfalls, tardiness, sick pay, and plant accidents. On-the-job drinking has become a problem to the degree that some plant managers are furnished breath analyzers. Per capita consumption of pure alcohol reached 2.5 gallons in 1971, an increase of over 50 percent in a ten-year period.

According to a government spokesman, crimes against the state include acts aimed at overthrowing the socialist order and those that upset the peaceful and constructive work of the people. Such political crimes are open to wide interpretation and in former days encompassed practically any offense the secret police forces deemed worthy of their attention. The number of people tried for political offenses fell rapidly after Stalin's death in 1953 and to near zero by 1956. In the aftermath of the revolt there was a large number of political trials for a few years but, after the series in which former Premier Imre Nagy was executed, they have become increasingly rare. The regime counted 180 political trials in 1967 but only fifty-five in 1970. Most of these were not serious, and in most instances the crimes were allegedly committed because their perpetrators were under the influence of alcohol. According to a government spokesman, by 1970 only one or two serious cases of espionage or conspiracy against the state were being investigated each year.

The Law and the Courts

Hungary's traditional legal system had been influenced by Roman law but, in contrast to it, had no real codes. The accumulation of "legal custom" was compiled in greatest detail in 1517. This sixteenth-century compilation was modified in succeeding centuries—partly in writing, partly by unwritten custom—but there was little hurry to enact the modifications into formal law. A criminal code was finally published in 1878. Its general portions were rewritten in the early 1950s, but the articles pertaining to specific crimes remained much as they were until the entire code was republished in 1961. The first formal civil code was published at that time.

Both codes and a decree on criminal procedure were again republished in the early 1970s. Revisions at that time aligned the legal system more closely with the constitution as it was amended in 1972. Terminology is also more precise and definitive and reflects the experience that has been acquired by law enforcement agencies and judicial staffs in the period since the communist takeover. The revised codes do not greatly alter the basic emphasis on individual rights, and they do not reflect a change in the concern of the regime toward crimes against the state as compared with crimes against the person. Defense of the state and the system remains paramount. Sentences authorized for antistate crimes are in general more severe than are those for crimes against individuals or personal property.

Because the courts are administered by, and are responsible to, the Ministry of Justice, they do not constitute a separate or independent branch of the government. The ministry defines their role as defending the society by teaching the people to respect the laws and the social order and by punishing those who do not. At the same time, they are charged with safeguarding the rights of individuals as they are established by the laws. First responsibilities are to the state and to the party; the individual merits protection when he is a cooperating and contributing member of the society. The law on the organization and function of the courts that became effective on January 1, 1973, defined the functions and duties of the various courts and legal personnel in far clearer and more precise terms than was formerly the case (see ch. 8).

Penal Institutions

After the communist takeover and until 1961, the penal system included labor or internment camps and prisons with three classes of disciplinary regimes. Reforms associated with the 1961 penal code did away for a short time with the differing disciplinary regimes. The experiment failed, however, and since then there have been four classes of prisons or prison regimes. Penitentiaries are the maximum security institutions and maintain the most severe of the regimes. At the other extreme, local jails hold those sentenced to short terms for minor crimes or, for example, those under the influence of alcohol who must be detained for a short time. Between the penitentiaries and the jails are two classes of prisons, their differences reflected in the severity of the regime and the physical security of the institution. Two or more prison classes may be located within the same complex, either in separate buildings or in different sections of the same buildings. Courts determine the initial class of disciplinary regime to which a newly sentenced inmate is assigned in consideration of the gravity of his crime and his criminal and prison history. Prison administrations may transfer inmates to more or less severe regimes, depending upon their conduct and cooperation within the institution.

Penal institutions are charged with an urgent responsibility for the rehabilitation of their inmates. The amount of effort that can be devoted to such programs varies widely, both because of the space and facilities available and because of the attitude and competence of prison administrations. Whatever other projects are available, however, all inmates who serve sentences of more than a few days' duration, and who are physically able, are required to work. Some of them work in the prison complex, others at enterprises or construction projects, usually under guard. If projects are distant from the prison, inmates may be housed at or near the work area, in whatever permanent or temporary facilities that may be available.

Labor camps—of the type that had a complete prison administration but minimal facilities for the inmates—probably no longer exist. They were a common phenomenon of the early years of the communist regime and were used again after the 1956 rebellion was put down, but the national leadership claimed that all of them had been abandoned by 1960.

Insofar as it is possible, prisoners are segregated within the prisons. Juveniles are separated from adults, men from women, recidivists and those having committed serious crimes from those serving first, short-term sentences. On the other hand, inmates considered trustworthy,

294

particularly if they are at or near the ends of their sentences, may be authorized to work unguarded outside the confinement area.

Prison populations were high during the Stalinist period, but between 1953 and 1956 most inmates serving sentences for political and economic crimes against the state were released. Large numbers of people were again confined during the last days of 1956 and during 1957 for their participation in the 1956 uprising. A majority of them were released by the general amnesties of 1963, and most of the remaining amnestied during the next few years. Rehabilitation trials have also erased the criminal records from many of those who died while serving sentences after secret trials. Partly to enable them to bring foreign currencies into the country, charges have been removed from those charged only with emigrating from the country illegally at the time of the uprising. Such persons may return to the country to visit relatives.

CHAPTER 16

ARMED FORCES

All of the regular military establishment is included in the Hungarian People's Army, which was created after the communist takeover in 1949. Most of this army consists of ground forces, although there is a small air and air defense force and a very small naval force, which operates on the Danube River. Soviet troops have been stationed in the country since World War II.

The armed forces have been almost completely reorganized since 1956. Such change was required in part by the Warsaw Treaty Organization (Warsaw Pact) in 1955. In addition, the forces proved unreliable in the revolt of 1956, some of them actively supporting the rebellion. Since 1956 much effort has been expended on improving the caliber of leadership, raising troop morale, and enhancing the professional status of career military personnel. Programs involved in this effort had a dual purpose: improving the potential for combat operations and assuring that men in a proud and competent army would remain loyal to their commanders and to the regime.

Personnel practices in the forces are similar to those of the other Warsaw Pact members. Men in the lowest grades are acquired by universal conscription. Most of them are taken from the group that is called up each year. The regular military services require less than one-half of those who are available for the draft, but certain police, border, and interior guard forces acquire their basic personnel from the same group of conscripts. A sizable portion of the officers and noncommissioned officers are career soldiers. All of them are volunteers, and they must sign up for longer tours of duty than the two years that are required of those who are drafted.

Skilled labor is in short supply in the country, but the forces draw a large portion of their men from those who have not yet started regular civilian work careers. Because they may be provided with training or work experience that is of value later, the time that conscripts spend on military duty is not usually considered an overall loss of productive manpower.

The expenses incurred in modernization have been relatively large, but they have been offset to some degree by the smaller than average size of the military establishment. The cost of maintaining the force in relation to the national budget is lower than the average in other Warsaw Pact countries.

HISTORICAL BACKGROUND

Hungarian soldiers have had a good reputation as individual fighting men since the first Magyar horsemen swept into the Carpathian Basin in the late ninth century A.D. They have been tough and determined soldiers, amenable to discipline and fiercely nationalistic in defense of their homeland.

The most massive Hungarian forces were employed during World War I when they fought as part of the Austro-Hungarian armies in alliance with the Central Powers. After the defeat of the Central Powers and the collapse of European empires, the Allies dictated the Treaty of Trianon, which stripped Hungary of more than 70 percent of its former territory and about 60 percent of its former population. The treaty also limited the Hungarian army to 35,000 men. Between the two world wars Hungary remained associated with, and to an extent economically dependent upon, Germany. With the rise of Adolph Hitler in the early 1930s, Hungary was encouraged to ignore the limitations imposed by the Treaty of Trianon. At the outset of World War II it had a substantial standing army and was able to achieve total mobilization of its manpower very rapidly.

Hungary was allied with Germany in the early part of World War II; much of the territory taken from Hungary by the Treaty of Trianon was briefly restored, and about 250,000 Hungarians fought on the eastern front. The greater portion of this force, however, was defeated and almost destroyed in 1943 in the Battle of Voronezh. This defeat broke the back of the Hungarian forces and removed nearly all of the enthusiasm for the war from the population at home. During the next year Hungary adhered to an unofficial neutral status. During that time, for example, Allied war planes flew unmolested over the country and were free to rendezvous over its territory for attacks on Austria and Romania. As the tide of the war changed in the east, Hitler's forces occupied the country.

Despite the fact that there were sizable Hungarian forces fighting beside Soviet armies at the end of the war, Joseph Stalin considered their efforts of little importance. Stalin concurred in reestablishing the Trianon borders of the country and even ceded a small additional parcel of territory to Czechoslovakia.

The forces formed under Soviet tutelage date their existence from late 1945. As after World War I, the post-World War II forces were limited—this time to about 65,000 ground forces and a token number of others. The early forces included security troops that were difficult to distinguish from those of the army. The combined strength of the regular army and of security forces organized into army-like units grew rapidly to three or four times the prescribed treaty limit. The rise in personnel strength was accompanied by a parallel effort to acquire politically reliable personnel who would defend the regime which, as of the early 1950s, had not acquired what it considered an adequate power base or sufficient popular support.

Hungary was one of the charter members of the Warsaw Pact, which was formed in 1955. The modernization of the Hungarian forces, however, was delayed until after the 1956 rebellion when—despite efforts that had been lavished on the forces to make them reliable—the army disintegrated. Not only had a portion of its men been actively sympathetic with the rebelling population, a few units had even joined the dissident forces.

Reorganization of the establishment, beginning in 1957, involved an even greater emphasis on personnel reliability, political controls, and continuing political and ideological education. The forces have been required to participate in large numbers of exercises in cooperation with Soviet units stationed in the country and also in most of the Warsaw Pact maneuvers conducted in the area. A political directorate was established within the forces to work parallel to the operational organization, and the political indoctrination of the troops received as much emphasis as combat training. Although the organization has been held to lower personnel strengths than were maintained up to 1956, the men are better paid and better equipped, and more effort is expended on improving conditions of service that contribute to better morale. By 1971, 80 percent of the army officers had been replaced, and all of the younger group were from peasant and worker backgrounds—backgrounds considered more politically desirable. Spokesmen for the regime have generally expressed satisfaction with their potential combat capability and their probable reliability in any future internal crises.

GOVERNMENTAL AND PARTY CONTROLS

The top leadership in both the government and party organizations retain tight controls over the armed forces. These controls are intended to ensure that the military is unable to become powerful and separate to a degree that it could question, pressure, or threaten the regime.

The minister of defense is the link between the military establishment and the government. His is an appointed position, as are those of the other members of the Council of Ministers. Upon appointment, whether he has had a civilian or a military background, the minister of defense assumes the highest active military rank. In peacetime he is customarily a colonel general; in wartime he would become a general of the army. His position is primarily political, but he takes direct command of the armed forces during the more important of their maneuvers. Colonel General Lajos Czinege, who was appointed to the post in 1960 and still occupied it in early 1973, was a party functionary who had no earlier military career experience.

The Main Political Directorate of the armed forces is responsible to the minister and is within the structure of the military organization. Its purpose is to ensure the correct political orientation of the troops and their officers. The political directorate has staffs at all levels of the military organization that are responsible for political education and indoctrination in the units. In addition, these staffs supervise sports programs and arrange off-duty recreational activities. The political staffs participate in all propaganda and agitation programs, whether initiated by the Communist Youth League (Kommunista Ifjusagi Szovetseg—KISZ) or by the directorate itself.

Party control of the Ministry of Defense is assured by high-ranking party officials who concurrently occupy top ministry positions. In 1971, for example, the minister of defense and the chief of the general staff were members of the party's Central Committee. Most service officers, including all of the higher ranking ones, are party members. At lower levels in the service organization, the party has cells at any base or in any unit that has three or more party members. In 1970 the party lowered its age for new members to age eighteen and expanded its recruiting program among conscripts. As a result, during that year 60 percent of the new party members in the army were conscripts.

Many more of the conscripts are KISZ members than party members, however. They are near the median age for KISZ membership and are at the point where its programs are most appealing. That party-sponsored youth group has recovered considerably since 1956, when it fell into such low esteem that it had to be totally reorganized. Much effort was expended on making programs attractive. The KISZ does not have as large a membership as authorities would prefer, but its membership is sufficiently active to be considered a constructive and influential force among the conscripts.

Political officers and leaders in party cells and KISZ units are directed to be on constant alert to discover potential political activists. Emphasis between 1957 and 1970 was on finding instructors to teach and disseminate propaganda—with appeals to study, logic, and reason. By 1972 authorities apparently believed that a majority of the young men were well-enough grounded ideologically by the time they were drafted that they would respond favorably to other influences. A new organization, named the Methodological Center, was established to produce films, periodicals, and other material having an emotional impact rather than a direct appeal to the intellect.

THE MILITARY ESTABLISHMENT AND THE NATIONAL ECONOMY

In the 1966-71 period the working-age population increased by 220,000 persons, and a further increase of 110,000 persons is anticipated by 1975. Thereafter, according to official population estimates, the number of working-age persons will decline by about 40,000 or 50,000 until 1985, when a resumption of the rising trend is expected to begin. In the early 1970s industrial managers complained about a growing labor shortage. Economists and public officials, however,

300

pointed to the existence of widespread underemployment. Drafting the majority of young men for two or three years of military service may intensify labor problems within the economy unless the government's drive for a substantial raise in labor productivity proves successful.

On the other hand, the cumulative effects of the many technical schools in the military that introduce conscripts to new skills, the work experience with complex equipment, and the discipline of military life that instills regular work habits are very beneficial in upgrading the quality of the youthful labor supply. Some officials commenting on the subject state that military service, in addition to upgrading the quality of the work force, also benefits the individual conscript and the national economy.

Defense expenditures in 1971 amounted to approximately 3.6 percent of the national income, slightly less than average for the Warsaw Pact countries. Costs of modernizing the forces' equipment and pay increases for servicemen caused the percentage to rise during the late 1960s but, since 1970, the increase in defense costs has been approximately matched by increases in the national income.

ORGANIZATION AND MISSION

The regular armed forces are those that are designed primarily to combat forces of an enemy power. They are organized under the Ministry of Defense and are its primary, if not total, responsibility. All the regular forces are included in the Hungarian People's Army, but they are separated into ground, air and air defense, and naval elements. The army is pledged to cooperate in any major Warsaw Pact military operation and to defend the country against any invading force. Its major units are committed to specific Warsaw Pact roles in the event of a major war.

The general staff is immediately below the minister of defense and is responsible to him. It is the highest purely military agency in the country and coordinates the functions of the services and the political directorate and allocates their share of military appropriations and common services. It has equally important operational and planning functions, the most important of which is responsibility for producing the country's defense plans and preparing the forces to execute them. For peacetime work it plans the forces' participation in Warsaw Pact exercises. For such exercises it must determine the extent of participation by the ground, air, and naval elements and define the roles that each force must play.

Ground Forces

About 90 percent of the personnel of the Hungarian People's Army are in the ground forces. Their numbers, however, include some air defense personnel and most of those in administrative, logistic, military police, and other organizations that are common to or that support the entire army. Ground force combat units consist of six divisions, which are the largest basic unit in the services, and a few special purpose units. The major units are not maintained at full strength.

Divisions are patterned after those of the Soviet army and have the same regimental structure. Four motorized-rifle divisions each have one tank, one artillery, and three motorized-rifle regiments. Two tank divisions each have one artillery, one motorized-rifle, and three tank regiments. The motorized-rifle division replaces the World War II rifle division and is called motorized because its equipment includes sufficient vehicles to carry all personnel when the division moves.

Air and Air Defense Forces

The air element of the air and air defense forces is small, consisting of nine squadrons of combat aircraft, a few transports and helicopters, and an assortment of trainers. All of the combat types in the 1972 force were Soviet-built MiG-19s and MiG-21s and were designed for use in the air defense role. A few of them have been used, however, for ground support in troop exercises.

The air defense mission is shared with the ground forces. Ground units in the force include antiaircraft artillery, surface-to-air missiles, radar units to detect incoming aircraft, and radar units to control and direct fighter aircraft. The ground forces man air defenses for their own units and installations. Area defenses are usually manned by air force personnel.

Naval Forces

The Danube River is large and important enough to warrant a waterborne force to defend it. Hungarian naval forces include about 125 ships that are designed to patrol the river, mine it if necessary, and sweep mines that might be laid by an enemy. The navy would also, as in a 1971 summer exercise, defend friendly forces crossing the river or oppose enemy crossings.

Vessels include gunboats, river patrol craft, minelayers, minesweepers, and a large assortment of miscellaneous craft. None are designed for combat against anything other than lightly armed river boats, and none would operate anywhere other than in the Danube River.

FOREIGN MILITARY RELATIONS

In the aftermath of World War II Hungary entered into an agreement with the Soviet Union known as the Treaty of Friendship, Cooperation, and Mutual Assistance. During the next two or three years similar treaties were signed with the other East European countries that were at the time in the sphere of Soviet influence. The German

Democratic Republic (East Germany) was at that time the Soviet Zone of Occupied Germany, and the first such treaty between it and Hungary was signed at a later date.

The initial treaties were to be effective for twenty years. Those with the Warsaw Pact countries have been renewed as they expired, although Warsaw Pact ties are more specific and, as such, more binding. Similar bilateral treaties exist between all of the Warsaw Pact countries and, in aggregate, they constitute a pledge that each one of them will come to the defense of any other member that is threatened. The treaties are subject to wide interpretation, and a threat to the communist party or to the socialist regime in any one of them may be considered an external threat by strict party ideologists, even though military forces of no other nation are involved.

With the exception of the brief period in 1956 when the rebellious regime severed its ties with the pact, Hungary has been an active participant in a major portion of Warsaw Pact activities. Reorganization of the armed forces after 1956 limited their capability to cooperate fully for several years, and the country's public opinion has not supported all pact activities wholeheartedly. Party and governmental leaders, however, see multinational maneuvers as vehicles for raising the professional standards of the forces and for making it habitual for the forces' commanders to adhere to the pact organization and to respond to orders from pact headquarters. In 1968, therefore, Hungary joined in the Soviet-led invasion of Czechoslovakia, although there was sentiment among the people in opposition to the invasion.

Hungary has also been a strong supporter of all efforts to reduce armaments and to improve international relations. In an effort to widen its contacts, military delegations have visited defense ministries and combat units in an increasing number of countries outside the Warsaw Pact alliance. During 1971, for example, official groups visited Austria, Yugoslavia, and Finland. A similar number of visiting military delegations have also been received in Budapest. Hungary's military academies have accepted a number of foreign students, most of them North Vietnamese, during the late 1960s and the early 1970s.

MANPOWER, TRAINING, AND SUPPORT

Manpower

Personnel in the regular armed forces in 1972 represented slightly less than 0.5 percent of the total male population, about 3.1 percent of the male working force, and 4 percent of the men in the eighteen- to forty-nine-year-old military age group. These percentages were lower, but not significantly so, than the averages for Warsaw Pact countries and also than those for Europe as a whole.

There were approximately 2.5 million males in the military age group in 1972. Of them about 75 percent, or under 2 million, were physically fit and available. The group of physically fit male youths that reaches the draft age of eighteen each year numbers only a little more than 75,000, and population statistics indicate that this number will not increase until about 1980. About two-thirds of those eligible are called up each year. The army requires the largest portion of them; the remainder serves in border guard and internal police forces, which draw their basic personnel from the same group of conscripts.

Training

All equipment and tactical doctrine for the armed forces have been Soviet or copied from Soviet models since 1945. Training has necessarily been geared to that equipment and doctrine from that time, but the emphasis increased after 1955, when the Warsaw Pact alliance was formed. Cooperation within the alliance has required standardization of training programs among all member countries to enable all armies to understand common orders and to assure that they make the same responses to them. It has also been necessary for units in each nation to attain combat readiness at the same season of the year in order to participate in annual joint maneuvers. The largest of these maneuvers are usually held in late summer or early autumn.

To fit into the Warsaw Pact pattern, individual training for conscripts begins immediately after induction, with strenuous physical training, instruction on individual weapons and small arms, and long sessions of military drill and political education. Preinduction military training has usually been minimal, and inductees are rarely in required physical condition when they enter the service. The early weeks of training, therefore, are exhausting. Training proceeds from individual weapons in small combat units to larger weapons or more complex equipment and integration of the group and the equipment into larger unit exercises. The annual training cycle usually ends when the troops are ready to participate in the large-scale summer or autumn maneuvers.

Noncommissioned officers—including the sergeant major and ensign grades, which the army classes as higher than noncommissioned officer but lower than commissioned officer rank—usually have positions requiring a special skill, a limited area of interest, or authority over a small group or unit of equipment. As such, most of their training is received in special technical schools. Most such schools are set up within military units. The main base for general administrative noncommissioned-officer training is the Central Noncommissioned Officer School. As in the case with the other specialized schools, its graduates are prepared for better jobs and promotions, but its diplomas are the equivalent of those from civilian technical schools and are not university-level degrees.

Curricula in all of the military academies whose graduates receive commissioned officer rank have been raised to the university academic level. Direct commissions are sometimes given, but they are increasingly awarded to conscripts who already have civilian university degrees in addition to outstanding service records. Because both sources of new officers contribute men having higher education, the percentage of those with university degrees is rising rapidly.

The highest level military educational institution is the Miklos Zrinyi Military Academy. It serves mainly as a command and general staff college, preparing junior officers for service at higher ranks. It also provides broader background knowledge to those who have trained or served in a limited or specialized area, preparing them for combined arms operations or for a greater variety of career assignments. The academy also has one- and two-year reserve officer training courses for party, state, and mass organization leaders.

The other academies differ in curricula and the kind of degrees presented. They usually have four-year academic programs for cadets, however, and accept their students from among secondary school graduates. They also may accept transfers from other universities or they may take first-year students who have not completed secondary school if the applicant has military service experience that is considered an adequate substitute. In all cases, candidates for admission are required to have Hungarian citizenship, be physically fit, have no criminal record, be twenty-one years of age or under, and be able to show moral and political integrity and a sense of commitment. Academy graduates receive bachelor degrees and are commissioned as sublieutenants. Dates of commissioning ceremonies may not coincide with graduation exercises, as classes from all of the academies are commissioned simultaneously.

One of the academies specializes in air defense, communications and electronics, and chemical and biological warfare. The academy providing air force officers has pilot training and aircraft maintenance programs. A third academy serves both the regular forces under the Ministry of Defense and the police forces under the Ministry of Interior. It has special police and border force courses in addition to tank and artillery programs. The political academy provides intelligence officers, officers intended for political indoctrination and agitation programs, as well as officers designated for the political directorate's chain of command. Bachelor of science degrees in engineering are awarded by the military science and technical academies; bachelor of arts degrees in social or political science areas are given by the political academy (see ch. 15).

Enlisted men remain in the reserve forces until age fifty; officers, until age sixty. The rapid turnover of personnel in the regular forces, occasioned by the release of conscripts after their short two-year tours of active service, provides a steady and large source of reservists. It is both expensive and difficult to keep large numbers of men in satisfactory physical condition and up-to-date on newer equipment, and those who remain on a fully qualified inactive reserve status until the upper age limits of their commitment constitute a minute percentage of the total. There are efforts, however, to hold as many as possible of those who keep themselves fit and who remain interested.

The Hungarian National Defense Association—the Defense Sports Association until it was reorganized and renamed in 1967—directs the largest portion of the reserve activities that are conducted outside regular military units. It holds sports competitions, sponsors social activities, and supports flying clubs. Although most of the effort appears to emphasize sporting events or social affairs, there are basic requirements to encourage physical fitness and to keep men current on weapons firing and on the use of new weapons and otherwise renewing military expertise. Competitions, for example, sometimes include races in which portions of the course have simulated radiation contamination, water crossings under simulated fire, or other combat-type obstacles.

Regular units also devote some time to reserve training. A few reservists are called to short periods of active duty at all times of the year, but the greatest numbers are called during the summer to participate in small unit maneuvers, most of which are scheduled in the early or midsummer season.

When most of the mandatory duty tours were reduced to two years during the early 1960s, it became apparent that poor physical conditioning and ignorance of basic military fundamentals on the part of conscripts resulted in most of their time being spent on elementary basic training. Insufficient time remained during which they could be used effectively. Beginning with the academic year 1968/69, a new five-year national defense educational program was introduced into the primary and secondary schools. The elementary program included a group of general courses with classes in defense of the country, civil defense, drill competition, and marksmanship. The more advanced high school program added courses in topography, military engineering, and military physical education to the basic programs.

About 700,000 students were enrolled by the third year of the program, and the first cycle of students to complete the advanced secondary program was graduated in the spring of 1972. Although it was too early to assess whether or not the army could reduce its time spent on basic training, authorities expressed satisfaction with early results. The program evoked student interest, as evidenced by absenteeism being lower than average on days devoted to the home defense courses. More important to the evaluators of the program was the fact that, in the 1972 draft, a larger percentage of inductees with the premilitary training volunteered for career assignments.

The party-sponsored mass organizations of the country contribute to the school system's premilitary training and also sponsor programs of their own. The Hungarian National Defense Association cooperates in these activities with the Workers Militia and the KISZ, but it has primary responsibility for premilitary as well as military reserve training. Premilitary courses include radio telegraphy, diving, driving, parachuting, and pilot training. The association's flying classes throughout the country, for example, have more than 10,000 young people in various phases of training. Most members begin working with model planes and advance to gliders. If they show aptitude, they are given medical examinations and further testing to determine their fitness for military flying. Some who qualify are selected for forty-five-day intensive courses, which include ground school and power flight training.

Requirements on the mass organizations, eliciting greater assistance from them, have increased steadily. Pleas for increased efforts from them usually came first, and it occasionally took much longer to effect increases in their budgets that would permit them to perform the additional work. As an example, the Hungarian National Defense Association 1971 budget to support flying clubs, which was continually being cut while costs were rising by 30 to 40 percent, was only one-fifth what it had been ten years earlier. When it was finally recognized that the federation could not meet increased demands for flying instruction under such circumstances, its allocation was increased in 1972. New support will permit, within three years, increases in aircraft from 120 to 200, in flying hours from 20,000 to 50,000, and in instructor pilots from 110 to 230.

Morale and Conditions of Service

Since their near disintegration in 1956, the forces have had an uphill battle to make service life acceptable, to inspire loyalty and, at the same time, to respond satisfactorily to constantly increasing requirements that have been levied on them. Housing has been chronically scarce, budgets have been tight, and the social status of servicemen has been low. It has been difficult to produce trained men, and it has been doubly difficult to retain them in the military service after they have been provided with a skill. Measures to improve conditions have included doubling the pay of conscripts, the increase beginning in 1969. Further legislation, enacted in 1971, provided for better pensions, improved care of dependents, and increased survivor benefits.

Legislation passed in 1971 attempts to make officer service a more attractive career. According to military spokesmen, the law provides officers with advantages that guarantee "unequaled material and moral recognition." Among the advantages, provisions for advancement promised that a new sublieutenant can become a lieutenant colonel before he is fifty-five years old, even if he receives only the regularly scheduled promotions. Pay at all levels has been increased, and fringe benefits were made more liberal. These include up to thirty-seven days' annual leave, complete family medical care, travel discounts, and a promise of improved housing. Small status symbols have not been overlooked and, as one such gesture, officers have for the first time in many years been authorized to carry their own personal sidearms. Commensurate with improved social status, higher level educational attainments are required of the officer, but opportunities to acquire them are being made available with advanced mid-career courses at the military academies.

Another section of the 1971 law offers the conscript better opportunities if he signs up for an extended tour of duty following his mandatory service. If he can meet a group of slightly more stringent requirements than those that are demanded of a basic soldier, he signs a four-year commitment. Because he is immediately promoted to a low noncommissioned officer grade at which he has had no experience, however, his first sixty days are a trial period. During those two months either he or his commanding officer may terminate the contract. Once the trial period is over, the new noncommissioned officer becomes eligible for an award for extra service, leave and vacation privileges, disability and length-of-service pensions, and opportunities to acquire a secondary education or a technical school degree.

Medicine

Medical care is provided to all military personnel through the medical services of the armed forces or through the state medical service. Military medical staffs are responsible for sanitary and safety standards, food inspection, and preventive medicine, in addition to their services to military personnel. Servicemen get all the usual and routine medical attention in their units, but in an emergency they can use any state medical facility. On the other hand, civilians may avail themselves of military medical assistance when circumstances warrant.

Special education of medical personnel within the military is limited to subjects that are peculiar to, or that need extra emphasis in, military medicine. These include treatment of battle casualties, care of radiation casualties and victims of chemical and biological warfare, and mass treatments for epidemics. The army's medical units are a primary source of assistance during natural disasters. At such times their mobility and evacuation capabilities are superior to those that are otherwise available.

Military Justice

Military tribunals are part of the country's court system and, as such, are responsible to the minister of justice as well as the minister of defense. At the highest level there is a military collegium in the national Supreme Court that can review cases from lower military tribunals or can elect to try certain of the most serious cases. Other than within the Supreme Court, military courts are separate and have no appeal or review relationships with county and district civil courts.

Military court jurisdiction is ordinarily limited to cases involving military personnel or cases that involve civilians on military installations or in relation to any aspect of the country's defense. There are occasional instances when certain other cases may be referred to military courts and, during wartime or during a national emergency when parts of the country are under martial law, the jurisdiction of these courts would be broadened considerably.

Military courts have a judge and two or more lay assessors whose functions are similar to their equivalents in civilian courts. Military judges are professional military officers who have university law degrees. The law states that such judges are elected, but presumably only as many lawyers as are required in its courts would be assigned to any single unit or base. Lay assessors are chosen from all ranks and are also elected. Officers are selected at officers' meetings; noncommissioned officers, at noncommissioned officers' meetings; and privates, at troop meetings. Additional numbers of lay assessors are appointed because all members of a court must have rank at least equal to that of the defendant on trial.

Logistics

Logistics—usually called rear services in Soviet and East European armies—are administered by one of the major directorates under the minister of defense. Except for such major items as aircraft and ships, all equipment and maintenance are handled by ground force logistics personnel.

Modernization of the forces since 1957, particularly since the mid-1960s, has increased the costs of the equipment and has added to maintenance problems. Career incentives of the 1971 laws on conditions of service were, in part, an effort to come to grips with the problem of retaining skilled personnel. In hope of reducing costs, a parallel effort has been directed toward expanding the capabilities of industry in order to produce more defense matériel locally.

Small arms, ammunition, and explosives have been produced locally for several years. Hungarian vehicles, including amphibious reconnaissance craft, armored personnel carriers, light artillery pieces, and trucks, are also in local production and have been introduced into the forces. Precision instruments and components for telecommunications and electronic equipment are also being acquired from local industry. All equipment has to be standardized to the degree that it can be integrated with that of other Warsaw Pact armies, but in several cases items of local design have been accepted as standard for the pact. Riverboats are built in Budapest shipyards, but all tanks, aircraft, heavy artillery, and more complex electronic equipment are acquired from the Soviet Union or other Warsaw Pact countries.

To guide and direct further research, primarily in the planning and requirements area, an army scientific collegium was formed in July 1972. Such a body was deemed necessary because the leadership has observed that complex military equipment items become increasingly more costly and also become obsolescent in ten to fifteen years. These leaders have concluded that careful study is essential in order to acquire the most satisfactory equipment at the least cost. The collegium is headed by the chief of the general staff, who is also a first deputy minister of defense. His immediate staff includes the chief of the Main Political Directorate and the deputy for scientific research, both of whom are also deputy ministers. The edict establishing the collegium defined it as an advisory body to the Ministry of Defense and described its functions as the debating of scientific questions affecting the armed forces in order to propose changes that scientific progress might make applicable to the army.

Ranks, Uniforms, and Decorations

The army has approximately the same number of ranks that are found in typical military organizations, but they are grouped into six classifications, the names of which do not in all cases translate readily to those used by other armies. Commissioned officer ranks, however, are standard and range from sublieutenant to general of the army. They include four general officer ranks—brigadier, lieutenant, and colonel general and general of the army. Field grades are major, lieutenant colonel, and colonel. Junior officers begin with sublieutenant and advance through second and first lieutenant to captain.

Enlisted grade nomenclature departs from that used by most of the world's armies. The three lowest grades—private first class, corporal, and lance sergeant—are called noncommissioned officers. The next three grades—sergeant, sergeant major, and company sergeant major—are called regimental sergeants major; in armies of most countries these would also be included among the noncommissioned-officer grades. Above the regimental sergeants major, but below the lowest commissioned officer rank, are two grades that are translated as ensign, which are the equivalent of warrant officers in other armies.

Rank insignia consists of shoulder boards for officers, ensigns, and higher grade enlisted men. Lower grades wear patches on shirt or blouse collars. Rank is indicated by the amount of ornamentation and the number of stars on the shoulder board. Officers have gold piping around the edges of the boards; ensigns and enlisted men have silver. General's stars are placed upon a solid gold braid background. Junior officers' boards are bare of braiding; those of field grades are partly braided. Except for the outer braiding, boards of the higher grade enlisted men resemble those of junior officers. Background colors and bronze devices identify service branches.

Uniforms are brownish olive drab. Enlisted men wear heavy wool in winter and a lighter colored cotton in the warm season. Officers wear the same colors, but the materials are wool worsted for winter and either cotton or tropical worsted for summer. The most frequently seen uniforms are the dress, service, and field uniforms. The service uniform is worn for most light duty work, recreation, and informal social occasions. It has a comfortably fitting blouse, and its long trousers are worn with low shoes. In summer a lighter weight, light-colored shirt takes the place of the blouse. The dress uniform consists of the same basic blouse and trousers but is worn with extra ornamentation, and the trousers are tucked into high boots. Officers wear a Sam Browne belt and, on the most formal occasions, a sword. Field uniforms include high boots into which the trousers are tucked. In summer the officers' field uniforms include a short jacket, Sam Browne belt, and sidearm; enlisted men's uniforms have a cotton shirt, which may be worn with sleeves rolled. A heavy overcoat is added for winter.

Twelve decorations were still being awarded in 1972 for extraordinary achievement, special merit, or outstanding performance. Another twenty-four are authorized to be worn but are no longer awarded. A few of those have been discontinued, but most of them were applicable to earlier service, such as in World War II or during the communist takeover after the war.

The highest ranking decoration is the Hero of Socialist Labor. Of those still being awarded, it is followed in order by the Medal of the Hungarian People's Republic, Order of the Hungarian People's Republic, Red Banner Order of Merit, and Red Star Order of Merit. Some of these decorations are awarded in two or more degrees, in which case the first degree is the highest class. The Order of Merit for Outstanding Service is frequently seen among the decorations of higher ranking military personnel. Although it ranks twenty-fourth in the list of thirty-six, it is one of a few decorations that is accompanied by a monetary award. An even more substantial pension supplement accompanies three or four of the more important decorations.

BIBLIOGRAPHY

Section I. Social

ABC World Airways Guide, CDLV, May 1972, ABC Travel Guides, Dunstable, Bedfordshire, England: ABC Travel Guides.

American Jewish Year Book, 1971, LXII. (Eds., Morris Fine and Milton Himmelfarb.) Philadelphia: Jewish Publication Society of America, 1972.

Andras, Emmerich, and Morel, Julius (eds.). *Bilanz des Ungarischen Katholizismus*. Munich: Heimat Werk-Verlag, 1969.

Baldwin, Godfrey (ed.). *International Population Reports*. (U.S. Department of Commerce, Series P-91, No. 18.) Washington: GPO, 1969.

Berki, R. N. "Evolution of a Marxist Thinker," *Problems of Communism*, XXI, No. 6, November–December 1972, 52–61.

Blumenfeld, Yorick. *Seesaw: Cultural Life in Eastern Europe*. New York: Harcourt, Brace and World, 1968.

Blunden, Godfrey. *Eastern Europe*. New York: Time, 1965.

Braham, Randolph L. *Education in the Hungarian People's Republic*. Washington: GPO, for U.S. Department of Health, Education, and Welfare, 1970.

Buti, Erno (ed.). *Public Education in the Hungarian People's Republic*. (Trans., Elek Mathe.) Budapest: Ministry of Education, 1968.

"Changes in the Standard of Living Reviewed," *Kozgazdasagi Szemle*, Budapest, October 1970. [Translated by U.S. Department of Commerce, Office of Technical Services, Joint Publications Research Service (Washington). JPRS: 52,082, *Translations on Eastern Europe: Economic and Industrial Affairs*, No. 395, 1970.]

Churchill, Winston S. *The Grand Alliance*. Boston: Houghton Mifflin, 1950.

Davis, Fitzroy. "East Europe's Film Makers Look West," *East Europe*, XVII, No. 5, May 1968, 27–31.

"Dealing with Hungary's Minorities," *East Europe*, XVIII, No. 1, January 1969, 31–32.

Degh, Linda. "Ethnology in Hungary," *East European Quarterly*, IV, No. 3, 1970, 293–307.

Deme, Laszlo. "The Society for Equality in the Hungarian Revolution of 1948," *Slavic Review*, XXXI, March 1972, 71–88.

Ekvall, David H. *Complete Guide to Eastern Europe*. New York: Hart, 1970.

Erdei, Ferenc. "The Changing Hungarian Village," *New Hungarian Quarterly* [Budapest], XXXVIII, 1970, 3-15.

Erdei, Ferenc (ed.). *Information Hungary*. New York: Pergamon Press, 1968.

The Europa Yearbook, 1971. London: Europa Publications, 1971.

The Europa Yearbook, 1972. London: Europa Publications, 1972.

"Fads in Schooling," *East Europe*, XV, No. 9, September 1966, 59.

Fejto, François, *A History of the People's Democracies*. New York: Praeger, 1971.

Fel, Edit, and Hofer, Tamas. *Proper Peasants*. Chicago: Aldine, 1969.

Ferge, Zsuzsa. "Social Mobility and the Open Character of Society," *New Hungarian Quarterly* [Budapest], No. 37, 1970, 83-98.

Fischer-Galati, Stephen (ed.). *East Europe in the Sixties*. New York: Praeger, 1963.

Fodor, Eugene (ed.). *Fodor's Hungary, 1970-71*. New York: David McKay, 1970.

Grant, Nigel. *Society, Schools and Progress in Eastern Europe*. New York: Pergamon Press, 1969.

Halasz, Zoltan. *Cultural Life in Hungary*. Budapest: Zrinyi Printing House, Pannonia Press, 1966.

Halasz, Zoltan (ed.). *Hungary*. Budapest: Corvina Press, 1963.

Hanak, Tibor. "Philosophy Under Kadar." Pages 65-73 in Editors of *Survey* (comp.), *Hungary Today*. New York: Praeger, 1962.

Helmreich, Ernest C. (ed.). *Hungary*. New York: Praeger, 1957.

Horthy, Nicholas. *Memoirs*. New York: Robert Speller and Sons, 1957.

Hungary. Ministry of Cultural Affairs. International Conference on Education. 33d Session. "Report on Educational Progress in the 1970/71 Academic Year." Geneva: 1971.

"Hungary." Pages 857-874 in *Encyclopaedia Britannica*, XI. Chicago: William Benton, 1969.

"Hungary." Pages 573-587 in *World Survey of Education*, V. Paris: United Nations Educational, Scientific and Cultural Organization, 1971.

"Hungary." Pages 139-148 in Louis Barron (ed.), *Worldmark Encyclopedia of Nations*, V. New York: Harper and Row, 1967.

"Hungary Revisited," *East Europe*, XV, No. 10, October 1966, 2-9.

Ignotus, Paul. *Hungary*. New York: Praeger, 1972.

————. "Literature Before and After," Pages 19-30 in Editors of *Survey* (comp.), *Hungary Today*. New York: Praeger, 1962.

Jane's World Railways, 1968-69. (11th ed.) New York: McGraw-Hill, 1969.

Jelavich, Barbara. *The Habsburg Empire in European Affairs, 1814-1918*. Chicago: Rand McNally, 1969.

Juhasz, William. "Freedom Under the Show: New Trends in Hungarian Writing," *East Europe*, XIV, No. 5, May 1965, 8-11.

Kaiser, Robert G. "Hungary's Farmers: Feudalism and the Future," *Washington Post*, August 20, 1972, A-16.

Kaiser, Robert E. "Searching for Jews in Eastern Europe," *Washington Post*, October 8, 1972, D-1, D-3.

Kaiser, Robert G., and Morgan, Dan. "Russia's Changing Empire," (A series.) *Washington Post*, December 17-27, 1972.

Kaldy, Gyula. *A History of Hungarian Music*. London: Haskell House, 1969.

Kampis, Antal. *The History of Art in Hungary*. London, Collet's, 1966.

Kertesz, Stephen. *Diplomacy in a Whirlpool*. Notre Dame: University of Notre Dame Press, 1953.

Konnyu, Leslie. *A Condensed Geography of Hungary*. St. Louis: American Hungarian Review, 1971.

Kosary, Dominic G. *A History of Hungary*. New York: Arno Press and New York Times, 1971.

Kovrig, Bennett. *The Hungarian People's Republic*. Baltimore: Johns Hopkins Press, 1970.

Macartney, C. A. *Hungary: A Short History*. Edinburgh: University Press, 1962.

Maday, Bela C. "Hungarian Peasant Studies." In Zdenek Salzmann (ed.), *A Symposium on East European Ethnography*. Research Reports No. 6, University of Massachusetts, Department of Anthropology. Amherst: 1970 (mimeo.).

―――― "The Significance of St. Stephen, King of Hungary, His Reign and His Era to Students of Humanities and the Social Science," *Congressional Record*, October 29, 1971, S17111-S17112.

Meray, Tibor. "Genealogical Troubles." Pages 31-39 in Editors of *Survey* (comp.), *Hungary Today*. New York: Praeger, 1962.

Miller, William J.; Roberts, Henry L.; and Shulman, Marshal D. *The Meaning of Communism*. Morristown, New Jersey: Silver Burdett, 1963.

Morgan, Dan. "Belgrade's Rocking to a 'Pop Socialist' Beat," *The Washington Post*, November 21, 1971, K-1, K-8.

――――. "East European Study Sees City Planning Crisis in Planned Society," *Washington Post*, June 22, 1972, 2-3.

Nagy, Karoly. "The Impact of Communism in Hungary," *East Europe*, XVIII, No. 3, March 1969, 11-17.

Parkin, Frank. *Class Inequality and Political Order*. New York: Praeger, 1971.

Pesci, Marton, and Sarfalvi, Bela. *The Geography of Hungary*. Budapest: Corvina Press, 1964.

Polinsky, Karoly. "Higher Technical Education in Hungary," *New Hungarian Quarterly* [Budapest], XII, Winter 1971, 110-116.

"Readying the Youth." *East Europe*, XVII, No. 9, September 1968, 45.

"School Dropouts." *East Europe*. XV, No. 12, December 1966, 50-51.

Schöpflin, George (ed.). *The Soviet Union and Eastern Europe*. New York: Praeger, 1970.

Schreiber, T. "Changes in the Leadership." Pages 39-48 in Editors of *Survey* (comp.), *Hungary Today*. New York: Praeger, 1962.

315

Seton-Watson, Hugh. *The East European Revolution.* New York: Praeger, 1955.

Shimoniak, Wasyl. *Communist Education: Its History, Philosophy, and Politics.* Chicago: Rand McNally, 1970.

Siklos, Laszlo. "Children from the Tanya," *New Hungarian Quarterly,* [Budapest], XXXVIII, 1970, 17-25.

Sinor, Denis. *History of Hungary.* London: Allen and Unwin, 1959.

Statistical Pocket Book of Hungary, 1971. Budapest: Statistical Publishing House, for Hungarian Central Statistical Office, 1971.

Statistical Pocket Book of Hungary, 1972. Budapest: Statistical Publishing House, for Hungarian Central Statistical Office, 1972.

Statistical Yearbook, 1970. Budapest: Statistical Publishing House, for Hungarian Central Statistical Office, 1972.

Szalai, Sandor. "Restratification of a Society," *New Hungarian Quarterly* [Budapest], No. 23, 1966, 24-33.

Tabori, Paul. "The Poet's Plight and the Poet's Power," *East Europe,* XV, No. 9, September 1966, 11-17.

Toma, Peter A. (ed.). *The Changing Face of Communism in Eastern Europe.* Tucson: University of Arizona Press, 1970.

UNESCO Statistical Yearbook, 1970. Paris: United Nations Educational, Scientific and Cultural Organization, 1971.

United Nations Educational, Scientific and Cultural Organization. "World Illiteracy at Mid-Century," *Monographs on Fundamental Education,* XI, 1957.

U.S. Bureau of the Census. *Estimates of Educational Attainment of the Population and Labor Force in Hungary: 1949-1971,* by Marjory E. Searing. (International Population Reports, Series P-95, No. 71.) Washington: GPO, 1958.

U.S. Department of Commerce. Office of Technical Services. Joint Publications Research Service—JPRS (Washington). The following items are from the JPRS series *Translations on Eastern Europe: Political, Sociological, and Military Affairs.*

"Begging in Budapest," *Nepszabadsag,* Budapest, September 19, 1971. (JPRS: 54,167, No. 420, 1971.)

"Conditions of Budapest Hospitals Discussed," *Nepszabadsag,* Budapest, September 13, 1968. (JPRS: 46,603, No. 33, 1968.)

"Decree on the Modification of Family Allowance Published," *Magyar Kozlony,* Budapest, December 29, 1971, 99. (JPRS: 55,142, No. 476, 1972.)

"Exchange Student Program Described," *Nepszava,* Budapest, CXIII, May 16, 1972. (JPRS: 56,175, No. 536, 1972.)

Hungarian Statistical Yearbook, 1970, Parts I and II, Budapest, August 16, 1972. (JPRS: 56,789, 1972.)

"Kadar Speaks on Education Resolution," *Nepszabadsag,* Budapest, July 2, 1972. (JPRS: 56,533, No. 556, 1972.)

"Over-Application to Universities, Colleges," *Magyar Nemzet*, Budapest, June 8, 1972. (JPRS: 56,723, No. 542, 1972.)

"Pardi Presents Five-Year-Plan Bill to National Assembly," (Pre-release of speech by Imre Pardi), Budapest, September 30, 1970. (JPRS: 51,629, No. 275, 1970.)

"Renovation of Hospital Network is Pushed," *Nepszabadsag*, Budapest, May 7, 1970. (JPRS: 50,604, No. 212, 1970.)

"Schooling of Worker-Peasant Youth Examined," *Tarsadalmi Szemle*, Budapest, XI, November 1970. (JPRS: 52,070, No. 298, 1970.)

"Shortcomings in Service Industries Reviewed," *Fagyelo*, Budapest, June 3, 1970. (JPRS: 50,830, No. 308, 1970.)

"Statistics on Communist Youth Federation and Students Reviewed," *Pedagogiai Szemle*, Budapest, April 1972. (JPRS: 56,081, No. 530, 1972.)

"Suicide Called Vital Problem," *Ifju-Kommunista*, Budapest, June 1970, 25. (JPRS: 56,263, No. 541, 1972.)

"University and College Officials for 1971-1972 School Year Listed," *Felsooktatasi Szemle*, Budapest, n.d. (JPRS: 55,422, No. 494, 1972.)

"Youth Guard Activities Described," *Nephadserey*, Budapest, XIX, May 6, 1972. (JPRS: 56,054, No. 528, 1972.)

Veto, Miklos. "The Catholic Church." Pages 58 64 in Editors of *Survey* (comp.), *Hungary Today*. New York: Praeger, 1962.

Volgyes, Ivan. "The Hungarian Tightrope," *East Europe*, XXI, No. 5, May 1972, 2-4.

Wolff, Robert Lee. *The Balkans in Our Time*. New York: W. W. Norton, 1956.

(Various issues of the following periodicals were also used in the preparation of this section: *East Europe* [New York], September 1966-September 1968; and *New Hungary* [Budapest], all issues January 1971-December 1971.)

Section II. Political

Aczel, Zamas. *Ten Years After the Hungarian Revolution in the Perspective of History.* New York: Holt, Rinehart and Winston, 1967.

Bagdy, Zoltan. "The Policy of Compromise: A Study of the Kadar Government, Recent Trends and Development in Hungarian Political Life, 1957-1962." Unpublished master's thesis. Washington: The American University, 1964.

Blumenfeld, Yorick. *Seesaw: Cultural Life in Eastern Europe.* New York: Harcourt, Brace and World, 1968.

Braham, Randolph L. *Education in the Hungarian People's Republic.* Washington: GPO, for U.S. Department of Health, Education, and Welfare, 1970.

Bromke, Adam, and Rakowska-Harmstone, Teresa (eds.). *The Communist States in Disarray, 1965-1971.* Minneapolis: University of Minnesota Press, 1972.

Brzezinski, Zbigniew K. "Communist State Relations: The Effect on Ideology," *East Europe,* XVI, No. 3, March 1967, 1-5.

Clews, John C. *Communist Propaganda Techniques.* New York: Praeger, 1964.

Darvasi, Istvan. "The Present Stage of 'Peaceful Coexistence,'" *East Europe,* XIX, No. 1, January 1970.

Editor and Publisher International Year Book, 1972. New York: Editor and Publisher, 1972.

Erdei, Ferenc (ed.). *Information Hungary.* New York: Pergamon Press, 1968.

Ergang, Robert. *Europe Since Waterloo.* Boston: Heath, 1967.

The Europa Yearbook, 1972. London: Europa Publications, 1972.

Farrell, R. Barry. *Political Leadership in Eastern Europe and the Soviet Union.* Chicago: Aldine, 1970.

Feron, James. "Kadar Seems Stronger than Ever in Stable, Affluent Hungary," *New York Times,* December 7, 1972, 16.

Frost, J. M. (ed.). *World Radio-TV Handbook, 1972.* Hvidovre, Denmark: World Radio-TV Handbook, 1972.

Griffith, William E. (ed.). *Communism in Europe: Continuity, Change, and the Sino-Soviet Dispute,* I. Cambridge: Massachusetts Institute of Technology, 1964.

Halasz, Zoltan. *Cultural Life in Hungary.* Budapest: Zrinyi Printing House, Pannonia Press, 1966.

Halasz, Zoltan (ed.). *Hungary.* Budapest: Corvina Press, 1963.

Helmreich, Ernest C. (ed.). *Hungary.* New York: Praeger, 1957.

Kaiser, Robert G., and Morgan, Dan. "Russia's Changing Empire," (A series.) *Washington Post,* December 17-27, 1972.

Kecskemetik, Paul. *The Unexpected Revolution.* Stanford: Stanford University Press, 1961.

Keesing's Contemporary Archives, 1971-72. London: Keesing's Publications, 1972.

Kemenes, Egon. "Hungary and the Developing Countries," *Hungarian Survey* [Budapest], No. 1, 1966, 97-107.

Kintner, William R., and Klaiber, Wolfgang. *Eastern Europe and European Security.* New York: Dunellen, 1971.

Kiss, Sandor. "The Kadar Imprint on the Hungarian Party," *East Europe,* XVIII, No. 3, March 1969, 2-9.

Kovrig, Bennett. *The Hungarian People's Republic.* Baltimore: Johns Hopkins Press, 1970.

Lindner, Laszlo. "Relations Between Hungary and the Latin American Countries," *Hungarian Survey* [Budapest], No. 1, 1968, 50-61.

Merrill, John C.; Bryan, Carter R.; and Alisky, Marvin. *The Foreign Press.* Baton Rouge; Louisiana State University Press, 1964, 121-122.

Nagy, Karoly. "The Impact of Communism in Hungary," *East Europe,* XVIII, No. 3, March 1969, 11-17.

Paal, Ferenc. "Hungarian Foreign Policy in 1965," *Hungarian Survey* [Budapest], No. 1, 1966.

Qualter, Terence H. *Propaganda and Psychological Warfare.* New York: Random House, 1962.

Roberts, Henry L. *Eastern Europe: Politics, Revolution, and Diplomacy.* New York: Knopf, 1970.

Sandor, E. "Hope and Caution," *Problems of Communism,* XIX, January-February 1970, 60-66.

Schöpflin, George (ed.). *The Soviet Union and Eastern Europe.* New York: Praeger, 1970.

Shaffer, Harry G. "Progress in Hungary," *Problems of Communism,* XIX, January-February 1970, 48-59.

Staar, Richard F. *The Communist Regimes in Eastern Europe.* (Rev. ed.) Stanford: The Hoover Institution, 1971.

Stanley, Timothy W., and Whitt, Darnell M. *Detente Diplomacy: United States and European Security in the 1970s.* Cambridge: Harvard University Press, 1970.

Statistical Pocket Book of Hungary, 1971. Budapest: Statistical Publishing House, for Hungarian Central Statistical Office, 1971.

Statistical Pocket Book of Hungary, 1972. Budapest: Statistical Publishing House, for Hungarian Central Statistical Office, 1972.

Statistical Yearbook, 1970. Budapest: Statistical Publishing House, for Hungarian Central Statistical Office, 1972.

Sugar, Peter F., and Lederer, Ivo J. *Nationalism in Eastern Euro*[Seattle: University of Washington Press, 1969.

"Television in Eastern Europe," *East Europe,* XV, No. 4, April 1966, 12-15.

Toma, Peter A. (ed.). *The Changing Face of Communism in Eastern Europe*. Tucson: University of Arizona Press, 1970.

Triska, Jan F. (ed.). *Constitution of the Communist Party-States*. Stanford: The Hoover Institution, 1968.

"The TV Season," *East Europe*, XVI, No. 2, February 1967, 51.

United Nations Educational, Scientific and Cultural Organization. *World Communications: Press, Radio, Television, Film.* (4th ed.) New York: UNESCO, 1964.

U.S. Congress, 89th, 2d Session. Senate Committee on Government Operations. *The Warsaw Pact, Its Role in Soviet Bloc Affairs.* Washington: GPO, 1966.

U.S. Congress, 91st, 2d Session. Senate Committee on the Judiciary. *World Communism, 1967-69: Soviet Efforts to Re-establish Control.* Washington: GPO, 1970.

U.S. Department of Commerce. Office of Technical Services. Joint Publications Research Service—JPRS (Washington). The following items are from the JPRS series *Translations on Eastern Europe: Political, Sociological, and Military Affairs.*

"Activities of Knowledge Spreading Society Described," *Elet es Irodalon*, Budapest, August 12, 1972. (JPRS: 56,851, No. 582, 1972.)

"Activities of the Patriotic People's Front," *Magyar Nemzet*, Budapest, April 27, 1972, 98. (JPRS: 55,928, No. 521, 1972.)

"Apro, Nyers Speak on Constitution Day," *Nepszabadsag*, Budapest, August 22, 1972. (JPRS: 56,964, No. 588, 1972.)

"The Cadre Policy of Our Party," *Ifju-Kommunista*, Budapest, August-September 1971, 8-9 (JPRS: 54,116, No. 416, 1971.)

"The Class Struggle in Contemporary Society," *Partelet*, Budapest, April 1972, 4. (JPRS: 55,980, No. 524, 1972.)

"The Development of State Work and Party Management," *Nepszabadsag*, Budapest, March 2, 1972. (JPRS: 55, 510, No. 500, 1972.)

"'Discovering Hungary' Book Series Reviewed," *Ifju-Kommunista*, Budapest, June 1972. (JPRS: 56,263, No. 541, 1972.)

"Election Law Modification Needed," *Allam es Igazgatas*, Budapest, July 1970. (JPRS: 51,233, No. 248, 1970.)

"Election Law Modifications," *Magyar Kozlony*, Budapest, October 14, 1970. (JPRS: 52,017, No. 296, 1970.)

"Electoral Reform Bill Passed by National Assembly," Budapest, October 3, 1970. (JPRS: 51,629, No. 275, 1970.)

"Expansion of Communist Youth Association," *Ifju-Kommunista*, Budapest, August 1968. (JPRS: 46,478, No. 30, 1968.)

"Hegedus Discusses the Social Problems of Communism," *Pedagogiai Szemle*, Budapest, November 1968. (JPRS: 47,475, No. 70, 1969.)

"Historians, Media Urged to Tell the Truth about Transylvanian Hungarians," *Tiszataj*, Szeged, August 1972. (JPRS: 56,813, No. 579, 1972.)

"Hungarian Editor of 'Peace and Socialism' Describes Work of Journal," *Partelet*, Budapest, March 1972. (JPRS: 55,447, No. 495, 1972.)

"Hungarians Join in Soviet Warnings Against 'Cold War' Television," *Orszag-Vilag*, Budapest, September 27, 1972. (JPRS: 57,235, No. 608, 1972.)

"Hungarian Trade Unions: Aims and Activities," *Praca*, Bratislava, December 31, 1969. (JPRS: 49,702, No. 178, 1970.)

"Janos Kadar Authors Lead Article in New Literary Magazine," *Kritika*, Budapest, February 1972. (JPSR: 55,472, No. 497, 1972.)

"Journalist Says It Is Safer to Ask Questions," *Nepszabadsag* (Supplement), Budapest, September 1972. (JPRS: 57,083, No. 597, 1972.)

"Local Party Election Results," *Magyar Nemzet*, Budapest, November 17, 1970. (JPRS: 51,929, No. 292, 1970.)

"Mass Media, Public Opinion Research Activities Described," *Elet es Irodalom*, Budapest, August 21, 1971. (JPRS: 54,067, No. 412, 1971.)

"Methods of Youth Federation Elections," *Magyar Ifjusag*, Budapest, December 1970. (JPRS: 54,451, No. 438, 1971.)

"MSZMP Daily Publishes Draft of Amended Constitution," *Nepszabadsag*, Budapest, March 26, 1972. (JPRS: 55,657, No. 507, 1972.)

"MSZMP Organizational Statutes," *Partelet*, Budapest, December 1970. (JPRS: 52,130, No. 303, 1971.)

"New 'Constitution' for Communist Youth Federation Described," *Ifju-Kommunista*, Budapest, August–September 1971. (JPRS: 54,116, No. 416, 1971.)

"'Our Neurotic Age'—A Hungarian Indictment," *Kortars*, Budapest, September 1971. (JPRS: 54,309, No. 430, 1971.)

"Party Committee Discusses Deficiencies in Socialist Thought," *Partelet*, Budapest, June 1972. (JPRS: 56,244, No. 540, 1972.)

"Party Membership Statistics: 1970–1971," *Partelet*, Budapest, December 1971. (JPRS: 54,690, No. 454, 1971.)

"Party Recruiting Among Draftees," *Nephadsereg*, Budapest, April 29, 1972. (JPRS: 55,980, No. 524, 1972.)

"The Party's Leading Role in the Construction of Socialism," *Tarsadalmi Szemle*, Budapest, August–September 1970. (JPRS: 51,653, No. 278, 1970.)

"Party Social Sciences Institute," *Partelet*, Budapest, June 1972. (JPRS: 56,244, No. 540, 1972.)

"Patriotic People's Front Presidium Meets to Discuss Front's Journals," *Magyar Nemzet*, Budapest, September 23, 1972. (JPRS: 57,180, No. 603, 1972.)

"People's Control Committees: Organization and Tasks," *Magyarorszag*, Budapest, August 22, 1971. (JPRS: 54,004, No. 409, 1971.)

"People's Control Committees: The Role of Party Activists," *Partelet*, Budapest, December 1971. (JPRS: 54,690, No. 454, 1971.)

"People's Front Activities Reviewed," *Magyar Nemzet*, Budapest, April 27, 1972. (JPRS: 55,928, No. 521, 1972.)

"Political Apathy of Youth Analyzed," *Valosag*, Budapest, January 1972. (JPRS: 55,270, No. 484, 1972.)

"Proposed Modifications of MSZMP Statutes," *Partelet*, Budapest, 1970. (JPRS: 51,822, No. 287, 1970.)

"Radio, Television Regulations Published," *Kozlekedesugyi Ertesito*, Budapest, September 26, 1970. (JPRS: 51,941, No. 385, 1970.)

"Resolution Establishing Council Bureau," *Magyar Kozlony*, Budapest, July 21, 1970. (JPRS: 51,283, No. 251, 1970.)

"Review of Constitutional Amendments," *Nepszava*, Budapest, April 16, 1972. (JPRS: 55,891, No. 519, 1972.)

"The Role of Party Organizations: A Discussion," *Partelet*, Budapest, January 1969. (JPRS: 47,475, No. 70, 1969.)

"Role of Youth Federation," *Ifju-Kommunista*, Budapest, December 1971. (JPRS: 54,868, No. 463, 1971.)

"Setting Up of Council Statutes," *Allam es Igazgatas*, Budapest, April 1971. (JPRS: 53,688, No. 390, 1971.)

"State Work and Party Management," *Nepszabadsag*, Budapest, March 2, 1972. (JPRS: 55,510, No. 500, 1972.)

"Struggle Against Bourgeois Propaganda in Zala Megye Described," *Partelet*, Budapest, June 1972, (JPRS: 56,244, No. 540, 1972.)

"Television Panel 'International Life' Accepts All Questions," (presented on Budapest television), Budapest, June 21, 1972. (JPRS: 56,569, No. 559, 1972.)

"Text of Draft Constitution," *Nepszabadsag*, Budapest, March 26, 1972. (JPRS: 55,657, No. 507, 1972.)

"TV-Radio Broadcasting Network and Telephone Web Expanding," *Nepszava*, Budapest, August 12, 1970. (JPRS: 51,380, No. 345, 1970.)

"Work of Mass Communications Research Center Described," *Magyar Nemzet*, Budapest, September 17, 1972. (JPRS: 57,083, No. 597, 1972.)

"Work of Propagandists Praised," *Nepszabadsag*, Budapest, June 29, 1972. (JPRS: 56,452, No. 550, 1972.)

"Work of Trade Union Propagandists Reviewed," *Munka*, Budapest, July 1972. (JPRS: 56,633, No. 563, 1972.)

"Youth Federation Journals to be Revamped," *Ifju-Kommunista*, Budapest, October 1972. (JPRS: 57,274, No. 610, 1972.)

Vajda, Imre. *The Role of Foreign Trade in a Socialist Economy*. Budapest: Corvina Press, 1965.

Vali, Ferenc A. "Hungary." Pages 71–86 in Adam Bromke (ed.), *The Communist States at the Crossroads*. New York: Praeger, 1965.

Wolfe, Thomas W. *Soviet Power and Europe, 1965–1969.* Santa Monica: Rand Corporation, 1969.

Yearbook on International Communist Affairs, 1968. (Ed., Richard F. Staar.) Stanford: Hoover Institution Press, 1968, 490–496.

Yearbook on International Communist Affairs, 1969. (Ed., Richard F. Staar.) Stanford: Hoover Institution Press, 1969, 696–701.

Yearbook on International Communist Affairs, 1970. (Ed., Richard F. Staar.) Stanford: Hoover Institution Press, 1970, 75–84.

Yearbook on International Communist Affairs, 1971. (Ed., Richard F. Staar.) Stanford: Hoover Institution Press, 1971, 72–84.

Yearbook on International Communist Affairs, 1972. (Ed., Richard F. Staar.) Stanford: Hoover Institution Press, 1972, 38–45.

(Various issues of the following periodical were also used in the preparation of this section: *East Europe* [New York], September 1967–June 1972.)

Section III. Economic

Buky, Barnabas. "Hungary's NEM," *Problems of Communism*, XXI, September-October 1972, 31–39.

Erdei, Ferenc (ed.). *Information Hungary*. New York: Pergamon Press, 1968.

Fel, Edit, and Hofer, Tamas. *Proper Peasants*. Chicago: Aldine, 1969.

Friss, Istvan. *Economic Laws, Policy, Planning*. Budapest: Akademiai Kiado, 1971.

Grzybowski, Kazimierz. "The Foreign Trade Regime in COMECON Countries Today," *International Law and Politics*, IV, No. 2, 1971, 183–211.

Halasz, Zoltan (ed.). *Hungary*. Budapest: Corvina Press, 1963.

Hont, J. "Major Tendencies in the Development of Hungarian Agriculture and Food Industry," *Acta Oeconomica* [Budapest], V, No. 3, March 1970, 193–208.

"Hungary," *East Europe*, XVIII, No. 4, April 1969, 46–47.

"Hungary," *East Europe*, XX, No. 6, June 1971, 40–41.

Markos, Gyorgy. *Ungarn Land, Volk, Wirtschaft in Stichworten*. Vienna: Ferdinand Hirt, 1971.

Minerals Yearbook, 1969, IV. Washington: GPO, for U.S. Department of the Interior, Bureau of Mines, 1971.

Osborne, R. H. *East-Central Europe*. New York: Praeger, 1967.

Pecsi, Marton, and Sarfalvi, Bela. *The Geography of Hungary*. Budapest: Corvina Press, 1964.

Pounds, Norman J. G. *Eastern Europe*. Chicago: Aldine, 1969.

Selucky, Radoslav. *Economic Reforms in Eastern Europe*. New York: Praeger, 1972.

Statistical Pocket Book of Hungary, 1971. Budapest: Statistical Publishing House, for Hungarian Central Statistical Office, 1971.

Statistical Pocket Book of Hungary, 1972. Budapest: Statistical Publishing House, for Hungarian Central Statistical Office, 1972.

Statistical Yearbook, 1970. Budapest: Statistical Publishing House, for Hungarian Central Statistical Office, 1972.

Statisticheskii Ezhegodnik, 1971. Moskva: Tipografiia Sekretariata, for Soviet Ekonomicheskoi Vzaimopomoshchi. Sekretariat, 1971.

Szabados, Joseph. "Hungary's NEM: Promises and Pitfalls," *East Europe*, XVII, No. 4, April 1968, 25–32.

Vajda, Imre, and Simai, Mihaly (eds.). *Foreign Trade in a Planned Economy*. Cambridge: University Press, 1971.

Wilczynski, J. *Socialist Economic Development and Reforms.* New York: Praeger, 1972.

Section IV. National Security

Baldwin, Godfrey (ed.). *International Population Reports.* (U.S. Department of Commerce, Series P-91, No. 18.) Washington: GPO, 1969.

Bromke, Adam, and Rakowska-Harmstone, Teresa, (eds.). *The Communist States in Disarray, 1965–1971.* Minneapolis: University of Minnesota Press, 1972.

Erdei, Ferenc (ed.). *Information Hungary.* New York: Pergamon Press, 1968.

Halasz, Zoltan (ed.). *Hungary.* Budapest: Corvina Press, 1963.

Helmreich, Ernest C. (ed.). *Hungary.* New York: Praeger, 1957.

Kintner, William R., and Klaiber, Wolfgang. *Eastern Europe and European Security.* New York: Dunellen, 1971.

Kovrig, Bennett. *The Hungarian People's Republic.* Baltimore: Johns Hopkins Press, 1970.

The Military Balance, 1972–73. London: Institute for Strategic Studies, 1972.

Soton-Watson, Hugh. *The East European Revolution.* New York: Praeger, 1955.

Statistical Pocket Book of Hungary, 1971. Budapest: Statistical Publishing House, for Hungarian Central Statistical Office, 1971.

Statistical Pocket Book of Hungary, 1972. Budapest: Statistical Publishing House, for Hungarian Central Statistical Office, 1972.

U.S. Department of Commerce. Office of Technical Services. Joint Publications Research Services—JPRS (Washington). The following items are from the JPRS series *Translations on Eastern Europe: Political, Sociological and Military Affairs.*

    "Advantages of Professional Military Career," *Nepszabadsag,* Budapest, April 4, 1972. (JPRS: 55,626, No. 505, 1972.)

    "Army Committee Reviews Agitation Work," *Nepszabadsag,* Budapest, June 30, 1972. (JPRS: 56,404, No. 548, 1972.)

    "Army Equipment, Training Changes," *Magyarorszag,* Budapest, October 15, 1971. (JPRS: 54,253, No. 426, 1971.)

    "Army Scientific Collegium Formed," *Nephadsereg,* Budapest, August 11, 1972. (JPRS: 56,754, No. 574, 1972.)

    "Causes, Prevention of Juvenile Delinquency," *Ifju-Kommunista,* Budapest, October 1970. (JPRS: 51,858, No. 290, 1970.)

    "Civil Defense Training System," *Polgari Vedelem,* Budapest, June 12, 1972. (JPRS: 56,404, No. 548, 1972.)

    "Court Reform Explained," *Nepszabadsag,* Budapest, June 11, 1972. (JPRS: 56,315, No. 544, 1972.)

"Criminal Statistics," *Magyar Hirlap*, Budapest, November 20, 1971. (JPRS: 54,641, No. 450, 1971.)

"Current System of Decorations and Awards," *Nepszabadsag*, Budapest, May 2, 1972. (JPRS: 55,868, No. 518, 1972.)

"Decrees on Armed Forces Service and Pensions," *Magyar Kozlony*, Budapest, June 1, 1971. (JPRS: 53,777, No. 397, 1971.)

"Defense Training in Primary, Secondary Schools," *Pedagogiai Szemle*, Budapest, May 1972. (JPRS: 56,404, No. 548, 1972.)

"Extended Service Procedures," *Nephadsereg*, Budapest, July 24, 1972. (JPRS: 56,594, No. 560, 1972.)

"Government Guard," *Nephadsereg*, Budapest, June 17, 1972. (JPRS: 56,404, No. 548, 1972.)

"Home Defense Federation," *Nepszabadsag*, Budapest, March 25, 1972. (JPRS: 55,733, No. 510, 1972.)

"New Law on Courts," *Magyar Kozlony*, Budapest, July 8, 1972. (JPRS: 56,633, No 563, 1972.)

"New Law on State's Attorneys," *Magyar Kozlony*, Budapest, July 8, 1972. (JPRS: 56,656, No. 565, 1972.)

"Paramilitary Links to Pilot Training," *Nephadsereg*, Budapest, September 16, 1971. (JPRS: 54,067, No. 412, 1971.)

"Police Officers' Academy Opens," *Magyar Nemzet*, Budapest, September 26, 1971. (JPRS: 54,210, No. 423, 1971.)

"Proliferation of Clubs and Associations," *Magyarorszag*, Budapest, July 9, 1972. (JPRS: 56,511, No. 554, 1972.)

"Requirements for Enrollment in Military Academies," *Ifju-Kommunista*, Budapest, February 26, 1971. (JPRS: 52,487, No. 318, 1971.)

"Reservist Training Exercise," *Magyar Hirlap*, Budapest, September 29, 1972. (JPRS: 57,149, No. 600, 1972.)

"Special Civil Defense Services Organized," *Polgari Vedelem*, Budapest, January 10, 1970. (JPRS: 49,904, No. 185, 1970.)

"Statistics on Communist Youth Federation and Students Reviewed," *Pedagogiai Szemle*, Budapest, April 1972. (JPRS: 56,081, No. 530, 1972.)

"Warsaw Pact Command, Soviet Aid Described," *Orszag-Vilag*, Budapest, September 29, 1971. (JPRS: 54,300, No. 429, 1971.)

"Youth Guard Activities Described," *Nephadsereg*, Budapest, May 6, 1972. (JPRS: 56,054, No. 528, 1972.)

"Youth Labor Camps," *Magyarorszag*, Budapest, July 2, 1972. (JPRS: 56,452, No. 550, 1972.)

GLOSSARY

COMECON—Council for Mutual Economic Assistance. Economic alliance founded in 1949 to further cooperation among member states. Members are Bulgaria, Cuba, Czechoslovakia, East Germany, Hungary, Mongolia, Poland, Romania, and the Soviet Union. Headquarters is in Moscow.

Euro-dollar—United States dollars held by foreigners in European banks and used to finance commercial transactions.

forint—The basic unit of currency. An artificial exchange rate, based on the gold content of the forint, is 10.81 per US$1 but is not used in practice. A rate of 27.63 forints per US$1 is used for most noncommercial transactions. Foreign trade transactions with the West peg the forint at 60 per US$1, and with COMECON countries, at 33.33 per US$1. Black-market rates range as high as 62.50 per US$1.

KISZ—Kommunista Ifjusagi Szovetseg (Communist Youth League). The official youth organization of the country; functions under the direct guidance and supervision of the party.

MSZMP—Magyar Szocialista Munkaspart (Hungarian Socialist Workers' Party). Known as the Hungarian Peace Party, it operated underground during the interwar period. The party emerged into the open after World War II as the Hungarian Communist Party. After forcing the Social Democratic Party to merge with it in 1948, the party eventually assumed the title by which it was still known in 1973—the Hungarian Socialist Workers' Party.

NEM—New Economic Mechanism (Uj Gazdasagi Mechanizmus). A long-range reform program, emphasizing decentralization, initiated in 1968 as a means toward greater efficiency in the overall economic system.

Patriotic People's Front—The umbrella organization for all other mass organizations; provides a façade of democratic practice, whereas, actually, it provides a means of party control.

SZOT—Szakszerveztek Orszagos Tanacsa (National Council of Trade Unions). The largest mass organization in the country, with a membership of about 3.4 million in 1970. The council is essentially a transmitter of party policy. The council acquired some influence in the field of workers' rights after the introduction of the New Economic Mechanism, but the union leadership is communist and therefore speaks first for the party.

Warsaw Treaty Organization (Warsaw Pact)—Military alliance founded in 1955. The Soviet minister of defense is traditionally the supreme commander of the joint Warsaw Pact forces. Members are Bulgaria, Czechoslovakia, East Germany, Hungary, Poland, Romania, and the Soviet Union.

INDEX

Academy of Marxism-Leninism: 104
Academy of Sciences: 125
adult education. *See* education
Ady, Endre: 113-114
Agricultural Youth Council: 290
agriculture: viii, 218, 243-262; collective
farms, viii, 4, 28, 129, 245, 246-251, 252;
credit, 252-254, 256, 260, 262; crop production, 259-261, 260 (table 10); education,
97, 100; fertilizers, 256; income, 250, 254;
investment, 251-252; labor, 48, 62, 82,
248-249, 251; land tax, 262; land use,
244-245; livestock production, 261 (table
11), 261-262; machinery, 254-256, 278
(table 12); marketing, 257-258; plant protective agents, 256-257, 260; prices, 257-
258; production, 258-263; state farms,
245-246; subsidies, 254, 255, 260, 262
air and air defense force: 7, 297, 302
airlines and airfields: ix, 48, 53; air police,
283
Albania: 180
alcohol: 289, 292, 293
Anda, Geza: 119
Andrassy, Count Gyula: 20
anti-imperialism, capitalism: 193
Arany, Janos: 112-113
architecture: 121-123
army: ix, 7, 297-311; administration, 7; conditions of service, 307-308; conscription,
7, 297, 300, 301, 304, 308; courts, 140, 141,
142-143, 308-309; effect on labor, 300-
301; foreign military relations, 302-303;
government and party control, 299-300;
ground forces, 7, 297; logistics, 309-310;
manpower, 303-304; morale, 297, 299,
307-308; organization and mission, 301-
302; ranks, uniforms, and decorations,
310-311; size, 297, 299; Soviet influence,
302, 304; training, 304-307; Youth Guard,
290
Arrow Cross parties: 24
Arpad dynasty: 10
art: 104
artists and intellectuals: 67, 109-125; censorship, 6, 109-110; European influence,

122, 123; party guidelines and subsidies,
6-7, 111; role in national crises, 6, 109;
writers' revolt of 1950's, 115
arts and sciences: 110-111
Attila Jozsef University: 99
Austria: 173; boundary with, 31, 41; television and radio, 292

Babits, Mihaly: 114
von Bach, Alexander: 19
Bakony Hills: 266, 267
Banki, Donat: 123
Baranyi, Ferenc: 115
Bardossy, Laszlo: 25
Bartok, Bela: 119
Batthyany, Count Lajos: 16
Battle of Voronezh: 298
Benjamin, Laszlo: 115
Bernath, Aurel: 122
Bethlen, Count Istvan: 23, 24
Bethlen, Gabor: 15
birth rate: 45-46, 47, 65
Blathy, Titus: 123
Bolyai, Janos: 123
boundaries: vii, 31, 41, frontier guard, 7,
286; post World War I, 2, 23; Vienna
Awards, 1938, 1940, 25
Brazil: 184
Brezhnev, Leonid: 149, 150, 178, 179-180
Buda: 45
Budapest: ix, 31, 34, 37, 44-45, 76, 264;
population, 41, 43, 46-47; port of, 50, 54
Bulgaria: 180

cabarets, satire in: 116-117
Carpathian Mountains: 33
Central Arbitration Committee: 137-138
Central People's Control Committee: 138
Charles III: 16
Charles IV: 22
Charles Robert of Anjou: 13
children: child-care facilities, 82; infant
mortality, 47, 70
Chile: 185
civil defense: 286-287
civil rights: 129, 132
climate: vii, 36-37, 243-245
clothing: 75, 79 (table 4), 80 (table 5)

coffeehouses: 113

communication (*see also* mass communication): viii, 79-80

communist party. *See* Hungarian Socialist Workers' Party

communist summit meeting, 1969: 179

Communist Youth League: 163-164, 199, 288, 289-291, 300

conscription: 7, 297, 300, 301, 304, 308

constitution: development, 12, 17-18, 128-132; 1946, 128; 1949, vii, 2, 27, 128-129; 129-130; revised, 127, 130-132, 134-135, 136, 138, 172, 175, 188-189

consumer goods: 78-81 (table 4)

Corvina Library: 121, 208

Corvinus Matyas (Matyas Hunyadi): 13-14, 121, 208

cost of living: 69, 77-78, 79 (table 4), 80 (table 5), 167, 257-258

Council for Mutual Economic Assistance: viii, 53, 169, 173, 174, 177-178, 185

Council of Ministers: vii, 3, 129, 133, 135, 136-139, 299; administration of mass media, 191 (fig. 1), 192, 193; duties and powers, 127, 138-139, 175; organization, 138 (fig. 5)

courts: viii, 139-143, 281, 293-294; county, viii, 141-142; district, viii, 140, 142; labor affairs, viii, 140, 141, 142; lay assessors, 141, 309; military, viii, 140, 141, 142-143, 308-309; reform, 1973, 139-140; Supreme Court, viii, 133, 141, 142, 308; supreme prosecutor, 142-143

craftsmen and artisans: 78-79, 120; dual income, 79, 80; gold and metal, 121-122

credit, agricultural: 252-254, 256, 260, 262

crime: 67, 289, 292-293; against private property, 281; against state, 281, 292-293

Croatia: 18

Csepel Island: 54

Csok, Istvan: 122

cultural agreements: 175

cultural clubs: 66

cultural relations: 169

culture: vii, 6, 24, 67, 109; Eastern heritage, 9; national renaissance (1700's), 16; of minorities, 129; propagation and dissemination, 193; Western orientation, 9, 12

currency: viii, 236-237; exchange rates, 238-239

Czechoslovakia: boundary with, 31, 41; 1968 Soviet invasion, Hungarian participation, 7, 110, 147-148, 149, 178, 180, 193, 303; trade with, 255, 267

Czingege, Colonel General Lajos: 299

dance: 120-121

Danube River: 32, 33-35, 41, 50, 51-52

Danube River conventions: 174-175

Deak, Ferenc: 19-20

death rate: 47, 70

Debrecen: 43, 45, 264

Deveny Gate: 33

Dinnyes, Lajos: 27

diplomatic relations: 178

discussion groups: 66

disease: 69, 70-71

districts: 43

Dohnanyi, Enro: 118

Dorati, Antal: 119

Dorog: 266

drainage: 33

Drava River: 33, 34, 35, 41, 52

Dubcek, Alexander: 7

Dunantul. *See* Transdanubia

economy (*see also* agriculture; industry; New Economic Mechanism): viii, 55, 128-129, 215-241; banking, 235-236; budget, 233-235; Committee on National Economic Policy, 155-156; currency, viii, 236-237; economic and labor disputes, 139-140, 141; five-year plans, 87-88, 221, 222-223; foreign loans, 24, 183; growth of personal incomes, 216; income and wage regulations, 217, 226, 227-231; investment policy, 216-217, 231-233, 234; military and, 300-301; national economic planning, 221-223; organization and structure, 217-221; party control, 218; price policy, 215, 216; socialized ownership, 132, 217-218; Soviet relations, 179; state subsidies, 225-226, 229; taxation, 217, 234, 262; theme of media, 193-194

education: viii, 79 (table 4), 79-80, 81, 85-107; adult, 90-91, 93, 105, 201; church schools, 6, 85, 86-87, 89, 92, 96-97; defense educational programs, 306; exceptional children, 102-103; films, 117, 211, 212; foreign students, 101; in minority languages, 56, 103, 129; party education, 6, 85, 87, 89, 104-105, 163-164; preschool, 93-94; radio, 201-202; school newspapers, 199; teachers, 90, 95, 101, 105-107; textbooks, 206-207; vocational and polytechnical, 6, 85, 86, 87-88, 89, 90-91, 96, 97-98, 100, 103-104; workers and peasants, 5-6, 64, 85, 86, 88, 89, 90-91, 98, 102, 104-105

elections: 127, 133, 134, 144-145; November, 1945, 1, 26-27, 128

electricity: 269-270, 271, 278 (table 12)

elevation: 31

League of Nations: 24
legal system. *See* courts
Lehar, Ferenc: 118
leisure: 82-83
libraries: viii, 187, 188, 208-210; administration, 192; Bibliotheca Corvina, 121, 208; national, 209-210; village, 208
life expectancy: 47, 69, 70
Liszt, Ferenc (Franz): 118
literature (*see also* artists and intellectuals; publishing): 16, 109, 111-116
Little Entente: 24
Little Plain: 32, 33, 38, 41
location (map): xiv
Lorand Eotvos University: 99, 210
Louis the Great: 13
Lukacs, George: 124
Lysenko, Trofim Denisovich: 110

Madach, Imre: 116
Magyar Kozlony: 135
Magyar Nemzet: 195, 196
Magyars: vii, 9, 10, 43, 55; percent of population, vii, 31
Makk, Karoly: 117
marriage and divorce: 65
Martinuzzi, Gyorgy: 15
Marxism-Leninism: viii, 6, 85, 87, 89, 104, 132, 159, 205, 287
mass communication (*see also* films; libraries; press; publishing; radio; television): 187-213; administration, 190-193; Agitation and Propaganda Department (Agitprop), 153 (fig. 6), 156, 159, 190, 191 (fig. 7), 193; effect of 1956 revolution, 187; freedom of expression, 187, 188, 189; Information Office, 190-192; government control, viii, 187-190, 200, 205, 207, 209, 211, 212; Institute for Cultural Relations, 192-193; propaganda, 111, 156, 159, 166, 188, 190, 203, 211, 212-213, 292, 300; themes, 193-194, 212, 213
mass organizations (*see also* Communist Youth League; Hungarian National Defense Association; Patriotic People's Front; sports clubs; trade unions; youth groups): 7, 66, 129, 147, 160-165, 187-213, 287-289, 306-307
Matra mountain range: 33
Mecsek Mountains: 33, 40, 265, 268
Medgyessy, Ferenc: 122
merchant marine: 54
Mezofold lowland: 33
Mezokovesd: 120
Mezokut: 120
Mindszenty, Cardinal Jozsef: 27, 29

minerals: 33, 40-41, 265-268, 269, 271, 278 (table 12)
mining and industrial region, population: 47
Ministry of: Agriculture, 97; Construction and Urban Development, 265; Culture, 91, 92, 93, 96, 99, 104, 106, 191 (fig. 7), 205; Defense, ix, 7, 299, 300, 301; Finance, 176; Foreign Affairs, 176, 192; Heavy Industry, 264; Interior, 27, 192, 195, 281, 283; Justice, 141, 142, 231, 293; Labor, 97, 141; Light Industry, 265; Metallurgy and Machine Industry, 176, 264; Transportation and Postal Affairs, 50
minorities: 9, 18, 19, 31; Croat, vii, 20-21, 46, 55; German, vii, 12, 46, 55; rights of, 129; Romanian, vii, 46, 55; Ruthenians, 46, 55; Serb, vii, 21, 46, 55; Slovak, vii, 46, 55; troops in World War I, 21, 22
Miskolc: 43, 45, 264
Molnar, Ferenc: 116
Moricz, Zsigmond: 114
mortality, infant: 47, 70
motor transport. *See* transportation
Mount Kekes: 33
Municipal Ervin Szabo Library: 210
Munkacsi, Mihaly: 122
Mura River: 41
music: 104, 117-119; folk music, 117-118, 119; national, 110, 119; rock, 119

Nagy, Agnes Nemes: 115
Nagy, Imre: 4, 28, 29, 110, 171
Nagy, Laszlo: 115
Nagyatudi-Szabo, Istvan: 23
Nagybanya: 122
National Assembly: vii, 3, 127, 128, 129, 130, 133-134, 136; duties, 133, 142, 175; elections, 144, 145
National Education Council: 91, 92
national health service: 71-73
national income: 218, 220-221
National Museum: 122
National Peace Council: 164, 165
National Savings Bank: viii, 235-236, 262
national security (*see also* security (secret) police): ix, 281-295; civil defense, 286-287; civil police, ix, 281, 282-283; frontier guard, 7, 286; Government Guard Command, 285; industrial guards, 285; internal security troops, ix, 7, 281, 284-285; liberalization, 282; Workers Militia, ix, 281, 283-284
National Szechenyi Library: 208, 209
National Women's Conference: 165
nationalism: 2, 9, 16-17, 187-188; as domestic danger, 190; conflict with socialism,

335

168, 193; historic, 14, 16; "irredentism," 2, 9, 67; literature, 113, 114
natural gas: 266, 278 (table 12)
natural resources (see also minerals): 129, 265-270
naval force: 7, 297, 302
Nazi Germany: 24, 25, 26; indemnities to Hungarian victims, 182
Nedudvar: 120
Nemeth, Laszlo: 114, 115
Neuman, Janos: 124
New Course program: 4, 28, 115
New Economic Mechanism: viii, 4, 29, 135-136, 140, 148-149, 166, 167, 216-232 passim, 264, 271; goals, 218; price system, 223-227, 258
1956 revolution: v, 1, 3, 4, 67, 171, 173, 297; amnesties, 295; communist control and reprisals, 29, 110, 115, 171; effect on party membership, 156-157
Northern Mountains: 33-43 passim, 244
nuclear power station: 269-270
Nyers, Rezso: 155-156
Nyugat: 113

Obuda: 45
oil: 40-41, 53, 266, 278 (table 12)

Paris Peace Treaty of 1947: 2, 170, 173
Parliament Library: 210
Patriotic People's Front: 7, 144, 145, 160-161, 222, 288
patriotism: 19, 67, 168, 188
peasants: 5, 57, 62, 63, 75, 79 (table 4), 80 (table 5), 120, 124; benefit payments, 69-70; customs, 56, 114; in armed forces, 299; National Peasant Party, 114; percentage of population, 61-62
Pecs: 43, 45
penal institutions: 281
penal system: 294-295
Pest: 45
Pest County: 41
Petofi, Sandor: 112
petroleum. See oil
Pioneers: 291
pipelines: 48, 48 (table 3), 49 (fig. 4), 49, 50, 52, 53
Poland: 180, 261
police. See national security
political attitudes and values: 165-168
Political Bureau (Politburo): vii, 3, 147, 153, 154, 155, 169, 175
Political College of the MSZMP: 104
political (secret) police. See national security
political prisoners: 28, 295

political subdivisions: 41-43
political trials: 7, 293
Polytechnical University of Budapest: 98
population: vii, 31, 45-48; age distribution, 45-46 (table 2); Budapest, 41, 43, 46-47; density, vii, 46-47; rate of growth, vii, 47; rural, 44 (table 1), 46; urban, 44 (table 1), 46
populist movement: 114
pottery: 120
Presidential Council: 3, 127, 129, 133, 134-136, 144, 175
press: 194-199; freedom of speech and press, 187, 189; governmental control, viii, 188, 190; historic, 194-195; MTI news agency, 191 (fig. 7), 192, 195, 196; periodicals, 113, 194, 198; Pravda pattern, 197; youth press, 198-199
private property: 67, 218; crimes against, 281
propaganda: 111, 166, 292, 300; Commission of Agitation and Propaganda, 153 (fig. 6), 156, 159, 190, 191 (fig. 7), 193; films, 211, 212-213; television, 203
public opinion surveys: 289
public order: 7, 287-291
publishing (see also names of authors): viii, 16, 109, 111-116, 187, 204-208; administration, 192; censorship, 188, 189, 204, 205; early, 111-112, 204; exports, 205-206; foreign works, 207, 208; nationalization, 205; official objective, 207; Rakosi regime, 110, 115; types of, 206 (table 8), 206-208
Puskas, Tivador: 199

radio: 111, 187, 199-202; foreign language, 202; freedom of expression, 189; government control, viii, 188, 192, 200; Hungarian Radio, 200, 201, 202; programs, 200, 201-202; Radio Budapest, 200
Radio Free Europe: 189
railroads: viii-ix, 48 (table 3), 48, 49 (fig. 4), 50
rainfall: 36-37, 243
Rajk, Laszlo: 189
Rakoczi, Prince Ferenc: 112
Rakosi, Matyas (see also Rakosi regime): 2, 211
Rakosi regime: 2-3, 4, 27-28, 110, 111, 115, 117, 170, 282
religion (see also Roman Catholic Church; Jews): vii, 9-10, 55, 56-57, 68, 91, 190; Calvinist, vii, 6, 56; church schools, 6, 85, 86-87, 89, 92, 96-97; Eastern Orthodox, vii, 6, 56; freedom of, 57, 129; Lutheran, vii, 6, 56; newspapers, 197; Protestantism,

vii, 6, 56, 112; State Office of Church Affairs, 57, 91; Unitarian, 6, 56
religious seminaries: 99
Renaissance period: 121
Rippl-Ronai, Jozsef: 122
rivers. *See* waterways
roads: ix, 51, 52
Roman Catholic Church: 27, 56–57, 66, 68, 197, 210; number of Catholics, vii, 6, 56
Roman period: 45
Romania: 7, 41; relations, 180–181, 266
Romantic Period: 112, 118
Royal Elizabeth University: 99
Royal Francis Joseph University: 99
Royal Istvan Tisza University: 99
Royal Peter Pazmany University: 98
Rudnay, Gyula: 123
rural life: 69, 81

St. Stephen's Crown: 11, 57, 68
Sarvis River: 52
satire: 116–117
science and scholarship: 123–125
security (secret) police: ix, 7, 27, 28, 29, 281, 285–286
Semmelweiss, Ignac: 123
settlement patterns: 43–45
Sigismund of Luxembourg: 13
Sino-Soviet dispute: 178
Sio Canal: 52
size: vii, 2, 23, 31
Smallholders' Party: 27
social insurance: 81–82
social organizations. *See* mass organizations
social system (*see also* peasants): 5, 57–62; classes, 5; communist "classless" society, 58–59; mobility of, 5, 57, 62–64; ranks and titles, 58; ruling elite, 5, 58, 59, 63, 147; working class, 5, 60–61, 63, 64, 131
social values: 60, 66–68; land ownership, 66–67
soils: 37–38, 234, 235
Soltl, Georg: 119
Soviet Union (*see also* World War II): 178–180; armed forces in Hungary, ix, 297; boundary with, 41; influence of, v, vii, 1, 9, 27–28, 89, 110, 170, 175, 193, 302, 304; Soviet army occupation of 1945, 1–2, 26, 170; trade with, 239, 255, 256, 265, 266, 267, 268
sports: 83, 104, 306
sports clubs: 7, 66, 165
Stalin, Joseph: 26, 28, 298
standard of living: 5, 69–83, 216; cost of living, 79 (table 4), 80 (table 5), 167, 257–258; diet and nutrition, 73–75; farm, 250, 254

State Development Bank: viii, 236
Stein, Aurel: 123
Stephen, King: 11–12, 68
suicide rate: 70, 292
Szabo, Dezso: 114
Szabo, Pal: 114
Szalay, Lajos: 123
Szazhalombatta: 53
Szechenyi, Ferenc: 208
Szechenyi, Count Istvan: 16–17
Szeged: 35, 43, 45, 264, 266
Szell, George: 119
Szent-Gyorgyi, Albert: 124
Szigeti, Joszef: 119
Szokolay, Sandor: 119
Szonyi, Istvan: 122
Sztojay, Dome: 26

Tatabayana: 266
taxation (*see also* agriculture, land tax): 217, 234, 262
Technological Documentation Center: 210
Teleki, Jozsef: 208
Teleki, Count Pal: 25
television: 81, 83, 187, 202–204 (table 7); government control, viii, 188, 192; Intervision, 202–203; opposition to satellite tv, 190
Teller, Edward: 124
temperature: 37, 38
theater: 116–117
Tisza River: 32, 33, 34, 35, 52, 269
topography: vii, 32 (fig. 2)
towns, classification as: 43–44
trade: viii, 169, 237–241, 255, 256; balance of, 184–185, 239, 240; EEC, 183; exchange rates, 238–239; exports, 240–241, 265, 267, 268; state monopoly, 238; with Soviet Union, 239, 255, 256, 265, 266, 267, 268, with West, 239–240
trade unions: 7, 66, 129, 132, 161–163, 287, 288, 291; administration of social insurance, 82; libraries, 205, 209; National Council of Trade Unions, 141, 142, 161; newspapers, 194, 195, 196, 197
Transdanubia: 32–47 *passim*, 53, 243, 244
Transdanubian Central Mountains: 33, 40
transportation: viii–ix, 48 (table 3), 48–54; 79–80 (table 4); automobiles, 51, 78, 81; cargo, 48 (table 3); passenger, 48 (table 3), 51
Transylvania, history: 11, 12, 14, 15, 18, 20, 25
treaties (*see also* Council for Mutual Economic Assistance; Warsaw Treaty Organization): 173–175, 184, 302–303

PUBLISHED COUNTRY STUDIES

(Area Handbook Series)

550-65	Afghanistan		550-151	Honduras
550-98	Albania		550-165	Hungary
550-44	Algeria		550-21	India
550-59	Angola		550-154	Indian Ocean
550-73	Argentina		550-39	Indonesia
550-169	Australia		550-68	Iran
550-176	Austria		550-31	Iraq
550-175	Bangladesh		550-25	Israel
550-170	Belgium		550-182	Italy
550-66	Bolivia		550-69	Ivory Coast
550-20	Brazil		550-177	Jamaica
550-168	Bulgaria		550-30	Japan
550-61	Burma		550-34	Jordan
550-83	Burundi		550-56	Kenya
550-50	Cambodia		550-81	Korea, North
550-166	Cameroon		550-41	Korea, South
550-159	Chad		550-58	Laos
550-77	Chile		550-24	Lebanon
550-60	China		550-30	Liberia
550-63	China, Republic of		550-85	Libya
550-26	Colombia		550-172	Malawi
550-91	Congo		550-45	Malaysia
550-90	Costa Rica		550-161	Mauritania
550-152	Cuba		550-79	Mexico
550-22	Cyprus		550-76	Mongolia
550-158	Czechoslovakia		550-49	Morocco
550-54	Dominican Republic		550-64	Mozambique
550-52	Ecuador		550-35	Nepal, Bhutan and Sikkim
550-43	Egypt		550-88	Nicaragua
550-150	El Salvador		550-157	Nigeria
550-28	Ethiopia		550-94	Oceania
550-167	Finland		550-48	Pakistan
550-155	Germany, East		550-46	Panama
550-173	Germany, Federal Republic of		550-156	Paraguay
550-153	Ghana		550-185	Persian Gulf States
550-87	Greece		550-42	Peru
550-78	Guatemala		550-72	Philippines
550-174	Guinea		550-162	Poland
550-82	Guyana		550-181	Portugal
550-164	Haiti		550-160	Romania

550-84	Rwanda	550-89	Tunisia
550-51	Saudi Arabia	550-80	Turkey
550-70	Senegal	550-74	Uganda
550-180	Sierra Leone	550-97	Uruguay
550-184	Singapore	550-71	Venezuela
550-86	Somalia	550-57	Vietnam, North
550-93	South Africa	550-55	Vietnam, South
550-95	Soviet Union	550-183	Yemens, The
550-179	Spain	550-99	Yugoslavia
550-96	Sri Lanka (Ceylon)	550-67	Zaire
550-27	Sudan	550-75	Zambia
550-47	Syria	550-171	Zimbabwe
550-62	Tanzania		
550-53	Thailand		
550-178	Trinidad and Tobago